Transportation for Livable Cities

Transportation for Livable Cities

VUKAN R. VUCHIC

CENTER FOR URBAN POLICY RESEARCH
Rutgers, The State University of New Jersey
New Brunswick, New Jersey

Second printing 2000

Published by the Center for Urban Policy Research
Civic Square • 33 Livingston Avenue • Suite 400
New Brunswick, New Jersey 08901–1982

Printed in the United States of America

Portions of the material contained in this book were previously published under the title *Urban Public Transportation: Systems and Technology* (Prentice-Hall, Inc., 1981 [ISBN 0139394966, Copyright TX 719-767]).

Library of Congress Cataloging-in-Publication Data

Vuchic, Vukan R.
Transportation for livable cities / Vukan R. Vuchic.
p. cm.
Includes bibliographical references and index.
ISBN 0-88285-161-6

1. Urban transportation—United States—Planning. 2. Urban transportation policy—United States. 3. Local transit—United States—Planning. 4. Urban transportation—Planning. 5. Urban transportation policy. 6. Local transit—Planning. 7. Urban transportation—Environmental aspects. 8. Automobiles—Environmental aspects. 9. Sustainable development. I. Title.
HE308.V83 1999
388.4—dc21 98–019218
CIP

Cover design: HELENE BERINSKY
Cover photograph: Courtesy TRI-MET, Portland, Oregon
Interior design/typesetting: Arlene Pashman

My wife Rada and I have always enjoyed traveling with our children because of their enthusiasm for the sights, history, and liveliness of New York, Paris, Munich, Hong Kong, San Francisco and other human-oriented cities.
It is their generation that should enjoy the increasing livability of cities.

This book is dedicated to our children – Monika, Boris, Lili and Victor – and their families.

Contents

List of Figures viii
List of Tables x
List of Photographs xi
Acknowledgments xv
Preface xvii

1 The Crisis of U.S. Cities and Metropolitan Areas: An Overview 1

2 The City–Transportation Relationship 23

3 How Did We Get Here? Transportation Policies and Practices in the United States 93

4 Urban Transportation Policies: United States and Peer Countries 128

5 Common Misconceptions in Urban Transportation 188

6 Transportation Policies for Livable Cities 227

7 Implementing the Solutions: Measures for Achieving Intermodal Balance 259

8 Cities and Transportation: What Is the Future? 320

Bibliography 335
Index 339

Figures

CHAPTER 1

1.1 The vicious cycle in urban transportation 8

CHAPTER 2

2.1 Cost characteristics of different transit mode categories 44
2.2 Urban trips served by regular transit and commuter transit 48
2.3 Time-area consumed per passenger on 4-km round-trip by three modes 56
2.4 Time-area consumed per passenger on 8-km round-trip by three modes 57
2.5 Areas required to transport 15,000 persons/hour by different modes 58
2.6 Average user travel cost curves for car and transit travel 61
2.7 Distribution of travel volume between auto and transit travel 62
2.8 Transportation policies for shifting individual equilibrium point toward social optimum 63
2.9 Classification of costs for car and transit travel 70
2.10 Direct costs of car travel under different conditions 75
2.11 Total costs of car travel under different conditions 75
2.12 Direct costs of urban travel by different modes 78
2.13 Total costs of urban travel by different modes 78
2.14 Conceptual classification of urban transport planning 83
2.15 Schematic presentation of urban transport planning levels 85
2.16 Planning sequence in urban transport 87

CHAPTER 3

3.1 1969 Plan for the Philadelphia Region in 1985 102
3.2 Consequences of different policies for relief of highway congestion 116

CHAPTER 4

4.1 Pedestrian areas, subway stations, parking, and stores, Munich 134
4.2 Initial pedestrian precinct and later redesign, Hannover 136
4.3 Change of modal split resulting from LRT opening, Hannover 137
4.4 Impact of different policies on future car use, the Netherlands 142
4.5 City center with five traffic cells, Gothenburg 153
4.6 Concept of integrated transport policy, Sydney 160
4.7 Passenger car ownership per capita, 1992 164
4.8 Average annual distance driven by car, 1990 165
4.9 Percentage of passenger trips in urban areas, car and other modes 166
4.10 Public support for transit- versus highway-oriented policies 170
4.11 Decision makers' perception versus surveyed public opinion favoring transit-oriented policies 172
4.12 Outlays for highways, transit, and related programs, 1981 and 1995 174
4.13 Price of gasoline in different countries, 1990 176
4.14 Revenue ratio, highway user taxes to government highway expenditures 178
4.15 Gasoline price versus use in selected industrialized countries, 1994 179

CHAPTER 6

6.1 Distribution of urban land between transportation and other activities 230
6.2 Total costs of urban travel by different modes and conditions 236
6.3 Policies toward modes and their impacts on intermodal balance 240
6.4 Impacts of different sets of policies on four sets of relative disutilities of different modes 242
6.5 Impact of auto disincentives and transit incentives on intermodal shift of travel and individual equilibrium points 246

Tables

CHAPTER 2

2.1 Estimates of subsidies to auto and truck users in the United States 68
2.2. Assumptions for travel costs of a round-trip 76

CHAPTER 4

4.1 Results of deregulation versus contracting 147

CHAPTER 5

5.1 Impacts of policies balancing transportation modes: examples of Munich and Stuttgart 222

CHAPTER 6

6.1 Occupancy of street area per person traveling by different modes and vehicle loadings 251

Photographs

CHAPTER 1

1.1 Popular low-density suburbs are served efficiently by car. 4
1.2 In high-density areas, congestion limits efficiency of cars. 6
1.3 Rapid growth of cities—a worldwide problem. 9
1.4 Pedestrian streets in older towns enhance their livability. 13
1.5 Superbly designed urban highways can serve low-density suburbs, but not urban cores, due to their large space consumption. 20
1.6 Modern traffic engineering can promote integration of cars, bicycles, and pedestrians. 21

CHAPTER 2

2.1 High-capacity radial freeway. 25
2.2 Highway congestion results in increased costs and wasted time. 26
2.3 Pedestrian traffic: a basic element of urban livability. 31
2.4 Shopping malls are pedestrian havens. 32
2.5 Design of shopping malls for auto access only prevents their interaction with surrounding areas. 33
2.6 Bicycle paths designed on sidewalks operate efficiently in many European cities. 34
2.7 Federal laws—ISTEA and TEA-21—have stimulated construction of bikeways in U.S. cities. 34
2.8 Freeways—category A highways—serve major corridors in large cities. 35
2.9 Compact metro stations fit well into centers of cities, but freeway interchanges occupy large areas. 38
2.10 Category B rights-of-way are often street medians used by LRT. 42
2.11 Metro systems have high performance due to exclusive ROW. 43

2.12 Houston uses many bus and HOV lanes for commuter transit services. 47
2.13 Congestion defeats mobility of cars and traps transit vehicles. 53
2.14 Comparison of street area taken by 69 passengers traveling by car and by bus. 54
2.15 Towing advertising trailers through congested streets: huge social (congestion) cost is not charged to the user. 72
2.16 The more accommodations for the car are provided, the less attractive the city is for people. 73

CHAPTER 3

3.1 At the height of car accommodation during the 1960s, car parks flooded cities.
a. Los Angeles 94
b. Vienna 95
3.2 Improved highway design for urban areas
a. Initial design of I-95 in Philadelphia separated city from the river. 105
b. Redesigned highway enables Old City access to the river. 105
3.3 Rapid transit allows car users to park in suburbs and ride trains to city. 106
3.4 New LRT systems have created efficient bus–rail intermodal networks. 107
3.5 Construction of "Add-a-lane" and a wide, paved divider defeated lane designation as "2+ HOV" in Hartford. 115
3.6 Demand for more freeway lanes continues to grow. 117

CHAPTER 4

4.1 Taming traffic in center city. 131
a. Shopping street Zeil in Frankfurt was heavily congested. 131
b. The same street after it became a pedestrian mall. 131
4.2 Intermodal solution in Karlsruhe. 138
a. Light rail transit on pedestrian street. 138
b. The same LRT train on railway tracks. 139
4.3 Street design for cars and pedestrians in a green environment. 140
4.4 Pedestrian area with transit in the center of Hannover. 181

CHAPTER 6

6.1 Soundwalls reduce negative impacts of major freeways on their surroundings. 254
6.2 Many cities design intermodal systems to encourage use of bicycles and transit. 256

CHAPTER 7

7.1 Excessive reliance on cars led to construction of six roadways with 18 lanes in a major corridor. 265

7.2 Attractive landscaping along roadsides and interchanges in Seattle. 266

7.3 Freeway ramp control is an efficient method to improve utilization of highways. 269

7.4 The Area Licensing Scheme is a simple and effective method of preventing CBD congestion. 282

7.5 Street design provides for cars, bicycles, and pedestrians. 288

7.6 Traffic taming is employed for a pedestrian crossing on a state highway that traverses the town center. 289

7.7 Pedestrian zone served directly by transit. 297

7.8 Diversity of light rail transit: high-speed line has a CBD distribution on streets. 302

7.9 Careful design of details enhances livability of cities. 313

CHAPTER 8

8.1 Intermodal system: pedestrians, cars, and buses. 331

8.2 Coordinated land use and transportation planning: high densities around metro stations. 332

Acknowledgments

The initial effort to assemble material for this book in a comprehensive document was a study analyzing urban transportation systems and policies sponsored by the Energy Foundation of San Francisco, as well as by a grant from the U.S. Department of Transportation University Transportation Centers Program. The support of these sponsors is gratefully acknowledged.

Drawing on material from his writings and several decades of work on urban transportation, the author also benefited greatly from participation of the Advisory Committee. Special thanks are due to committee members: Stephen H. Burrington, Conservation Law Foundation; Louis J. Gambaccini, then with SEPTA; Ronald J. Hartman, then with Amtrak; Professor Shinya Kikuchi, University of Delaware; Herbert S. Levinson, Consultant; Professor Edward K. Morlok, University of Pennsylvania; Professor John Pucher, Rutgers University; Professor Joseph L. Schofer, Northwestern University; Professor Elliott Sclar, Columbia University; and Jeffrey M. Zupan, Consultant.

The report on the initial project was later expanded, several chapters added, and materials elaborated and refined. The author is grateful for the assistance of the following persons in providing and reviewing text on various countries and cities: Professor Heinrich Brändli, ETH Zürich, Switzerland; Lawrence Dahms, MTC, San Francisco Bay Area; Ragnar Domstad, City of Gothenburg, Sweden; Professor Günter Girnau, VDV, Cologne, Germany; Professor Antonio Musso, University of Rome, Italy; Professor Peter Newman, Murdoch University, Perth, Australia; Professor Bo Peterson, SL, Stockholm, Sweden; Professor Matti Pursula, University of Technology, Helsinki, Finland; John Schumann, LTK Engineering Services, Portland, Oregon; Professor Gerald Steuart, University of Toronto, Canada; and Professor Jean-Claude Ziv, CNAM, Paris, France.

Special thanks are due several colleagues who reviewed portions of the text and contributed materials. First, Professor Emeritus Wolfgang S. Homburger, University of California–Berkeley, with his thorough knowledge of the subject area and editing expertise, provided extremely valuable comments and suggestions on all chapters. Portions of the manuscript were also reviewed and numerous suggestions made by Professor Robert Cervero, University of California; Thor K. Haatveit, City of Oslo; Shinya Kikuchi; Herbert S. Levinson; Thomas G. Matoff, LTK Engineering Services; Professor John Pucher; and Jeffrey M. Zupan.

Given the complex and dynamic topics concerning urban transportation, it was remarkable that there was a strong overall consensus among the committee members and reviewers with respect to the definition of problems and general approaches to the solutions. Yet, there were different views on defining the causes of problems and on feasibility of various policy and improvement measures. Thus, it was not surprising that this author has had reviewers' comments that suggested many statements should be "toned down," as well as those saying that the critical remarks should be stronger and more direct. Clearly, the content of this book is the author's responsibility and does not necessarily imply consensus by all participants and reviewers.

Several assistants worked with dedication and enthusiasm on the research and preparation for this book. They are Eric C. Bruun, Post-Doctoral Fellow, and then doctoral students Nikola Krstanoski, Young-Jae Lee, and Yong Eun Shin. Jeffrey Casello and Mario Semmler worked on the final stages of editing the manuscript and preparing the exhibits.

The author also wishes to thank Professor Norman J. Glickman, director of the Center for Urban Policy Research at Rutgers University, and Professor Robert W. Lake, editor in chief of CUPR Press and CUPR's associate director, for their assistance in publishing this book. Special recognition is also due Arlene Pashman, senior editor, for her expertise, precise work, and dedication in preparing the manuscript.

Finally, my wife, Rada, provided not only patience and understanding but consultations about portions of the text. As in all previous work, her support has been most valuable.

Vukan R. Vuchic
University of Pennsylvania

Preface

The beginning of the twenty-first century finds civilization heavily based in cities that have grown into large metropolitan areas. Many of these focal points of human activity face problems of economic inefficiency, environmental deterioration, and unsatisfactory quality of life—problems that go far in determining whether a city is "livable." A large share of these problems stem from the inefficiencies and other impacts of urban transportation systems. Actually, urban transportation in many ways reflects the general problems of advanced societies, such as the dichotomy between individual and social interests, the external impacts of a system's operation, and the relationship between market conditions and public service. This is illustrated below by several examples.

- *Unrestricted individual behavior collides with socially optimal behavior.* The need for modification of individuals' behavior in matters such as cleanliness of public areas, environmental protection, noise reduction, and the like has been recognized and effected by regulations, charges, and other measures. However, this problem has not been adequately addressed with regard to travel in cities.
- *There is a divergence between the immediate gratification of travelers and the larger long-range solution to urban transportation issues.* For example, every car driver desires ample highway and parking capacity; in the long term, however, meeting these desires leads to construction of excessive highways and so many parking facilities that the efficiency and environmental quality of urbanized areas are greatly diminished.

- *Transportation has major social, environmental, and other positive and negative side effects.* However, many of these invisible "externalities" are not reflected in the charges paid by users for transportation service.
- *Although transportation has some elements of free-market operation, it is also a complex system involving social and environmental factors that must be planned as a whole.* Citizens make travel choices based on their individual needs, but a comprehensive plan must be in place to coordinate those individual choices into an efficient transportation system. Unregulated market forces cannot achieve that: a comprehensive transportation system requires a strong governmental role.
- *Travel opportunities and costs affect the quality of life of individuals and population groups; transportation systems, therefore, must be planned not only for efficiency but for social and equity considerations as well.* Consequently, transportation policies must not be based on market forces and financial considerations only.
- *The structure and distribution of transportation costs between users and nonusers (private sector, government, and society in general) vary greatly among modes.* Most trips undertaken by car as well as by transit involve substantial direct or indirect public- and private-sector subsidies.
- *Transportation has a major impact not only on the physical form of cities but on their livability – the quality of their natural and man-made environments.* Transportation, therefore, strongly influences the ambiance of contemporary urbanized societies.
- *Inadequate understanding of these complex problems in urban transportation, compounded by the strong pressures exerted by special-interest groups, are serious obstacles to solutions that would serve the public good.*

This book gives an overview of the condition of transportation in cities and their suburbs. It shows that the conflict between the ubiquitous use of automobiles and the detrimental effect of traffic congestion on cities and the environment is neither fully understood nor resolved. Building more highways to solve traffic congestion is popular in the short run, particularly among an uninformed general public. Taken to its extreme, however, highway expansion ultimately exacerbates the problem of congestion and leads to cities that are much less livable. In some cities, major highways and transit systems are built without sufficient coordination with land-use policies and development controls. It is this conflict—excessive reliance on cars and deterioration of metropolitan areas due to congestion and its negative impacts—that Elmer Johnson, a former Vice President of General Motors, calls the "collision between cities and cars."

Chapter 1 discusses the dilemmas and options of metropolitan areas with respect to their basic transportation policies. At one end of the spectrum lies an attempt to restrict automobile use in a constrained urban space; at the other is the stimulation of maximum use of cars and the full adaptation of the city to vehicular traffic. The most rational goal, however, is to balance urban development with an integrated multimodal transport system. This last goal—achieving balanced development—is the most complex, but it is the only one that allows the use of *economies of aggregation* and the creation of *livable cities*. The concept of *livability* is a qualitative one; it represents the characteristic that "depends on the attractiveness of an area as a place in which to live, work, invest and do business."

In order to define and clarify the importance of a *balanced transportation system*, the relationship of cities and transportation is discussed in chapter 2. Transportation should be the city component that is physically and functionally integrated with other activities and services. It should not be suppressed; nor should it dominate the city's residential, cultural, social, industrial, and commercial activities.

No single mode of passenger transportation can satisfy the diverse needs of a metropolitan area. To provide a variety of effective services, particularly in medium-size and large metropolitan areas, passenger transportation must consist of complementary systems, including private, public, and paratransit modes. Among private modes, walking is most convenient for short trips. It is crucial for the livable city, but its importance is often underestimated. The car, which serves many different roles, dominates the category of private transport. For most trips, no other mode can provide similar performance and personal comfort. In high-density urban areas, however, due to its great demand for space, the private car causes congestion and becomes less efficient. Highway traffic in large metropolitan areas also produces negative impacts such as air pollution, noise, and accidents. Thus, in the long run, the human-based urban character and environment are degraded.

Transit plays numerous roles as well. In small cities, its social service and welfare functions dominate. In medium and large cities, however, transit should be more than mere social service: its high capacity, efficiency, and low space requirements allow varying densities of development and activities. Together with pedestrian traffic, and coordinated with the private car, transit gives the urban environment a human character. It offers the choice of travel without a car, which, in many cities, is the preferred option for most trips. Rail transit is actually the only mode that makes large cities possible with their diverse densities and human character. Moreover, in all cities, transit and paratransit have the important role of providing mobility for people who do not have cars or who, for one reason or another, do not drive.

The main feature determining the "performance/investment cost package" of transit modes is the type of right-of-way (ROW), which, in turn, strongly influences system technology. Category C ROW—streets—uses primarily buses, which often cannot compete with cars. Category B and A rights-of-way, respectively, partially or fully separated from other traffic, require substantial investment but provide service of much higher quality. Rail systems used on these ROW categories offer high-quality service that attracts riders and has great potential for interaction with urban form and human activities of cities.

The collision of cities and cars is caused primarily by the car's extremely high area requirements. For example, during peak hours, a trip by car consumes about 30 times more area than one by bus, and 40 times more than a trip on a rail line. The typical car commuter requires some 20 percent more area for parking than for work in an office. This space requirement results in the creation of dispersed urban developments that are poorly suited to walking. Eventually, this leads to the creation of *private* urban areas with few public activities or opportunities for social interaction.

Metropolitan areas with *balanced* multimodal transportation—pedestrian, car and transit—are superior in many respects to the two extreme solutions: restricting the car or rebuilding the city. These areas require less investment and lower operating costs, in addition to providing adequate transportation for everyone, something car-based and transit-based cities lack. In other words, metropolitan areas with balanced transportation provide an environment for *humans,* rather than for vehicles.

To achieve a balance between modes, it is first necessary to implement two sets of policies: *transit incentives* and *car disincentives*. These policies lead to shifting a portion of travel from car to transit, i.e., from individual selection to a socially optimal condition. Congestion, air pollution, cost, and the negative impact of excessive car concentration are reduced—to the benefit of all travelers, transit, and other drivers, as well as the overall urban-area population.

The pressure of steadily increasing car use, and the growth of vehicle-kilometers traveled (VKT) or vehicle-miles traveled (VMT), is fueled mostly by two forces. First, car use is subsidized in many ways—from government funds for highway construction (which exceed taxes collected from highway users), to tax deductions, the use of "company cars," and ubiquitous "free parking." Moreover, the social and environmental costs of cars—their "external costs," particularly significant in metropolitan areas—are not paid by car users in any form. Several recent studies of these costs, such as that by the Office of Technology Assessment (1994), estimate the total subsidy for highway transport in the United States to be between $400 billion and $900 billion per year.

The second factor driving increased car use is the cost structure of car use: 80 to 90 percent of the user costs of driving are fixed, independent of individual trips, whereas only 10 to 20 percent are direct, out-of-pocket costs that drivers consider when deciding whether to make a trip by car. As with any service offered at a price much lower than full price, this service is used far more than would be justified if car users had to pay the full cost of their travel.

In the real world, when out-of-pocket cost is substantially lower than full cost, the only significant deterrent to excessive driving is highway congestion. When highway capacity increases, it stimulates more driving and increases VKT, which results in higher indirect user costs and negative social and environmental impacts. Cost-based road pricing, which would be a major step in correcting this situation, is being discussed, particularly in the United States and Great Britain; but it remains far from politically acceptable, largely because the public is not informed about the costs of driving and purposes of corrective measures.

A review of developments in urban transportation in the United States is given in chapter 3. After World War II, the country adopted strong highway-oriented policies, which peaked in the federally sponsored construction of the National System of Interstate and Defense Highways. By contrast, until the mid-1960s, transit had no federal support. Transportation planning at that time consisted basically of extrapolating past trends without adequately defining goals for metropolitan areas and their quality of life. In this regard, the car was considered *the* mode of the future for urban travel.

These developments led to the "freeway revolt" of 1966, in which considerations of environmental and quality-of-life concerns eventually were introduced, and plans for extensive additional freeways throughout metropolitan areas were rejected. During the 1970s, significant innovations in transit and urban design were introduced, but the 1980s reversed much of this progress. Throughout most of its tenure (1981–89), the Reagan administration tried to terminate federal involvement in transit altogether, while increasing highway funding. This attempt to return to the policies of the 1950s did not succeed, however.

Several federal transportation acts since the 1960s have required the broadening of urban transportation planning to include all modes and entire metropolitan areas. The Intermodal Surface Transportation Efficiency Act (ISTEA) of 1991 is particularly significant because it requires the comprehensive planning and development of integrated multimodal systems. Recognizing that land use and transportation should be better integrated, the Act introduces various measures to reduce VKTs and their negative impact on metropolitan areas. Similar requirements are specified by the Clean Air Act Amendments of 1990. So far, however, the effectiveness of these laws has been limited, due to a lack of land-use controls in most states. An even greater obstacle to implementation of improvements is the institutional inertia of highway-oriented transportation departments and their neglect of all other modes. This bias is supported by various interest groups that benefit from present trends and oppose any innovations.

Chapter 4 presents an extensive review of transportation policies and practices in the developed countries that are considered to be peers of the United States. This review shows that most peer countries are more advanced than the United States in creating balanced transportation systems. Their transportation is more human-oriented at local levels and thus provides for convenient walking, bicycle, car, and transit travel. For regional travel, they offer not only highways, but also attractive transit capable of competing with car travel. Balancing these two modes is achieved by *transit incentive* and *car disincentive measures*. Modern, attractive rail and bus systems, integrated with extensive pedestrian areas, are the backbone of transport in the central areas of most cities in peer countries such as Germany, Norway, and Canada. Outlying areas are served mostly by cars, supplemented by walking, bicycles, and paratransit. Many cities in peer countries, such as Toronto, Melbourne, and Vienna, are distinctly more livable than typical car-oriented U.S. metropolitan areas of comparable size.

This situation triggers numerous questions. How can U.S. policies differ so much from the policies of peer countries, which have developed more livable cities? How can there be a denial of the problems in our metropolitan areas, or arguments made that present trends cannot be changed? How can there be sweeping criticism of efforts to improve transit and paratransit, which receive less than $10 billion of public funds annually, while there is no discussion of highway subsidies that are orders-of-magnitude greater? The debate in the United States about urban transportation abounds with inadequate understanding of the complex problems and relationships, incorrect statements, and lack of clear vision about the future of cities. This is the subject of chapter 5, which presents a collection of misconceptions—frequently used misleading statements, overgeneralizations, and confused concepts. Each statement, drawn from the literature or from public statements, is brief and is rebutted or clarified by a short explanation. Some issues mentioned are planning philosophy, the role of the car in urban transportation, and the characteristics and relationships of different transit modes and pedestrian travel.

Chapter 6 is a systematic review of the principles and policies needed to create efficient and livable cities. It defines the role of transport as well as its relationship to other activities. The need for balanced intermodal systems is pointed out, and alternative policies toward different modes are discussed. Coordinated policies of transit incentives and car disincentives usually are most effective in achieving the goals of efficiency and livability.

Drawing on experience with various measures for implementing solutions that have been used successfully in many cities, chapter 7 presents a review and evaluation of these measures. The sequence of actions aimed at achieving an intermodal balance should be to determine goals at the city level, then select the modes that will facilitate the determination of the required combination of modes. Various measures for achieving the desirable balance of modes are discussed. Among numerous design, operational, and economic (pricing) measures, particular attention is given to the various methods of charging for travel. The potential for reducing subsidies, especially parking, and for introducing various types of road pricing is discussed in considerable detail. Innovative designs and operational methods for traffic calming are also reviewed.

In closing, chapter 8 reviews the book, pointing out that, in recent years, most of America's peer countries have intensified their efforts to achieve a reasonable balance among different modes of urban transportation. The United States, in contrast, during the 1980s reversed such efforts and in many respects still follows the concurrent policies of *limited transit improvements* and *car-use incentives*. Policies for the latter are largely contrary to the spirit and requirements of ISTEA, to reduce VKT. The two sets of policies, combined, result in actions that are competing or mutually conflicting, while increasing the total costs of transportation, both highway and transit. Yet, economically rational measures such as raising the gasoline tax (a win-win action because it would take a step toward market-based pricing) that increase the out-of-pocket cost of driving and bring in large revenues with no adverse impacts, are not seriously considered. They are simply labeled "politically unacceptable" and dismissed, even by the writers purporting to argue for fiscal responsibility and market-based measures to better regulate urban transportation.

The current transportation crisis—increasing congestion, deteriorating transit, and neglect of pedestrians—cannot be corrected without significant changes in policies, planning effectiveness, and people's habits. Introduction of such changes requires a far-reaching effort in educating the public about the goals, problems, and benefits involved. People will not change their travel patterns and driving habits until they understand that these changes will, or could, result in a reduction of transportation costs for themselves and for the government; that they will improve the economic vitality of metropolitan areas; and that cities will be more attractive and livable.

Since the private car, the dominant mode of travel, is greatly underpriced relative to its costs, particularly on an out-of-pocket basis, road pricing, tolls, and other charges represent the most appropriate and effective measures to increase the efficiency of America's urban transportation. However, to introduce restraints, it is first necessary to have affordable, acceptable alternative transport systems. Thus, the provision of high-quality transit is a sine qua non for any major effort to control car use in urban areas and to slow down land consumption in suburbia and exurbia.

The serious problems in urban transportation, as well as the crisis of cities in general, require an aggressive search for solutions. The complex relationships between cities and transportation must be discussed. It is necessary to reach a clearer consensus on goals for metropolitan areas than the one now available. The experience of our peer countries also should be carefully considered. It would be self-delusional to ignore the numerous successful policies in other countries under the pretense that these policies cannot be transferred. Just as European countries and Japan learned much from the U.S. experience in developing highways and traffic engineering several decades ago, the United States can now learn from the more diverse experiences and sophisticated solutions in planning and implementing the multimodal transport systems for livable cities that have been achieved in peer countries. The setting of clear goals, application of a systems approach to urban transportation, and pursuit of coordinated rather than mutually conflicting policies are valid steps in all countries, regardless how their local conditions differ. Changing the trends in American urban transportation is a complex task, one that cannot be achieved overnight. But that is no excuse for not starting.

Reference

U. S. Congress, Office of Technology Assessment (OTA). 1994. *Saving energy in U.S. transportation.* Report OTA-ETI-589. Washington, DC: U.S. Government Printing Office.

Transportation for Livable Cities

1

The Crisis of U.S. Cities and Metropolitan Areas: An Overview

It is not unusual to hear Americans returning from Europe lavish praise on cities they have visited. "Why can't we have cities as lively and attractive as Brussels, Munich, or Oslo?" they ask. Similar comments are heard from people returning to Detroit, Dallas, or San Jose from Toronto, or even from some cities in Australia or Eastern Europe. American visitors are impressed by the human scale of the urban landscape in these cities. Pedestrian-friendly design encourages strolling in both commercial areas and residential neighborhoods. Tourists travel within and between cities by various modes of public transportation; renting a car is not necessary.

The metropolitan areas of the peer countries[1] analyzed in this book generally have freeway networks that are much less extensive than typical freeway networks in U.S. metropolitan areas, particularly in their central cities.[2] In most areas, freeways serve the region but do not penetrate and/or encircle the city core as they do, for example, in Columbus, Hartford, and Los Angeles. Car ownership, though lower than in the United States, is high enough to cause serious traffic congestion; but transit services in many cities provide an alternative to the usual congestion. They are far superior to the transit systems of U.S. cities. Pedestrians are not only given more protection, but urban design in most cases stimulates pedestrian travel. In addition, most European cities have numerous pedestrian-only streets and plazas, and in many of them auto-free zones are being expanded.

AN AFFLUENT COUNTRY WITH DETERIORATING CITIES

There is little doubt that, with respect to personal affluence, a large segment of the U.S. population ranks high in relation to corresponding groups in peer countries. A high standard of living, including extensive homeownership, is typical for large suburban areas. The condition of private affluence that so impresses foreign visitors to America stands in sharp contrast to the lagging public facilities and services, particularly in central cities.

The casual observations of American travelers reflect the fact that, with respect to livability and physical and social conditions, most U.S. cities are inferior to the cities in its peer countries. Actually, the problems of U.S. cities go very deep. Many are in crisis economically, socially, and physically. These problems are especially severe in the large inner-city areas surrounding central business districts, where 80 million Americans, or 30 percent of the U.S. population, live. Furthermore, large portions of inner-city areas in cities such as Chicago, Detroit, and Los Angeles are dilapidated—with thousands of boarded-up buildings, streets littered with trash, and neighborhoods and industrial buildings defaced by graffiti. Life in these areas is ridden with crime, drugs, vandalism, and poverty.

It is paradoxical that in the United States, one of the world's most affluent democracies, central cities house a disproportionately large percentage of the country's 40 million people who live below the federally defined poverty level. This concentration of poverty is interrelated with the existence of extensive ghetto areas and separation of minorities in cities, a condition that has been called "American Apartheid": although numerous U.S. laws prohibit segregation, de facto separation by race and economic class continues to exist in most metropolitan areas.

The condition of urban areas, whether they grow or decline, depends on myriad economic, social, and other factors. Various "economies of agglomeration"—that is, greater efficiencies in economic and social functions due to physical proximity—stimulate the concentration of activities and thereby lead to the creation and subsequent growth of cities. Decentralization, on the other hand, is caused by the attraction of homeownership, social problems that lead to separation, and various activities that require relatively large spaces. Transportation may exert either influence, agglomeration or decentralization, depending on the dominant mode, pricing policies, and other factors. In general, strong reliance on the private automobile favors suburb over central city. Travel by automobile is ideally suited to low-density areas with dispersed activities, whereas it is inferior to transit and walking in high-density areas and cities where space is at a premium and the automobile's impacts are particularly serious. Thus, *the more an area relies on transit and walking, the greater is its advantage over suburbs with respect to transportation choices, convenience, and overall cost of travel. The more an urbanized area relies on the automobile and neglects its alternatives, the more likely it is that its central areas will deteriorate.*

In recent decades, American cities have gone through periods of dispersal, or central-city decline; some reversal of this trend (gentrification in many cities such as New York and Philadelphia); then dispersal again. The migration of residents has been followed by the development of suburban shopping malls; somewhat later, businesses, too, began to move outward. Two factors have had a particularly strong influence on the outward movement of urban population: crime in the cities and the low quality of city schools. Contributing to this trend is the lower cost of agricultural land in suburbs, relative to the cost of lots in the central city, combined with tax deductions for single-family housing units built mostly in outlying areas.

Clearly, transportation has not been the only force at work in this trend. Other problems were growing. Nevertheless, heavy reliance on the private automobile undoubtedly has been a major contributor. The extremely low out-of-pocket cost of travel by automobile leads to an extensive trade-off of distance for other costs; thus, any problem or inconvenience in cities leads to the relocation of people and businesses to remote areas. Consequently, from the point of view of the individual, "escape" becomes an easier option in locational decisions than working on solutions to the problems of crime or schools, at least in the short run. In the long run, the aggregate effect of these individual decisions—personally rational, in light of government policies—is social and urban decay.

The lower quality of life in central cities has deterred large groups of people from living in them. The population dispersal into suburbs has resulted in a weakening of the tax base in cities, which further stimulates the concentration of poverty and social problems. *There has been a tendency when such problems occur to escape rather than face the problems and implement corrective actions.* Edward Rendell, mayor of Philadelphia, eloquently described the desperation that exists in many of the city's neighborhoods: "The real story can be understood by examining the plight of hundreds of thousands of each city's residents who are very much at risk, very much trapped in an existence that they had no part in creating—people who are trapped in a state from which they have absolutely no expectation of escaping without doing something illegal, like selling drugs or robbing a store" (Rendell 1994).

It is often said that the automobile has "freed" people to move out of the traditional city. This situation has led to the virtually unlimited growth of suburbs. Although "moving out" may be a desirable outcome for the

PHOTO 1.1
Popular low-density suburbs are served efficiently by car (Calgary, Canada). *(Vukan R. Vuchic)*

individual, the macrophenomenon of sprawling suburbs and poorly planned "edge cities" has generated serious problems—including those of high cost of infrastructure (particularly transportation); excessive consumption of land, energy and other resources; and social segregation (Bank of America et al. 1995; Pennsylvania Environment Commission 1998; Transportation Research Board 1998).

Much of the change in urbanized areas is being made step by step, with no integrated vision of the future metropolitan areas—their physical form, economic and social functioning, and quality of natural and man-made environment. In many ways, the present condition of metropolitan areas is not what it would have been if it had been clearly foreseen; nor is it a condition that can continue to develop without exacerbating the problems.

Today, the problems of metropolitan areas are deep and complex. Although economic, government, social, and cultural activities continue to be centered in cities or other "major activity centers," most of the growth is taking place in continuously spreading suburbs with scores of governments. Most suburban townships, villages, and boroughs have little professional planning expertise. Worse still, parochial attitudes toward the rest of the region often are very strong. This situation leads to inefficiencies and inequities. Within most metropolitan areas, there are significant differences among cities, townships, and counties in their taxation rates, employment opportunities, income levels, school quality, safety, and other elements that constitute their overall livability. These are by no means local problems of a few individual cities. Henry Cisneros, former Secretary of Housing and Urban Development, correctly stated, "There is no healthy country without healthy cities" (Cisneros 1993).

TRANSPORTATION SHAPES CITIES AND INFLUENCES THEIR LIVABILITY

Historically, transportation has been the critical factor in selecting the sites of most cities. New York, San Francisco, Naples, and Glasgow were founded around natural harbors; many Midwestern cities were established and grew as major railroad terminals, stations, or transloading points between railroads and boats on the Great Lakes (Chicago) or rivers (Pittsburgh and St. Louis). In fact, the vast majority of cities around the world are located around natural harbors and other transloading points. After their founding, transportation continued to play a strong role in the economy and in the physical growth of cities. Initially, the size of cities was constrained by the ability of the transportation system to provide supplies, particularly perishable goods. With the invention of the railway in England in 1825, this limitation was removed. Railways could now bring sufficient quantities of goods over great distances.

Another constraint on the growth of cities prior to the invention of mechanized transportation systems was the travel of people inside cities, which was limited by the slow speed of walking and horse-drawn coaches. The urban form that developed for these "walking cities" was highly concentrated: high-density housing with stores and factories within walking distance of residential areas (Schaeffer and Sclar 1975). When urban population increased rapidly, the high density often resulted in tenement housing and poor living conditions.

The invention of the electric tramway or streetcar around 1890 led to the introduction of much faster and cheaper transportation than had previously been available. The streetcar provided a high level of mobility as well as easy access to activities throughout an urban area. This newfound mobility—together with the potential for more jobs and higher earnings, for education, medical services, running water, and electricity—contributed greatly to the shift of population from isolated rural areas to cities.

PHOTO 1.2
In high-density areas, congestion limits efficiency of cars (Boston, Massachusetts). *(Ryan/Massachusetts Department of Highways)*

Thus, during this century, urbanization, combined with natural population growth, led to the rapid growth of cities. Then came "transit cities" with growing suburbs along major streetcar and suburban railway lines and the development of suburban centers. A radial urban form, with spokes emanating from the center city, was typical.

The next major development influencing travel and urban conditions was the widespread use of the private automobile, which changed conditions in cities dramatically. The great convenience of the car for individuals led to its extensive use. However, the space requirements of the automobile, which are much greater than for travel by any other mode, aggravated the problem of traffic congestion, especially in medium-size and large cities. Not only did the congestion defeat the major feature of the automobile—its high level of mobility—it led both to inefficiencies and to strong negative impacts of transportation on the urban environment. This has been the main reason for a serious problem of our age, one summed up in the brief phrase, "collision of cities and cars" (Johnson 1993).

The direct, negative impacts of vehicular traffic on the everyday lives of people in cities have been known and debated for a long time. However, not immediately understood were the negative impacts of excessive reliance on car travel in urban areas on their form, lifestyle, and social relationships. In the past two or three decades, however, the concept of quality of life, or livability of individual cities or areas, has been recognized as an important dimension (and problem) of contemporary societies.

Livability is generally understood to encompass those elements of home, neighborhood, and metropolitan area that contribute to safety, economic opportunities and welfare, health, convenience, mobility, and recreation. The United Nations and the Organization for Economic Cooperation and Development (OECD) include these elements in their definition of livability. A broader definition includes such factors as equality, learning, social attachment, and distribution of income. Although livability cannot be defined precisely or measured quantitatively, it is recognized as a very important concept and consideration in the societies of developed countries at the approach of the twenty-first century.

A number of elements comprising livability of an area depend, directly or indirectly, on the type and quality of its transportation system. Thus, the discussions of interaction between transportation and human environment, or, particularly, cities and automobiles, have intensified and progressed in most developed countries. In this respect, the United States has fallen considerably behind its peers.

THE AUTOMOBILE: BUILDER OR DESTROYER OF CITIES?

The rapid increase of car ownership occurred in the United States during the decades immediately preceding and following World War II. Other developed countries followed this trend somewhat later, mostly from the mid-1950s to the mid-1970s. In all countries, widespread ownership of cars has made possible much greater opportunities for people to select their housing, as well as their places of work, business, recreation, and other activities. This increased mobility offered far wider choices and higher living standards. The development of trucking eliminated the need for retail businesses and industries to be located close to railroad terminals or harbors and opened up new locations. As a system, however, the automobile–truck–highway transportation system led to the progressive dispersal of cities and to excessive vehicular travel volumes, which created negative impacts on the urban environment, both natural and man-made.

Consequently, for individuals, the automobile has ushered in an era of unequaled potential for personal mobility and all its concomitant benefits. Today, the private automobile is a basic component of life in every developed country. At the same time, excessive use of the automobile, together with an inadequately organized and poorly managed system of streets, highways, and parking facilities, has brought congestion and created inefficiencies throughout the entire transportation system. In other words, serious negative side effects, both physical and social, have resulted.

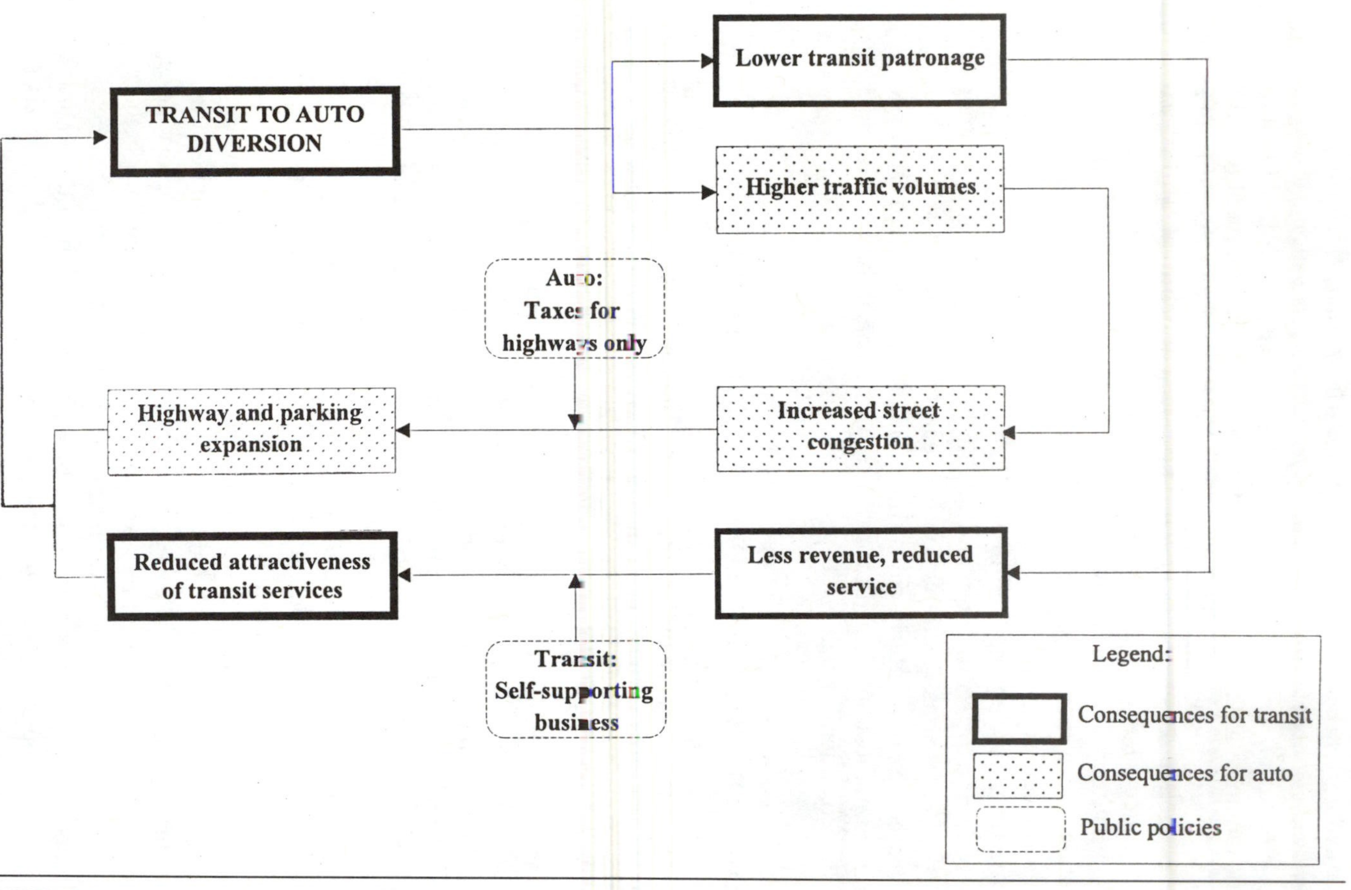

FIGURE 1.1
The vicious cycle in urban transportation intensifying shift of travel from transit to auto due to policies, 1930–1965

PHOTO 1.3
Rapid growth of cities—a worldwide problem (Seoul, Korea). *(Vukan R. Vuchic)*

The problem of excessive automobile traffic in U.S. cities was aggravated by failure to consider transportation as a system made up of different modes. In the early decades of this century, most cities had extensive transit systems. The importance of public transportation was generally recognized. For example, it was eloquently articulated by the Wilcox Commission, which analyzed the crisis of the transit industry (Federal Electric Railways Commission 1920). Yet, when widespread ownership of cars developed during the 1920s and 1930s, governments at all levels focused mainly on accommodating highway traffic while treating public transport as the domain of private transit-operating companies. Nor did governments show any awareness of the importance of pedestrian traffic to the quality of life in cities.

The results of these policies are known as the "vicious cycle of urban transportation," which is shown as a flowchart in figure 1.1. This cycle began when the widespread use of automobiles caused a logical shift of some travel from public transit to cars. Transit began to lose revenues, while its operating costs increased due to street congestion. Meanwhile, car travel suffered from congestion and lack of parking space. In such a situation it was necessary to develop policies aimed at the creation of a coordinated, intermodal transportation system, which is vital for efficiency and livability of cities. However, instead of creating these policies and treating transportation as an intermodal system, palliative policies were applied separately for different modes. Transit was still considered a "private business" with its own financial problems; its crucial role in the vitality of cities was overlooked.

Pressures for wider streets and more parking space were given much more attention. Funds for construction of highways were provided by governments; a permanent supply of funds was secured when taxes and funds were earmarked specifically for highway construction. As figure 1.1 shows, instead of balancing modes, these policies stimulated a further shift of travel from public transit to auto, thus closing the vicious cycle and leading eventually to the "automobilization of cities" and the downgrading of all other modes of travel into second-class transportation. Only much later (after 1970), with federal assistance and new initiatives, was high-quality transit developed, for instance, in such cities as San Francisco, Washington, San Diego, and Portland.

The problem of overreliance on a single mode of passenger transport—the private car—is not limited to metropolitan areas. The problems in intraurban and interurban travel differ somewhat, however. Long-distance travel by car in rural areas may not appear to have direct negative impacts that are as serious, such as air pollution and noise. On the other hand, studies of the national transportation system increasingly point to such nationwide problems as extremely high total cost of highway transportation, including widespread subsidies to car travel, the high social costs of accidents, and the heavy burden of oil imports on the country's trade balance. Another problem is the isolation of people who do not own cars or cannot drive, which is sometimes even more severe in rural than in urban areas. Many of these problems are neither well-known nor understood by the public.

URBAN TRANSPORTATION POLICY DILEMMAS

The conflict between the city and the automobile in the United States has been very serious since the 1920s, with a respite during World War II. The debate over this problem and its possible solutions covers a wide range of opinion. The extreme pro-automobile argument is that the private car is so beneficial that cities should be rebuilt to accommodate its unlimited use. Streets should be widened; extensive networks of freeways and parking facilities should be built throughout metropolitan areas. This thinking prevailed when federal and state laws were adopted that prohibit the use of gasoline and other highway-related taxes for any other purpose except investment in highways (known as "non-diversion laws"). Despite their effectiveness in financing highways, these laws have proven damaging because they prevent intermodal coordination and stimulate further increase in reliance on highway travel.

Federal and some state non-diversion laws have since been revised to allow certain other uses of highway-related taxes, desired to increase efficiency of transportation systems, as required by ISTEA. Yet, extremist lobbyists continue to oppose such changes, considering only their narrow, short-term interests, as illustrated by a recent statement by William Fay, president of the Highway Users Federation: "The highway funding landscape is obstructed by non-highway diversions, subsidized and poorly patronized mass transit projects, and littered with unaffordable luxuries promoting bicycle riding and historic preservation."

Critics of this view point out that this argument is simplistic because it overlooks the fact that car travel is greatly stimulated by both direct and indirect subsidies; that car drivers do not pay for the negative impacts their travel imposes on society and the environment; and that unlimited promotion of highway travel leads to the continuous dispersal of activities, which, in turn, results in increased travel distances. Moreover, in the long run, excessive dependence on car travel, to the neglect of other forms of transportation, is largely self-defeating because it leads to regeneration of highway congestion, which decreases the efficiency of highway travel.

For decades, the problem of collision between cities and cars has been debated in many countries. The approaches, analyses, recommendations, and implementation of policies have varied greatly, however, as have their results. Whereas some countries pursue generally logical transportation policies coordinated with urban redevelopment and growth, others take counterproductive measures that often lead to mutually conflicting goals. The problems resulting from such confusion will be discussed in chapter 3.

Looking at this problem in perspective, the policies governing the relationship of cities and cars can be grouped into three general categories. One policy favors the traditional city, whereas the opposite policy stimulates unlimited use of the private car. Between these two extremes lies a broad group of intermediate policies seeking to establish an optimal relationship of cities and the demand for travel in them. In simplified form, these three policies can be defined as follows:

1. *Restrict auto travel to fit the city*. This policy is based on the concept that cities have great social and historic value, neither of which should be sacrificed to provide unlimited travel by car in urban areas.

2. *Reconstruct the city to allow maximum travel by auto.* To achieve this, the city must be virtually redesigned and built in a different form. The physical and social character of urban areas changes drastically.
3. *Balance development.* Coordinate adjustments to the city with an integrated multimodal transportation system.

The first policy, *restrict auto travel* (that is, adjust transport systems to fit other activities and constraints in the traditional city), has been used successfully in some historic city centers and in sections of cities of varying sizes, particularly in Europe, Japan, and, in the most effective way, in Singapore. This policy has the advantage of preserving the human character of cities while avoiding the negative side effects of motor vehicle travel and traffic congestion. However, if this kind of development is pursued not as a consistent policy but simply by default—lack of any adjustments to streets and arterials—it will result in chronic congestion and inefficiency. Excessive suppression of auto traffic may also deprive the city of the benefits of the high personal mobility offered by the automobile, with its numerous contributions to business and social activities, as well as recreation. The second policy, *reconstruct the city* for extensive vehicular traffic, is pursued when a city follows the simplistic policy of "building itself out of congestion." As traffic volume reaches the capacity of a city's facilities and congestion sets in, transportation authorities try to solve the problem by building additional lanes, streets, parking, and, above all, a large "saturation freeway network" intended to serve major traffic flows throughout the metropolitan area. The negative impact of these actions on the city's physical form and livability is considered secondary to the convenience of travel by car. Any inconvenience to those who cannot or do not choose to use private cars is neglected as well.

This policy has been pursued by many cities, primarily those that grew rapidly in recent decades, such as Dallas, Houston, and Los Angeles. Both physically and socially, these cities have become very different types of human settlements from cities with extensive, direct human interaction and social life. They have developed extensive freeway networks, major arterial roads with strip commercial developments, and sprawling suburbs. Transit has been degraded to a social welfare service for those who do not have cars or cannot drive. Walking is inefficient or impossible because of the considerable distances between destination points, the lack of attractive sidewalks, and the need to cross wide streets and extensive parking facilities. Teenagers, the elderly, tourists, and other categories of people who travel easily in such cities as San Francisco, New York, or London

PHOTO 1.4
Pedestrian streets in older towns enhance their livability (Stade, Germany). *(Vukan R. Vuchic)*

suffer in Houston, Phoenix, Detroit, and Indianapolis from limited mobility. They often are dependent on chauffeuring by others when they want to travel. Virtually all activities in these auto-based metropolitan areas are heavily influenced by, adjusted to, and dependent on, car travel.

Ironically, the reconstruct-the-city policy aimed at accommodation of car travel and truck transport has failed in its main goal: elimination of highway congestion. Having built hundreds of miles of freeways and huge parking structures that dominate not only suburban landscapes but also central cities, these metropolitan areas suffer from highway congestion at least as severe as that of cities with much more limited freeway networks. Moreover, a significant portion of the population—non–car owners—suffers from much lower mobility than it had prior to the rebuilding of these cities.

The third policy, *balanced development*, is based on the concept that a city is a complex system of myriad activities and services, one of which is transportation. The optimal functioning of a city is achieved when all its functions and services are coordinated; in other words, transportation must efficiently serve and interact with other functions. It should neither be suppressed (as in the restrict-auto-travel policy) nor should it dominate other functions and ways of life (as it does in the reconstruct-the-city policy). It will be shown in later chapters that this policy represents the only method capable of achieving efficient urban transport, as well as high-quality environment and life—that is, *an efficient and livable city*.

During the 1950s, when major legislation for highway construction was enacted, there was little understanding of the consequences of large-scale accommodation to automobile travel. For this reason, the reconstruct-the-city policy was for a long time the basis for urban transportation planning. As a result, in the collision between cities and cars, cars have been winning. In large areas of most U.S. cities, numerous buildings have been destroyed to make room for highways, parking lots and garages, gasoline stations, and similar facilities. Moreover, in most cities, pedestrian traffic has been badly neglected during the design and operation of streets, plazas, and other public places. This has further contributed to the lower attraction of urban living and the deterioration of large urban areas, particularly central cities.

In summary, transportation is by no means the only reason for the urban crisis in the United States. Obviously, the problems are broader and deeper. They include unemployment, race relations, inadequate schools, lack of a comprehensive public health care system, and the economic and environmental deterioration of urban areas. *However, the practices associated with excessive automobilization—continuous expansion of the highway system, construction of huge parking facilities even in the cores of cities, as well as extensive subsidies of auto travel, paralleled by neglect of transit and other alternative modes of travel—have been major contributors to the urban crisis.* They have further aggravated many urban problems, both in the short and the long run.

THE UNITED STATES AND ITS PEERS: DIVERGING URBAN TRANSPORTATION POLICIES

The United States experienced the rapid growth of automobile use, with its enormous benefits as well as problems, several decades before its peer countries. There have been, however, substantial differences in the attitudes and policies that evolved. Generally, cities in the United States made a far greater effort to accommodate cars than did most cities in the peer countries of Western Europe, Japan, Australia, and Canada. These countries came much sooner to the awareness of the problems the city–car collision causes, and they developed policies which, in many ways, are diametrically different from those followed in the United States.

Peer countries had much to learn from the U.S. experience in traffic engineering, operations and control, and freeway design. Their development during the 1950s resembled that in the United States during the 1930s. However, the acute problems caused by heavy motorized traffic in cities developed rather quickly in Europe and Japan because their cities and street networks were less adaptable to large-volume vehicular traffic than were the grid patterns with wide streets typical of American cities.

It is important to mention that attitudes and policies toward cities in the peer countries are distinctly more positive. For example, in the United States, federal subsidies by means of tax exemptions of housing loans, and federal regulations in the housing loan program favoring the single-family house with garage (but no requirement for pedestrian access or transit service), greatly stimulated the growth of low-density suburbs while decreasing the attraction of living in central cities. In most European countries, policies and financing stimulate historic preservation and urban renewal. Many historic buildings and private houses in cities like Amsterdam, Hannover (Germany), and Zurich have been renovated utilizing tax incentives. Although control of land use and suburban growth vary greatly among countries, policies in peer countries generally are much more supportive of maintaining existing urban areas and preventing the development of large "brown areas"—abandoned housing and industrial buildings in cities—which greatly contribute to the blight in most U.S. cities. The Netherlands does not allow development of outlying, totally car-based shopping centers. The national government of Australia has a "Better Cities Program" which incorporates a set of policies coordinating urban form and intermodal transportation systems. Many were developed based on explicit decisions in a number of countries that "car-based cities" or the "Los-Angelization of cities" must be prevented. The emphasis on retaining and enhancing the human character of cities developed earlier in many peer countries than it did in the United States.

Despite variations in the methods of planning and plan implementation among countries, land-use controls based on a broad concept of public welfare are used more widely in most peer countries than in the United States. American attitudes toward property rights often conflict with controls and thus work in opposition to the development of a more humane urban environment. This mind-set, compounded in recent years by the prevailing NIMBY ("not in my backyard") sentiment, was not always an American tradition. For example, in 1910, President Theodore Roosevelt, a Republican, said: "Every man holds his property subject to the general right of the community to regulate its use to whatever degree the public welfare may require it." The NIMBY attitude has taken hold in many other countries but, in most cases, it is not as entrenched as it is in the United States.

Finally, another example of differences in attitude is found in the development of new towns and suburban areas. In most peer countries, major residential, commercial, and civic activity complexes are built around rail transit stations. These complexes incorporate convenient bus stops, elaborate walkways, and attractive pedestrian plazas and facilities. Along with new towns with coordinated multimodal transportation, they are found not only in the well-known example of Stockholm, but also in Amsterdam, Frankfurt, Sydney, and Tokyo.

During the first half of the twentieth century, the United States was a leader in the coordination of planned developments with intensive land use around transit stations, with good street access and elaborate pedestrian facilities. For example, many suburban towns were founded and developed around railroad stations in Philadelphia (Main Line), Cleveland (Shaker Heights), the New Jersey suburbs of New York City, and numerous other places. But, in view of the American preoccupation with cars and highways since the 1950s, often all other modes have been practically eliminated from consideration in designing new developments and towns.

A good example of the car-only orientation—the town of Reston, Virginia—was designed during the 1960s for a population of 100,000. It was widely touted as an example of the best in American city planning. However, although it is near Washington, D.C., there was no provision for transit services in the plans. Bus service was later organized by citizen initiative to provide an alternative to total car dependence for commuting to Washington. Many suburban residential and office developments have neither transit access nor even pedestrian walkways. Only in recent years have the concepts of "traditional neighborhoods" and "transit-oriented developments" been invoked to introduce the idea that human-based design and availability of facilities—not only for cars, but also for bicycles, transit, and pedestrian activities—offer a higher quality of life than total car dependence.

Thus, America's peers have been much more active in implementing various balanced-development policies. The proliferation of urban deterioration due to excessive use of cars has been widely discussed and analyzed, and in many other countries, innovative measures have been introduced to address the problem. Not only academics, planners, engineers, and civic leaders, but also the general public is aware of the transportation difficulties contemporary metropolitan areas face and of the trade-off between the individual convenience of unlimited driving and the social goal of a livable city.

It will be argued later that the present differences between the United States and its peers in urban transportation are not as extreme in laws and officially proclaimed policies as they are in implementation. Underlying this situation is the dichotomy between U.S. laws concerning transportation and actual practices in metropolitan areas. The reasons for the differences between the United States and its peers in urban transportation policies and practices, and their consequences—including selected lessons U.S. cities can learn—are analyzed in the following chapters.

THE VITALITY OF CITIES REMAINS CRUCIAL

The serious crisis of cities in the United States is the subject of numerous studies and discussions. With the continuing growth of "edge cities" and the decay of many parts of central urban areas, the opinion is sometimes heard that cities are much less important now than they were in the past—that with rapidly increasing service industries, decreasing manufacturing, and growth of telecommunications, cities may not be needed in the future. What the form of settlements will be, or the type of living that goes on in them, is seldom discussed, however.

This view represents an apology for current uncoordinated policies and actions, and it has several obvious flaws. First, although the suburban share of activities has been increasing steadily, the importance of central cities to the economic and social health of entire urban regions remains crucial. Second, the diminished-importance view is based on the assumption that present trends are part of a natural process, so that the future scenario toward which present trends lead is an inevitable one. Actually, the trends are strongly influenced by numerous social and economic policies, from subsidies to single-family housing to tax deductions for auto travel. Thus, present trends are neither natural nor inevitable. Third, in many metropolitan areas, the trends in recent years point toward growing urban transportation problems and deteriorating social and economic conditions rather than toward viable, and livable, cities and suburbs. Fourth, urban sprawl and "edge city" developments are not only inefficient in initial use of resources such as land, construction of highways, and utilities, but also in their operation (Burchell et al. 1999; Pennsylvania Environment Commission 1998).

These problems and inefficiencies in metropolitan areas compound national problems of excessive use of resources, particularly energy. Transportation is the leading consumer of oil in the United States, which now imports more than 50 percent of the oil it consumes. The cost of these imports, exceeding $50 billion per year, is the largest import expenditure item; automobiles and their parts are the second-largest import item. Thus, the excessive reliance on highway transportation represents a major contributor to the country's negative trade balance, which weakens its economic strength and international competitiveness.

It is remarkable that in the United States and Great Britain, many analysts of urban transportation downplay the existing problems in cities, failing to recognize the problems that arise from total reliance on car travel. In his extensive analysis of contemporary cities, Altshuler (1979) claims that urban transportation has been a "resounding success." Any unbiased observer of urban transportation in American cities can easily see how unrealistic this statement is. Several Transportation Research Board committees analyzing urban transportation have also adopted the "inevitability hypothesis"—that the present problems are not serious and that major changes in the trends are not possible anyway.

In 1996, a major article in *The Economist* presented an extensive analysis of the serious problems car traffic causes in cities but focused on cleaner engines as the solution to the problem! The same tendency to consider air pollution as virtually the only problem caused by car travel in cities is found in publications by Sperling (1995, 1997). His focus is also on developing electric or other types of "clean cars." The fact is that air pollution, however serious, is only one aspect of the problem of excessive use of cars in metropolitan areas. Sperling fails to see the importance of other modes. Actually, he severely criticizes transit—as though it were a problem, rather than an underutilized component of the solution. He even claims that the trends in European countries are essentially the same as those in the United States, lagging only by a time interval. Descriptions of policies in peer countries presented in chapter 4 of this book show clearly that differences in urban transportation between the United States and other developed countries are due not only to different historic and various local conditions, but to fundamental differences in attitudes and policies and, consequently, in trends in transportation developments.

Confusion about the future of metropolitan areas leads, by default, to inaction and further accentuation of the problems. It represents the clear denial of a serious economic and social problem the country is facing while preventing rational planning and implementation of coordinated policies leading to the positive goal of efficient and livable cities.

Several basic facts concerning the importance of urbanized areas, and the role transportation plays in their vitality or in their problems, are outlined here.

Fact 1

In developed, industrialized countries, metropolitan areas house more than two-thirds of the population. Thus, urban problems—be they economic, environmental, safety, welfare, social, or cultural—affect a vast majority of each country's population, either directly or indirectly. Healthy metropolitan areas are therefore clearly of great importance for the country's vitality, prosperity, and economic competitiveness. The excessive separation of different economic and ethnic groups of the population, between central cities and suburbs, or among different areas, represents an obstacle to solving economic and social problems. The present transportation system contributes to this problem in two ways.

First, car travel fosters the spatial separation of activities and the segregation of residential areas. High-quality public transportation usually contributes to mixed land uses, stimulating the creation of major activity centers and more diversified residential developments (apartment buildings, town houses, and single-family units). The strong bias toward cars over all other modes leads to separated rather than diversified, integrated land uses (Weyrich and Lind 1996).

Second, the present gross underpricing and ubiquitous subsidies of car travel, found in the United States far more than in its peer countries, leads to its overuse. Cheap mobility leads to the trade-off of longer travel for land values. It is often less expensive for individuals to abandon buildings and entire areas in central cities and move to remote locations than to renovate old infrastructure. This is one of the main reasons for the existence of extensive areas with skeletons of abandoned factories and houses in most U.S. metropolitan areas. Further, the people who remain in these areas have a greatly diminished chance of finding employment and maintaining a reasonable quality of life. The downward spiral of social and economic decline is thus accelerated.

Fact 2

Certain activities—such as some industries, recreation, and housing for a large portion of the population—are performed more efficiently or preferably in low-density settings. Others—for example, many governmental functions, services, consulting, banking, and educational activities—are optimally performed in high-density areas. Various social and cultural activities—such as concerts, conventions, sport events, and parades—also require high concentrations. *To permit easy functioning of all these diverse activities, the urban transportation system must be capable of serving efficiently a variety of densities and travel volumes. Only a multimodal system, consisting of private and public transportation modes, is capable of meeting this need.*

Fact 3

The increasing car dependence is not sustainable. If the present trends in urbanized areas are allowed to continue and worsen, the United States will increasingly suffer from the lack of diverse densities and of efficient activity centers—the strong economies of agglomeration that cities inherently

PHOTO 1.5
Superbly designed urban highways can serve low-density suburbs, but not urban cores, due to their large space consumption (Austin, Texas).
(Texas Department of Highways and Public Transportation)

provide. This places U.S. metropolitan areas, and the entire country, in a very unfavorable situation vis-à-vis its peer countries.

Fact 4

Regardless of the degree of car ownership, *there will always be a significant segment of the population who cannot use a private car.* It is an advantage

PHOTO 1.6
Modern traffic engineering can promote integration of cars, bicycles, and pedestrians (Eindhoven, Netherlands). *(Vukan R. Vuchic)*

of urbanized areas that they can offer high-quality public transportation and many developments based on walking access. These prevent the creation of second-class citizens—those not owning cars and those who cannot or do not want to drive.

In conclusion, metropolitan areas are centers of every country's activities, of its economy, social life, and residential living. Their prosperity depends greatly on healthy central cities, and their form and vitality are closely tied with the type of transportation system; that is, they depend on the composition of the utilized modes.

Notes

1. Other developed, industrialized countries, primarily those in Western Europe, the Far East, Australia, and Canada, are referred to in this book as United States peers, or simply as "peer countries."

2. The term "city" usually refers to a traditional city surrounded by suburbs and undeveloped areas, together comprising a metropolitan area. In addition to this strict definition, the term is used in this study in a broader sense, referring to urbanized (built-up) or metropolitan areas. Thus, for instance, the

discussion of "collision of cities and cars" will cover entire metropolitan areas, rather than "core cities" only.

References

Altshuler, Alan. 1979. *Current issues in transportation policy.* Lexington, MA: Lexington Books.

Bank of America et al. 1995. *Beyond sprawl: new patterns of growth to fit the new California.* San Francisco, CA: Bank of America.

Burchell, Robert W., et al. 1999. *Eastward Ho! development futures: paths to more efficient growth in Southeastern Florida.* Report prepared by the Center for Urban Policy Research, Rutgers University, for the Florida Department of Community Affairs and the U.S. Environmental Protection Agency.

Cisneros, Henry G., ed. 1993. *Interwoven destinies.* New York: W. W. Norton.

(The) Economist. 1996. Taming the beast – living with the car. June 22. pp. 3–18.

Federal Electric Railways Commission. 1920. *Proceedings and final report.* Washington, DC: U.S. Government Printing Office.

Johnson, Elmer W. 1993. *Avoiding the collision of cities and cars: urban transportation policy for the twenty-first century.* Chicago, IL: American Academy of Arts and Sciences and the Aspen Institute.

Pennsylvania 21st Century Environment Commission (PEC). 1998. Report to Governor Ridge. Harrisburg, PA: PEC. September. Available on the World Wide Web at: http://www.21stcentury.state.pa.us

Rendell, Edward G. 1994. *The new urban agenda.* Report issued by the Mayor's Office, City of Philadelphia, Pennsylvania.

Schaeffer, K. H., and E. Sclar. 1975. *Access for all: transportation and urban growth.* Hammondsworth, UK: Penguin.

Sperling, Daniel. 1995. *Future drive: electric vehicles and sustainable transportation.* Washington, DC: Island Press.

______. 1997. A new agenda. *Access* (Fall). University of California at Berkeley, Berkeley, CA. pp. 2–9.

Transportation Research Board. 1998. *The costs of sprawl – revisited.* TCRP Report 39. Report prepared by Robert W. Burchell et al. for Transportation Research Board, National Research Council. Washington, DC: National Academy Press.

Weyrich, Paul M., and William S. Lind. 1996. *Conservatives and mass transit: Is it time for a new look?* Washington, DC: Free Congress Foundation and American Public Transit Association.

2

The City–Transportation Relationship

The dynamic growth and changes in cities and metropolitan areas require that their transportation systems be further developed and modified. The types of transportation systems, in turn, influence the growth, characteristics, and environment of the cities and metropolitan areas. Thus, there is continuous interaction between the city, on one side, and its transportation system, which consists of the infrastructure and the operation of its different modes, on the other.

The serious transportation problems many cities face are largely the result of policies and planning that failed to take into account the long-term relationship that exists between a city and its transportation. Many of the decisions made during policy formation and implementation tend to focus on the improvement or construction of individual modes and facilities, with no consideration being given to the long-term impact of the overall transportation system. Finally, transportation policies often neglect the needs of the great variety of activities and groups of urban residents that have a stake in the outcome.

An understanding of the basic role of transportation in urban areas is essential to the use of the systems approach that needs to be taken in planning urban transportation. This role depends on the different systems and modes involved, on their immediate impact on facilities, as well as their long-term impact on cities – in other words, on the urban environment and desired quality of life.

CITIES AND THEIR TRANSPORTATION

Every city represents a concentration of human activities such as housing, industry, government, commerce, education, and social interaction. This complex system of activities can function efficiently only with assistance from various services: food and water supplies, transportation, communications, health, and police and fire protection.

Transportation is often referred to as the "lifeblood of cities" because it provides the essential link among activities and, in the long run, to a large extent, it helps shape the city. The urban resident lives in one place. He or she goes to work at another place, shops or visits at yet another. Each of these activities usually requires travel from one point to another. If the activities are located close to each other, the trips are short and can be performed by nonmotorized modes, such as walking or bicycle. This is typically the case in city centers, major activity centers, and university campuses. *If cities are large, however, and travel distances are great, faster motorized and higher capacity systems, or different transportation modes, are needed.* Cars, buses, and trains meet this need.

This description of the function of transportation and its role in cities defines the basic requirements. On one side, *transportation must provide efficient service for the movement of people and goods*; on the other, *transportation should be one of the components of the city that is physically and functionally integrated with other activities and services.* Transportation facilities should not dominate other activities, nor should the transportation system severely constrain urban environment and quality of life.

A common problem that affects development of transportation in metropolitan areas has been the tendency to consider one mode of transportation as "the best," and thus favor that mode in planning and financing, to the neglect of other modes. This is especially the case with the private automobile. Studies performed in many countries as early as the 1960s (Buchanan 1964; Fitch 1964; Hollatz and Tamms 1965) point out the need to understand both the advantages and the disadvantages of auto use in urban areas. Most of these studies strongly emphasize the importance of transit and pedestrian travel.

Travel needs in cities vary greatly by location, time, distance, and other characteristics, as well as by category of traveler. These diverse needs are best met by providing the services of different systems, or modes, of transportation. These modes—including walking, bicycle, car, bus, and rail transit—vary greatly among themselves: in performance (speed, reliability, availability, frequency of service, and so on); in cost (both initial investment and operating); and in the space occupied by a person traveling by a

PHOTO 2.1
High-capacity radial freeway (San Francisco Bay Area). *(Vukan R. Vuchic)*

specific mode. This last aspect determines the capacity of each facility and thus the area required for the movement of people and goods in a city.

In areas of concentrated activity, the extensive use of low-capacity modes, particularly the private automobile, leads to congestion, which results in unreliable, low-speed travel, higher costs, and deterioration of the area's environment and attractiveness. Transit systems, with their greater capacity, make higher-density development feasible because transit and walking can serve the high volume of people generated by such developments.

In a transportation system designed to be car-oriented, buildings are likely to be separated by considerable distances to provide for roads and parking, and this makes walking less attractive and even difficult. Neglect of pedestrians makes urban areas less safe and the use of transit less convenient. These conditions lead to further dependence on the automobile and to the creation of an environment that is car-oriented rather than human-oriented. Such conditions are less conducive to diverse social, recreational, and business activities than are those urban areas that provide different modes of intracity travel. Thus, the selection of transportation modes—specifically, the respective roles given transit, cars, bicycles, and pedestrians—is an extremely important decision in determining the character of, and quality of life in, urban areas.

PHOTO 2.2
Highway congestion results in increased costs and wasted time (San Francisco Bay Area). *(Bob Colin, CALTRANS)*

TRANSPORTATION REPRESENTS A SYSTEM

The complexity of selecting transportation systems and modes for each urban area is often underestimated. Incremental decisions are frequently made to provide solutions to immediate problems that may not lead to long-range efficiency of the transportation system. For example, in recent years, the U.S. Department of Transportation, along with many metropolitan area leaders, has often stated that the main goal in improving transportation is "to solve the highway congestion problem." This statement confuses symptom with cause. Congestion is a consequence of inappropriate policies and inadequate planning; it is not the fundamental problem of transportation. *Multimodal planning*—planning highways, streets, transit systems, pedestrian facilities, and other modes in a coordinated manner—has, in theory and on the basis of the experience of progressive cities, been recognized as an essential goal for urban areas. In practice, in many metropolitan areas, only rudimentary beginnings of such planning can be found.

The experience of many countries in recent decades shows that solutions to the problems of urban transportation, especially in medium-size and large cities, can be found only through a *systems approach,* which requires:

- A thorough knowledge of the characteristics and impacts of different transportation modes
- Treatment of transportation as a functional system consisting of different modes integrated for optimal performance
- A concerted effort to balance the behavior of individuals with the efficiency of the transportation system and, ultimately, the metropolitan area
- Consideration of the short- and long-range roles and impacts of different modes on the man-made and the natural environment
- Recognition of social and equity aspects: the need to provide the entire population with a reasonable level of mobility
- Use of transportation modes that will enable and stimulate creation of human-oriented urban areas
- Preparation of an evolutionary implementation plan for achieving a livable city

Complexity of Urban Transportation Modes

Inadequate understanding of the role and impacts of urban transportation systems has often led to confusion in transportation planning. For example, several theoretical analyses of hypothetical cities, using minimum cost as the only criterion, have been made to compare different modes of transportation. Differences in transport systems—with respect to performance, operating characteristics, passenger attraction, and positive and negative impacts—were disregarded. The economists Meyer, Kain, and Wohl (1965) published *The Urban Transportation Problem,* which, for many years, misdirected transportation analysis among many academics who had little familiarity with urban transportation. Their study found that rail transit is, under virtually all conditions, "inferior" to bus and car.

Not only is this finding conceptually incorrect, but it runs contrary to dozens of plans and studies for real-world cities. The conclusions of Meyer et al. (1965) have been disproved by the fact that there has been extensive construction of different rail transit modes since the 1960s on all continents and with great success. In North America, the number of metropolitan areas with rail transit has nearly tripled since publication of their book. The success and positive impacts of BART in San Francisco, Metro in Washington, and the San Diego Trolley are so clear that the perennial academic critics of these systems have become lonely voices. People have repeatedly voted to extend these systems. What, then, caused such a discrepancy between theory and the real world? The answer is: an incorrect methodology for comparison of modes, combined with the biases of people who emotionally favor a single mode (in this case, the car) because they fail to understand the more complicated but far superior concept of multimodal systems.

Urban transportation modes such as the bicycle, car, bus, or train vary greatly in their performance, the level of service offered, and, most important, ability to attract passengers. In the terminology of economists, modes differ not only in their supply but in their demand characteristics as well. In planning new transportation systems and selecting among modes, one must carefully consider the differences in their attraction of users-passengers, as well as their short- and long-term impacts. The fact that many of these impacts are qualitative and cannot be expressed in monetary values, or that many of the benefits and costs are transferred to others, must not become reasons for ignoring them. Indeed, in some instances, user and nonuser benefits outweigh the system investment and operating costs; this is the case with "free" transportation services such as parking in shopping malls, bus shuttles (Denver), and fare-free light rail services (Buffalo) in central business districts (CBDs).

Because of differences in infrastructure, service, and passenger attraction, modes differ fundamentally in the role they play in metropolitan areas, in shaping land use, and in their impacts on quality of life. For example, freeways and streets differ greatly; they have relative advantages and disadvantages—in their attraction of users, their impacts on the surroundings, and their roles in metropolitan areas. So, too, do rapid transit and light rail transit (LRT), LRT and buses, and cars and bicycles.

Comparison of such fundamentally different modes as rapid transit, buses, and cars by cost alone disregards some of the most important goals and criteria that must be included in transportation planning. With such a methodology, studies searching for the "lowest cost" mode often find that buses are "better" than rail transit, or that unregulated jitneys are "more efficient" than buses. This search for a single "optimal mode" is unrealistic because "superiority" of modes depends heavily on the prevailing conditions and planning goals. Also, fundamental deficiencies in this methodology are clearly demonstrated by the fact that if the same analysis is applied to all modes of urban transportation, one would reach the absurd conclusion that motorcycles are superior to all other modes of urban passenger transportation. They are cheaper and faster than cars, while their great inferiority in safety and comfort are not considered in the simple "minimum cost" model used in the Meyer et al. (1965) study and in several later ones that adopted the same methodology.

Real-world problems are more complex. Comparison of multidimensional systems cannot be done on a two-dimensional diagram of costs versus travel volume. Translating to the real world, a realistic comparison of bus and rail transit must include such factors as the stronger passenger attraction and land-use impacts of rail transit. Or, a comparison of travel modes cannot ignore the fact that services provided by unregulated jitneys in Manila or Istanbul would meet none of the comfort and safety standards adopted in Western countries, or that few people would like to reduce their costs by riding motorcycles rather than driving cars. Thus, an excessively simplified theoretical approach cannot lead to valid conclusions.

There is often a tendency to search for solutions to urban transportation problems in exotic technology. For decades, monorails provided the image of a "system of the future." So far, however, they have remained only that—a system of the future—because rail transit systems are superior to them in virtually all applications. "Group Rapid Transit" (GRT), twelve-passenger vehicles operating, supposedly, at one- to two-second intervals behind each other, were researched without any defined potential role in urban transportation. Personal Rapid Transit, or PRT—an imaginary system of vehicles with three to four seats, which would be operated automatically on an extensive network of elevated guideways, claimed to fit any city—was discussed and promoted from the late 1960s to mid-1970s. The PRT system was proposed for several cities (for example, Minneapolis, Denver, and Gothenburg, Sweden), but in each case it was deemed infeasible, both operationally and economically. Yet, recently the same concept has been revived. Currently, an effort is being made to build a PRT line in a Chicago suburb. The inherent incompatibility of expensive, grade-separated guideways and small, automated vehicles unable to handle a large volume of passengers remains a problem that cannot be "resolved."

Since 1990, research and development in "Intelligent Transportation Systems" (ITS) has been given large government financing, funding projected to amount to $40 billion over the next twenty years. This program of applying contemporary communications technology to highway and transit systems will contribute significantly to traveler information and to the safety and reliability of transport systems. However, it will not solve the basic problems in urban transportation: the city–car conflict and achieving balance among transport modes for efficient, livable metropolitan areas. In many cases, if ITS increases the capacity of freeways leading to central cities, it may lead only to an increase of travel volume, expressed as vehicle-kilometers traveled (VKT) or vehicle-miles traveled (VMT). This would intensify all its negative impacts (Topp 1995). Critics of this effort and these huge expenditures point out that the ITS program is being promoted by a coalition of more than 500 organizations, nearly 40 percent of which are nontransportation industries. This coalition of interested companies, including IBM, AT&T, Rockwell, and the three major U.S. automakers, are advisors to the U.S. Department of Transportation (DOT) on this effort; yet, the goals of many components of this program are at best vague, if not questionable (Lowe 1993).

The problem all these efforts have in common is that they are attempting to find solutions to urban transportation via new technology alone, whereas *the core of the urban transportation problem is actually based more on shortsighted policies and poor organizational procedures than on technological inadequacies.*

The confusing claims and conflicting actions about different transport modes and the role of different transportation technologies would not be so prevalent if the city–transportation interaction were better known, if problems were correctly diagnosed, and if the characteristics of different modes were properly understood. Toward this end, a brief but systematic review of the family of urban passenger transportation modes is presented.

PRIVATE, PUBLIC, AND FOR-HIRE TRANSPORT

The basic classification of urban transportation systems is functional, that is, on the basis of their type of use, their availability to travelers, and the type of service provided. Each of the following categories — private, public transport (transit), and for-hire (paratransit) — has distinctive characteristics and a particular role in cities.

Private Transportation

This category — which includes walking, bicycle, motorcycle, private car, and similar modes — gives the user the greatest freedom of movement with respect to time and place. Aside from that feature, private modes (particularly pedestrians and cars) differ greatly among themselves in their characteristics and impacts on the environments they are in.

PHOTO 2.3
Pedestrian traffic: a basic element of urban livability (shopping street in Stockholm). *(Vukan R. Vuchic)*

Walking, or pedestrian traffic, represents the basic, ubiquitous mode of travel that is by far the most efficient means of transport for short-distance trips. As Bovy (1973) pointed out, every trip begins and ends on foot, even if only to and from a car. Walking is more convenient, cheaper, and usually faster than any vehicular trip for travel up to 400 meters (1,300 feet). In attractive areas, people walk much greater distances. The major limitations of walking are low speed, effort required (particularly on hilly terrain), obstacles in areas where pedestrian traffic is neglected, and inconvenience of walking in inclement or extreme weather conditions. Fruin (1971) presents extensive—in many ways, definitive—material on the pedestrian as a transportation system, at both the micro and the macro scales.

Due to its superior characteristics for diverse, short, high-density trips, walking is by far the most convenient and efficient mode of travel in such areas as transportation terminals, major building complexes, downtown areas, public squares and plazas, shopping streets, suburban malls, and university campuses. Therefore, it is of critical importance for efficiency and user attraction to design these areas and facilities for the utmost convenience, safety, and attraction to pedestrians, and to give this mode preferential treatment over vehicular traffic, or full separation from it.

PHOTO 2.4
Suburban shopping malls are pedestrian havens. *(Vukan R. Vuchic)*

In addition to the function of travel, pedestrian traffic is a fundamental component of livable cities. Most people would agree that a basic feature of the livable city is the ability to walk in pleasant surroundings. Cities that have a high rate of crime in streets, poor facilities for pedestrians, no protection for people from vehicles or inclement weather, and few attractions along pedestrian facilities cannot be considered human-oriented, attractive, or livable.

Bicycle transportation is the most economical vehicular mode of transportation. It is far less comfortable than the car, it requires effort on the rider's part, and it is vulnerable to inclement weather and hilly terrain. At the same time, it is attractive to those interested in physical exercise and in the bicycle's convenience for short trips in cities, suburbs, parks, campuses, and so on. Because of its much lower negative impact compared to car travel, countries and cities concerned with environmental protection usually have a policy of promoting bicycle travel.

Following a period in the 1960s when it appeared that cars might eventually replace bicycles, physical recreation and the environmental aspects of urban living have led to a revival of interest in the bicycle. Thus, whereas bicycles are used extensively in developing countries such as China and India, due primarily to their low cost, they are used as an attractive and

PHOTO 2.5
Design of shopping malls for auto access only prevents their interaction with surrounding areas. *(Vukan R. Vuchic)*

efficient mode by substantial portions of the population in several developed countries, particularly the Netherlands, Denmark, and Germany. In many U.S. cities, too, interest in bicycle use is increasing. However, most city and state departments of transportation still tend to ignore this potentially useful mode of travel; they neither provide bicycle facilities nor enforce the traffic laws essential for safety and convenience.

The convenience and appeal of bicycle use depends on numerous local conditions, such as climate, topography, design of streets, traffic regulation, and population characteristics. As a system, the bicycle mode has the advantages of higher capacity and lower negative impacts than autos, motorcycles, mopeds, and other forms of private vehicles.

The *highway transportation system* consists of networks and facilities (roads and streets) that can be classified in three categories:

Category C—urban streets, which serve primarily local traffic accessing the served area;

Category B—arterials, some of which are partially grade separated multilane roadways serving mostly through traffic; and

Category A—freeways or divided, controlled-access highways, which serve only through traffic.

PHOTO 2.6
Bicycle paths designed on sidewalks operate efficiently in many European cities (Munich). *(Vukan R. Vuchic)*

PHOTO 2.7
Federal laws—ISTEA and TEA-21—have stimulated construction of bikeways in U.S. cities (Boulder, Colorado). *(Mario Semmler)*

PHOTO 2.8
Freeways—category A highways—serve major corridors in large cities (Sao Paolo, Brazil). *(Eduardo Vasconcelos)*

In addition to serving *moving traffic*, the highway transportation system includes facilities for *stationary traffic*, such as terminals and car parking, which have a particularly strong impact on urban environment because of their high consumption of space.

Among highway vehicles—which include bicycles, cars, buses, and trucks—cars are the dominant mode of travel in developed countries, particularly in the United States. The private car gives its user great personal convenience and independence in time and direction of travel, short travel time, and personal comfort. These advantages make the car an extremely attractive mode, particularly for individual users, families, and small groups. As a system, however, the auto/highway mode is limited in its urban applications. It causes congestion at relatively low traffic volumes (a traffic lane on a local or an arterial street reaches congestion when cars on it carry between 700 and 1,400 persons per hour). Its social cost, created by congestion and negative environmental impacts, can be high, especially in urban areas. Its average energy consumption per person-kilometer (-mile) is much higher than that for any other mode. Finally, highway accidents lead to large social and personal costs.

The most important but often overlooked impact of extensive reliance on the car is its long-term impact on the form and character of urban areas—weakened social relationships, deterioration of historic and human-oriented cities and towns, greater segregation of social groups, more pollution, higher impact on urban infrastructure, and so on. This problem is attracting the increasing attention of planners and civic leaders around the world.

Car ownership is now extremely high in the United States (about 90 percent of American households own at least one automobile), yet it is important to bear in mind that this mode is not available to everybody. There are several significant categories of the population who either cannot or do not want to use a car. The first, and largest, category is nondrivers: young people, the elderly, or simply those not qualified as drivers, either by circumstances or by choice. This is a sizable group when it is considered that only about 67 percent of the U.S. population are licensed drivers. Although the nondriver group includes babies, children, and very old persons (who travel much less than those in the middle-age licensed-driver group), nondrivers represent a significant portion of the population. Finally, there are the drivers who would prefer not to drive on city streets with heavy traffic, or on frequently congested suburban highways and regional freeways. Many elderly persons with reduced abilities must drive when there is no convenient alternative system.

Among nondrivers, many use automobiles indirectly—for example, children driven by parents. Although chauffeuring is an "American tradition," from a systems point of view, it represents an extremely inefficient mode of transportation. To illustrate, suppose that a mother drives her 14-year-old child to a music lesson, then returns home. An hour later, she drives to fetch the child. This total "operation" amounts to four vehicle trips in order to make two required person-trips—all to transport a child to a lesson and back. The observed average occupancy for these four trips is 1.5; actually, since the mother is not counted (she is merely a chauffeur), the functional average occupancy is only 0.5 persons per vehicle. *For every kilometer the person (child) had to travel, two VKTs were driven.* Obviously, the energy consumption, as well as all negative impacts of VKT for this type of transport, are extremely high. This is in addition to the time and effort the mother devoted to chauffeuring.

The second category (largely, but not completely, included in the first category) are low-income people who do not own cars. In cities where there are considerable concentrations of these people (ranging from 15 to 25 percent of families), they usually can use transit (where it offers adequate services) or walk to most destinations. In rural areas, non-car owners often represent groups with virtually no mobility. This group has been increasing since deregulation of bus systems in the 1980s caused the cessation of bus service from hundreds of towns in the United States and Canada.

The third population category consists of people who are non-car users by choice. They live mostly in cities and find it more convenient and economical not to own an automobile, relying instead on walking, transit, taxis, and occasionally car rentals. Many in this group are licensed drivers.

To a large extent, the size of each category depends not only on age distribution, economic status, and other characteristics of the population, but also on the availability and quality of alternative modes for travel.

In heavily auto-dependent cities such as Detroit and Houston, the gap in mobility between car users and non-car users is extremely large. The third category above is the truly disadvantaged. People who are, by choice, non-car owners, and those who choose to use transit, are an extremely small group in these cities, because it is seldom convenient to use transit and to walk safely in cities totally adapted to cars.

Public Transportation or Transit

Once the main carrier of persons in cities, transit lost its dominant role when automobile ownership increased and reached nearly saturation levels. This has been especially true of U.S. and Canadian cities. Yet, despite its greatly decreased role, transit remains very important; its potential for contributing to the solution of the urban transportation crisis, particularly in central cities, is much greater than is generally recognized. This important role is a result of two basic features of transit:

1. *As a public system, transit is open and available to most of the population,* rather than only to vehicle owners. Thus, in cities, it represents a basic service, and it is one of the significant functional advantages of cities over rural areas.
2. *Transit has far greater transporting capacity, lower area requirements, and fewer negative side effects per passenger trip than does the auto/highway system.* Therefore, it is better suited than cars to meet the demand for high-density travel that exists in medium-size and large cities. These advantages make possible the efficient functioning of the city, with all its diverse activities and densities—a fundamental requirement of urban areas.

Transit has numerous, different roles in metropolitan areas, from transporting children to schools to serving as a distributor for intercity bus, rail, and air travel to and from terminals, to carrying commuters to work. These roles can be aggregated in two major categories. One is *to serve mostly "transit captives"*—people with no access to cars and those who cannot drive or who choose not to drive. This is largely a social service, since most transit users lack a convenient, alternative means for travel. Although this role is

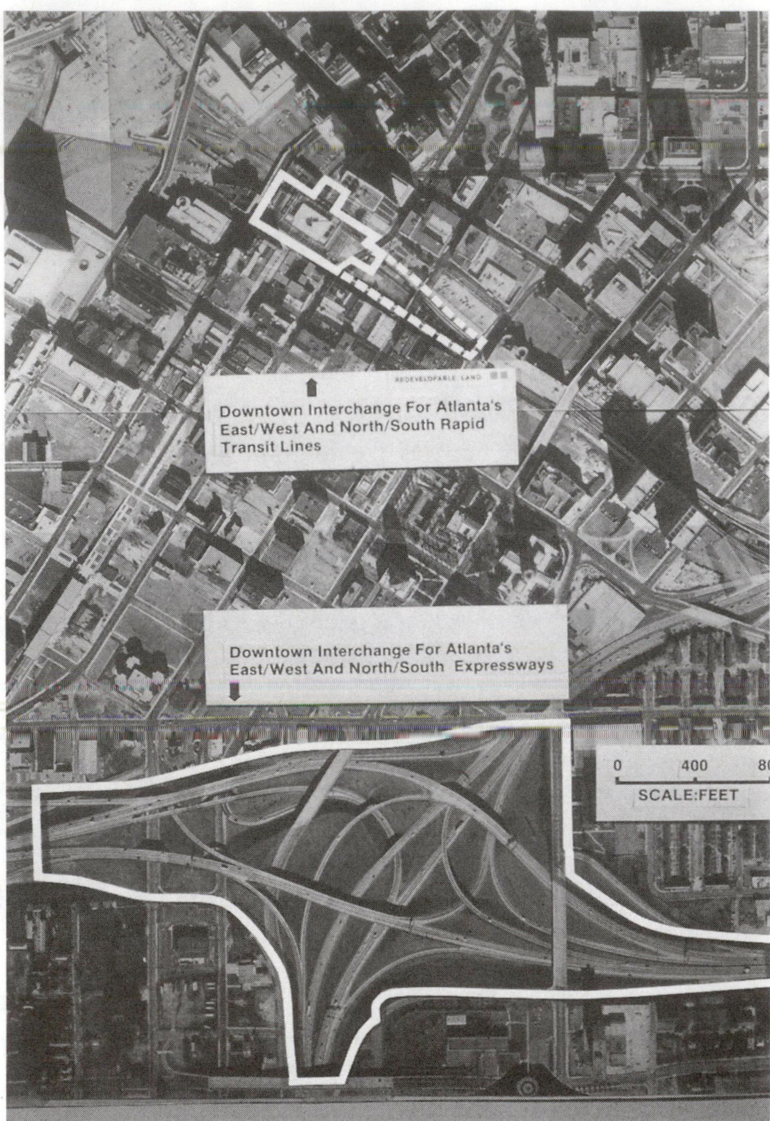

PHOTO 2.9
Compact metro stations fit well into centers of cities, but freeway interchanges occupy large areas; with associated parking facilities, the urban environment is broken up. *(Richard Stanger)*

needed in all cities, it is particularly essential in areas with large numbers of children, elderly, low income people, and other non-car users.

Another role of transit is to serve as *a convenient and competitive carrier for "choice riders"*—those who have access to private vehicles but find transit equally or more attractive on the basis of travel time, cost, convenience, and other features. This is most commonly the dominant role of transit where it carries a large volume of people in medium-size and large cities, in and among major activity centers, and similar areas. One of the fundamental characteristics of a city should be *the ability to travel conveniently without having to own or operate a car*. The requirement to have and operate a car is often an imposition on individuals as well as a source of high, uncompensated social costs. Transit provides such a service. In addition, due to its high capacity, it makes far fewer demands on the urban environment: it produces fewer air pollutants, consumes less energy, and uses less space per trip than the car.

The low space requirement per trip makes transit much better suited for transporting large passenger volumes in metropolitan areas with diverse activities than the car. As noted, the car has by far the highest space consumption of all modes. *Transit represents the only transportation system that makes it possible to have large cities that both function efficiently and have human character*. This is confirmed by urban development in recent decades. A review of cities worldwide shows that cities that are economically strong, socially healthy, and livable are not auto-based; they have multimodal transportation that includes extensive and efficient transit systems (Newman and Kenworthy 1989a; Newman, Kenworthy, and Robinson 1992). They also have extensive and attractive facilities for pedestrians.

Paratransit

This category includes various transport modes that, by their characteristics, fall between private cars and transit. Taxis, jitneys (in developing countries), dial-a-ride, and other types of demand-responsive minibuses (in developed countries) usually provide public service, so that they are available to everyone. Their fares typically are considerably higher than transit fares, but they provide services that are more personalized.

Paratransit thus plays a complementary role to that of the car and transit. For example, in large cities, taxis offer premium-fare personalized service more conveniently than private cars, whereas demand-responsive minibuses can provide transit service in low-density areas more economically than regular transit. In many cities, paratransit is the most efficient mode for providing services to the disabled.

THE FAMILY OF URBAN TRANSIT MODES

The attractiveness to passengers, effectiveness, and economic efficiency of transit systems greatly depend on utilization of the most appropriate transit modes for each particular application. For any set of operating conditions, it is necessary to consider one or several modes that provide the appropriate "performance/investment package" (that is, offer required service for an appropriate level of expenditures). To make a proper analysis, it is necessary to understand the performance characteristics and costs of different modes, then match them to local conditions and project the demand for the type of service each mode would provide, and, finally, select the most appropriate mode among those available.

It is common to classify transit modes by their vehicles and technology—for example, bus, trolleybus, rail, or monorail. People have long been familiar with buses, streetcars/trams, metros, and cable cars. In recent decades, however, there have been numerous inventions and developments of transit systems, not only in vehicular technology but also in system designs and operational concepts. For example, buses today are not always only transit vehicles operating on streets; in some cases, they operate on exclusive bus lanes or on separated busways, which give such systems considerably higher performance.

Rail systems in particular have been extensively diversified. Instead of using only streetcar/tramway lines operating mostly on streets (in Zürich and Toronto) or fully separated, much higher performance metros (New York and Paris), many new rail systems have been built with mostly, although not fully, separated rights-of-way (ROW). Separated tracks allow use of higher capacity vehicles, much higher operating speeds, reliability, and greater comfort than streetcars or buses can provide in mixed street traffic. This development has led to the evolution of a new mode—light rail transit (LRT), exemplified by the systems in Boston (Green Line), Hannover, Nantes, and Sacramento. Although laypeople often confuse streetcars with LRT, the two modes consist of quite different "investment/performance packages." So do LRT and metros, although some systems combine the features of both modes (Chicago, Frankfurt, and Rotterdam).

Transit systems and modes are defined by three basic characteristics:

1. *Type or category of ROW;*
2. *Technology* (mainly, highway or rail vehicles); and
3. *Type of operation* (local, express, special)

(Vuchic 1981)

These characteristics are, to some extent, interdependent. Technology depends heavily on the type of ways or paths on which a transit system operates; for transit lines operating on streets, buses are the dominant technology. The greater the extent of separate ROW provided, the more logical and advantageous it is to use rail vehicles or trains with electric traction. Because the investment cost of a transit system increases sharply with the degree of separation, it is logical that, with higher-quality ROW (partially or fully separated), higher-performance technologies be used. Therefore, whenever ROW is fully separated on an entire line, rail technology becomes distinctly superior. It is logical that, for fully controlled systems, high-performance features be utilized, such as high-capacity vehicles/trains, electric instead of diesel traction, and positive (fail-safe signal) control—all of which can be used by guided rail systems but not by steered ones (buses).

Buses can also be used successfully on partially or fully separated ROW, as is the case on a sizeable network of busways in, for example, Ottawa and Curitiba (Brazil); on an O-Bahn (guided bus) line in Adelaide (Australia); and an exclusive trolleybus tunnel in Seattle. All these systems benefit from full separation from other traffic on substantial portions of their lines, though none is separated over its entire length (so that they do not have the above-described features of rapid transit). These lines and systems have the advantage of lower investment than would be required for full separation of the entire line, and they utilize the ability of buses to branch out on outer sections of lines, which are under certain conditions more useful than the advantages of the total separation characteristic of rapid transit. Consequently, there are no "bus rapid transit systems"; all fully separated transit systems use guided, electrically powered vehicles. However, many "Semirapid Bus Systems" or "Bus Transit Systems" (BTS) utilize extensive sections of separated ROW and have correspondingly higher performance than do regular buses operating on streets.

The same concepts of rapid and semirapid transit modes apply to rail systems. Many LRT systems have extensive sections of fully separated ROW—at-grade (Calgary and St. Louis), aerial (Cologne and San Diego), or in tunnels (Boston and Frankfurt). Yet, because these systems are not fully separated over entire lines and cannot take full advantage of such ROW, they are semirapid, not rapid, transit. Several rail lines, consisting primarily of LRT elements but fully separated ROW—such as the Norristown Line in Philadelphia, Line 8 in Gothenburg, and the Manila LRT line—are defined technically as Light Rail Rapid Transit, or LRRT. Their vehicles, though basically of the LRT type, take advantage of numerous features of rapid transit systems, such as full signalization, high-level platforms, and

PHOTO 2.10
Category B rights-of-way are typically street medians used by light rail transit. *(Vukan R. Vuchic)*

high maximum running speed. Thus, like the term "bus rapid transit," "U-Bahn" designation for LRT lines in some German cities, or "Shaker Rapid" for LRT in Cleveland, Ohio, these names, although popular, are professionally incorrect designations.

Clearly, the type of ROW, the basic infrastructure component of transit systems, determines more than other components both the investment cost and the performance of transit systems. Because of its significance, it is important to define ROW types. Right-of-way, according to Vuchic (1981), is classified into three categories—C, B, and A.

Category C. This category consists of streets or roads with mixed traffic. It requires little, if any, investment. Generally, however, transit services in this category are not competitive with auto travel with respect to speed and reliability: transit vehicles travel together with cars, but they are delayed by having to stop for passengers. Consequently, street transit, comprising services provided by buses, paratransit vehicles, trolleybuses, and streetcars (also known as trams or trolleys), are the modes with the lowest "performance/investment package" of all transit categories. They tend to serve predominantly transit-captive ridership—that is, travelers who cannot use cars.

PHOTO 2.11
Metro systems have high performance due to exclusive ROW (category A) and large, comfortable electric vehicles. *(Paul Myatt, Washington Metropolitan Area Transportation Authority)*

Category B. This category of ROW is partially separated. Typically, transit tracks (or, sometimes, lanes) are placed in a strip of land, such as a curbed street median, physically separated from other traffic. At intersections transit vehicles cross streets at grade, usually under signal control. Transit modes with ROW category B require a considerable investment, but they also have a significantly higher performance and stronger passenger attraction than modes with ROW category C. The most typical mode in this category, designated as semirapid transit, is Light Rail Transit—LRT; Bus Transit Systems—BTS (buses on busways that exclude other vehicles) also belong in this category. While the LRT and BTS systems typically use ROW category B, they may also have line sections of ROW categories A or C.

Category A. This ROW category is fully separated and used by transit vehicles or trains only. It requires very high investment for construction of its aerial structures, tunnels, separated stations, and other infrastructure. The systems with ROW A always have guided technology, usually rail, which inherently offers much higher capacity, reliability, and safety than transit vehicles, steered or guided, operating on streets and highways. The

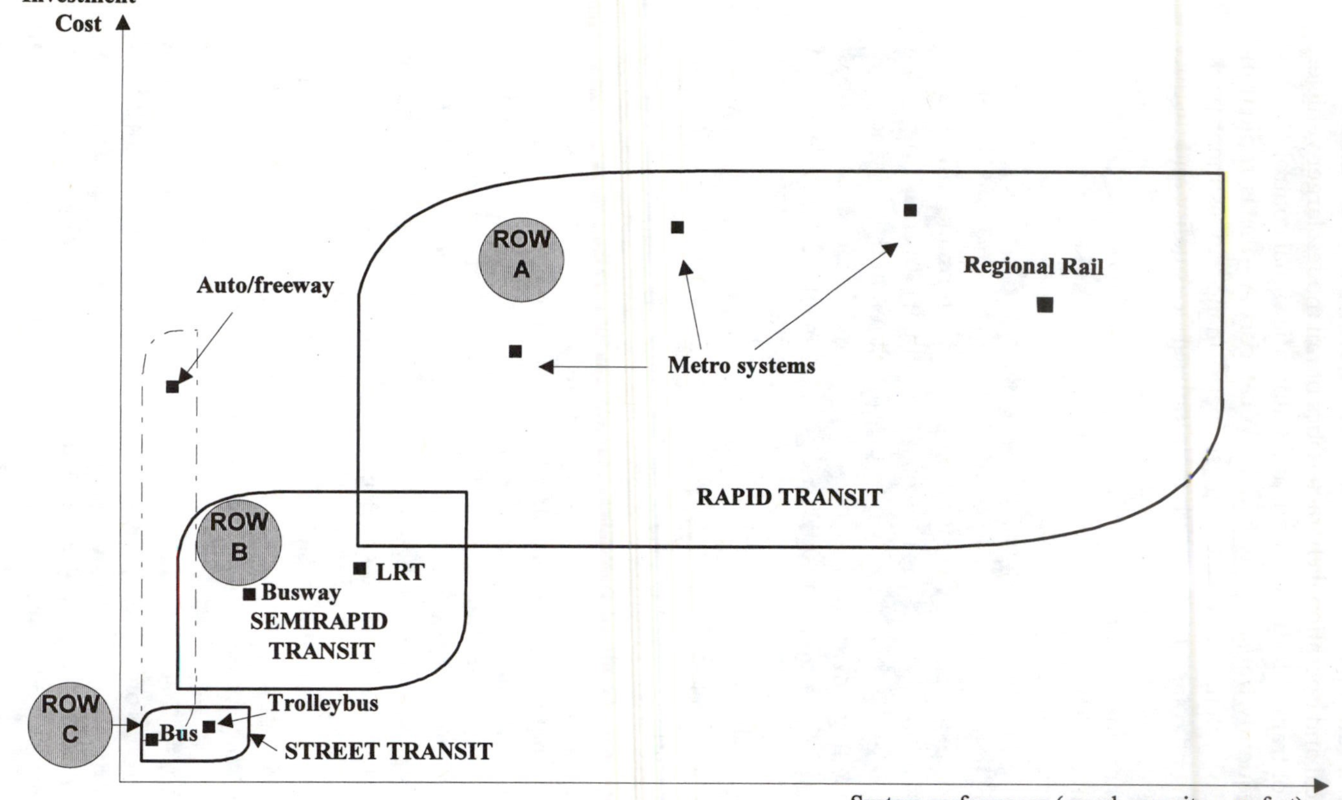

FIGURE 2.1
Performance/investment cost characteristics of different transit mode categories

features that full separation from other traffic brings are best utilized by the technical and operational characteristics of rail modes: larger vehicles, operation of trains, electric traction, and automatic signal control.

Consequently, transit modes with ROW category A—that is, rapid transit or metro systems—offer the highest "performance/investment package" among all transit modes. With their high service quality and distinct lines and stations, they are competitive with car travel and attract considerably higher ridership than street transit modes, *ceteris paribus*. Although the high investment cost limits the size of metro networks, *where large passenger volumes can be attracted, rail rapid transit is operationally superior and has a better performance/cost package than any other mode.*

As explained above, the main set of features to be considered in selecting a transit mode for a given situation is the "performance/investment package"—in other words, the type of system obtained versus how much must be invested. When these two features of different transit modes are plotted on a diagram (figure 2.1), one obtains three distinct sets of modes, which are grouped by their ROW categories. Street transit (category C) represents low investment and low performance modes; rapid transit (category A) is the highest performance/highest investment mode; and semirapid transit modes with ROW B are between these two categories.

This diagram shows that the ROW category is the basic feature determining the performance and cost of transit systems. Through performance, it determines attraction of passengers and competitiveness of transit with the private car. Moreover, the impacts of transit on land use and quality of life in a city depend on the infrastructure of transit systems. Thus, *ROW category is the most important physical component determining the role of transit in urban transportation*. Transit services operating on ROW category C, typically buses, cannot attract passengers from cars unless there is strict parking control or some other deterrent to car use. The most effective use of investment funds to achieve a transit system competitive with cars is to provide separate ROW, that is, category B or A.

The specific vehicle-way technology—minibus, articulated bus, LRT, AGT, or others—actually is a secondary decision in the choice of modes. Technology is largely a technical consequence of ROW category and performance requirements—for example, needed capacity, comfort, speed, safety, and operating cost. For transit services on urban streets (category C) with low to moderate passenger volumes, buses usually are the most effective mode because they offer the highest service frequency and require the lowest investment. The higher the volume, and the longer the lines, the more it becomes necessary to provide higher capacity and speed, respectively. This can best be achieved by transit on partially or fully separated rights-of-way, which, in turn, make rail modes such as LRT, metro, or regional rail the superior choice because they offer considerably higher performance and are more attractive to passengers. They make better use of the investment required for construction of separate ROW.

The diagram in figure 2.1 leads to the following conclusions regarding urban transit modes:

- The modes arranged by their performance–investment cost characteristics represent a *family of transit modes*. This family covers an extremely broad set of characteristics, ranging from paratransit that serves most efficiently low-volume, dispersed travel, through buses on streets and LRT, to metro and regional rail, which are suited to high-volume corridors and networks, usually found in large metropolitan areas.
- There is no single "best" mode. For each set of conditions—such as capacity and speed requirements, physical features, and available investments—one or a few modes are possible candidates. In virtually no situation would such diverse modes as paratransit and regional rail, or minibus and LRT, offer similar services and be close competitors.
- It would be incorrect to claim that one major mode is always better than or inferior to another. As has been shown, this "alchemist research" has been a common error in theoretical studies that compare modes in hypothetical situations on the basis of cost alone, while overlooking the differences in performance and attraction of passengers.

An important classification of transit services is one that is based on the type of trips they serve and the role they play in urban transportation. Two major categories are defined, regular transit and commuter transit.

Regular transit offers services on an integrated network, usually consisting of numerous lines and different modes, with convenient transferring. This basic transit category serves travel throughout the urban area (the "many-to-many" pattern shown in figure 2.2a), from early morning to late evening. This is the basic transit service that all groups of population can use for any trip purpose they need. In large metropolitan areas, regular transit typically consists of a rail network supplemented by buses for extensive area coverage; buses also serve, together with park-and-ride and other modes, as suburban feeders to rail or express bus lines.

PHOTO 2.12
Houston uses many bus and HOV lanes for commuter transit services.
(American Public Transit Association)

Commuter transit provides service exclusively for commuters traveling between suburban areas and the city center or other major activity centers. Thus, it provides "many-to-one" and "one-to-many" types of travel during the morning and afternoon commuting hours, respectively (figure 2.2b). Commuter transit supplements regular transit. Usually it is provided by bus lines operating during peak hours only, often in unidirectional, high-occupancy-vehicle (HOV) lanes, such as Shirley Corridor bus lines in Washington, D.C., and many lines in Houston and Seattle. Some commuter rail lines also operate only during peak hours. In addition, vanpools or paratransit vans, sometimes utilizing HOV facilities, represent typical commuter services.

A number of rail systems, often popularly known as "commuter lines"—such as New Jersey Transit, Chicago Metra, and MARC in Washington, D.C.—are misnomers. Representing regular transit, they are increasingly being designated as "regional rail" (SEPTA's division in Philadelphia) because they offer services throughout the day and serve all trips, including an increasing number of "reverse commuters"—workers who live in central cities but work in suburbs.

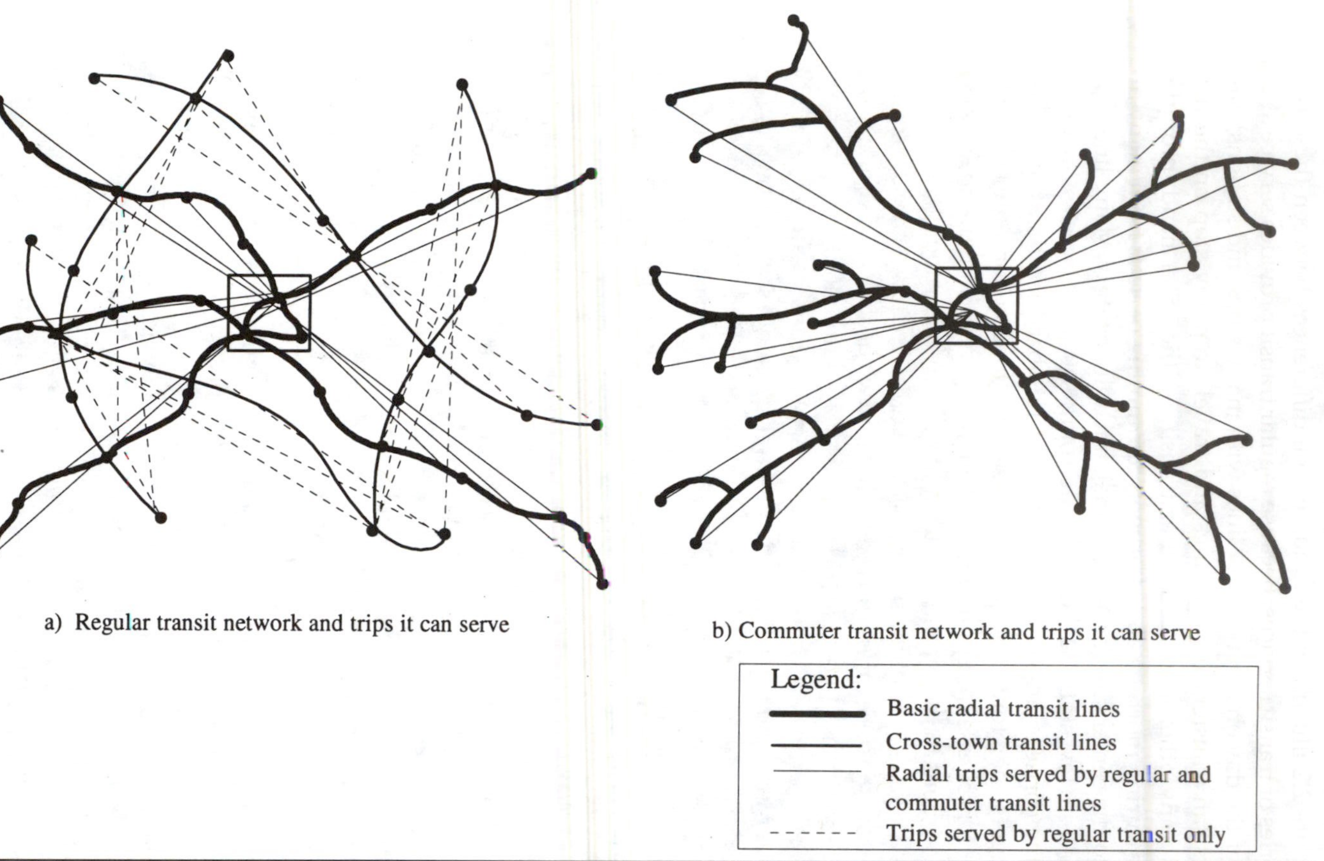

FIGURE 2.2
Urban trips served by regular transit (a) and commuter transit (b)

Figure 2.2 illustrates the fundamental differences between these two categories of transit services. Because regular transit provides service at all times of the day on a network of lines with many stops and stations, passengers can transfer between lines and travel from any stop on the network to any other stop. Commuter transit, on the other hand, provides service during morning and afternoon commuting periods from many areas into the center city (or another major activity center). Many lines run express with few stops, so there is limited or no service between stops along the same corridor and no convenient transfers between the radial lines. Passengers, therefore, cannot use these services for any noncenter-oriented trips or for reverse commuting (trips from center city to suburban employment locations in the morning, with returns in the afternoon).

As a result of the different types of networks, stopping schedules (serving all stops versus express runs between only two or a few stops), and times of operation, these two transit categories play different, though overlapping, roles in urban transportation. Regular transit can serve many noncenter-oriented trips that commuter transit cannot serve (shown in figure 2.2a by dashed lines). On the other hand, commuter transit sometimes can offer faster or more direct service than regular transit for commuters who work in the center city.

These major differences in the roles regular and commuter transit can play are often overlooked by some highway planners and even by city planners for many U.S. metropolitan areas. These planners consider the car to be the basic carrier of urban passenger transport, with transit as "assisting mode" for peak-hour commuters into and out of city centers. This policy of treating the car as the only mode of travel except during peak commuting periods overlooks the fact that a substantial portion of trips cannot be served by car even when it is the dominant mode. This is the case not only during peak hours but throughout the day. If these trips are not served, the city has much lower overall accessibility than cities with adequate services for both types of travel by both modes—car and transit. Furthermore, the effort to shift *all* travel to private cars leads to excessive negative effects of congestion, particularly in large urban areas with a high concentration of activities.

Lack of high-quality regular transit services places a hardship on such population groups as teenagers, the elderly, tourists, choice transit riders, and others; it also leads to serious environmental deterioration in the urban area. Consequently, large cities that rely on cars and commuter transit only are at a serious competitive disadvantage in comparison with cities that have good regular transit services, even if the car has a dominant role.

TRANSPORT SYSTEMS' COMPOSITION RELATED TO CITY SIZE

Urban transportation represents a complex system that involves the interests of individuals as well as society as a whole. Often, these interests conflict and must be reconciled. Similarly, short- and long-term solutions often conflict, and both must be considered in making planning and policy decisions.

Bearing in mind the characteristics of private and public transport systems defined above, it is obvious that their relative roles should vary with population size and density in a metropolitan area. Although such local conditions as topography, physical form, and other characteristics of the city always influence transportation to some extent, the relative roles of private and public transport can be defined for cities of different sizes.

Small Cities

In small cities and urban areas such as Waterloo, Canada; Lancaster, Pennsylvania; or Klagenfurt, Austria, the problem of traffic congestion is less severe than in large cities. Therefore, if good street design and traffic regulation are applied, most travel in these areas can be accomplished by private car while preserving the livability of the town or city. The need for transport of non-auto users, is, however, significant, and transit must provide this social service.

Thus, the role of transit in small urban areas is primarily, if not exclusively, one of social service. Its role as the efficient carrier of large numbers of passengers and its contribution to lower traffic congestion are relatively minor. Transit services cannot economically provide the frequency of service required for transit to be competitive with the automobile, particularly if ample parking is provided and subsidized (that is, users do not pay for it directly).

The fact that transit cannot play a major role in small urban areas implies neither that transit, bicycle, and pedestrian travel should be neglected nor that transportation planning need not be related to urban design and land-use planning. Without planning, even relatively small cities can suffer from frequent congestion, unattractive public areas, and social isolation of large population groups. Towns or suburban areas with land use planned and facilities designed for convenient pedestrian travel to schools, neighborhood stores, business areas, and major activity centers, which also are served by transit, can offer more efficient and livable environments than unplanned areas with extensive urban sprawl, which rely solely on facilities for travel by car.

As city size increases, traffic problems such as congestion, increased costs, and negative impacts intensify. In medium-size cities, such as Bonn, Germany; Salerno, Italy; or Edmonton, Canada, the advantages of transit in alleviating these problems become more important. The treatment of pedestrians becomes critical for serving many trips in high-density urban centers and for giving the city a human character. The relative roles of cars, transit, and pedestrians should therefore change in favor of the latter two modes.

Large Cities

In large metropolitan areas such as Sydney, Montreal, and Philadelphia, and even more so in very large ones such as Buenos Aires, Chicago, and Paris, transit should play the dominant role in carrying major passenger flows, in making it easier for many trips to be made by transit or walking than by driving a private car. Central business districts, as well as many major activity centers throughout metropolitan areas, should be served by high-quality (frequent, reliable, and comfortable) transit. Where this is not the case—that is, when large metropolitan areas such as Leeds (England), Detroit, and Phoenix have only bus transit in mixed traffic and in some cases no Sunday service at all—their transportation systems are, from the point of view of both present and potential users, inadequate and inefficient. In these cities, transportation presents a rigid ceiling to growth and achievement of socially healthy, livable regions. Even Seattle, which has many elements of a livable city, has lower mobility by transit than its peers with transit services on separate right-of-ways—for example, Ottawa with busways and Portland (Oregon), Vancouver, and Toronto with rail systems. Lagging considerably behind its peers, Seattle, in 1996, approved by referendum construction of initial rail lines and upgraded bus service.

In addition to good transit service, and as its support, cities must have extensive pedestrian facilities. Well-planned bicycle facilities can also be effective in such areas as major boulevards and green areas, university campuses, school complexes, and residential suburbs. In some cases, the physical condition of many streets and boulevards in central cities may lend themselves to introduction of bicycle facilities. Although extensive bikeway systems usually are associated with cities in several European countries (for example, the Netherlands, Denmark, and Germany), many U.S. towns and university campuses have, in the past couple of decades, been successful in providing for and promoting bicycle use.

During the 1980s, the concept of traffic calming in residential areas, pioneered and successfully developed in Europe, was applied in a number of areas in the United States, Australia, and other parts of the world. This was followed by efforts to develop neotraditional residential neighborhoods, transit-oriented developments (TODs), and similar innovative designs. In their concept, strict land-use zoning, which contributes greatly to the separation of activities and population groups and results in excessive dependence on car travel, is eliminated and replaced by integrated designs of multipurpose areas that provide for shorter trips, convenient walking, transit use, and abundant social contact. This represents a departure from the extensive suburban sprawl, total reliance on the car, and social isolation typical of neighborhood designs based on rigid zoning laws that were standard practice during the 1950–1980 period. A recent technical report on this subject by the Institute of Transportation Engineers (ITE 1997) points out that street designs for many suburban developments in the United States were based on standards from the 1950s that required wide, straight streets for evacuation in the event of nuclear attack!

CAUSES AND CONSEQUENCES OF TRAFFIC CONGESTION

The car offers its user an extremely attractive mode of travel. It is available at all times for movement to myriad destinations, in excellent comfort, with high speed and reliability on publicly provided streets or highways, usually with no direct charges. The car, however, takes up a large area, so that high concentration of its use, which occurs in metropolitan areas, results in congestion that tends to diminish some of its advantages. The convenience of travel by car—its speed, reliability, and safety—is reduced, while parking becomes inconvenient, time-consuming, and expensive. In large metropolitan areas with balanced transportation systems (that is, with high-quality transit, attractive pedestrian facilities, and so on), travel *without* a car is often more convenient than travel *by* car.

In addition to the reduced efficiency and inconvenience of the transportation system, the high concentration of cars has a number of negative environmental effects, including noise, air pollution, accidents, and generation of developments that are unsafe and unpleasant for pedestrians and social interaction. Thus, such a system negatively affects the quality of life.

Because the car is responsible for a high proportion of air pollution over regions, a succession of laws and regulations concerning exhaust standards has resulted in "cleaner cars" and significant decreases in pollutant production per VKT. This progress, however, has been offset by a steady increase in the volume of travel, so that the problem of auto-generated

PHOTO 2.13
Congestion defeats mobility of cars and traps transit vehicles (Reforma in Mexico). *(Vukan R. Vuchic)*

pollution remains a serious one, particularly in high-density areas where most VKTs are generated and the largest volumes of people are directly affected. In addition, traffic accidents impose a serious toll on society, one that far exceeds their material damages and monetary compensations.

The inherent physical problem with private automobiles in urbanized areas is that each trip by car requires a large area for vehicle movement and storage (parking). When a large volume of traffic is concentrated in urban areas, streets become congested, thus defeating the potentially high mobility of cars. The congestion also impedes all other traffic using streets, such as transit, trucks, and emergency vehicles. The car causes travel time losses and other inefficiencies and has negative impacts on the man-made and natural environments of urban areas (Burrington 1994; Johnson 1993).

Several methods can be used to compare areas occupied by travel of one person using different modes of transport. One method is to use the *time-area concept,* which consists of computing the paths vehicles occupy during their movement and the area they occupy while parked; path and parking area are then multiplied by the duration of occupancy and divided by the average number of persons the vehicle carries to obtain the time-area consumption per person-trip.

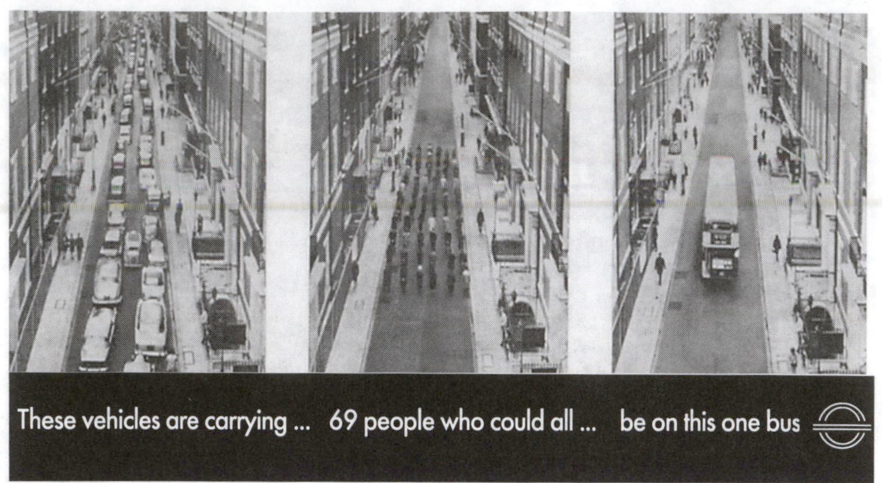

PHOTO 2.14
Comparison of street area taken by 69 passengers traveling by car and by bus. *(©London Transport)*

This time-area concept, analyzed in depth by Bruun and Vuchic (1995), is expressed by consumed area-time (square meter-hours) per person-trip. It has several advantages over the conventional concept of capacity, or "throughput," of a facility, measured by persons per hour. First, the time-area concept includes both basic elements of "consumption"—area and time of area occupancy. Second, this unit allows incorporation of both movement and stationary portions of a trip in a common unit. And third, due to these features, time-area provides a common denominator for different modes, thereby making possible a clear and easy comparison of land requirements for travel of persons by such modes as walking, car, and bus.

The time-area consumption by different modes varies with conditions, such as time of day (changing traffic volumes, trip lengths, and so on), vehicle occupancy, speed, and safety conditions of different modes. Two cases developed by Bruun and Vuchic (1995) are presented here. They represent a typical local urban round-trip with a length of 4 kilometers (2.5 miles) by three modes—car, bus, and rapid transit—for peak period and for off-peak travel. Peak-hour travel assumes, for car, bus, and rapid transit, average speeds of 20, 15, and 30 kilometers per hour (km/h) and occupancies of 1.2, 60, and 1,200 persons, respectively. The values for off-peak travel change to speeds of 30, 20, and 30 km/h, occupancies of 4 for car, 15 for bus, and 300 for rapid transit. No access time or distance is assumed for car travel (door-to-door), but 100- and 200-meter walks, respectively, for getting to and from bus and rapid transit.

The results of computations for these two sets of trips are plotted on two diagrams in figure 2.3. The horizontal dimension shows duration of travel components in minutes, plotted from the origin to the left, to show the joint time of arrivals by all modes. The vertical dimension shows occupied-area modules in square meters per person. The numbers shown for each mode represent these times and areas, as well as their product—time-area, which are represented graphically by the rectangular areas for each mode of travel.

The two diagrams reflect the fact that peak-hour travel speeds by bus and auto are lower than in off-peak travel (travel times are longer). Average auto occupancy is lower during the peak periods, whereas bus and rapid transit load factors are higher at those times. For walking access to transit stations, pedestrian speed, and the module remain unchanged at all times.

Figure 2.3 shows that car travel has shorter duration (mainly due to assumed door-to-door travel), but that car travel's total time-area of occupancy (area of the rectangle) is much larger than for bus and rapid transit because of its low occupancy. The difference in time-area occupied among modes is particularly great during peak periods. Thus, car users tend to put the highest claim on road resources (area) at the very time the maximum numbers of vehicles are on the road.

The diagram in figure 2.4 shows the peak-hour trip from figure 2.3a. It includes not only the time-area occupied for travel but also for parking, assuming an eight-hour stay (typical for work trips). The time-area consumed for this trip is shown in figure 2.3a, compressed at the beginning and end of the diagram because the time dimension is plotted at a much smaller scale to accommodate the eight-hour period. Note that the module for parking is somewhat lower than the module for driving at low urban speeds; this results from the lower area occupancy of a parked car than of a moving one. Yet, because of its long duration, parking dominates time-area consumption. For bus and rapid transit modes, land areas they occupy for movement are plotted, but they do not require areas for parking.

These computations exhibit all the advantages and limitations of theoretical models. They clearly show the influence of different elements on the consumption of time and area in three modes while representing only those cases with assumed conditions. Conditions for different types of travel in cities vary considerably. The three presented cases, typical for certain conditions, lead to the following conclusions about the problem caused by the extensive use of private cars:

- During peak hours, a trip by car may consume up to 25 times more time-area than the same trip made by bus, and more than 60 times the time-area consumed by rapid transit.

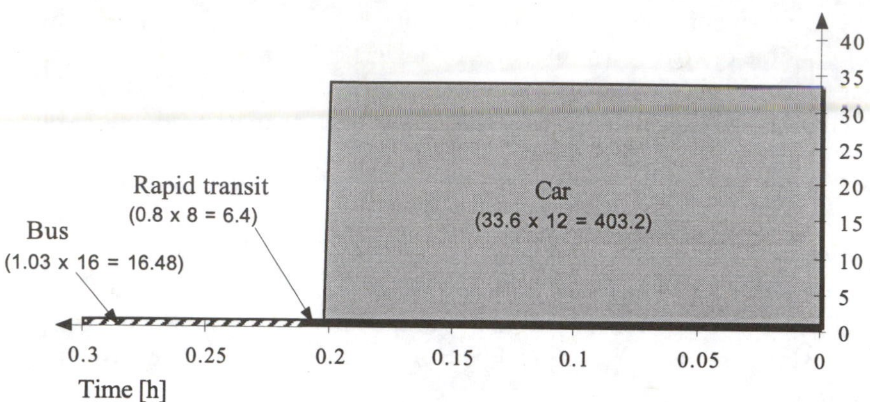

a. Peak-period travel

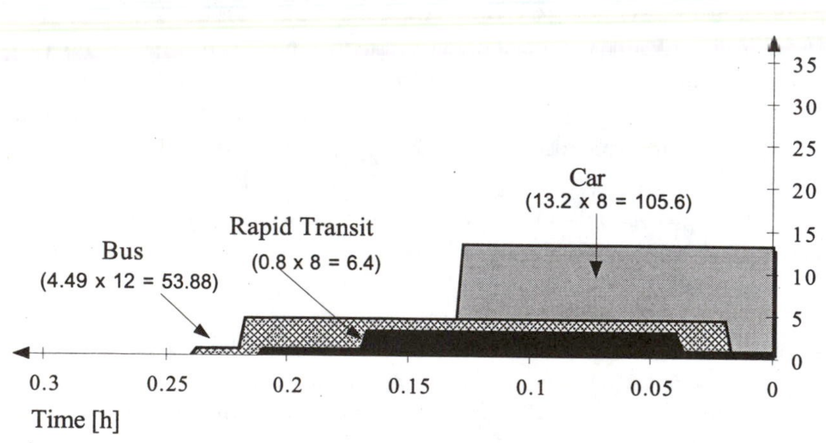

b. Off-peak travel

FIGURE 2.3
Time-area consumed per passenger on a 4-km round-trip, using three different modes

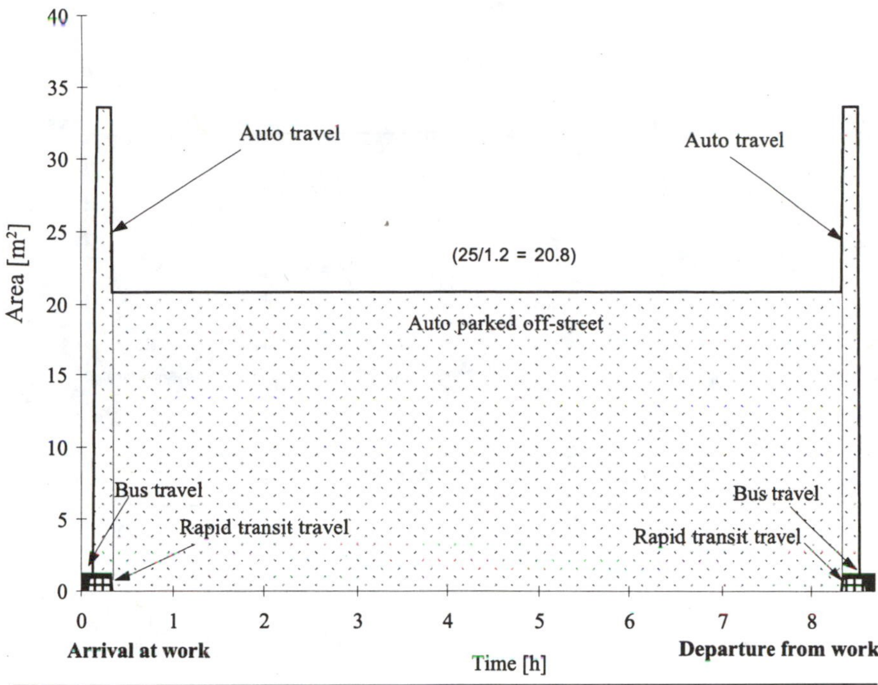

FIGURE 2.4
Time-area consumed per passenger on an 8-km round-trip, using three different modes

- Car trips take an extremely large area for parking, an area transit modes do not need. As another relative measure of this consumption, it may be mentioned that the area a car commuter needs to park his/her car is about 20 percent larger than the average area that person occupies in an office for work.

Another way of illustrating the differences in capacities of various modes of urban transport is to sketch the facilities required for transporting 15,000 persons per hour (prs/h) by different modes, shown in figure 2.5 (adapted from Vuchic 1981). This volume is found in many transit and freeway corridors in medium and large cities, since even facilities carrying only 5,000 to 7,000 prs/h obtain flow rates of 15,000 to 20,000 prs/h during 15–20 minute periods – factors which then dictate the design capacity. Line capacity reserves – capacities that could be provided on the same fixed facilities by adding more vehicles or trains – are also given, since they influence comfort, reliability, and efficiency of operation, as well as the potential to

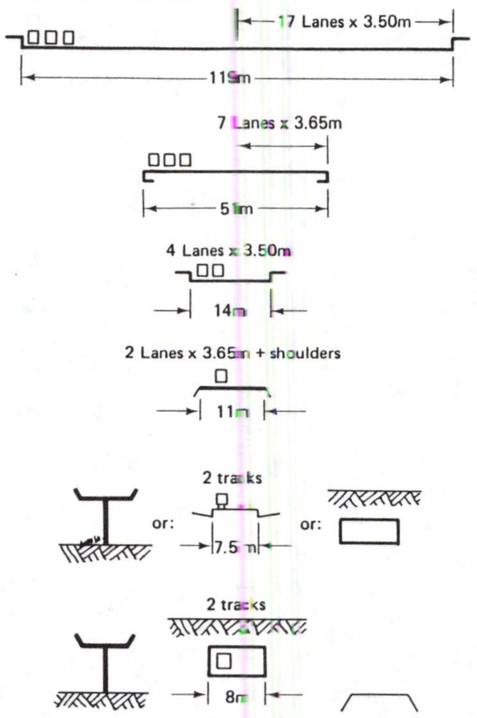

Mode	Schematic of right-of-way (ROW)	Line capacity reserve	Terminal area requirements
Private autos on street (Persons/vehicle: 1.3 Maximum freq.: 700)	17 Lanes x 3.50m 115m	None	Parking: 23 m^2/person For 15,000 people 34.5 ha (85 acres)
Private autos on freeway (1.3; 1800)	7 Lanes x 3.65m 51m	None	Same as above, plus interchanges
Regular buses (ROW C) (75; 100)	4 Lanes x 3.50m 14m	None (station and way capacities reached)	Each station 20 x 80 m on the surface
Semirapid buses (articulated, ROW B) (100; 90)	2 Lanes x 3.65m + shoulders 11m	None (station capacity reached, way capacity not)	Each station 25 x 100 m on the surface
Light rail transit (2 articulated car trains) (400; 50)	or: 2 tracks 7.5 m or:	33%	Each station from 12 x 50m on the surface to 20 x 90 grade separated
Rail rapid transit (1000; 25 RGR, 1000; 40 RRT)	2 tracks 8m	67-167%	Each station from 20 x 100 to 25 x 210m grade separated. No surface occupancy

FIGURE 2.5
Areas required for transporting 15,000 persons per hour by different modes (Vuchic 1981)

accommodate growth. Terminal areas are included as a significant component of space consumption by different modes.

The values assumed for this comparison are typical for operations of different modes under capacity conditions. For example, in figure 2.5, an average car occupancy of 1.3 has been assumed—a value too high for commuting but lower than that for some recreational trips. The capacity of a street lane was assumed to be 700; for a freeway lane, 1,800 vehicles per hour. For regular buses, occupancy was assumed to be 75—that is, including about 35 standees, as is typical during peaks. Frequency of Rail Rapid Transit (RRT) trains of 40 per hour is quite high, but a train capacity of 1,000 persons is conservative: many trains, such as those in Washington, San Francisco, Toronto, or New York, can exceed this number by 20–100 percent. Thus, for capacity conditions in major cities, the computed capacities are all realistic.

Figure 2.5 shows that an automobile on a street occupies by far the largest area: 17 lanes per direction plus 34.5 hectares (85 acres) for parking. Autos on freeways require fewer lanes (seven per direction) but the same parking area. The area requirements decrease progressively for bus and rail modes, with LRT and rapid transit systems using rights-of-way only eight meters (25 feet) wide, with additional areas for stations. These two modes have considerable spare capacity.

As mentioned, the preceding two models are general, and their numerical values cannot be applied exactly to any given situation without considering numerous local factors, such as transportation network form and travel fluctuations in direction and time. The models, however, show that the greater the share of trips in a city by car, the larger the area that must be used for transportation. In an extreme, theoretical case, the area dedicated to transportation in a city where only cars are used would be many times larger than the area utilized for the same purpose in a city where travel is done only by transit and walking.

By implication, then, a given sector of an urban area where development is car-based has much less land available for all nontransportation activities than if the development were served by transit, paratransit, bicycle, and walking. One reason is that for every office building to which all its occupants come by car, an area larger than the office building must be built for parking its employees' cars. Or, put another way, for a city with a given population and certain activities, a much larger area would be needed if the city is car-based than if it relies on other than car modes. If the required large area is not provided for cars, congestion results, with all its negative consequences. If, however, space for cars is provided, the character of the area changes and trips become longer, further exacerbating the problem of the large areas assigned to transportation.

It can also be concluded that a car-based development has a much lower limit on activity densities than a development that relies on non-car modes. For this reason, *cities that are entirely auto-based have a "ceiling" on the diversity and density of activities that can be served in major activity centers.* Efficiency of operations and potential growth of large activity concentrations (for example, office and apartment complexes, university campuses, sport arenas, shopping areas) are impeded by the limited capacity cars can provide.

This kind of analysis of capacity and area consumption by various modes of transportation is sometimes criticized as irrelevant. Because the United States has lots of land, who cares how much is used for transportation? This argument is invalid for several reasons.

First, the availability of land in Montana or Maine is irrelevant to the needs of such metropolitan areas as Boston, the San Francisco Bay Area, or Los Angeles, which have physical constraints and limited land available for expansion. Second, development at extremely low densities, typical in recent decades, consumes large amounts of land that has value for other purposes, such as agriculture or nature preservation. Third, municipal costs increase considerably as density decreases (Transportation Research Board 1998). Most important, however, is the fact that economic and social activities are much less efficient in metropolitan areas that do not provide diverse densities and economies of agglomeration—a basic reason for the existence of the city or metropolis in the first place (Bank of America 1995; Cisneros 1993; New South Wales Department of Transport 1993; Persky et al. 1991).

INDIVIDUAL EQUILIBRIUM AND THE SOCIAL OPTIMUM IN TRAVEL CHOICE

In urban transportation, similar to human behavior in many other respects, there is a significant difference between the choice of travel mode individuals make as their own optima and the distribution of passengers among modes that results in operating the most efficient system—the social optimum. In most situations, every person selects a travel mode that offers him or her travel at the lowest cost, or, more precisely, lowest disutility consisting of travel time, cost, reliability, safety, and other elements. The condition resulting from such individual choices is designated as "individual equilibrium" (IE). This condition is also known as "Wardrop's First Principle of Traffic Flow Distribution." John Wardrop was the first person to clearly define this phenomenon for highway traffic distribution through a street network based on travel times (Wardrop 1952). The IE

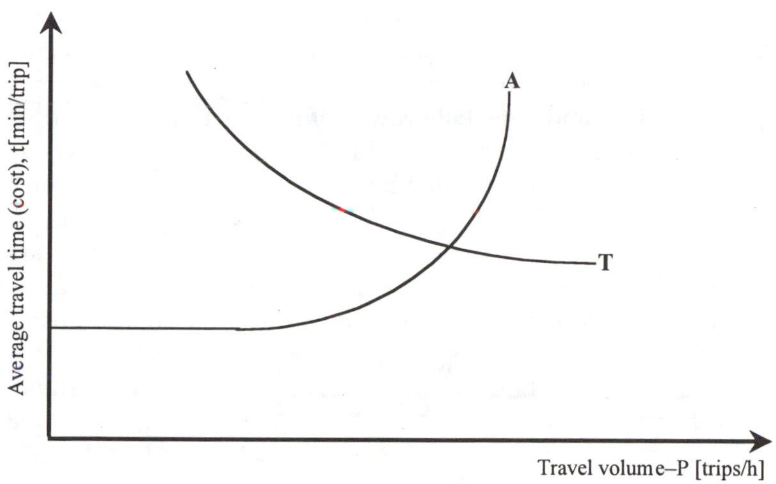

FIGURE 2.6
Average user travel cost curves for auto and transit travel

condition usually results in aggregate disutility for all travelers that is not at its minimum. Passenger distribution that achieves the minimum average disutility, or the lowest total user disutility of transportation, is designated the "social optimum" (SO), or "Wardrop's Second Principle of Traffic Flow Distribution."

Thus, when each person selects his or her preferred mode of travel, the resulting situation is not, from the system's point of view, optimal. This relationship of uses of different modes and user transportation disutilities—for simplicity, referred to here as "costs"—can be explained by two specially designed diagrams.

If the average cost of highway or street travel in an urban area is shown as a function of traffic volume on it, one obtains the curve "A" on the diagram in figure 2.6. The corresponding cost of travel by transit is plotted on the same diagram as curve "T." Line A—auto cost per person-kilometer (person-mile)—increases with volume, because congested traffic results in higher costs. Line T—transit cost per passenger—decreases when travel volume increases, because transit lines offer higher frequencies of service; thus, passenger waiting time decreases and operating costs are spread over a larger number of riders. This reflects the fact that, generally, transit lines with high ridership offer better service and are more economical to operate than lightly traveled lines.

The question is, if there are P persons per hour traveling along the same urban corridor, and they can choose to travel either by auto or by

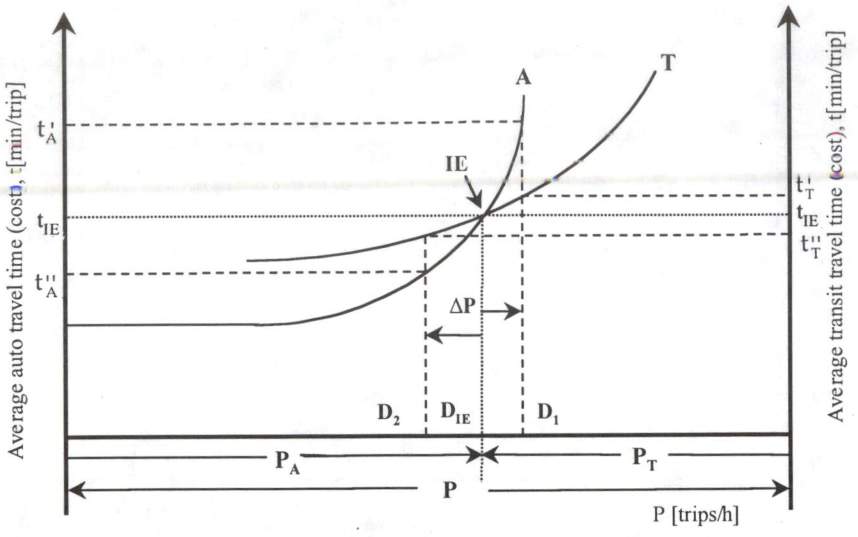

FIGURE 2.7
Distribution of travel volume P between auto and transit travel

transit, how will they distribute themselves between these two modes? This distribution can easily be obtained graphically when a diagram with travel volume P on the abscissa is plotted with the A curve (auto user costs) from the left, and the T curve (transit costs per passenger) from the right toward the left, as shown in figure 2.7. Then, the intersecting point, designated as IE, represents the equilibrium condition reached when each person selects the lower travel cost between the two options. In that situation, P_A persons travel by auto, while P_T use transit. The total travel cost for all travelers is represented by the area under the horizontal line, t_{IE}, through IE.

If some transit riders were to switch to auto, so that the passenger distribution moved from D_{IE} to point D_1 on the right, the cost of travel by either mode would increase. Auto costs would go from t_{IE} to t'_A, transit costs from t_{IE} to t'_T. Transit travel, however, would have lower cost than auto travel; some passengers would therefore switch back from autos to transit, until the distribution would return to the IE point. The same return to IE would occur if some auto users switched to transit—that is, if the distribution line moved to the left, to point D_2. The difference between the two costs would lead some travelers to shift back to autos until IE distribution was reestablished. Thus, the distribution at point IE is stable; whenever a shift between the two modes in either direction occurs, travelers would, of their own volition, return to the original distribution.

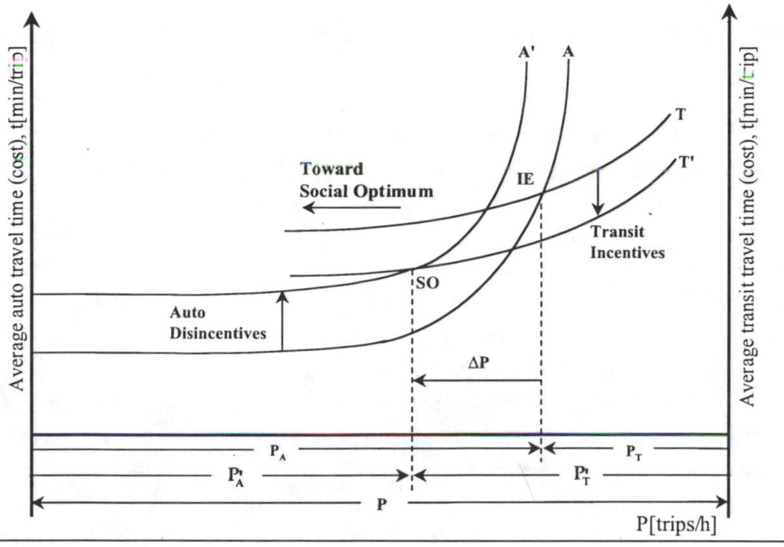

FIGURE 2.8
Transportation policies for shifting the individual equilibrium point toward social optimum

It is important to note that, if the distribution of trips is moved to D_2 (i.e., some auto users shift to transit), costs on *both* modes would decrease (to t''_A and t''_T, respectively). Both groups would then enjoy lower costs. Therefore, it is obvious that the social optimum distribution of travel is to the left of IE—that is, when a certain amount of auto travel is shifted to transit. How, then, can such a distribution, closer to SO, be achieved and maintained as stable? Two sets of policies and measures can be used, preferably in a coordinated manner, to achieve this goal:

1. *Transit incentives.* A set of measures that result in decreased disutility of transit travel, such as increased frequency of service, reliability, comfort, lower fares, and construction of a higher-quality transit mode.
2. *Auto disincentives.* Measures that increase monetary costs or decrease the convenience of auto travel, such as higher gasoline taxes, parking charges, limitations on street and parking capacity.

The diagram in figure 2.8 shows how the two sets of measures, transit-use incentives and auto-use disincentives, result in a shift of the equilibrium point: transit incentives move the T curve down to T ', whereas auto disincentives move the A curve up to A '. The result is a shift of travel volumes from auto to transit so that the distribution goes from the individual optimum IE toward the social optimum SO, resulting in a reduction of the total transportation cost, including transit and auto. This shift of travel between modes represents the main challenge to improving transportation in most cities.

Similar to the supply-demand graphical analysis, equilibria, trade-offs, and other curves of this nature, the average cost curves used here present general relationships rather than exact quantitative values. They are extremely useful in illustrating some of the most important concepts and intermodal relationships in urban transportation. They also show clearly the purposes and impacts of different transportation policies.

The concept of individual equilibrium (IE) and social optimum (SO) is fundamental to determining rational urban transportation policies. Urban transportation systems operations based on IE are much less efficient and cause more serious negative impacts than their operations at SO travel distribution. Yet, despite its importance, this concept is generally unknown, not only to the public but to many professionals as well.

Coordinated policies intended to shift the distribution of travel from the IE to the SO condition in the United States are rare. The few cases include traffic control measures that close freeway ramps and divert additional traffic to alternate routes when volume on the freeway approaches the saturation level. These measures usually increase travel times of the diverted vehicles, but they prevent breakdown of the flow on the freeway, which would drastically increase the travel times of the majority of vehicles. This traffic control measure therefore results in lower average travel times than in the conditions when each driver would select his or her individual minimum-time path—that is, when the driver entered the freeway. In most cases, the social and environmental consequences of such diversions are not directly considered in implementation of these measures.

The implementation of transportation policies and regulations to change intermodal distribution of travel from IE to SO is even more limited. A number of cities have introduced transit incentives, which vary from improved service quality to the introduction of exclusive bus lanes and construction of rail transit. However, the other part of coordinated intermodal policies—auto-use disincentives—is rare because of intensive resistance from special interest groups. Sometimes, too, such measures are resisted by the public because of the natural tendency of people to look only at their personal short-term interests. Another problem in implementing this kind of policy is that the negatively affected individuals are users of specific facilities and thus are concentrated in a limited area. Therefore, they can more easily be organized in their opposition than beneficiaries who support change and innovations. Usually, the latter group is more numerous but is dispersed and thus difficult to organize.

Because of these implementation difficulties, even some effective measures have been eliminated after their implementation, due to pressures from drivers of single-occupancy vehicles (SOVs), which actually impose by far the highest social costs among all modes. This was the case with Santa Monica Freeway HOV (high-occupancy vehicle) lanes in 1976. Another good example is the conversion of nearly all busways into HOV facilities that decrease benefits to transit users (Leman et al. 1994; Vuchic et al. 1995). In some cases, highway user lobbies prevent a transit improvement until an equivalent improvement has also been made to the parallel highway (for example, the widening of freeways parallel to new LRT lines in Portland, Oregon, and Salt Lake City, Utah). These developments represent an irrational policy of incentives to transit and car, i.e., public investments in two competing facilities with an IE distribution, rather than intermodal policies moving travel distribution toward a more efficient SO intermodal system.

Thus, in most situations, particularly in the United States, in urban transportation, the individual equilibrium rather than the social optimum applies; and that is one of the reasons for inefficiencies. Upgrading from IE to the more efficient SO conditions has numerous obstacles, but the basic one is lack of understanding of these two conditions and a tendency to look at transportation on a short-term basis, through individual facilities, rather than treating transportation as a system and planning for its improvement on a permanent basis.

TRAVEL COSTS, CHARGES, OPEN AND HIDDEN SUBSIDIES

Governmental policies in urban transportation are implemented largely through financial decisions: investment in the construction of facilities, subsidies or taxation of transportation systems operation, and so on. User costs of travel, on the other side, have a strong influence on the behavior of travelers. There are many discussions of costs in urban transportation; yet, the problem is so complex that many of its aspects are overlooked or misunderstood. Quality of service, particularly travel time, also plays an important role in user behavior and selection of mode. These considerations should be taken into account in many demand-estimation models, as well as in planning and designing specific transportation systems. The analysis in this section focuses, however, on user costs because of their strong impact on the behavior of the population, on the roles of different modes, and thus on all metropolitan transportation and cities.

Costs of Travel by Different Modes

Travel characteristics of urban populations—such as mode selection, number, and length of trips—depend greatly not only on the total costs travelers must pay but on the method in which they pay. Travelers consider for which services there are charges (transit fares, parking) and how these compare among travel alternatives. They pay the most attention to out-of-pocket expenditures. For longer modal decisions, some travelers include their own fixed costs, such as car depreciation and maintenance; but few travelers pay attention to the costs they, as users, incur but do not pay (social, environmental, and long-term impacts). Thus, in most cases, *decisions about travel are influenced more by the structure than by the total cost.*

The impacts or costs that transportation exerts on nontravelers, as well as impacts and costs to the entire metropolitan area and environment, now receive more attention because of their growing influence, positive or negative, on the livability of cities and society as a whole. There is a distinct dichotomy, however, between these two categories of transportation costs and impacts: users consider primarily their own costs, whereas transportation experts and public officials are concerned with the impact of the transportation system.

Walking and bicycling. These modes usually require very low or moderate investment. Sidewalks, pedestrian street crossings, and streets that bicycles use typically require minimum investment. Special facilities for pedestrians—plazas, overpasses, attractive pedestrian zones, separate bicycle paths with some grade separations, and so on—may require a substantial investment in infrastructure, although the investment is far lower than that for high-performance transit or highway facilities. By their very nature—persons walking or themselves providing motive power on simple vehicles—and representing the basic human elements in any city, pedestrian and bicycle modes never involve a charge to users. Use of these modes, therefore, depends mostly on the types of trips and attractiveness of facilities, but not on users' cost considerations.

Transit systems. In most cases, transit systems need public resources for infrastructure construction and vehicle purchases, as well as partial subsidies for operating costs. User costs consist of transit fares; in West European and U.S. metropolitan areas, they cover a portion of operating costs, typically 20 to 90 percent. In the United States, federal funds for transit investments—together with planning, research, and financing of urban facilities related to transit lines—amount to $3 billion to $5 billion per year in recent decades, with nearly no increases between 1981 and 1985. Although this funding is far less than the needs of metropolitan areas and is negligible in comparison with funds for highway facilities that compete with transit, transit funds, to a much greater extent than highway and related funds, are subject to criticism by various lobbies.

Highway/street system, auto/truck transport. These systems involve by far the largest financing because they serve the largest share of urban travel. However, financing these systems, and the car user charges involved, require particular attention because the current practice of high investment and low user charges for car travel together represent the most critical factor among urban transportation problems.

In addition to its inherent attractiveness to users, discussed in the preceding section, car travel is strongly stimulated by several aspects of transportation costs and charges, which users and society pay in different forms. A number of present practices that are particularly prevalent in U.S. cities and their suburbs make car use extremely attractive and lead to excessive driving. This condition results in a large number of discretionary trips, i.e., trips of marginal value to the traveler or those that would not be made if car travel were priced more realistically. This condition also creates the tendency for increasing trip lengths and decreasing car occupancy. These phenomena result in an ever-growing increase in the use of cars, i.e., a trend toward increasing VKTs and use of SOVs.

For analysis of costs of car travel in urban areas, it is necessary to view the entire process of transportation in perspective. As a major economic and social function, transportation always involves benefits and costs, not only to travelers but also to other groups. This is particularly true in urban and metropolitan areas where transport, especially passenger car use, affects both one's surroundings and the environment. In the long term, the entire social life and livability of cities and their surroundings is influenced by transportation. The form of charges and payments for driving represents a complex combination of users' direct and indirect costs, government expenditures, and societal direct and indirect impacts.

Estimates of Urban Transportation Costs and Subsidies

Considering the entire highway transportation system, what is the distribution of its costs? Who pays for highway travel? In this complex question, the focus is on the costs of car travel in metropolitan areas.

There is a widespread belief in the United States that "highway users pay their way." This belief was influenced by the concept of the Highway Trust Fund (HTF), which is funded by taxes on fuel (gasoline and diesel

TABLE 2.1
Estimates of Subsidies to Auto and Truck Users in the United States

Study Author	*Year*	*Total Annual Subsidy ($ billions)*
Lee	1991	330
Voorhees	1992	631
World Resource Center	1992	400
Ketcham and Komanoff	1993	730
National Resources Defense	1993	378–660
Transport Policy Institute	1994	935
Office of Technology Assessment (U.S. Congress)	1994	447–899

Source: Holtzclaw 1995; Pucher 1995

oil) and on other highway-related taxes. The Trust Fund finances much of the capital investment in major highway categories, particularly for the Interstate System and, more recently, the National Highway System; but it does not cover many other costs, such as highway maintenance, traffic regulation, and parking.

A number of studies of costs for highway transportation, and the allocation of these costs, have been made in recent years by individual researchers and organizations. Some comprehensive ones are listed in Table 2.1. These studies vary considerably in scope (costs of one or several modes, different types of trips, and so on), in their assumptions (total or marginal costs, impacts and externalities, and others), and in their objectives (planning purposes, taxation, equity analysis). Table 2.1 presents their estimates of total annual subsidies for highway travel, i.e., the costs of car and truck transport not paid by the users but instead passed along to the general taxpayer. Despite the differences among the studies, which are logical because of the complexity of the subject, there are several issues on which they have reached a rather clear consensus regarding costs of car and truck driving:

- The cost of driving varies greatly among different trip categories—for example, urban versus rural areas, peak versus off-peak. Allocating costs to different groups that pay for them—such as government, employers, users, society—also differs among modes, times of day, and locations. Thus, the share a driver pays, and how much he or she is subsidized by others, varies greatly among trips.

- Car driving in urban areas includes a large share of indirect costs and externalities, most of which are of a qualitative nature not conducive to exact assignment of monetary values.
- For most car trips, particularly in urban areas, the user pays only part of the costs of that trip because he or she is not charged for the social, environmental, and other indirect costs. The subsidies are paid by governments (taxpayers), employers (who also pass a portion to the governments as tax deductions or to other customers through price increases), other travelers, and society at large.
- Although the estimated amounts of total subsidies for car and truck transport vary somewhat, they are all within the range of, roughly, $400 billion to $900 billion per year. Given the abovementioned differences among studies in approaches and methodologies, these results are surprisingly consistent.

Thus, the claim that car users pay their costs is overly simplistic and inaccurate. Actually, highway user taxes defray only part of the country's total highway transportation costs. *Most car trips are subsidized.* A variety of costs, ranging from extensive tax-free use of company cars to "free" parking for employers or customers, are commonly not paid by the users. These costs represent far greater hidden subsidies than the total amount of government and private subsidies to all other modes (transit, bicycle, or pedestrian facilities) combined.

Computing the averages for all categories of travel, the OTA study (1994) estimates that car drivers pay about 60 percent of the total cost of their travel. The remaining 40 percent consists of costs of highway construction, maintenance and control (traditionally subsidized by all three levels of government), "free" parking (subsidized by employers, store owners, schools, federal tax laws, and so on), and various social and environmental costs absorbed by society.

The Structure of Car-Use Costs

Approaches to cost analysis in the studies discussed vary somewhat due to the different objectives of their analysis. Utilizing selected approaches and data from these studies, a review and analysis of costs of travel by different modes is presented from the perspective of travelers. This approach is used because the emphasis here is on the behavior of people in urban areas and the impact of their travel decisions.

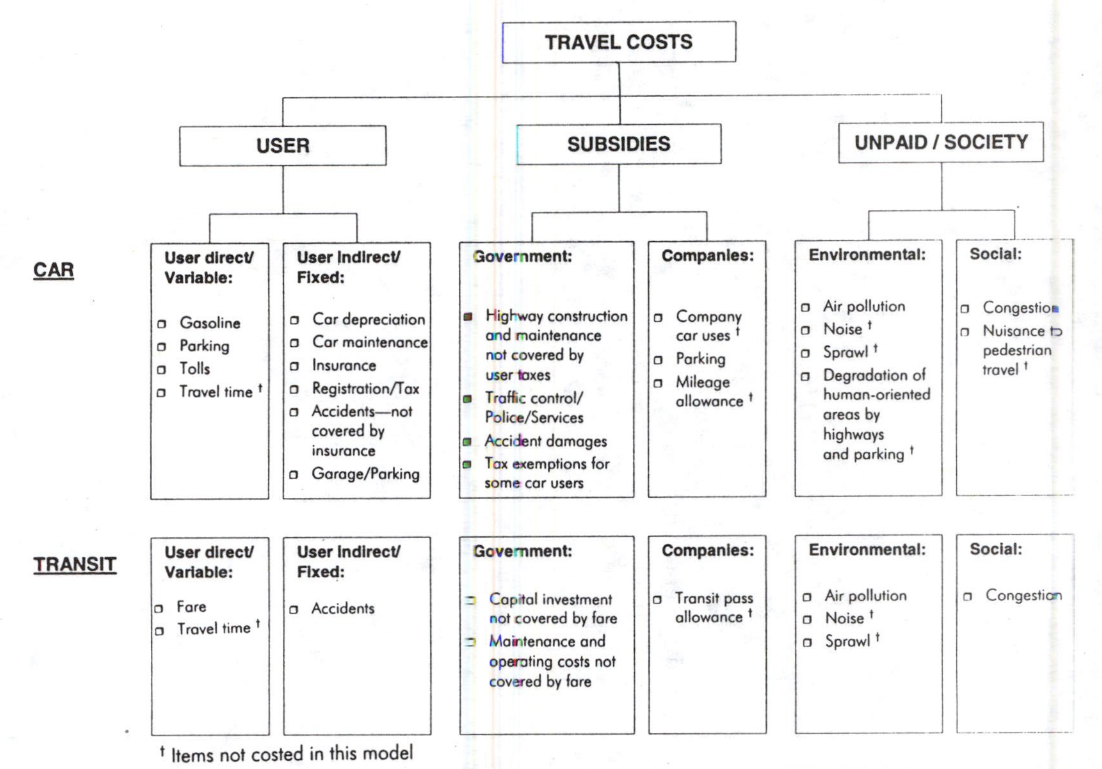

FIGURE 2.9
Classification of costs for car and transit travel

Figure 2.9 presents a classification of costs of travel by car into three major categories, each divided into two subcategories. For comparison, transit travel costs are also included in the figure and classified on the same basis.

User costs represent all the costs users pay. They consist of two subcategories – *user direct* and *user indirect* costs. User direct, or variable costs, are those that the user pays for each trip. User indirect, or fixed costs, are expenditures for owning and operating a car that are not directly related to each trip or the distance traveled. Urban travelers also incur other disutilities, such as travel time, convenience of driving or comfort of not driving, safety, and security. These elements are not included in the following analysis because they are mostly qualitative; although they can be quantified, the factors used in quantification may vary greatly among trips and thus divert attention from the largely monetary analysis discussed here.

Subsidies are the costs of car travel paid by sources other than car users. There are two major contributors of subsidies: governments, including local, state, and federal or national; and companies/agencies, which, as employers, retailers, or other organizations, cover directly or indirectly part of the travel costs of their employees, customers, or the general public.

The *unpaid costs* category refers to negative impacts or costs that cars (or highway transport in general) impose on third parties or nonusers: society and the entire urban environment. They are classified by their impacts as social and environmental costs.

Each category will be briefly discussed, then its estimated values will be included in graphical models of travel costs by different modes.

User costs must be analyzed by their two distinct categories. *User direct costs* for car travel consist mainly of gasoline, parking, and toll expenditures. These costs are sometimes referred to as "out-of-pocket costs." They have by far the strongest impact on user behavior. Most drivers tend to consider these costs carefully while disregarding many costs that are fixed or that depend only indirectly on the amount of travel, despite the fact that the latter costs are often far greater than out-of-pocket costs.

User indirect costs include the costs of owning a car, including its depreciation, maintenance, insurance, uncovered accident costs, registration, and tax. Some of these costs, such as maintenance and a portion of insurance, are dependent partly on the distance driven or number of trips performed. Others, such as car depreciation and registration, are largely or entirely independent of the amount of car travel. As such, the contribution of these

PHOTO 2.15
Towing advertising trailers through congested streets: huge social (congestion) cost is not charged to the user. *(Vukan R. Vuchic)*

costs to the total costs on a per-trip or per-kilometer/mile basis decreases with increasing distance traveled per year. Its consideration in the analysis of travel costs depends on how analytical the individual user is and what accounting method is used.

Subsidies include a large variety of costs that governments and public and private agencies contribute to the cost of car travel, mostly in an indirect way. As shown in figure 2.9, government subsidies include expenses for street and highway construction and maintenance that are in excess of revenues collected as car-user taxes, costs of traffic control, police and emergency services, and others. A very large but well-hidden subsidy is that in the form of tax exemptions for the cost of car trips for business and similar purposes.

Subsidies by companies and agencies are also numerous but are not always recognized as such. "Free" parking, a standard practice for virtually all employers, stores, schools, and other institutions except in city centers, probably is the largest subsidy to car travel. Use of company cars and various "mileage allowances," or full payments for car use, are subsidies often not given for travel by any mode other than cars.

PHOTO 2.16
Impact on livability: the more accommodations for the car are provided (highways, streets, parking), the less attractive the city is for people. *(U.S. Department of Transportation, Federal Highway Administration)*

Unpaid costs—costs imposed on and absorbed by third parties or society at large—are mostly difficult to quantify, and they are greatly dependent on traffic conditions and surrounding area.

Social costs include time, inconvenience, and other consequences of highway congestion that directly affect other travelers while indirectly affecting entire areas and their populations. These costs are extremely high in large metropolitan areas. Interestingly, studies by the Texas Transportation Institute have found for eight consecutive years that the most congested metropolitan area in the country is Los Angeles, the leading area from the 1940s through the 1980s in attempts to solve all its transportation problems by constructing a larger and larger freeway network.

Environmental costs vary greatly among locations with geographic, topographic, and climatic conditions. For example, some metropolitan areas, such as Denver, Los Angeles, Mexico City, and Sarajevo, have topographic and climatic conditions conducive to the retention of polluted air and creation of smog. Traffic volume—or, more specifically, VKT—plays a major role in the production and concentration of air pollution. In low-density areas with low traffic volumes, the negative impact of air pollution, as well as noise, is usually low or even negligible. In large cities, however, it increases, often reaching high values during peak hours, even when computed on a per-trip basis. In some areas, it represents a chronic condition, one with a major negative impact on the environment of the entire area. For this reason, many cities, at critical times, impose emergency restrictions on automobile use. This has been done in recent years in Mexico City, Paris, Seoul, and other cities. In the United States, a strict Clean Air Act and its amendments were passed. Such measures often have a stronger impact on transportation planning and regulations than most other transportation laws.

An important social cost concerns the negative direct impacts of car travel on pedestrian traffic and the long-term detrimental impact on the human character of the city—one of the main topics in this book.

The costs of travel by transit are simpler. User cost consists primarily of the fare. Subsidies include mostly governmental contributions to infrastructure investments and operating costs of transit. Social and environmental costs tend to be considerably lower than the corresponding costs of car travel.

Graphical Illustrations of Cost Structures

It is obvious from figure 2.9 that the structure of costs involved in passenger travel, particularly in urban areas, is complex. Because cost plays an important role in traveler behavior, it will be useful to explain the components and relationships of travel costs by graphical presentation of travel costs of car and transit travel under varying conditions. Figures 2.10–2.13 show typical costs for selected situations. They are based on estimates of costs of driving reported by the American Automobile Association (AAA) (Urban Transportation Monitor 1995) and the information derived from recent studies by Litman (1992, 1995) and Burrington (1994). Several cost items computed by various researchers, such as the cost of urban sprawl and various environmental impacts, were not included in these diagrams because they are extremely difficult to estimate, particularly in relation to individual passenger trips or distances traveled. Travel time costs, although important, are not included because their quantification unit varies by trip and conditions, which may have a large effect on the relationships of other cost components.

Because of the combination of fixed and variable costs, the diagrams are more accurate when they represent values for individual trips, rather than costs per unit of travel distance. Each graph shows numerical estimates for the conditions specified, such as 20-km round-trips, during peak

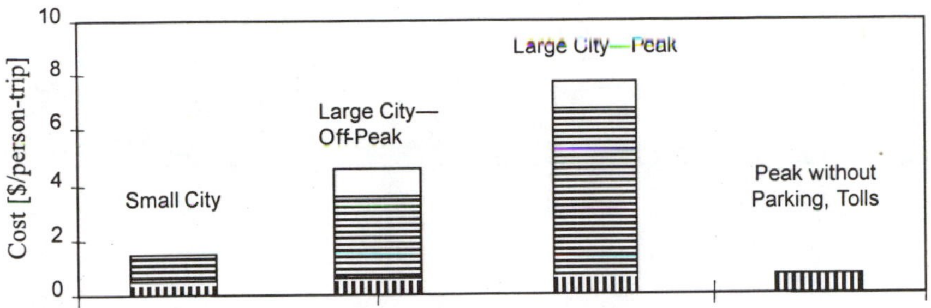

FIGURE 2.10
Direct costs of car travel under different conditions

Source: See text.

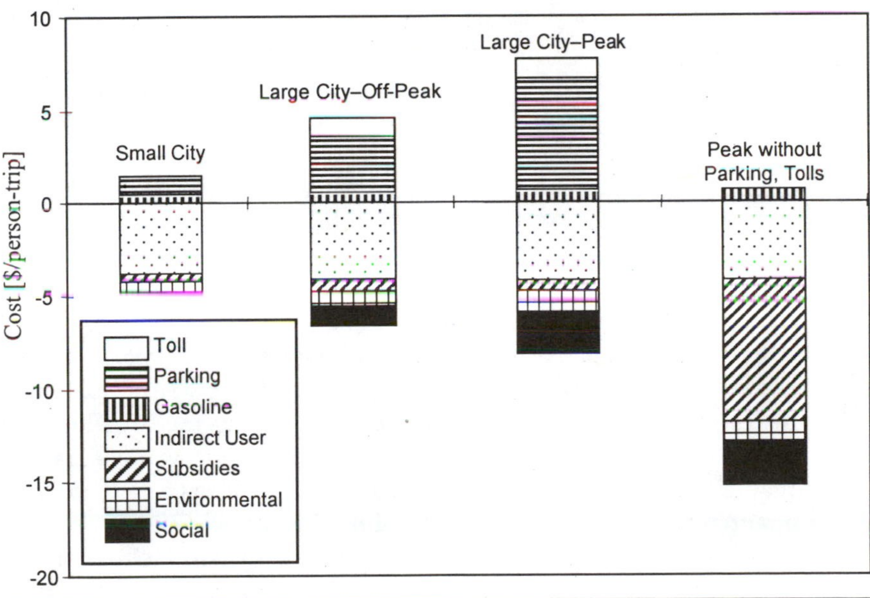

FIGURE 2.11
Total costs of car travel under different conditions

Note: Negative signs are used to distinguish indirect from direct costs; they do not imply negative values.

Source: See text.

and off-peak periods, small and large city, and so on. For the shares of fixed costs and unpaid costs assigned to a single trip, several assumptions have been made about the volume of travel by car and by transit. For example, unit costs for car travel are greater for peak than for off-peak

TABLE 2.2
Assumptions for Travel Costs of a Round-trip

	Size of City	
	Large	*Small*
Assumption:		
Two-way trip length	20 km / 12.5 mi	20 km / 12.5 mi
Parking cost		
Off-peak	$3.00	$1.00
Peak	$6.00	$2.00
Toll per round-trip	$1.00	
Transit fare	$2.50 for bus/metro $4.00 for express bus/ regional rail	
Auto occupancy	1.2 persons/vehicle	1.2 persons/vehicle

Source: See text.

conditions due to congestion, increased pollution, and other factors. With transit, different unit fixed costs are assumed for two different modes. The specific values used for these graphical cost models, presented in table 2.2, are selected from the sources referenced above.

Due to the importance of direct costs in travelers' decisions, two diagrams show out-of-pocket costs only, while two others show all costs. These diagrams of total costs present all indirect costs below the base line, to emphasize the fact that they usually are not considered by travelers for individual trips. Included are user fixed costs and the costs carried by the government or imposed on society but not paid by travelers.

Figure 2.10 shows out-of-pocket costs for a car trip in four situations: a small city, a large city during off-peak period, the same location during peak hours with parking and a toll charge, and the same peak period trip with "free parking" and no tolls. The diagram shows that direct costs of car travel in the small city are quite low. They increase rapidly in a large city during off-peak and then peak hours, due mostly to parking and toll charges. Without parking and toll charges, shown as the fourth case, out-of-pocket cost is very low even for peak period travel.

Figure 2.11 shows total costs for the car trips presented in figure 2.10. The indirect costs, shown below the base line, consist of the remaining three major categories of costs shown in figure 2.9: user fixed costs, subsidies, and unpaid costs, which are divided into social and environmental costs.

The two diagrams shown in figures 2.10 and 2.11 illustrate the fact that the level of costs car users consider in deciding whether to make a trip, and how far to travel, represent a small portion of the total costs. Figure 2.11 also shows that the total costs car trips incur typically include substantial user fixed costs, as well as costs borne by society, which represent a form of subsidy.

Figure 2.12 shows the comparison of car out-of-pocket costs with those of two different transit trips—a typical urban trip and a long, regional commuting trip. The figure shows that, with parking charges, car travel is more expensive than transit. Providing "free parking," however, creates a situation in which many commuters who select a mode on the basis of direct costs believe that they "save money" only by driving. This confirms the experience of many cities that "free parking" is a major—often the most important—factor in the encouragement of car commuting. It may represent the dominant obstacle to diversion of trips from cars to transit or to any other mode.

Figure 2.13 shows the total costs for the same four cases. The subsidies for transit include operating subsidies and a certain value for infrastructure investment. The latter amount may vary from none for bus transit on streets, which has virtually no infrastructure, to extensive for rapid transit or busways, which have substantial investment costs. In the plotted case of regional travel, it was assumed that express buses use freeways, while regional rail operates on existing rail lines, so that neither involves a major investment in infrastructure.

The four diagrams of car travel costs in urban transportation and their comparison with transit costs lead to the following important observations.

1. Travel costs by both car and transit vary considerably with location and time of travel. Total car travel costs are particularly high in large cities during peak hours because of parking, social, and environmental costs.
2. The direct, out-of-pocket cost of car travel consists mainly of the cost of fuel, which is extremely low, and parking fees and tolls, when these are charged. When parking is subsidized ("free"), which is the case virtually everywhere except in city centers, the direct cost of auto travel is virtually negligible.
3. Because most people decide how far to travel and which mode to choose on the basis of direct costs only, this cost structure greatly stimulates driving. This follows the fact that underpriced services are overused. The ultimate distortion of pricing in urban travel occurs when people who drive company cars treat their travel as entirely free.

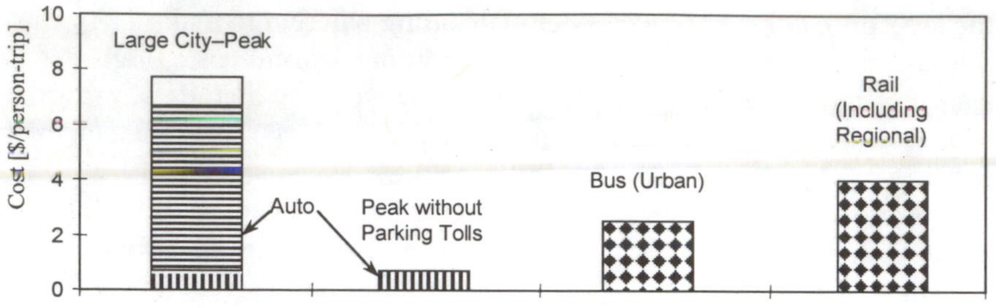

FIGURE 2.12
Direct costs of urban travel by different modes

Source: See text.

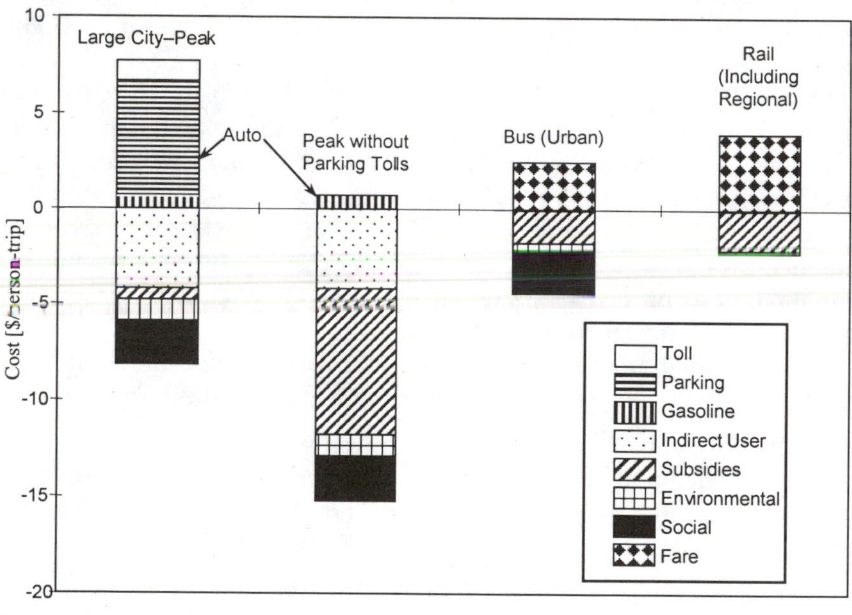

FIGURE 2.13
Total costs of urban travel by different modes

Note: Negative signs are used to distinguish indirect from direct costs; they do not imply negative values.

Source: See text.

4. With respect to costs, the low direct cost of driving renders fully priced transit noncompetitive with the car. Thus, underpricing car driving through direct subsidies, and its consequent unrealistic cost structure, results in the need to subsidize transit.

5. The direct costs represent, in most cases, the "tip of the iceberg" of the total costs of car travel. Based on the AAA's 1995 estimates (Urban Transportation Monitor 1995), on average, direct costs of driving amount to only 13 percent, fixed costs 87 percent, of user costs. Fixed costs consist of depreciation, insurance, repairs, and other costs not directly dependent on individual trips.
6. Social costs of driving (mostly congestion imposed on other street and highway users, including car and truck drivers, transit riders, and pedestrians) and environmental costs (affecting society at large) are not paid by car users at all.
7. Environmental costs and the impacts of highway travel are not paid by users, either. They represent another major cost element of the "under-the-surface portion of the iceberg." The total indirect costs, including the user's fixed costs, subsidies, and unpaid costs absorbed by society and the environment, amount, in the case shown, to more than 92 percent of the total costs.

Illustration of the Problem of Low Marginal Pricing

These two factors—subsidy of car use and its cost structure—represent the main obstacle to achieving realistic pricing and an efficient intermodal balance in metropolitan areas. A thorough understanding of this problem is important. For that purpose, a parallel situation is described in a hypothetical example of different methods of food pricing and consumer behavior in response to it.

Suppose that Mrs. Saver spends an average of $100 for her weekly food shopping. Then the supermarket offers a subscription plan for its customers. Those who pay an annual subscription of $4,420 (equivalent to $85 per week for 52 weeks) can purchase all items at 15 percent of their prices. What would happen?

If Mrs. Saver continued to purchase the same items and quantity of food as before, her expenditures would continue to average $100 per week: $85 through annual subscription, plus the weekly shopping for $100 at 15 percent—$15 out of pocket. However, faced with food available to her at a mere 15 percent of its full price, Mrs. Saver will find it very attractive to purchase both higher quality and greater amounts of food than before: filet mignon would replace ground beef. Actually, she can now purchase twice the amount of food she bought before, while paying only 15 percent more! Thus, although her total payments for food would increase slightly, Mrs. Saver would find that expenditure very attractive because of its extremely high marginal return!

This example shows how the cost structure of a product or service influences human behavior. Decisions to purchase an item usually depend on its marginal rather than its total cost. If a large portion of the cost is fixed, low marginal cost stimulates excessive purchase of items. That is, it leads buyers to purchase and consume far more than they would if they paid the full price directly. This excessive buying of goods at less than their full cost eventually forces the supermarket to raise the subscription price. Then, consumers who purchase fewer goods will have higher expenses because they will subsidize those who purchase an excessive volume of goods. Total consumption and total expenditures for food are thus increased, and cost distribution becomes inequitable, subsidizing the big spenders.

The impacts of this behavior would be even more complex in the case where production of some food items leads to environmental damage that is not compensated through the price of the product; or, when some items are imported, using foreign currency and affecting the country's international balance of trade. Then the excessive purchases by Mrs. Saver would cause both uncompensated environmental damage and a worsening of the country's financial stability.

This example of the impact of different pricing structures on Mrs. Saver's shopping behavior, and the impacts of this behavior on the costs imposed on others, including the country's international monetary stability, represents a close parallel of the costs and impacts of car use in the United States, exemplified by a driver who shall be referred to as Mr. Racer.

The AAA estimated in 1995 that, on average, the total user cost of driving a car amounted to about 45 cents per mile. Since Mr. Racer purchased his car two years ago, insurance and maintenance costs are paid a couple of times per year; he thus disregards these costs and considers only his out-of-pocket cost when deciding whether or not to drive. That cost amounts to only about 6 cents/mile (4 cents/km); that is, it is extremely low. If Mr. Racer has to pay a toll or a parking fee, the out-of-pocket cost becomes much higher and has a far stronger influence on his decision whether to use transit, to drive, how far to drive, or not to make the trip at all, than if he faces only the cost of gasoline.

Considering only the direct cost of 6 cents/mile (4 cents/km), Mr. Racer will be inclined to drive much more than if he had to pay 45 cents for each mile out of his pocket. This leads to virtually ignoring the cost of driving in human behavior and in trading many other activities and goods for ever longer trips. If prices in different stores should be compared, if a child should be chauffeured to three different points—all these trips simply will be made without any effort to combine or replace them in order to reduce costs. At such a low cost of driving, it is not worth making an effort to economize on travel distances.

Mr. Racer's excessive driving contributes to congestion and all its negative consequences. But these problems do not influence his behavior much because he does not have to pay for them. He will change his travel habits only if congestion becomes intolerable or a better alternative, such as good transit service, is available. Nor is his behavior influenced by the disastrous impact of oil imports on the huge international trade deficit (see chapter 1). The weakening economy and value of the dollar may affect Mr. Racer eventually, but not in a way he would notice and thereby change his travel behavior.

There is another problem with this cost structure of car use. Because travelers decide on mode selection on the basis of out-of-pocket costs, transit fares must be low enough to compete reasonably with car travel. Total cost of providing transit services can never be as low as 6 cents/mile (4 cents/km), which Mr. Racer faces when deciding on a trip for which he would have free parking. This situation leads to the need for substantial transit subsidies.

Consequently, in addition to numerous indirect subsidies to auto travel, it is the structure of costs for driving, with only 10 to 20 percent of it being out of pocket, that results in the need for large transit subsidies. Meanwhile, extreme congestion or high prices for parking usually are the only caps on demand for auto travel.

Although this problem is inherent in the structure of costs of private and public transportation, it is more acute in the United States than in its peer countries. Being much more aware of this problem and the need to have a balanced transit–auto–pedestrian system in urban transportation, countries like Italy, Germany, and Sweden have far higher charges for car travel than are found in the United States. High gasoline taxes, particularly, are aimed not only at increasing the overall cost of driving but are specifically intended to increase its out-of-pocket cost, as well as to compensate for the high social and environmental costs drivers otherwise do not pay. The high generation of revenue and disincentives for consumption of imported oil, considered to be in the countries' national interest, are additional reasons for the high gasoline taxes. This is demonstrated by the fact that even some large oil exporters, such as Great Britain and Norway, have high gasoline taxes.

In addition to short-term congestion and other problems, excessive automobile use, facilitated and induced by low out-of-pocket costs, subsidies, and unpaid costs, is, in the long run, a strong stimulus to dispersal of activities and extensive urban sprawl, which, in turn, increases municipal costs and creates other problems (Burchell 1999).

THE FOUR LEVELS OF TRANSPORTATION PLANNING

The description of various physical, operational, and policy aspects of cities and their transportation systems in the preceding sections indicates that most current problems are created by a failure to understand transportation as a system that interacts with most other activities in cities. To analyze the types of deficiencies in the process of transportation system planning, design, and operation, it is useful to analyze how the relevant activities—policy, planning, financing, construction, and operation—are performed at different levels, from individual facilities to the complex interrelationship of the transportation system with the city or metropolitan area. This section classifies and analyzes the present state of planning at different levels.

Planning, organization, and operation of urban transportation can be classified by its objects, scope, and domain into four levels, from individual system elements to the overall city/urban area level. The four levels, shown schematically in figure 2.14, are:

Level IV: Individual Facilities

such as a boulevard, intersection, pedestrian area, or bus line;

Level III: Single Mode Network or System

for example, a street network, network of bicycle lanes, or regional rail system;

Level II: Multimodal Coordinated System

which incorporates streets and freeways, different transit modes, pedestrian zones, and the like; and

Level I: City-Transport Relationship

or coordination between the transportation system and the city, its physical components and all other functions, such as economy, housing, social conditions, and myriad others (the highest level of planning and operational integration).

A review of practices in different cities shows at what levels the most common successes and failures, as well as typical problems, are.

Level IV planning and operation are, in most cases, performed satisfactorily. There are many well-designed and efficiently operated streets, freeways, regional rail lines, and pedestrian plazas. Designing and operating a single facility is technically the least complicated; moreover, it is usually financed from a single source or several pooled sources, and it is performed

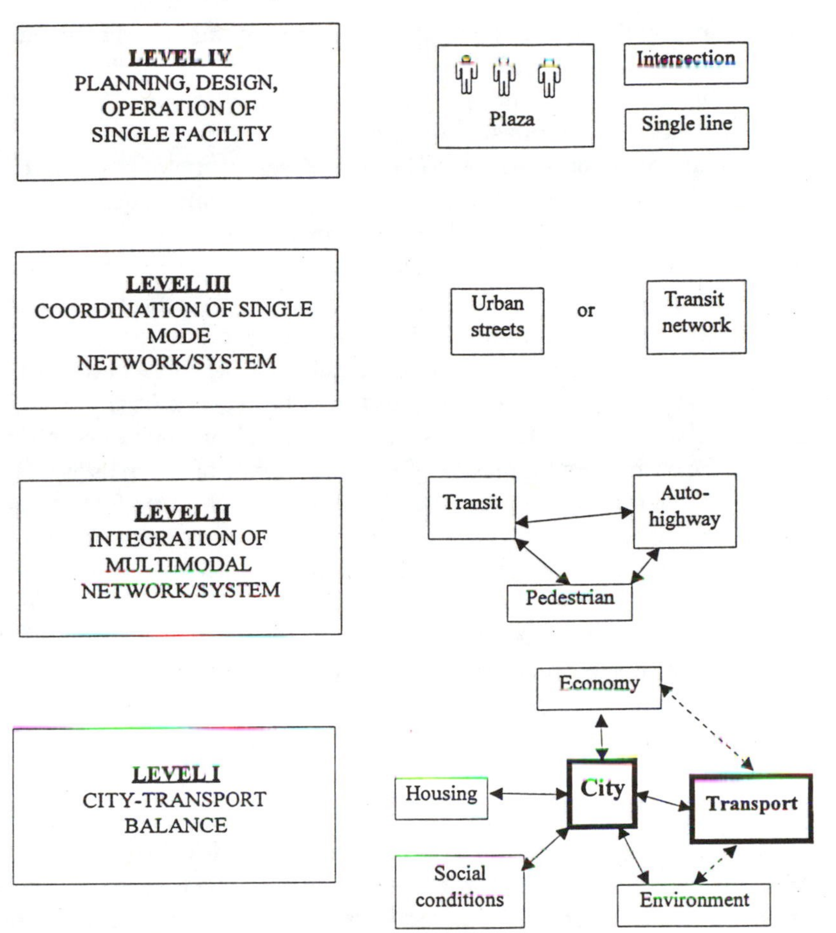

FIGURE 2.14
Conceptual classification of urban transport planning

by a single agency, such as a department of streets, transit agency, parking authority, or the like.

Level III requires more coordination than Level IV, but networks of individual modes are usually under the same jurisdiction, with joint financing and unified control. If jurisdictional problems do not exist (for example, street networks are shared by different municipalities, or there are two different transit planning agencies), inefficiencies may occur.

Level II supersedes single-mode jurisdictions, such as a street or highway department, a trucking or a transit company. It involves a higher-level organization, usually a regional or state government agency. The need for Level II planning has increasingly been recognized in recent decades. For example, the Intermodal Surface Transportation Efficiency Act of 1991 (ISTEA) placed great emphasis on intermodal coordination. In practice, however, many problems remain to be solved before the necessary cooperation, particularly in cities and metropolitan areas, can be achieved.

The obstacles to this higher level of transportation system planning include much more complex, technical, and operational considerations in coordinating different modes than are required for single modes, and they involve separate jurisdictions for different modes. Another serious obstacle is often the narrow, modally oriented mentality of personnel and professionals in many agencies in charge of different transportation modes. The extensive debates about "highways versus transit" or "bus versus rail," created by the narrow single-mode expertise of many professionals as well as by the emotional biases of some professionals and others, are often stronger than efforts to develop efficient, well-coordinated multimodal systems.

Some persons working for individual agencies, such as highway, bus transit, or regional rail, have limited knowledge of other modes and even harbor biases against them. Instead of cooperation among different modal agencies, this attitude often leads to counterproductive intermodal competition, highway-versus-transit attitudes, treatment of pedestrians as "obstacles to vehicular traffic," and so on. The emotional bias toward or against individual modes of transportation is also strong among theoretical analysts of urban transportation, as discussed in chapter 5.

Level I is the highest level of urban planning and development coordination. This is where transportation as a functional system is planned in relation to other activities, such as residing, economic and social activities, and the environment (figure 2.14). This planning is the most complex, both theoretically and practically; but, in the long run, it is most important for metropolitan areas. Special arrangements are required for organizing, financing, planning, and implementing transportation systems and for their coordination with other activities. Without Level I planning, cities can seldom achieve satisfactory levels of efficiency and livability. The increasing efforts to achieve more sustainable forms of urban development will further increase the need for such planning.

The problem in most cities is not only insufficient or inadequate planning at Level I, but inability to implement its results. The planning—including land use, zoning, transportation networks, and facilities—usually is performed by regional or official metropolitan planning organizations (MPOs) according to legal mandates. In many states and countries, however, these regional governmental organizations lack the power to implement plans if

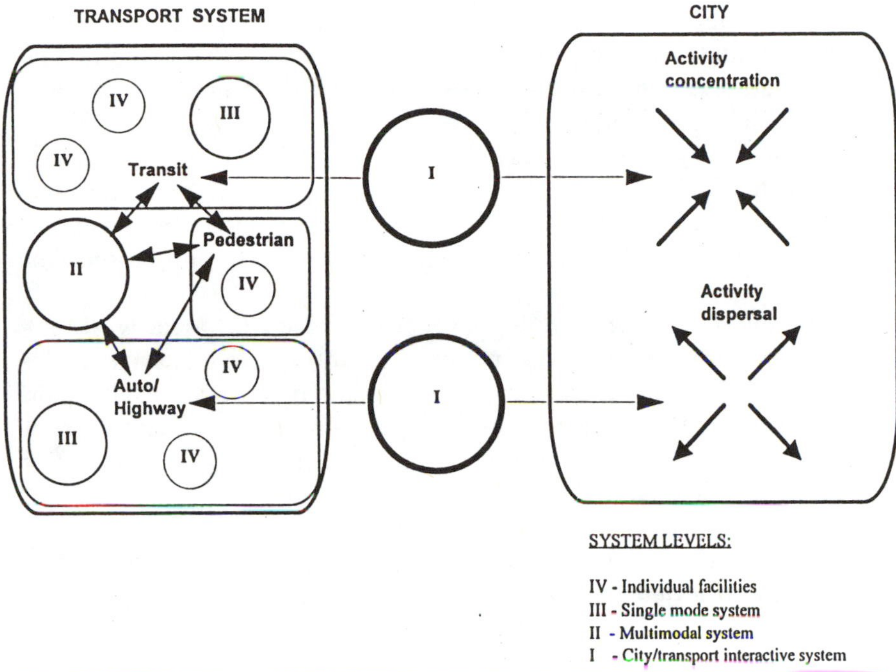

FIGURE 2.15
Schematic presentation of urban transport planning levels

individual counties, townships, and other local units do not comply. Thus, local interests and political and lobby pressures tend to defeat much of Level I work, which is most critical for achievement of both transportation system efficiency as well as a city's livability.

This classification of urban transportation planning can provide insight into its scope and organization. The conceptual schematic diagram in figure 2.15 shows the relationship of different components of planning. Projects at Levels IV and III are within modes—highway or transit; Level II planning is intermodal and encompasses, for example, pedestrians, transit, and auto/highway; and finally, Level I planning relates the entire transportation system, consisting of all modes, to all other activities in the city. The long-range impacts on the city of individual modes or their combinations are analyzed at this level. In general, transit systems tend to create conditions for concentrated activities, while an auto/highway system influences predominantly the dispersal of activities, as shown in the diagram.

This difference in the impacts of the two systems on the social character of an urban area is pointed out by Weyrich and Lind (1996): "Historically, transit helped foster community, just as the automobile helps undermine it." They point out that when people use transit, they walk from their homes to transit stops, often meet neighbors face to face and get to know each other, which helps a neighborhood become a community. "In contrast, . . . the average [car] commuter gets in his car in his garage, turns on the heat or air conditioning and radio, hits the bar on the garage door opener, and sallies forth. He does not see any neighbors; at most he sees their cars. . . . Each driver is isolated in his car, which does nothing to build a sense of community. Indeed, it works against it."

The concept of four planning levels can be related to real-world activities. For example, the ISTEA requirement for intermodal systems development is intended to raise the level of planning to the transportation system, or Level II, and to include its impacts on the urban environment and livability, i.e., Level I, rather than support independent projects at Levels IV and III only.

On the other hand, transit deregulation in Great Britain was based on the claim in the White Paper entitled "Buses" (Department of Transport 1984) that transit deficits represent the most critical transportation problem in British cities. That claim placed the focus of attention on a problem at Level III (transit system) while ignoring the fact that Britain had been far behind most of its European peer countries in coordinating its multimodal transportation systems with urban development. In other words, it had neglected activities at Levels II and I. Indeed, one of the results of the British deregulation of buses has been prohibition of multimodal transit companies, which represents legal prevention of constructive work at Levels III and II. Deregulated bus systems have thus been degraded to Level IV planning and, to some extent, Level III. Planning and system management at Levels II and I are eliminated from the planning and organization of urban transportation systems.

This classification can also be used to gain a proper perspective on the overall handling of urban transportation and its role in cities. If planning focuses on individual facilities (Level IV) while their interactions with other modes and their impacts on the city (Levels III, II, and I) are not considered, such a transportation system may stimulate urban development that is neither efficient nor livable. This sequence of planning, based on Level IV, has been the cause of many problems and conflicts between transportation and cities.

The theoretically correct sequence of planning is shown in figure 2.16. Definition of the type of society and city should be developed first on the basis of societal goals; that definition (overall character and physical form

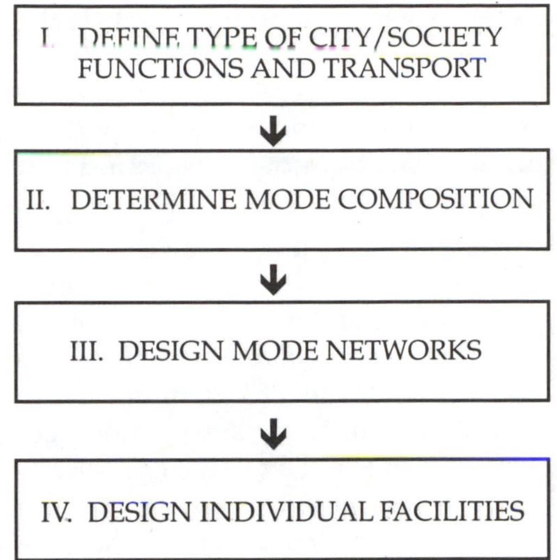

FIGURE 2.16
Planning sequence in urban transport

of the city) should then be used to determine the optimal composition of transport modes. With basic balance among modes defined, planning should proceed to individual system networks and facilities.

SUMMARY AND CONCLUSIONS

The basic interactions between metropolitan areas and their transportation systems have been discussed in this chapter. Also, characteristics of different urban transportation modes and their optimal roles in cities are presented, and the main factors contributing to the excessive use of the private car are described. Here, the main points presented are summarized briefly.

1. As focal points of contemporary societies, metropolitan areas depend greatly on various services. As the "lifeblood of cities," transportation has a particularly strong influence not only on physical conditions of metropolitan areas but on the quality and style of life in them.
2. Transportation must be considered a system that is integrated with diverse activities in metropolitan areas. To serve these activities, transportation service must be efficient and available to all subgroups of the population.

3. No single mode of transportation can satisfy the diverse needs of a metropolitan area. To provide diversity in service types, capacities, speeds, and other elements, particularly in medium- and large-size metropolitan areas, a transportation system must consist of a set of complementary modes including private, public, and paratransit systems.
4. Among private modes, walking is crucial for livability of cities. Underestimation of its role and its neglect in urban planning and design at macro and micro scales have been major problems in many cities, particularly those that focus only on highway transport. As a matter of fact, most cities that want to enhance social life and livability stress encouragement of pedestrian activities as one of their primary goals. For longer trips, the car dominates private modes and serves many different roles. In many suburban areas, the car is by far the most efficient mode for most trips. As urban density increases, however, the efficiency of the private car decreases, and the congestion it creates produces many negative impacts.
5. Transit also plays many roles, but in small cities its social service is dominant. In medium- and large-size cities transit becomes crucial. Its high capacity, efficiency, and low space requirements per person-km (-mile) allow different densities of development. Together with pedestrian traffic, transit ensures human character of the urban environment and enhances a city's overall efficiency and attractiveness.
6. The main feature determining the "performance/investment cost package" of transit modes is the category of its right-of-way, which strongly influences system technology. For transit services on ROW category C—streets, buses usually are best suited and most economical, although they often cannot compete with cars. ROW categories B and A, partially or fully separated from other traffic, require high investment but provide much higher service quality. Rail systems, used on these ROW categories, represent a much higher quality of service, which attracts riders and has a strong interaction with urban form and quality of life.
7. The "collision between cities and cars" is caused by the very high area requirements of the car compared to any other mode. An example showed that during peak hours, a trip by car consumes about 25 times more area than a trip by bus and 60 times

more than a trip on a rail line. A car commuter takes more area for parking than for work in his or her office. This space requirement results in dispersed urban development that is poorly suited to walking. In the long run, it results in urban areas designed for total car dependence for travel and for a high level of privacy, but limited social activities.

8. Metropolitan areas with balanced multimodal transportation—pedestrian, car, and transit—are superior to those served by only one mode, be it paratransit (in some developing countries), transit (in countries with low car ownership), or car (many recently developed North American urbanized areas). The advantages of multimodal over unimodal systems are numerous. They require lower investment and operating costs. Every person has mobility. Their physical environment is human-based. And they allow both privacy and diverse social activities.

9. There are two types of distribution of travel among transportation facilities or modes. Individual equilibrium, based on individual travelers' short-term choices, often results in inefficient system operation: congestion, excessive cost, and misallocation of charges for travel among modes. Social optimum distribution results in lower average costs or disutilities for all travelers. In the case of distribution between cars and transit, a shift of a certain amount of travel from cars to transit would result in reduced costs to both car and transit users. The most effective way to achieve such a shift is to implement transit-use incentive and car-use disincentive measures. Such measures have been proven effective where public authorities have sufficient authority to plan and implement transportation as a multimodal system and the public has a reasonably good understanding of relative efficiencies and impacts of different modes. In the United States, strong opposition to car-use disincentives presents a major obstacle to implementation of the social optimum condition in travel distribution among modes in most cities.

10. Complex problems of costs, charges, and subsidies in urban transportation were discussed. Several recent major studies have shown that car travel, not only transit, is heavily subsidized. The most important problem, however, is not just the subsidy but the fact that car travel has extremely low out-of-pocket costs, which leads to excessive driving. This driving, in turn, creates many indirect costs for other travelers and on society in general,

which car users do not pay. Thus, subsidies of car use lead to dispersal of activities and urban areas and many indirect social and environmental costs.

11. To clarify the planning and organization of transportation in metropolitan areas, four Planning Levels are defined, from individual facilities and modes (Levels IV and III, respectively) to the level at which different modes are integrated and, finally, the relationship between the metropolitan area and its transportation system (Levels II and I, respectively). Most present-day problems in urban transportation are caused by failure to develop and implement effective policies at Levels I and II.

References

Bank of America et al. 1995. *Beyond sprawl: new patterns of growth to fit the new California.* San Francisco, CA: Bank of America.

Bovy, Philippe. 1973, 1974. *Amenagement du territoire et transports.* Lausanne, Switzerland: École Polytechnique Federale.

Bruun, Eric C., and Vukan R. Vuchic. 1995. The time-area concept: development, meaning, and application. *TR Record* 1499: 95–104. Washington, DC: Transportation Research Board.

Buchanan, Colin, et al. 1964. *Traffic in towns.* London, UK: Her Majesty's Stationery Office (HMSO).

Burchell, Robert W., et al. 1999. *Eastward Ho! development futures: paths to more efficient growth in Southeastern Florida.* Report prepared by the Center for Urban Policy Research, Rutgers University, for the Florida Department of Community Affairs and the U.S. Environmental Protection Agency.

Burrington, Stephen H. 1994. *Road kill: how solo driving runs down the economy.* Conservation Law Foundation (CLF), Boston, Massachusetts. May.

Cisneros, Henry, ed. 1993. *Interwoven destinies.* New York: W. W. Norton.

Department of Transport. 1984. *Buses.* London, UK: Her Majesty's Stationery Office (HMSO).

Fitch, Lyle, and Associates. 1964. *Urban transportation and public policy.* San Francisco, CA: Chandler.

Fruin, John J. 1971. *Pedestrian planning and design.* New York: Metropolitan Association of Urban Designers and Environmental Planners.

Hollatz and Tamms. 1965. *Die Kommunalen Verkehrsprobleme in der Bundesrepublik Deutschland.* Essen, Germany: Vulkan-Verlag.

Holtzclaw, John. 1995. America's autos and trucks on welfare: a summary of subsidies. *Mobilizing the Region* 15. February 3.

Institute of Transportation Engineers (ITE), Transportation Planning Council Committee 5P-8. 1997. *Traditional neighborhood development: street design guidelines*. Washington, DC: ITE. June.

Johnson, Elmer W. 1993. *Avoiding the collision of cities and cars: urban transportation policy for the twenty-first century*. Chicago, IL: American Academy of Arts and Sciences and the Aspen Institute.

Leman, C. K.; P. L. Shiller; and K. Pauly. 1994. *Rethinking HOV: high-occupancy vehicle facilities and the public interest.* Annapolis, MD: Chesapeake Bay Foundation.

Litman, Todd. 1992. *Transportation cost survey.* Olympia, WA: Evergreen College.

______. 1995. *Automobile dependency as a cost.* Victoria, B.C., Canada: Victoria Transport Policy Institute.

Lowe, Marcia D. 1993. Smart cars: a really dumb idea. *Seattle Times.* December 16.

Meyer, J.; J. Kain; and M. Wohl. 1965. *The urban transportation problem.* Cambridge, MA: Harvard University Press.

New South Wales Department of Transport. 1993. *Integrated transport strategy for Greater Sydney.* First release for public discussion. Sydney, Australia: New South Wales Department of Transport.

Newman, P., and J. Kenworthy. 1989a. *Cities and automobile dependence: an international sourcebook.* Aldershot, UK: Gower.

______. 1989b. Gasoline consumption and cities: a comparison of U.S. cities with a global survey. *Journal of the American Planning Association* 55: 23–37.

Newman, P.; J. Kenworthy; and L. Robinson. 1992. *Winning back the cities.* Australia: Pluto Press (Australian Consumers' Association).

Persky, J.; E. Sclar; and W. Wiewel. 1991. *Does America need cities?* Washington, DC: Economic Policy Institute.

Pucher, John. 1995. Budget cutters looking at wrong subsidies. *Passenger Transport.* Washington, DC: American Public Transit Association. March 13.

Real Estate Research Corporation. 1974. *The costs of sprawl: detailed cost analysis.* Washington, DC: U.S. Government Printing Office.

Topp, Hartmut H. 1995. A critical review of current illusions in traffic management and control. *Transport policy* 2, 1: 33–42.

Transportation Research Board (TRB). 1998. *The costs of sprawl – revisited.* TCRP Report 39. Report prepared by Robert W. Burchell et al. for Transportation Research Board, National Research Council. Washington, DC: National Academy Press.

Urban Transportation Monitor (UTM). 1995. Numerous statistical data and information items. Burke, VA: Lawley Publications. May.

U.S. Congress, Office of Technology Assessment (OTA). 1994. *Saving energy in U.S. transportation.* Report OTA-ETI-589. Washington, DC: U.S. Government Printing Office.

Vuchic, Vukan R. 1981. *Urban public transportation: systems and technology.* Englewood Cliffs, NJ: Prentice-Hall.

Vuchic, Vukan R.; S. Kikuchi; N. Krstanoski; and Y. E. Shin. 1995. Negative impacts of busway and bus lane conversions into high-occupancy vehicle facilities. *TR Record* 1496: 75–86. Washington, DC: Transportation Research Board.

Wardrop, John G. 1952. Some theoretical aspects of road traffic research. *Proceedings of the Institute of Civil Engineers.* Part II. London, UK. pp. 325–378.

Weyrich, Paul M., and William S. Lind. 1996. *Conservatives and mass transit: Is it time for a new look?* Washington, DC: Free Congress Foundation and the American Public Transit Association.

3

How Did We Get Here? Transportation Policies and Practices in the United States

This chapter reviews urban transportation policies and planning in the United States, both stated and actual, over the past few decades. It also places these policies—and, particularly, their implementation—in the context of the larger society. Thus, it provides a more complete picture of these policies and practices and their importance to the functioning and livability of American cities.

FEDERAL POLICIES 1956–1991: HIGHWAY DOMINATION

Probably the most important legislation affecting transportation and cities in United States history was the Federal Aid Highway Act of 1956 and its companion, the Highway Revenue Act of 1956, enacted during the Eisenhower administration. The first authorized a 66,000-km (41,000-mile) "National System of Interstate and Defense Highways," while the second financed the program through increased fuel taxes, excise taxes on tires, and weight taxes on commercial vehicles. The system was designed to connect at least 90 percent of all urban areas with a population over 50,000. Revenues collected to finance the undertaking were put in the newly created Highway Trust Fund (HTF), which could be used only for highway purposes.

The initial aim of the Interstate Highway System network was that it be a national system for intercity travel and freight transport. However, being funded at a level of 90 percent federal and 10 percent state investment, with no local match, the construction of interstate highways was an offer local governments found hard to refuse. It was even harder to refuse when such alternatives as public transportation received *no* federal funds. As a result, many cities made decisions that were later criticized as damaging to the human orientation of urban environments. They demanded more extensive interstate networks than initially planned; thus, as much as 20 percent of the entire interstate network's mileage was built in metropolitan areas (Weiner 1992).

The Interstate Highway System proved to be the skeleton transportation network in metropolitan areas around which all other facilities were planned. Instead of building basic freeway networks in urban regions coordinated with high-quality transit systems, many cities constructed ubiquitous freeway networks that extended even into high-density, formerly human-oriented city centers. At the same time, transit services were reduced

PHOTO 3.1
At the height of car accommodation during the 1960s, car parks flooded cities.
(3.1a, p. 94): Los Angeles CBD *(California Department of Highways)*
(3.1b, above): Vienna, Austria *(Vukan R. Vuchic)*

to buses operating in mixed street traffic, while walking became unattractive and sometimes dangerous. While during this era of rapid growth in auto ownership the public generally supported construction of highways and freeways, failure to maintain even minimum acceptable levels of transit, pedestrian, and other modes was not supported by the public. Nor was that policy in the interest of metropolitan areas' economic prosperity or livability. Contrary to the belief that Americans left transit because of their "love affair with the automobile," actually, in large part, they reacted logically to policies that strongly promoted car use and led to the degradation of all other modes of travel.

Following the introduction of federal support for single-family housing in the form of tax exemptions for loans, the two Federal Highway Acts of 1956 provided further impetus to suburban development. They stimulated adjustments in urban areas to a single mode of transport—car travel—while contributing to the deterioration of central urban areas and their human character.

The major positive (+) and negative (–) impacts of the two Federal Highway Acts of 1956 can be summarized as follows:

- \+ With the rapid growth of highway transportation, the country responded by making a major commitment to provide a national network of high-quality highways, superior in economy, speed, safety, and other respects to traditional roads and streets.
- \+ The basic *concept* – that the high-quality national network of highways should be in the domain of the federal government – followed the long, well-proven tradition of federal involvement in promoting transportation systems of national significance. This tradition included the construction of the National Highway around 1800, the Erie Canal in the 1820s, assistance to railroads during the second half of the nineteenth century, and strong promotion and major investments in the air transportation system since 1910.
- \+ Financing through a dedicated Highway Trust Fund has a number of advantages of user taxation, such as the correlation of revenues to the amount of car travel, availability of a stable and predictable source of funds, and others.
- \+ The freeway system allowed use of the great mobility that auto and truck transport offer for longer trips throughout metropolitan areas. Urban growth and enhanced choice of residential and business developments were made possible through this increased mobility.
- \- The Federal Highway Acts of 1956 were aimed not at creating an optimal transportation system that utilizes a coordinated set of modes (pedestrian, auto, paratransit, bus, rail transit) but rather gave an enormous boost to one mode only – the highway (automobile and truck), thus greatly reducing any opportunity to achieve a balanced intermodal system.
- \- Getting huge public works projects at 10 percent of their cost for states, and at no cost to cities, induced many metropolitan areas to build as many freeways and interchanges as possible, even in densely populated urban centers or along attractive waterfronts. Seattle, Hartford, Houston, and many other cities followed this strategy. Without comparable funding, such programs as modernization of streets and pedestrian facilities, traffic engineering for capacity improvements, and other measures more conducive to a human-oriented urban environment than freeways were neglected. The United States, which had invented traffic engineering in the 1930s, lost ground in these endeavors during the 1950s and 1960s to a number of its peers, such as

Germany, Switzerland, and the Scandinavian countries. Today, many concepts and engineering techniques in the design and regulation of vehicular, bicycle, and pedestrian traffic, transit priority, and other measures are much more developed in several peer countries than in the United States.

- Neither the general relationship between transportation and land use (and thus its influence on the shape and character of metropolitan areas) nor specific impacts of different modes were taken into account in these federal highway acts. Major consequences of the single-mode-based planning were largely overlooked. Little attention was given to such issues as the negative spatial impacts of freeways, which in some corridors were built with four roadways and up to 16 lanes; environmental impacts of large traffic volumes on metropolitan areas; and reduced efficiency of areas due to large surface and multistory parking facilities occupying prime land in urban centers. These problems were recognized only later, by which time the human character of cities had eroded greatly.

The impact of massive amounts of virtually "free" money for one mode only on metropolitan transportation planning was strong and largely negative. The "area transportation studies" during the period 1956–1970 – CATS in Chicago, TCATS in Twin Cities, PATS in Pittsburgh, LARTS in Los Angeles, and many others – presented their reports as "transportation plans" for metropolitan areas; but this designation was not justified by their contents. These documents were not based on true planning processes, nor did they adequately encompass all transportation modes. In an evaluation of these studies, The Brookings Institution (1969) stated: "In the U.S., the principal objective of most urban transport studies has been . . . the design of freeway systems for the metropolitan area. Thus, the emphasis has been on forecasting future auto travel, with transit travel regarded as a residual to be subtracted from total trip generation before the resulting trips are assigned to the highway network. These highway planning studies have been little concerned with the relative performance of alternative modes." The fundamental deficiencies of these studies are briefly described below.

Deficient planning methodology: Though presented as planning processes, the studies generally represented the development plans for future scenarios obtained by extrapolation of past trends. Correct planning must first define goals for the metropolitan area and objectives for its transportation system. It utilizes extrapolation of trends to examine what the future would be if past trends were to continue. Then it must analyze the *desirability* of such a future scenario. If the scenario is economically and physically feasible, and it is also desirable, policies and plans should aim at achieving it. If, however, the scenario is infeasible, or if it conflicts with the adopted goals and objectives, policies and plans should be formulated that will modify the existing trends so as to reach the specified goals.

Using the period of rapid changes as the basis: This conceptual flaw in the planning process was compounded by the fact that the 1950s was a period of rapid growth of car ownership and use, accompanied by declining transit, which meant that future projections based on extrapolation of trends from that period show a sizable increase of "demand" for auto and truck travel. The assumption was that the projected demand for auto travel was unrestricted and must be accommodated. This thinking led to many undesirable, even physically infeasible, plans. For example, in many cities, projected parking "demand" in the central business district (CBD) would have physically displaced most other activities. In Philadelphia, the "freeway-dominated" plan would have required an increase of off-street parking capacity from 30,000 to 90,000 parking spaces, which would have increased areas occupied by parking into a dominant land use, totally changing the human and historic character of the city.

Space requirements of different modes ignored: In most metropolitan area transportation plan reports, as well as in numerous other publications about urban transportation, such as Meyer, Kain, and Wohl (1965) and their ideological followers, the physical requirements and problems caused by unrestricted auto travel were, for the most part, ignored. "Future Highways and Urban Growth" (Wilbur Smith and Associates 1961), which focused on this problem, claimed that the construction of extensive networks of freeways in cities was beneficial in virtually all respects. Parking demand was estimated by extrapolation, thus assuming continuing extensive subsidy of parking by employers, merchants, and businesses. Environmental impacts and decreased livability of metropolitan areas as a result of full accommodation of car travel received little or no attention.

Computer models suppressed creativity: With the introduction of computers and the ability to handle large volumes of data, urban planning shifted from the earlier qualitative, architecturally based planning to mathematical modeling and quantitative analyses. These new capabilities made it possible to augment the traditional, mostly subjective planning by more factual, quantitative analyses. Soon, however, it became clear that the new quantitative tools had led to a drastic reduction in reliance on experience, judgment, and creativity in the development and evaluation of plans. The mechanistic benefit–cost analysis became the dominant selection criterion.

As is pointed out by Kuhn (1962) and many subsequent writers, this methodology resulted in serious neglect of the non-monetary and non-quantitative aspects of policies and plans. Such plan parameters as the value of travel time had a major bearing on evaluation outcomes. By assuming different values for such elements, relative "values" of plans could easily be changed. The emphasis on time favored high-speed facilities such as freeways and regional rapid transit systems, which stimulate urban sprawl while neglecting inner, human-oriented central city areas.

Freeway impacts not understood: Most plans from the 1955 to 1970 period presented saturation-type freeway networks without examination of the impacts that construction of such enormous structures would have on the form and character of the local urban environment, particularly on the CBD, major activity centers, and historic areas. Despite criticism that many railroad yards or embankments built in the late 1800s had "strangled" cities, new plans for cities such as Chicago, Hartford, and Columbus led to deep penetration of freeways into high-density urban cores, including "inner loops" of elevated freeways around central business districts. These freeways have had a "strangulation" impact similar to that of the condemned railroads, as exemplified by the deterioration of large CBD areas in Detroit and Los Angeles. Plans for the total orientation to car travel, with minimal supporting roles for other modes, thus became self-fulfilling prophecies. Among numerous examples of the disregard of negative environmental and aesthetic impacts of freeways in sensitive alignments was the Embarcadero Freeway in San Francisco, which was planned to block the entire coastline from the Bay Bridge to the Golden Gate Bridge (one section of it was built and, after a long controversy and damage by the 1987 earthquake, torn down); the double-deck Alaskan Way Viaduct along Puget Sound in downtown Seattle; and the plan for construction of an elevated six-lane offshore freeway that would have blocked the entire world-famous Waikiki Beach in Honolulu from the Pacific Ocean.

Vision of city and modes unclear: The future urban scenarios, travel modes, and their mutual relationships were not clearly defined. It was simply assumed that the vast majority of people would use their cars for travel in all areas and at all times. Transit use would be mainly in peak hours and in most cases would consist of buses for which, it was claimed, no special facilities were needed. Inability of buses operating in mixed traffic to compete with the car was not recognized in most transportation studies of the 1950s and 1960s. Only in a few major corridors with heavy travel was the need recognized for a transit system on separate right-of-way. Full-scale rail rapid transit was the only transit option considered for such applications.

Lack of financing for transit system investments contributed heavily to this "unimodal" approach to urban transportation planning and neglect of transit, as well as of all non-highway-based modes.

Human element neglected: The importance of pedestrian travel for local areas (CBDs, activity centers, neighborhoods, access to terminals, commercial and school zones, university campuses, and the like), and for a viable social life, community activities, and livable cities was not recognized. In the planning process, modal split usually did not have pedestrian trips as a category, although in many areas this mode may amount to 20–30 percent of trips. By not including this mode, benefits to pedestrians were not incorporated as a criterion in evaluating alternative transportation plans. This omission further contributed to the failure to develop multimodal transportation systems that utilize the advantages of each mode according to the needs of specific areas, users, communities, and urban environment.

Critics of this process and its results have pointed out that such a narrow approach to transportation policies and planning was destroying not only large residential areas in cities but also the human lifestyles and a complex system that was gradually defined as the "urban environment"—man-made and natural (Appleyard et al. 1976, 1981; Jacobs 1961; Mumford 1961). Reliance on the private car as the only solution to transportation needs in metropolitan areas led to physical, economic, and social problems; and criticism grew of the actions that led to rebuilding entire cities to fit the needs of car travel. These discussions and a study of urban transportation initiated by the Kennedy administration, later reported by Fitch et al. (1964), led to new action by Congress, which passed the Federal-Aid Highway Act of 1962. This law was clearly intended to ensure that all major investments in transportation facilities be based on broad planning that encompasses all modes (Level II) as well as interactions between transportation and other activities in metropolitan areas (Level I).

Until 1962, states and localities conducted their own transportation planning largely by themselves, with technical guidance only from the federal government and such quasi-governmental agencies as the American Association of State Highway Officials (AASHO, now the American Association of State Highway and Transportation Officials [AASHTO]). The federal government provided financial assistance almost strictly by formula, with few strings attached.

The 1962 Act required that any federal aid project in an urbanized area (defined as having 50,000 or more population) be based on a "Continuing, Comprehensive, and Cooperative (3C) Urban Transportation Planning Process." This legislation required that, to continue receiving federal funding, each urban area have such a process in place by July 1, 1965.

The Act prompted changes in planning practices. It required planning at the metropolitan or regional level instead of the city or county level. It also called for new cooperation between state and local governments and provided funds to create this new process by allocating 1.5 percent of all federal highway funds to planning and research. Numerous procedures and mathematical models were created to assist analysts, thus greatly increasing the professionalism and technical sophistication of planning.

The "Comprehensive" component of the 3C process required that ten basic elements be included: economic factors affecting development; population; land use; transportation facilities, including those for mass transit; travel patterns; terminals and transfer facilities; traffic control features; zoning ordinances; financial resources; and, finally, social and community factors (Weiner 1992). The "Continuous" component meant that the plan must be periodically updated. The "Coordinated" component meant not only that different levels of government must work together but also that different divisions at the same level must coordinate all related projects being planned in the same region. It was this law that prompted the creation of most of the metropolitan planning organizations (MPOs) in existence today, as it was thought that such an agency was the only way to coordinate plans in jurisdictionally fragmented metropolitan regions.

The first significant federal aid aimed specifically at urban public transportation came with the passage of the Urban Mass Transportation Act of 1964. The Act allowed up to two-thirds federal funding for capital costs of mass transportation projects (but only 50 percent for those regions that had not developed their 3C planning process). It also included a provision for research, development, and demonstrations pertaining to mass transportation.

Although, initially, the actual funds appropriated for transit research and development were very low, particularly in light of the serious neglect of transit for a long period prior to that time, their availability resulted in initiation of a significant federal effort to reverse the degradation of transit from earlier decades. Under the leadership of the Urban Mass Transportation Administration (UMTA), many innovations, experiments, and developments in transit were conducted during the 1970s. UMTA sponsored technological developments and new vehicle designs such as articulated buses and several rail vehicle models. It had a crucial role in the promotion of various types of paratransit services, in bringing the Light Rail Transit (LRT) concept to the United States, and in introducing self-service fare collection. Its successor, the Federal Transit Administration (FTA), is now continuing that effort.

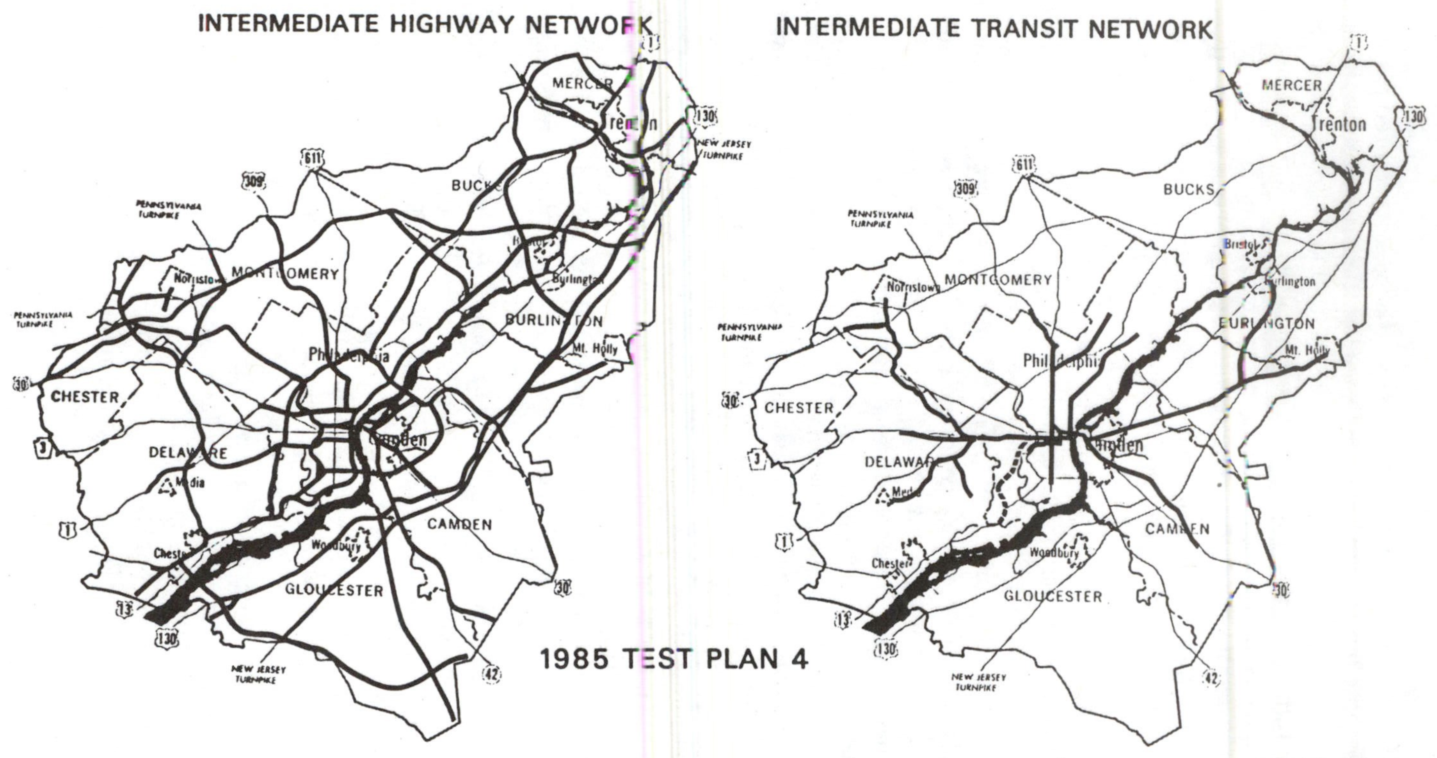

FIGURE 3.1
Urban transportation planning studies in the 1960s proposed extensive freeway networks, but no major extensions of transit; from the 1985 Plan for the Philadelphia Region (Delaware Valley Regional Planning Commission [DVRPC] 1969)

Despite the clearly stated intent and specific requirements of the 1962 Act, which were to improve and broaden transportation planning, to a large extent, the practice of narrow, freeway-dominated planning continued. For example, the 1985 Regional Transportation Plan for the Philadelphia Tri-State Area, published as late as 1969 (DVRPC 1969), was still based on the "saturation freeway network" concept. Figure 3.1 shows the "intermediate" network for highways, as well as its much smaller transit counterpart. Due to a major change in public and political attitudes and the later-adopted federal provision that freeways can be "traded in" for transit projects, most freeways from the 1985 Plan were subsequently deleted.

The changing attitudes toward the environment, cities, public interest, and public participation in decision making that swept the country in the late 1960s and early 1970s had a major impact on urban transportation. The "Freeway Revolt"—which started when citizen groups in San Francisco protested the planned extension of the criticized Embarcadero Freeway, another freeway through the famous Golden Gate Park, and several similar projects in 1966—led to a reexamination of transportation plans not only in the San Francisco Bay Area but also in Boston, Los Angeles, Washington, Philadelphia, and most other metropolitan areas. The above-mentioned weaknesses of these plans made the freeway-dominated plans largely indefensible when submitted to open public scrutiny. As a result, most freeways not built by the early 1970s were deleted from the plans.

How could the 1962 Act be bypassed? The problem was that the philosophy and practices from the freeway era before 1962 were retained and were put in the format and planning steps required by the new law:

- The basic technique of extrapolating past trends continued to be used and was incorrectly presented as "planning."
- Planning organizations had few professionals with expertise in transit systems or in any mode of transportation other than highways. Pedestrians and bicycles continued to be ignored.
- Interaction between land use and transportation was used to compute trip generation; using transportation systems to shape the metropolitan area, however, was not seriously considered because of the inability of most planning agencies to control land use.

The need to diversify the transportation system and better utilize existing facilities was reflected in the Transportation System Management (TSM) Program, promulgated by the federal government in the late 1960s (revitalized by the 1991 Intermodal Surface Transportation Efficiency Act [ISTEA]). TSM emphasized the need for:

- Better utilization of streets and other existing facilities through low-cost improvement measures
- Increased utilization of different modes, particularly transit, and their coordination with car travel
- Utilization of not only physical improvements but also operational and economic measures (pricing) intended to optimize utilization and coordination of different modes

Thus, a new federal requirement specified that planning must have two components, the long-range plan and the shorter-range TSM element.

The rapidly increasing public concern for protection of the environment and quality of life in metropolitan areas led to another milestone in federal transportation policy: creation of the National Environmental Policy Act (NEPA) of 1969. NEPA required that an environmental impact statement (EIS) be prepared for any legislation or major action, investment, or project that would affect the environment significantly. Closely following was the Clean Air Act of 1970, with its later Amendments, which placed the federal government squarely in control of policies that affect the environment. NEPA created the Environmental Protection Agency (EPA), whose first action was to set ambient air quality standards. Concern for clean air went on to become a driving force in subsequent federal transportation legislation and policies.

Yet another major milestone came with the Urban Mass Transportation Assistance Act of 1970. For the first time, there were long-term federal financial commitments to transit projects. This Act also declared that the elderly and handicapped had the same right to transportation as the rest of the population. Additional acts throughout the 1970s allowed use of the Highway Trust Fund for transit projects, though under restricted conditions. This legislation also created operating assistance grants. This was an attempt to revive a floundering transit industry and create a countermeasure to the overwhelming support given highway transportation. The planning process became even more complex as additional regulations were issued. In particular, the Clean Air Act Amendments of 1977 required that state and local governments jointly create a State Implementation Plan (SIP), demonstrating how each region would reach compliance with clean air standards.

During the 1980s, the attitude of the federal government toward transportation changed significantly, from promoting and coordinating different modes to a return to distinctly pro-highway actions and policies. President Ronald Reagan's call for travelers to pay a greater share of transit's costs resulted in reduced assistance to transit and a sharp increase in fares.

PHOTO 3.2
Improved highway design for urban areas.

(3.2a, top): Initial design of I-95 in Philadelphia separated the city from the Delaware River. *(City of Philadelphia, Pennsylvania)*

(3.2b, bottom): Redesigned highway has a cover, giving Old City access to Penn's Landing on the river. *(Pennsylvania Department of Transportation)*

PHOTO 3.3
Intermodal transportation systems: rapid transit allows thousands of car users to park in the suburbs and ride trains into the central city (PATCO line from New Jersey to Philadelphia). *(Vukan R. Vuchic)*

At the same time, no effort was made to increase car users' payments to cover their costs. During its early years, the Reagan administration actually wanted to terminate all federal assistance to public transportation, including urban transit and Amtrak. Investment in highways was increased, while transit investment remained nominally the same for many years (see chapter 4, figure 4.12). Expressed in constant dollars, transit assistance actually decreased from 1981 to the mid-1990s.

When the Surface Transportation Assistance Act (STAA) of 1982 was being prepared, it was noted that the quantity of deferred maintenance of the transportation infrastructure was beginning to mount, and the Interstate Highway System was not yet complete. The estimated cost of building the remaining 10 percent or so of its length was estimated at $40 billion, that is, an amount similar to the initial estimate for construction of the entire network. These spiraling costs were due not so much to inflation as to stricter requirements for meeting the environmental criteria required for approval of environmental impact statements. Higher fuel taxes and commercial vehicle taxes were authorized to bring in additional revenue. The gasoline tax was increased by only five cents per gallon, of which one cent went to a Mass Transportation Account of the Highway Trust Fund.

PHOTO 3.4
New light rail transit systems in many cities have allowed creation of efficient bus–rail intermodal networks (Los Angeles Blue Line). *(Richard Stanger)*

The STAA also represented the beginning of a change in federal policy, as states and local governments were given increasing latitude in the use of both highway and mass transportation funds. Shortly after passage of the Act, new urban transportation planning regulations were issued that greatly reduced the federal prescription for how the process should work, concentrating instead on what its goals should be. MPOs could now be whatever the state and local government agreed upon, thus swinging the pendulum back toward the era of local control of the planning process, similar to that before the Federal Highway Act of 1962. The reauthorization bill in 1987 did not change this basic policy, and it remained basically unchanged until the end of 1991.

ISTEA was, in many ways, a major departure from previous federal transportation policies. For the first time, it stressed the *intermodal* nature of travel and the need to use each mode most efficiently. It also recognized the impotence of most MPOs in the real world of transportation planning, the failure to link transportation planning with land use, and the dominance of highway planning at the expense of all other modes. Under the Intelligent Vehicle Highway System (IVHS) Act , ISTEA funded new research and development intended to explore the benefits of information systems to improve the efficiency of existing facilities and increase the attractiveness of alternatives to the private automobile. This program was later redesignated the Intelligent Transportation Systems (ITS) Act.

It was recognized that there were difficulties in obtaining funds from highway projects for non-highway projects, as both state and federal laws often prohibited such "diversions," so that ISTEA has new provisions for "flexible funding" from a larger percentage of the total funds than before. This allowed unprecedented latitude to use federal funds for the combination of modes that is judged most effective in the particular region. In addition, new requirements have been introduced that were designed to make regional transportation plans more effective than in the past. The requirement that the MPO must make a long-range plan for the region and a Transportation Improvement Plan (TIP) that is consistent with it has been retained.

Furthermore, each state was required to develop, establish, and implement six different management systems: (1) highway pavement, (2) bridges, (3) highway safety, (4) traffic congestion, (5) public transportation facilities and equipment, and (6) intermodal transportation facilities and systems (U.S. Department of Transportation 1992).

ISTEA has provisions for withholding federal funds from states that fail to comply with its requirements. Thus, there are penalties for nonexistent or ineffective state—and, indirectly, regional—plans. Of particular interest is the traffic congestion management system provision in ISTEA. This provision contains several requirements and stipulations directly aimed at reducing congestion through reduction of VKT (VMT) rather than by the traditional self-defeating policy of increasing highway capacities. The Act states that highway lanes that "significantly increase" capacity for single-occupant vehicles can no longer be funded from several key programs unless they are part of an approved traffic congestion management system.

Under ISTEA, clean air concerns continued to be central to transportation policy. A special fund under the Congestion Mitigation and Air Quality (CMAQ) program of ISTEA has been targeted for projects in regions classified as "non-attainment areas," that is, areas not satisfying federal air quality standards. Many regions are still not in compliance with air quality standards, which, once again, have been strengthened by the Clean Air Act Amendments of 1990. This fund represents a significant portion of ISTEA funds intended specifically for alternatives to single-occupancy vehicle (SOV) travel.

ISTEA: PROGRESS AND MAJOR OBSTACLES

Has ISTEA actually changed the way planning is done and implemented? A few years after its enactment, it is obvious that there have been significant steps toward transportation planning that takes a long-range view, a view that considers not only transportation per se, but its interaction with the entire economy and society. The effectiveness of ISTEA, however, is severely limited by the fact that its advanced policies and principles, aimed at solving the serious crisis of transportation in metropolitan areas, require major changes in the long-standing practices that have caused the crisis. These practices are deep-rooted and are strongly defended by interest groups. An overview will be useful here.

Compared with previous transportation acts, ISTEA represents very progressive legislation. It defines the fundamental problems in urban transportation and makes a significant step forward by promoting a systems approach to transportation. ISTEA emphasizes that the goal in transportation planning—improving accessibility (rather than maximizing VKT)—can be achieved most efficiently by utilizing coordinated intermodal systems, rather than highways alone. It states explicitly that congestion should be mitigated by discouraging SOV use, by promoting alternatives to cars, and by development of intermodal systems. ISTEA also requires a stronger role for MPOs in coordinating regional efforts to achieve intermodal solutions optimal for the region. Considerable flexibility in funding is allowed; thus, strict earmarking of funds for different modes, with the major share going to highways, has been relaxed considerably.

In the United States, however, there is a long tradition of conditions and practices that prevent effective multimodal planning and have deep-rooted bias favoring the car over all other modes. Not only do the conditions that prevented effective 3C planning required by the 1962 Act continue to exist, but they represent even greater obstacles to the more complex multimodal urban transportation planning required by ISTEA. They are summarized below.

- In many states, the legal jurisdiction of governments gives such strong home rule to local governments—cities, townships, boroughs, sometimes counties—that regional planning is extremely difficult. MPOs have no overriding powers over these units.
- Despite greatly improved, sophisticated planning techniques, such as models for coordinated land use/transportation plans, the basic approach continues to be extrapolation of trends, rather than development of creative plans that lead to defined goals. When projected developments are undesirable, plans should lead to changes of the current trends.

- The plans developed by MPOs resemble more closely collections of independent, often competing, wish lists of individual townships and counties than they do a coordinated plan designed to achieve a region's goals. The decision process of MPOs often consists of political trading of individual projects among local officials from different counties, rather than the pursuit of an overall regional goal.
- Planning of different modes (highway, transit, bicycle systems) continues to be separated rather than integrated, for several reasons: funding is still, for the most part, modally provided; each mode is planned by a separate agency; most professionals are mode-oriented. Those in the last group usually have limited knowledge of modes other than the one they are working on. Many have an emotional bias toward *their* mode, so that lack of mutual professional understanding is often aggravated by animosity among modal groups. Strong emphasis by ISTEA on an intermodal approach has been a useful step toward amelioration of this problem in recent years.
- Both investment and operating costs of all modes are subsidized. Usually, however, the funds, particularly those for infrastructure maintenance and improvements, are insufficient, creating continuous competitive attitudes among modal organizations for any funds that may be shared.
- Adequate financing of major projects, especially those for transit and other alternatives to car travel, is often prevented by lobbies. For example, highway and oil company lobbies, extremist anti-tax groups, and even some consumer organizations develop enormous propaganda against every cent of gasoline tax increase, although gas prices at different pumps, even along the same street, may vary by 10 to 15 cents per gallon! Moreover, the price of gasoline during the 1990s has been lower in constant dollars than at any time since the 1930s!

In addition to special-interest lobbies, public opinion about gasoline taxes and prices is often misled by politicians' populist stands. The low point in this misinformation of the public was reached during the 1996 presidential campaign. Republican candidate Bob Dole claimed that an increase in gas prices of 15 to 20 cents per gallon (4 to 5 cents per liter), the result of world oil market fluctuations, caused "hardship for hard-working groups" and suggested that a 4.3 cent per gallon (1 cent per liter) tax earmarked for deficit reduction be repealed. This proposal was criticized by most transportation experts and economists from all sides of the political spectrum as unsound. An increase in price of 20 cents per gallon (5 cents per liter) amounts to less than 1 cent per mile (0.6 cent per kilometer), or about 2 percent of the total cost of driving. Repeal of the 4.3 cents per gallon tax would recover about 20 percent of that 1 cent per mile, but it would mean a loss of $5 billion in federal revenues at a time when the country was desperately trying to decrease the budget deficit. Despite this lack of logic, the Democratic candidate, incumbent President Bill Clinton, did not openly criticize this proposal, but instead managed to avoid it through legislative procedures.

With each 1 cent per gallon bringing a revenue of $1.1 billion per year nationally, an increase of 25 to 30 cents per gallon (6 to 8 cents per liter) could provide sufficient funds for investment in all modes. Any such increase in the cost of driving would have a positive, though moderate, impact on reducing the underpricing of car use, which, as shown in chapter 2, has had extremely negative consequences.

- The various modes of urban transportation are still funded mostly from different sources and have different degrees of certainty. When some elements of a comprehensive plan receive funding but others do not, the coherence and balance of the plan are undermined. Specifically, highway investments are generally paid for through a combination of user fees and subsidy from general revenues, whereas transit increasingly is financed by taxes unrelated to transportation such as the sales tax, which often requires approval by a public referendum. Thus, transit investments are subject to numerous opportunities not only for public scrutiny but for opposition and negative propaganda as well, while highway funding flows through well-established channels with no specific public referenda.
- Numerous biases remain in funding that favor highway over travel by other modes. For example, employers' "free" parking for employees was fully tax-deductible (that is, federally subsidized), whereas employer contribution to transit monthly passes was limited to $15; if the amount was greater than $15, all tax exemptions were lost. Congress in the mid-1990s imposed a limit on the parking tax exemption of $170 per month while increasing the transit pass tax exemption to $65. Despite this correction, the subsidy of car travel over transit use remains about 2.5 times greater, contradicting statements in the law that transit use should be encouraged and SOV use discouraged.

- The goals and relationships of transportation modes are not clearly defined. In implementation, the private car continues to be favored over transit, whereas pedestrian and bicycle needs have received attention and financing only since 1991 in both regional and local planning, and in street design.
- Utilizing the classification of planning into four levels, most transportation planning in metropolitan areas includes little effective planning at Level I (the city-transportation relationship), and there is some planning at Level II (intermodal coordination). Collections of separate plans from Levels III and IV, which are compiled by MPOs, cannot result in effective, coordinated regional plans.

Consequently, similar to the situation in which the 1962 Transportation Act was introduced, ISTEA is being weakened by underlying deficiencies in the organizational setup of governments, by political forces defending continuation of past trends, and because a largely uninformed public does not have an adequate explanation of the causes of problems and trade-offs among alternatives. For example, unlike their peers in other developed countries, residents of U.S. metropolitan areas do not fully understand that car driving is subsidized. Nor are many of them aware that car driving, in addition to its great benefits, has certain negative impacts on cities and suburbs. The importance of improving pedestrian facilities and stimulating lively public areas so that, in the long run, crime will be reduced (as pointed out by several authors from Jacobs [1961] to Cisneros [1993]), is not fully recognized. Nor is it broadly understood that cities, particularly large metropolitan areas, cannot be economically efficient and livable without high-quality, attractive transit systems and good treatment of pedestrians.

BYPASSING ISTEA: FREEWAY WIDENING UNDER HOV LANE DISGUISE

One of the most obvious examples of the methods used locally to avoid and contradict the ISTEA spirit, and even its explicit requirements, is the wave of highway construction projects in many metropolitan areas.

Construction of new highways or the widening of existing ones in metropolitan areas not only increases the direct use of SOVs but causes further diversion of travel from HOVs, transit, and other modes. ISTEA, therefore, discourages such construction except in certain special situations. Meanwhile, HOV use is strongly encouraged, and many metropolitan areas are introducing HOV lanes and facilities. The argument often is given that HOV lanes are being built instead of general-purpose lanes. There are, however, two ways for providing HOV facilities:

1. Conversion of one or more existing general purpose lanes – *"Convert-a-lane"*; and
2. Construction of new HOV facilities – *"Add-a-lane"* (or roadway).

There is a great difference between these two methods of providing HOV lanes. "Convert-a-lane" meets ISTEA's intermodal coordination requirement by improving travel conditions for HOVs and decreasing the capacity for SOVs. It directly encourages shifting travel from the least productive mode, SOV, to higher-capacity HOVs, thus increasing the productivity of the existing highway. Inevitably, it causes dissatisfaction among SOV users. Their opposition to this efficiency measure was validated in 1977 by a court decision in the infamous case of the Santa Monica Freeway in Los Angeles.

Faced with chronic congestion on a 20-km-long section of the 10-lane Santa Monica Freeway, California's Department of Transportation (Caltrans) converted one out of five lanes per direction into HOV, or "Diamond," lanes. The initial increase in congestion in the four general traffic lanes led to a lawsuit against this project, and 21 weeks after its start, a judge stopped the project and asked for additional environmental impact studies. Instead of providing such information, Caltrans decided to drop the project, proclaiming that convert-a-lane projects were "not politically feasible."

Actually, within the 21 weeks of operation, the project was well along toward achieving its goals. Buses and HOVs experienced a travel time reduction of about five minutes, while cars had an average travel time increase of 24 seconds, with somewhat increased variability. The total number of people carried increased 3 percent, while the number of vehicles decreased 7 percent. In their final week of operation, HOVs reached 269 percent of the riders they had carried at the beginning of the project, while the number of transit bus riders more than tripled (Billheimer et al. 1977; Homburger et al. 1996).

The judge presiding over this case decided on the basis of the project's legal aspects—that is, those concerning Planning Level IV primarily. Caltrans then neglected to raise its evaluation to Planning Levels III and II. Moreover, highway authorities across the country have cited this case as "proof" that the convert-a-lane concept is "infeasible" regardless of the broader aspects of the system. Thus was missed a chance to raise transportation decisions to the systems level. Actually, the decision is controversial even as a project (Level IV), because it gives preference to a portion of highway users over the interests of the entire population and the overall public interest. It also favors highway users who occupy a much greater share of the facility over those who use the facility and area resources several times more efficiently.

"Add-a-lane" is more popular with SOV users for obvious reasons, but it is much more expensive and environmentally damaging than convert-a-lane. Although add-a-lane improves travel conditions for HOVs by separating them from general traffic, removal of these vehicles from regular lanes increases capacity for SOVs. Thus, add-a-lane removes the main stimulus for people to use more efficient modes, HOVs or transit, while in effect causing an increase of VKT. Therefore, the results are clearly contrary to ISTEA requirements (Leman et. al 1994; Vuchic et al. 1995).

The strategy outlined below for bypassing and actually contradicting the ISTEA requirements for creating coordinated multimodal systems has been used in one metropolitan area after another.

1. Publicize the need for HOV facilities, purportedly to reduce VKT and increase the efficiency of highways.
2. Propose introduction of HOVs. Since "the public is opposed to introducing any restrictions in existing lanes," claim that it is necessary to build additional HOV lanes rather than convert existing ones into HOV lanes. This evasion of any disincentive to SOV use, which practically defeats intermodal coordination, is proclaimed to be a "political reality."
3. Claim that, because HOVs will enjoy better travel conditions, many drivers will leave their cars in order to carpool; that is, they will shift from SOVs to HOVs. This is contrary to fact. In most cases, SOV use will become even more attractive because drivers' travel will improve. Under such conditions, there actually will be a diversion of travel from HOVs to SOVs, unless other disincentives are introduced, such as road pricing or parking controls and charges. Until recently, however, these actions were limited to theoretical studies. It should be mentioned that the first significant application of road pricing in the United States was the opening of new lanes on U.S. Highway 91 in southern California, which have time-variable tolls and free passage for HOVs. Thus, SOVs have the option of fast trips on the toll lanes or slower, less reliable travel on old, often congested, "free" lanes. This innovative concept, aimed at increasing efficiency of traffic flow, particularly during peak hours, may bring significant results.

PHOTO 3.5
Construction of "Add-a-lane" and a wide, paved divider defeated any purpose for lane designation as "2+ HOV" on I-84 in Hartford, Connecticut. *(Vukan R. Vuchic)*

4. When HOVs are defined as vehicles with four or more passengers ("4+") and HOV facility use is not near capacity, build pressure for "better utilization of capacity" by lowering the limit to "3+" and then to "2+" HOVs, thus creating even more capacity for SOVs in general-purpose lanes. Gradually, some metropolitan areas have converted all HOV facilities into a "2+" regime, and some have opened them to general traffic, thus completing the "by-passing of the law circle" (Leman et al. 1994).

Thus, based on a series of deceptive statements and gradual changes that are contrary to ISTEA requirements, the final result is construction of additional highway capacity, increased SOV use and VKT, decreased transit use, and further reliance on one mode—all away from the goal of achieving a multimodal, coordinated urban transport system. This process has been called a "Trojan Horse" tactic for increased driving and use of SOVs.

Examples of these developments abound across the country. Interstate 84, north of Hartford, Connecticut, has been greatly widened, with new

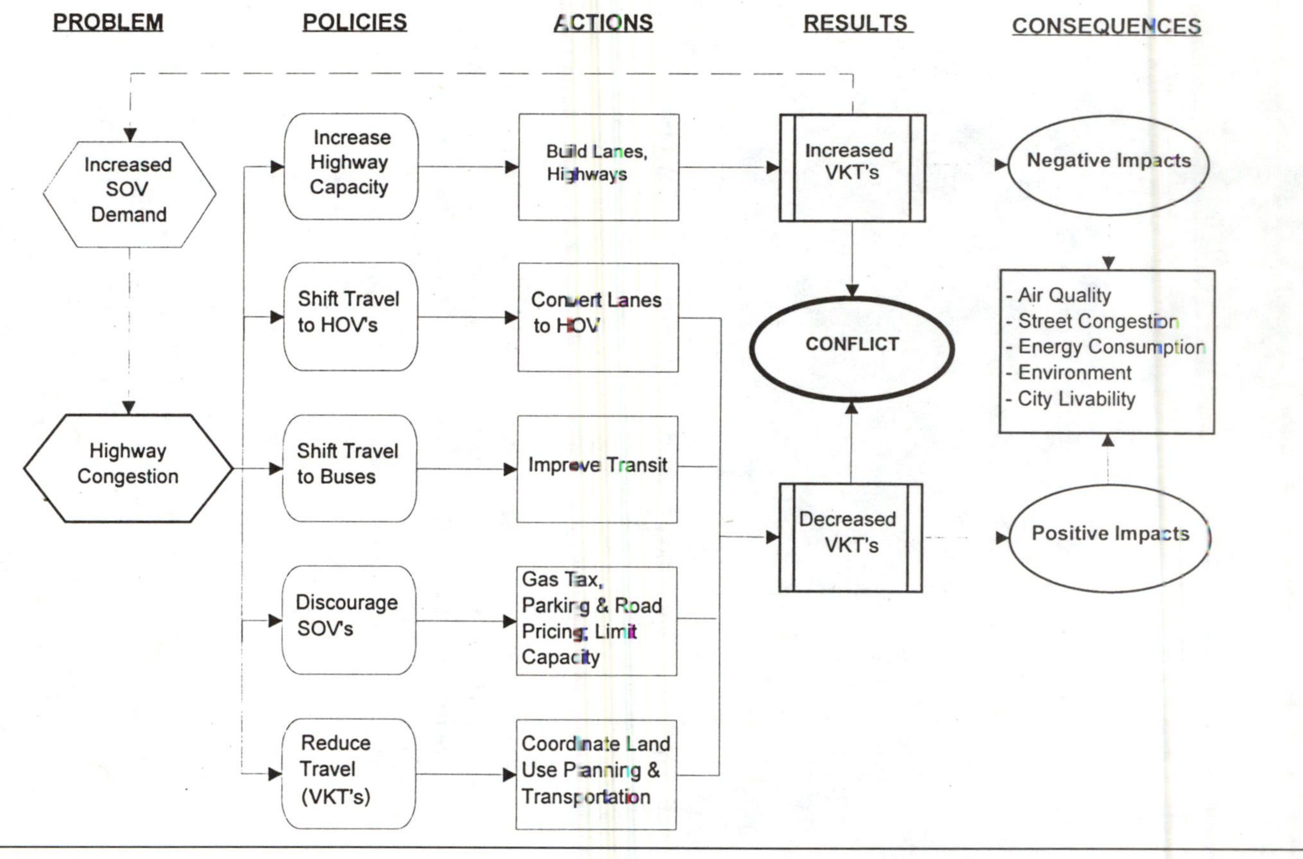

FIGURE 3.2
Consequences of different policies for relief of highway congestion

PHOTO 3.6
Without realistic pricing or disincentives for auto use, demand for more freeway lanes continues to grow (Los Angeles). *(Vukan R. Vuchic)*

HOV lanes added, separated by wide paved strips intended to be "dividers." Thus, there is a pair of extremely wide paved roadways in which, by this very widening and increased capacity, the need for HOV lanes has been diminished. Similar addition of 3+ HOV lanes was made on Interstate 5 in the Puget Sound region. According to a report released by the Puget Sound Regional Council (1995), these lanes, subsequently downgraded to 2+, attracted about 1,000 HOVs during peak hours from general purpose lanes. However, this diversion then generated an increase of traffic volume in the general-purpose lanes by 1,000 SOVs per hour during peaks. This corroborates the hypothesis mentioned above: add-a-lane results in increases, rather than decreases, of SOVs and VKT. Despite the need to return the facility to 3+ regulation, Washington State's Department of Transportation has not taken that action.

The flowchart in figure 3.2 shows five alternative methods for alleviating highway congestion. Whereas four of the alternatives result in a reduced number of VKT, add-a-lane HOV construction actually increases the number of VKT. Thus, if trip-reduction measures are applied in the same area where new HOV lanes are constructed, the latter measure works directly against the former. Such investments are made in mutually conflicting projects, increasing transportation expenditures while moving away from ISTEA-defined goals.

Redesign of freeways to increase vehicular capacity is another way to bypass the requirement not to increase the use of SOVs. In a number of cities, freeways were designed to high safety standards: 12-feet-wide (3.66-meter-wide) lanes, and adequate shoulders on both sides of the roadway to serve as breakdown and safety lanes for emergency stopping, maintenance equipment, and so on. On many freeways in Los Angeles, Atlanta, and other cities, shoulders have been incorporated and mainline roadways restriped to provide a greater number of narrower lanes (11 feet/3.35 meters wide). This results in a loss of emergency lanes and thus less safe operations. Safety, then, has been sacrificed to increase vehicular capacity, primarily to allow increased use of SOVs and VKT.

On the positive side, ISTEA has drawn attention to the serious deficiencies in our transportation systems and at least raised issues for discussion. It has also given stimulus to changes in the metropolitan areas and states that have initiatives and are actively working to change the traditional methods of planning, which had obviously failed. New directions in state-level planning and innovative actions of several MPOs, such as planning peak-hour pricing on bridges in the San Francisco Bay Area, are good examples of this positive trend. So far, however, most of these proposals, including the Bay Area bridge pricing modifications, have stalled at the level of political decision making. Public understanding of complex urban transportation issues remains inadequate, so that special interest groups exert pressures on political leaders, which they cannot overcome without strong public support.

Most states continue to have inadequate planning mechanisms and resources for non-highway modes. Also, they still have little control over factors complementary to transportation, such as land use. But a few states are leading the way to integrated planning; for example, the states of Washington and Oregon have passed growth management laws requiring that metropolitan regions draw boundaries inside which future development shall take place. These laws have already prompted long-range land-use plans which will help to contain sprawl and promote travel patterns less dependent on the automobile. A higher goal is to promote more livable communities.

ISTEA has also stimulated intermodal activities and development of different modes. New Jersey and Pennsylvania, for example, have developed plans for strong promotion of bicycle use.

CHANGING PUBLIC ATTITUDES

An increasingly knowledgeable public is now not only permitted but demands to participate in planning when there is a likely impact on local communities or areas. There is more skepticism about the wisdom of official plans that are highway-dominated and the politicians and professionals promoting them than was the case several decades ago.

In the late 1960s and building momentum in the early 1970s, the public increasingly demanded to express its views about environmental issues. Air pollution, noise, land conservation, historic preservation, nuclear plant safety, chemical waste, and numerous other issues about the human and natural environments became central to public discussions.

As mentioned, the Freeway Revolt, which began in San Francisco in 1966, was the first major public expression against official transportation plans after the passage of the Interstate Highway Act in 1956. Criticism quickly spread to other metropolitan areas across the country. The automobile and, especially, the freeway were often criticized as symbols of environmental damage and waste, as well as disregard for the livability of communities slated for freeway construction. The public demanded that some solution be found other than construction of more freeways. In a few cities, such as Portland (Oregon) and Sacramento, state and local contributions scheduled for construction of specific freeways were diverted to LRT systems. Until ISTEA in 1991, diversions were minimal; freeways were built with up to 90 percent federal funds, but the federal share could not always be diverted to anything other than highway projects. Interstate highways remained federally sponsored at the 90 percent level, a contribution higher than that for any other transportation projects.

To combat this funding inequity, and to finance alternatives, many regions passed local bond issues or taxes. In the San Diego region, for instance, sufficient local funds were raised to finance construction of major parts of a new LRT system—with *no* federal financial contribution. That the public would demand a local community to forgo federal money and jobs, and instead vote to increase its own taxes, provides strong evidence of changing public attitudes.

This is not to say that all public demands have been motivated by concerns for a more livable city—decreased pollution, energy conservation, and other broad societal goals. There is also the "Not In My Backyard" attitude, known as the NIMBY syndrome. In its worst form, it is merely the selfish hypocrisy of wanting a new facility but requesting that others suffer the negative consequences. In its best form, it is the feeling of being unjustly singled out to shoulder the burden of the greater community. In all cases, it concerns local interests trying to override overall project goals.

Fierce, organized resistance at the local level has been responsible for many aborted transportation plans. This is true not only of highway-related projects but of urban public transportation and airport projects as well. When plans are not waylaid, implementation costs skyrocket as numerous environmental mitigation measures are added, sometimes arguably involving excessive protection of certain individuals or communities. It is now commonplace to install noise barriers along freeways. In a few cases, such as on Mercer Island outside Seattle along Interstate 90, elaborate and very expensive lids have been built over freeways. In conclusion, many impact-mitigation measures required by the public have been justified; in other cases, however, excessive and unrealistic NIMBY-based demands have become serious obstacles to construction of needed highway, transit, and airport projects.

This situation is further exacerbated by a series of unfunded mandates imposed mostly on transit projects. Examples include expensive requirements of the Americans with Disabilities Act (ADA) for facilities retrofitting, and far more stringent clean engine requirements for buses than for other vehicles. Although ADA requirements represent worthwhile national standards for improving the living conditions of disabled persons, failure to provide special funds for transit systems to meet these requirements is highly inequitable. Since these funds must be allocated from already inadequate transit resources, the social measure of accommodating the handicapped is not borne by society but by transit users alone.

THE PRESENT SITUATION: AGGRAVATING URBAN TRANSPORTATION PROBLEMS

In the late 1990s, many events are affecting the problem of urban transportation as well as the condition of metropolitan areas in general. Trends in the United States are not encouraging.

There is little doubt that the United States faces serious problems in urban transportation. Recognizing this, ISTEA and its successor, TEA-21 of 1998, mandated several measures that should bring major changes in present practices and traveling habits. A number of studies and proposals for action have focused on inefficient transportation as one of the problems contributing to the deterioration of metropolitan areas (Cisneros 1993; Johnson 1993; Persky 1991; Rendell 1994). These and many other studies strongly point to the need for changes in present practices and trends. Yet, most current trends and proposals for legislation run contrary to the recommendations found in ISTEA, TEA-21, and in the quoted studies. A brief review of major current developments and attitudes follows.

- Some ISTEA mandates being followed continue to have a major positive impact on broadening metropolitan planning procedures. Interest and participation by local governments has increased, and many innovations are being introduced in MPO activities. Also, intermodalism is actively promoted by a special office in the U.S. Department of Transportation.
- Obstacles to implementation of ISTEA provisions are, however, formidable. Enforcement of the Employer Trip Reduction Program has virtually been discontinued, as have numerous other initiatives intended to reduce VKT and, particularly, SOV use. As discussed above, the HOV concept is being used to increase freeway capacity while claiming that SOV use is being discouraged. Actually, that also leads to an increase in VKT and directly contradicts the requirements and spirit of ISTEA.
- Car-use disincentive measures are extremely difficult to implement because industry lobbyists interested in maximizing highway transportation stimulate complaints by motorists and then proclaim them to be "political realities" that prevent implementation of such measures. Thus, industry lobbies organized a multimillion-dollar campaign against any possible agreements that could be reached at the Kyoto Conference on World Climate in 1997. With no effective restraints on SOVs, the growth of VKT continues and congestion worsens. This situation will continue as long as car drivers pay only a small fraction of their costs out of pocket while continuing to enjoy numerous indirect subsidies. Present conditions will be further aggravated unless travel habits are changed, and they will not change as long as the conditions that have created the present extreme car dependency continue.
- At the time of this writing, a new transportation act is being planned. While there is strong bipartisan support for an act that would extend the basic policies of ISTEA with some modifications (the National Economic Crossroads Transportation Efficiency Act, or "NEXTEA"), extreme highway lobbies are trying to defeat the concept and spirit of intermodalism of ISTEA and return to the one-sided transportation policies of the 1950s, that is, to those highly favorable to highways only. The allocation of funds proposed by the Clinton administration continues the trend of large increases in highway funding and much less funding for transit and Amtrak.

- The Intelligent Transportation System (ITS) is a program that is claimed to promise great improvements for urban transportation, and it has been given ample funding. Several component programs of ITS will result in improved vehicle safety, travel information, and traffic management and lead to increased safety and better utilization of highways. In addition, transit systems will benefit from advanced information systems for the public and for operations control.

- The ITS program has some serious shortcomings, however, as discussed in chapter 2 (Lowe 1993). They lie in the fact that its components are not integrated into a total transportation system. Moreover, they are not coordinated with overall urban transportation goals and policies. For example, the following basic issues have not been resolved.

  - If freeway capacity is enhanced by Advanced Vehicle Control Systems (AVCS) programs, that will result in increased VKT. This runs counter to the goal of reducing VKT.

  - If the Advanced Traffic Management Systems (ATMS) program allows optimal distribution of traffic throughout a network, many streets and arterials will experience increased traffic volumes. This is contrary to the requirements to reduce vehicular movements or "tame traffic" in local streets and neighborhoods and to make metropolitan areas more livable.

  - Advanced controls are being focused on freeways. How can a freeway network with advanced controls interact with local urban streets, many of which lack conventional traffic engineering controls?

These and other fundamental questions about the ITS program have been raised and remain open. Its critics make strong arguments, claiming that the entire ITS program neither justifies such large funding nor is likely to fulfill many of its promises. Moreover, many of these results, such as increased highway capacities without consideration of the total highway network and multimodal transportation system, are likely to conflict with the goals of national transportation policies.

- Many proposals debated in Congress represent a major leap backward in transportation policies. For several years during the 1990s, the federal budget contained increased funding for highway and air transport, but drastic cuts for Amtrak and several categories of transit funding. This trend is contrary to all efforts to improve intermodal balance in transportation in metropolitan areas. Congress recently took a similar negative attitude toward environmental legislation: many proposals were produced that were aimed at watering down or eliminating existing legislation protecting clean air, water, and natural resources. Again, these actions contradict the worldwide trend of increasing concern for environmental protection.

- Reduction of unfunded mandates and excessive regulations is, in principle, a positive effort that Congress is pursuing. Much of this effort, however, is misdirected. For example, helmet laws to protect motorcyclists are being repealed, resulting in a drastic increase of deaths and injuries; speed limits and their enforcement have been relaxed, also contributing to an increase in the number of highway deaths. On the other hand, the unfunded entitlement provisions of the Americans with Disabilities Act, and the obstructive 13C provision requiring labor union endorsement of all transit investments, remain intact.
- The greatest "free lunch" in transportation continues. Congress seems to have little interest in reducing the extensive subsidies to car use, from tax exemptions for many trip categories made by car, to "free" parking in the public and private sectors. While cuts for transit are explained by "fiscal constraints," this plausible conservative philosophy is not extended to greater highway and car use subsidies. Nor is a gas tax increase, which could easily solve all problems of funding in transportation and contribute to budget deficit reduction, even seriously considered. Although most officials agree that major increases in the gasoline tax would be in the national interest, the populist stands by some politicians arouse the instinctive desire of the public for free services. With any negative public reaction, it is proclaimed that gas tax increases are "politically unrealistic."
- The concept of "livable cities" is being promoted by the Federal Transit Administration and by the U.S. Department of Transportation. Although many current activities will greatly decrease chances to improve quality of life in metropolitan areas, it is important that public awareness of this concept continues to be raised.
- Confusion of means and goals and pursuit of minimum short-term cost continue to be widespread in the literature about urban

> transportation. There is a major gap between many academic writings and real-world developments with respect to various aspects of urban transportation, particularly in discussions about different modes. For example, the mayors and civic leaders of numerous cities—including Atlanta, San Francisco, Boston, Washington, and Portland—point to their rail systems as great assets for economic viability, attractiveness, and mobility of all economic and racial groups in the city and entire region; yet, many theoreticians make sweeping statements that rail transit is "infeasible" or "wasteful."

The biases and narrow views of many theoreticians who analyze urban transportation deserve some attention. Inadequate understanding of transportation system characteristics and impacts is found in many papers on this subject. For example, in his numerous writings criticizing BART and claiming that a bus system would have been cheaper and offered better services, Webber (1977) described a bus system that would use freeways and then branch out on streets to numerous local areas; it would have express and local services, frequencies would be tailored to demand, and so on. While such a system sounds attractive to laymen, it overlooks a number of inferior features in real-world applications. Webber's proposal of a bus system supposedly superior to BART actually represents the bus system provided by AC Transit at the time Bay Area residents voted to fund construction of BART. Such bus services were neither satisfactory for that time nor could they meet the region's needs for future growth.

Other examples of misunderstood characteristics and impacts of transportation modes are the proposals by Downs (1992), who argues that "off-road transit systems . . . are costly but divert relatively few commuters off roadways." Not only is this statement factually incorrect, but it disregards the fact that the value of independent transit systems is not limited to diversion of present car users. Such systems also influence land development, generate new activities, increase mobility for people without cars, and enhance the livability of areas they serve. All these impacts have been observed, for example, in Washington, D.C., since the opening of its Metro. The ability of Metro to attract car drivers is demonstrated by the high demand for park-and-ride at its suburban stations. Downs also suggests that *additional* HOV lanes are preferred to both converted ones and rail, despite the counterproductive impact of these lanes on VKT reduction and intermodal balance.

Where does this divergence between civic leaders and population asking and voting for transit funding, and theoreticians claiming that transit is the "wrong solution," stem from? The underlying problem is the difference in the scope and perspective of these studies. An excellent example of the problem is the recent detailed study of transit in Boston by Gomez-Ibanez (1996). Focusing on the transit agency's financial deficit as the central problem of transportation in Boston [*sic*], the author claims that the main reason for increasing deficits is the effort of the transit agency to increase ridership and extend services. A suggested solution is to "rethink commitment to maintaining or increasing transit and commuter rail ridership."

Gomez-Ibanez's analysis of transit finances is both detailed and useful. Its goal, however, is to minimize the cost of transit rather than consider transit as an efficient means to achieve a livable metropolitan area. How can one analyze financial aspects of transit without considering other modes and the role transit plays in a city like Boston? First, one cannot ignore the fact that Boston is one of the most livable cities in the country, and that ubiquitous, convenient, reasonably priced transit is an essential component of that livability. It is not difficult to show that shifting transit riders to cars would be counterproductive to the lifestyle and urban environment. Thus, the author's recommendation for scaling down transit while reducing transit subsidies would aggravate transportation problems if the entire system were considered. Gomez-Ibanez analyzes the problem at Level III and reaches conclusions that are contrary to those an analysis at Levels II and I would reach.

Finally, how can one be concerned with public expenses for transit in Boston and not mention public expenditures for the Central Artery reconstruction in the same city—the most expensive urban transportation project in history? Thus, this author considers transit as a problem rather than as an underutilized solution toward the goal of a city's livability. A tree (Level III) hides the forest (Levels II and I).

In addition to overgeneralized, often biased statements about transport modes, a recurring theme in the writing of many theoreticians is that increasingly they agree that there are serious problems in urban transportation but argue that policies cannot change the trends. The solutions they offer tend to be minor modifications of present practices, such as cleaner cars, hopes that the ITS program will improve the efficiency of vehicular travel, or that people should be encouraged to work at home. Even Johnson's (1993) astute description of the "collision of cities and cars" shows the same bias against transit as an important contributor to improvements, proposing only minor modifications of the present trends. In his report, the imaginary PRT system—an infeasible concept—is afforded more coverage than rail and bus transit!

The present situation, including the negative trends, actually is being made possible partly due to the limited information the public has about urban transportation. Better understanding of the problems and relationships in urban transportation, along with better information about potential solutions here and in peer countries, is essential for efforts to improve efficiency and livability of cities and metropolitan areas.

References

Appleyard, Donald, with M. Sue Gerson and Mark Lintell. 1976. *Livable urban streets: managing auto traffic in neighborhoods.* Report prepared for Federal Highway Administration, U.S. Department of Transportation. Washington, DC: U.S. Government Printing Office.

_____. 1981. *Livable streets.* Berkeley, CA: University of California Press.

Billheimer, J. W.; R. J. Bullemer; and C. Fratessa. 1977. *The Santa Monica Freeway diamond lanes.* Report UMTA-MAA-06-0049-77-12. Washington, DC: UMTA.

Cisneros, Henry, ed. 1993. *Interwoven destinies.* New York: W. W. Norton.

Downs, Anthony. 1992. *Stuck in traffic: coping with peak-hour traffic congestion.* Washington, DC: Brookings Institution.

Fitch, Lyle, and Associates. 1964. *Urban transportation and public policy.* San Francisco, CA: Chandler.

Gomez-Ibanez, Jose. 1996. Big city transit ridership, deficits, and politics. *APA Journal* (Winter).

Homburger, W. S.; J. W. Hall; R. C. Loutzenheiser; and W. R. Reilly. 1996. *Fundamentals of traffic engineering.* 14th ed. Berkeley, CA: University of California, Institute of Transportation Studies.

Jacobs, Jane. 1961. *The death and life of great American cities.* New York: Vintage Books.

Johnson, Elmer W. 1993. *Avoiding the collision of cities and cars: urban transportation policy for the twenty-first century.* Chicago, IL: American Academy of Arts and Sciences and the Aspen Institute.

Kuhn, Tillo. 1962. *Public enterprise economics and transport problems.* Berkeley, CA: University of California Press.

Leman, C. K.; P. L. Shiller; and K. Pauly. 1994. *Rethinking HOV: high-occupancy vehicle facilities and the public interest.* Annapolis, MD: Chesapeake Bay Foundation.

Lowe, Marcia D. 1993. Smart cars: a really dumb idea. *Seattle Times.* December 16.

Meyer, J.; J. Kain; and M. Wohl. 1965. *The urban transportation problem.* Cambridge, MA: Harvard University Press.

Mumford, Lewis. 1961. *The highway and the city.* New York: Mentor Books.

Persky, J.; E. Sclar; and W. Wiewel. 1991. *Does America need cities?* Washington, DC: Economic Policy Institute.

Puget Sound Regional Council (PSRC). 1995. *Trends.* Seattle, WA: PSRC. October.

Rendell, Edward G. 1994. *The new urban agenda.* City of Philadelphia, Office of the Mayor.

U.S. Department of Transportation. 1992. Summary: Intermodal Surface Transportation Efficiency Act of 1991. Pamphlet FHWA-PL-92-008. Washington, DC: U.S. DOT.

Vuchic, V. R.; S. Kikuchi; N. Krstanoski; and Y. E. Shin. 1995. Negative impacts of busway and bus lane conversions into high-occupancy vehicle facilities. *TR Record* 1496: 75–86. Washington, DC: Transportation Research Board.

Webber, Melvin. 1977. *The BART experience: What have we learned?* Monograph No. 26. Berkeley, CA: University of California, Institute of Urban and Regional Development.

Weiner, Edward. 1992. *Urban transportation planning in the United States: an historical overview.* Washington, DC: U.S. Department of Transportation.

Wilbur Smith & Associates (WSA). 1961. *Future highways and urban growth.* New Haven, CT: WSA.

4

Urban Transportation Policies: United States and Peer Countries

The basic problems in urban transportation—the collision of cities and cars and the conflict between short-term individual interest and long-term social interest—have for years existed in the cities of developed countries. The United States and its peer countries—Western Europe, East Asia, Australia, and Canada—have faced similar problems and dilemmas in their metropolitan areas. However, most of these countries approach urban transportation quite differently from the United States. The differences in approach are too great to be explained by different historic and physical conditions. Most significantly, the gap between the approaches of the United States and its peers increased considerably during the 1980s and 1990s. It is therefore appropriate to review and compare the policies, experiences, and achievements of the peer countries and cities with those of U.S. metropolitan areas.

This chapter presents brief descriptions of transportation developments in several peer countries and their cities. Their common features are then discussed and compared with policies and practices in the United States, emphasizing those particularly relevant to efforts to solve the present crisis of transportation and of metropolitan areas in general. This chapter does not, by any means, imply that transportation solutions and designs applied successfully in Vienna or Hong Kong should be directly replicated in Detroit or Houston, or vice versa. The message of this discussion is that countries can learn a great deal from each other's experiences, positive and negative, in handling the complex problems of urban transportation. The success of Munich, Melbourne, or San Francisco in achieving a livable city should not be ignored by other cities because of a vague excuse that their practices are irrelevant elsewhere. Improving the economic efficiency of transport, avoiding mutually conflicting policies, and enhancing the livability of metropolitan areas are common goals. Measures in support of these goals can, to a large extent, be shared.

DEVELOPMENTS IN SELECTED PEER COUNTRIES AND CITIES

The countries, metropolitan areas, and cities discussed in this chapter have been selected because of their similarity to conditions in U.S. metropolitan areas or because of the lessons that can be learned from their success or failure.

Germany

Facing the problem of increasing motorization and congestion in metropolitan areas, with their negative impacts on transit as well as on the human character of cities, the West German government in the early 1960s appointed a group of urban planners and transportation experts to study the problem and make recommendations. This "Committee of Experts" submitted a report (Hollatz and Tamms 1965) that spelled out the basic principles for urban transportation planning. For example, the report stated that everyone in a metropolitan area should have available some form of transportation. Urban planning should avoid extremely high densities, which lead to congestion, as well as extremely low densities, which make the provision of transit services infeasible. The need for balanced, complementary roles of private and public transportation (auto and transit) to achieve an efficient transport system was noted. The authors emphasized the goal of achieving environmentally friendly, livable metropolitan areas.

The Hollatz and Tamms report also presented a specific plan for financing transportation investments in metropolitan areas that became the basis for the Urban Transport Financing Act adopted by West Germany's Parliament in 1967. The plan was designed to take about 30 years to implement and to require an investment of about 38 billion marks ($10 billion in 1967 money) of federal investment. A gasoline tax surcharge was earmarked to finance this fund, which would be used for urban road and transit improvements at a 55:45 ratio, later often changing to increased transit share. With some variation among the West German states, this federal money amounted to 60 percent of the investments, matched by another 40 percent of state and local road and transit funds. The amounts of federal assistance changed over time, but the Act has remained basically the same.

Today, some three decades later, the results of the Urban Transport Financing Act are impressive. Metropolitan areas have networks of freeways and streets with the latest traffic engineering techniques and innovative design features. In central areas, the emphasis is on rail transit, mostly on right-of-way (ROW) categories B and A. Rail and bus transit directly serve pedestrian malls and zones, which now exist in most German cities and towns. Many cities also have extensive bicycle facilities in their streets, on sidewalks or on separate paths. "Traffic-calming" techniques are used extensively in many residential areas in cities and suburbs as well. These consist of various design and traffic control measures aimed at reducing vehicular traffic volume and speed and at facilitating nonmotorized trips and activities. Monheim (1994) estimates that there are about 2,000 applications of traffic-calming techniques in Germany.

Despite very high auto ownership, car use in many sections of cities and their suburbs is controlled by traffic-calming measures, discouraged by high gasoline taxes and parking prices as well as by attractive alternatives for travel, notably the excellent urban transit and long-distance railway services. This situation maintains a reasonable balance between the two major motorized modes of urban travel, while the sensitivity toward pedestrians and bicycles is credited for the fact that Germany today has some of the most efficient and livable urban areas in the world.

How did Germany ameliorate the problems typical of the period of growth in car ownership? Actually, the common trends did occur: increasing motorization in Germany since the 1950s resulted in considerable losses of transit ridership, growth of suburbs, and dispersal of activities. Essentially, these trends are similar to those in the United States. However, they developed to a far lesser extent; the balance among modes has been kept much more stable than in U.S. metropolitan areas. The policies of implementing coordinated multimodal transportation systems in metropolitan areas are recognized as an essential factor in maintaining viability and improving the quality of life in metropolitan areas.

Since the mid-1980s, transit ridership in Germany has increased, due not only to the continuing improvements in quantity and quality of services, but also to operational concepts and innovative marketing. Examples of such innovations are the introduction of cheap, strongly marketed "Ecopass" transit tickets, "Semester Tickets" for students, and "Job Tickets" for employees. These tickets have become popular with commuters

4.1a Shopping street Zeil in Frankfurt was heavily congested.

4.1b The same street after it became a pedestrian mall.

PHOTO 4.1
Taming traffic in center city. *(Studiengesellschaft für unterirdische Verkehrsanlagen–STUVA, Köln, Germany)*

and many other segments of the population, including students, tourists, and shoppers, because they eliminate out-of-pocket payments and thus make transit more competitive with car travel. Their acceptance has been stimulated by the increasing concern for the environment.

Paralleling excellent alternatives to car travel, intermodal balance is assisted by policies of increasing the costs of driving. Car registration, a driver's license, and, particularly, gasoline, involve costs that are several times higher in Germany than in the United States, while tax deductions, free parking, and other subsidies are less extensive. This is actually a national policy pursued in most peer countries (Pucher 1988, 1995). The purpose of increasing the cost of driving is not punitive; rather, it is intended to reduce the problem of very low out-of-pocket costs, which stimulate excessive driving, as well as to make drivers pay at least a partial compensation for the social and environmental costs of driving.

Taking a broader view of cities in general, Germany has experienced basic trends of sprawling suburbs, competition from outlying shopping centers, and greater demand for the funding of urban transportation, similar to the United States and other developed countries. Although the population of Germany is more homogeneous than that of the United States and Canada, there are considerable immigrant groups and social divisions. However, efforts to maintain the traditional values of cities and their social life have strongly influenced Germany's urban transportation policies.

The massive destruction of German cities during World War II provided an opportunity to build extensive freeways and parking facilities. This was not done, however, because the concept of the "auto-based city" (*Auto-gerechte Stadt*) was rejected as undesirable by the Committee of Experts (Hollatz and Tamms 1965) and by the leading transportation planner, Friedrich Lehner (Lehner 1961, 1969), as well as in the discussions that continued during the 1970s and 1980s. It was even explicitly stated that the example of Los Angeles must not be followed. Coordination of transportation with land-use planning is difficult and faces many obstacles; planning, policies, and supporting legislation, however, have generally resulted in the trend toward modernized, yet human-oriented, livable cities with economically viable central areas. Higher population densities, historic values, and living habits have been major factors in this attitude toward cities.

Considering these conditions, most German transportation experts believe that it is not at all likely that the conditions in German cities will ever approach the serious problems of deterioration found in U.S. cities. In spite of high car ownership, many cities and their suburbs have become more livable in recent decades. Following are some examples of developments in several major cities.

Munich was one of Europe's most congested cities during the 1950s and 1960s. Tramways, trucks, cars, and pedestrians streamed through the medieval gate toward the central square at Rathaus at extremely low speed in heavily polluted air. Based on a comprehensive plan initiated in the late 1960s to revitalize the city by developing an integrated multimodal transport system, several major changes were introduced:

- Twelve radial regional rail (S-Bahn) lines were electrified and integrated by constructing a tunnel through the central city that allowed the creation of six diametrical lines. This change resulted in an increase of daily ridership on this network from 150,000 to more than 600,000.
- A rapid transit (U-Bahn) system was built under the central city and later extended to cover a much larger area.
- A set of streets comprising a ring around the city center was improved to accommodate higher traffic volumes, while streets inside the ring were interrupted and diverted at many points to discourage auto travel through the area; parking facilities around the ring were improved.
- The most congested street, Neuhauser/Kaufinger Strasse, was converted into a pedestrian street, as were numerous adjoining streets, creating one of the largest pedestrian zones in Europe. The reorganized central area is shown in figure 4.1.

As a result of these changes, the modal split of travel into the central area changed in the early 1970s by 12 percent in favor of transit. For a mature city with high auto ownership, this was a drastic change. Related to this change, Munich has become world-renowned as an attractive, livable metropolitan area.

Improvements of all modes have continued to take place in Munich ever since this major reorganization, which was focused on the target date of the 1972 Olympic Games. Highways are being improved, but not expanded, in the central area, where pedestrian and transit travel are given distinct and effective priorities. As a result, the amount of driving per capita has stabilized, while the modal split has shown additional growth in favor of transit (see chapter 5). These trends show that a stable, balanced transportation system has been achieved and that the livability of the city and its suburbs has not only been retained but significantly enhanced. A coordinated intermodal transportation policy was a crucial element of this success.

Hamburg began to modernize and build extensions of its U-Bahn system during the late 1950s. Organization was a major problem, however.

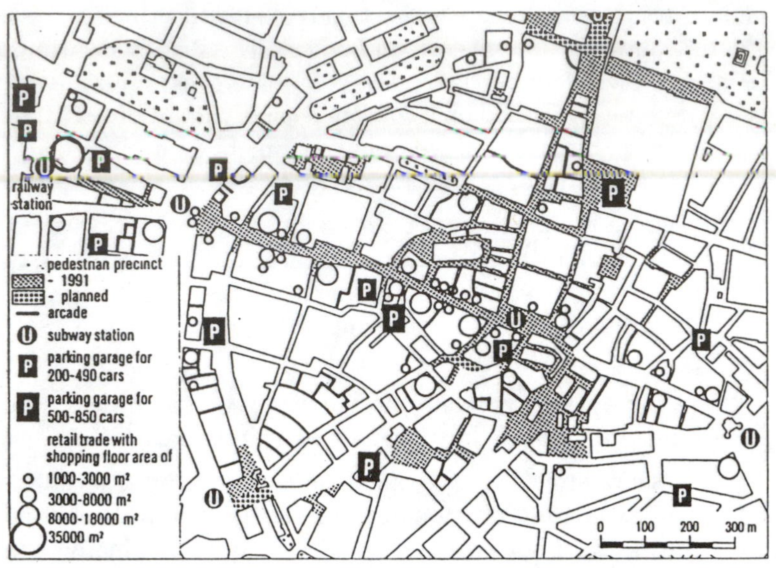

FIGURE 4.1
Center of Munich: pedestrian areas, subway stations, parking, and stores
Source: Monheim 1994

While the transit agency operated the U-Bahn (metro) and buses, its S-Bahn (regional rail) system belonged to the Federal Railways. There were also several other rail, bus, and ferryboat companies. This caused problems for passengers: uncoordinated services, multiple fares, and incomplete information.

Faced with the increasing attraction of car travel, transportation authorities decided that passengers should not be inconvenienced by the fact that there were different operating agencies. To compete with a single ride by car, transit should provide a single fare and transfers with minimal inconvenience and delay. To achieve this, the concept of "Transit Federation" *(Verkehrsverbund)* was developed. The Federation, an umbrella organization, was founded to perform such joint functions as planning, scheduling, and public relations. It schedules all services, which partner agencies then perform; they collect fares and turn revenues over to the Federation, which redistributes them on the basis of costs of performed services, using the unit costs agreed on in the contract (Homburger and Vuchic 1972).

Introduction of the Federation in 1965 resulted in a substantial increase in transit ridership and in use of transfers, because the obstacles of double fares and long waits were removed. The success was such that many other metropolitan areas in Germany, the Scandinavian countries, Austria, and Switzerland later founded similar transit federations.

Hamburg was an innovator in numerous other respects. It was the first city in the world to operate rapid transit trains with one-person crews and among the first to introduce a full self-service fare-collection system. Today, parallel with construction of highways serving the region and, particularly, suburban areas, Hamburg has good bicycle path networks, pedestrian zones, and a viable central city, as well as many suburban activity centers, all served by arterial streets and major stations of rail and bus lines. Limited parking capacity is used to prevent excessive flow of cars into the city center.

Cologne pursued a policy of incremental upgrading of its streetcar network into a high-quality LRT system supplemented by buses. The LRT mode was also used to replace a regional rail line to Bonn, so that now a single LRT line goes from a suburb in Cologne through a center city tunnel, uses a median ROW category B in a major circumferential boulevard, then proceeds at speeds reaching 100 km/hour along a former railway ROW category A to Bonn, where it again goes through a center city tunnel to end in a suburb. This is one of the best examples of innovation in designing an LRT line utilizing various ROW categories and operating regimes of what used to be streetcar, metro, and regional rail modes.

The Ruhr Region, including 21 cities and towns and stretching from Düsseldorf over Duisburg and Essen to Dortmund, was Germany's major industrial region. With decreasing mining and steel industry activities, increased mobility for workers was created by construction of a regional transit system that serves all these cities. A Regional Transit Federation was organized, so that 21 previously independent local and intercity rail and bus transit systems are now functionally integrated.

All other cities in the former West Germany with populations between 400,000 and 1,000,000 have used these policies to follow a similar development process. Thus, such cities as *Frankfurt, Stuttgart, Düsseldorf, Duisburg,* and *Essen* have rebuilt central city areas. Their plans include modernization of street networks, construction of off-street parking, transit systems that consist of high-quality LRT networks coordinated with buses, regional rail, and some dial-a-ride services in suburbs. Excellent intermodal transfer facilities have also been provided.

Bremen differed from its peers in its approach to center city area design and traffic solution. Already, during the early 1960s, the city developed a comprehensive intermodal plan based on a new concept of "traffic cells." The road around the center city was improved to handle more vehicular traffic, while the central area was divided into four sectors, or "traffic cells." Vehicular traffic was routed to the circumferential road and was allowed to enter each cell but was prohibited from traveling *between* cells. Thus, the

FIGURE 4.2
Hannover: Initial pedestrian precinct (left) and further redesign stage (right)
Source: Monheim 1994

central area remained accessible by all modes, but traffic volume in it was drastically reduced, and pedestrian areas were improved.

Light rail lines follow the dividing boundaries between the cells so that they do not intersect cross traffic. Speed and reliability of transit services in the once most congested part of the city were thus improved, without construction of tunnels. This concept of reducing vehicular traffic and favoring pedestrian and transit in the central city (which was historically designed for people) was so successful that it was adopted by several cities in other countries, including *Gothenburg* in Sweden and *Besançon* in France.

Street and highway designs in Germany have numerous innovative features aimed at improved environmental aspects and taming traffic, while the capacity of arterials is increased by advanced traffic engineering. These transportation concepts are recognized as contributing to the economic and environmental viability of metropolitan areas and to the elimination of slums.

Coordination of transportation with urban planning in recent decades has varied among cities. *Hannover* is known as a particularly good example of such planning. Construction of LRT tunnels in the central city was part of a plan that included construction of a major pedestrian area and seven department stores (figure 4.2). This reorganization of transport and reconstruction of the central city resulted in a significant shift of travel from cars to other modes, as figure 4.3 shows. The new intermodal balance increased the orientation of the urban environment to people rather than vehicles. It is the attractiveness and efficiency of such central cities that keeps them economically prosperous and competitive with outlying activity centers.

Karlsruhe, a city with a population of only 280,000, has drawn much attention in recent years with its major innovation in intermodalism.

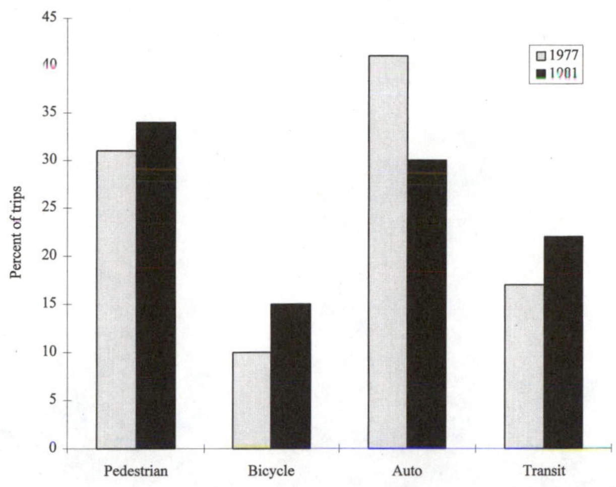

FIGURE 4.3
Change in modal split as a result of LRT opening in Hannover, Germany
Source: Verband öffentlicher Verkehrsbetriebe 1986

Following extensive preparations of organization, operation, and rolling stock, its transit was extended over intercity railway lines. Several of its LRT lines run on streets and in a pedestrian mall in the center city, then proceed to railway tracks to go to suburbs as far away as 60 kilometers. This merger of urban and regional services has resulted in passenger increases of 30 to 50 percent, and on some lines up to 240 percent (Brandl and Axhausen 1998). *Saarbrücken* has used this concept for its new LRT system, which opened in 1997. Several other cities in different countries are planning similar mergers of urban and regional rail lines.

France

Trying to cope with increasing traffic congestion during the 1960s, *Paris* authorities improved traffic engineering, constructed a belt freeway ("Peripherique"), and attempted to control parking in the central city. The famous Paris Metro was aging and becoming less acceptable to an increasing segment of the public. Influenced by transportation studies of highway-oriented metropolitan areas in the United States during the 1960s, increased efforts to accommodate greater use of cars were considered. In 1968, however, an environmental movement led to a change of views and policies. The option of accommodating car travel as much as possible was rejected as incompatible with the desirable human orientation and character of urban areas. An efficient and attractive Metro was considered vital to the progress of the entire metropolitan area, though it needed to be supplemented by a higher-capacity system serving the entire region.

PHOTO 4.2
Intermodal solution in Karlsruhe.
4.2a Light rail transit on pedestrian street. *(Mario Semmler)*

4.2b The same LRT train on railway tracks. *(Siemens–DUEWAG)*

Since the 1960s, the Metro has been greatly improved and modernized. A new "regional metro" (RER—Réseau Express Régional) network was built and is continuously being expanded. Introduction of numerous exclusive bus lanes on Paris boulevards during the 1970s resulted in a substantial increase in the number of bus passengers. The pressure of automobile traffic has continued, however; thus, there are plans for construction of a major underground toll road through the central area to serve through traffic and decrease congestion.

Traffic congestion was also increasing in other French cities , but there was no attractive transit alternative because bus service on busy streets was slow and unreliable. A major change in national policy toward urban transportation occurred in 1973, when a law was introduced stipulating that all companies with more than nine employees pay a special tax earmarked for transit investments. Initiated in Paris, the law was later expanded to include all cities with more than 300,000 inhabitants.

With newly available investment funds for transit and related urban improvements, the situation changed drastically. Many cities began construction of higher-quality transit systems and reorganized traffic in central areas that favored pedestrians. Four large cities—*Lyon, Marseilles, Lille,* and *Toulouse*—built new rapid transit systems, while a number of medium-sized cities—such as *Nantes, Grenoble, St. Etienne, Strasbourg,* and *Rouen*—

PHOTO 4.3
Street design for cars and pedestrians in a green environment (France).
(Vukan R. Vuchic)

built new LRT lines, most of which run through pedestrian areas. These cities also reorganized entire transit networks to take full advantage of the new rail systems.

Nantes, with a population of about 300,000, is a good example of this upgrading of services. When its new LRT line opened in 1985, a number of bus lines were restructured, shortened, or extended to feed it. Transit ridership increased by 25 percent, of which more than a third represented former car users. Public information and marketing were used to promote the upgraded multimodal system.

Grenoble, a city of 400,000, has, since the 1970s, pursued policies favoring transit. In 1987, a new rail line was opened through the core of the city, which has been extensively reorganized to reduce car entry and expand the pedestrian zone. The line running through this pedestrian area has more the character of a modern tramway than a high-speed LRT. Trolleybus and bus lines have been realigned to reduce duplication and to feed the rail line. The city is now typical of historic towns, with modern facilities and a strong emphasis on social life and tourist attractions.

The best-known small city with a new traffic concept is *Besançon*. With less than 200,000 inhabitants, bus service was more appropriate than rail. Suffering from increasing traffic congestion, the city developed a plan for reorganization of traffic in the central area, using the traffic cells concept pioneered by *Bremen*, Germany. After a public referendum, the plan was implemented; it resulted in the creation of pedestrian-dominated areas served by buses and a considerable reduction of car traffic. Interestingly, this concept is similar to the plan for the redesign of *Fort Worth*, Texas, proposed in the 1960s by the well-known architect and urban planner Victor Gruen, but never implemented. Few residents complained about the inconvenience of reduced access by car; most enjoyed the improved quality of life and revival of the unique, historic character of the city's core area.

The Netherlands

When auto ownership began to grow rapidly during the 1950s, Dutch cities, similar to their peers in France, Great Britain, and the United States, tried to accommodate the increasing volume of traffic. One of the measures proposed was to "get rid of old-fashioned tramways." Urban planners, however, emphasized the need to keep cities livable and human-oriented. Under pressure from citizen groups, transit policies were reversed. In many cities, tramways were upgraded into LRT systems, and transit preferential treatments, which favor rail and bus vehicle movements, were introduced. Bus, LRT, and metro lines have been integrated with national railways, which provide regular headway services on an extensive network, resembling a "national rapid transit network."

The Netherlands is a world leader in developing several urban design-transportation concepts. The best known is the *woonerf*, a residential area that includes streets for pedestrians, areas for children, delivery facilities, limited parking, and slow car-driving. Thus, cars are not excluded, but instead are integrated into an environment predominantly oriented to residential and related activities. These areas provide an excellent diversity of coexisting functions and modes of transport.

Bicycle use in the Netherlands is legendary. The role of bicycles is significant in all towns and metropolitan areas. Nationally, 8 percent of person-kms is traveled by bicycle (Matsoukis and van Gent 1995), but its share in some small towns is as high as 40 percent. Bicycles are used by persons of all ages and for trips of various purposes. This mode, facilitated by flat terrain, is strongly encouraged by the construction of extensive facilities, from special lanes and signals to independent bikeway networks.

As in other peer countries, rising affluence in the Netherlands has resulted in continuing growth of car ownership and in pressures to

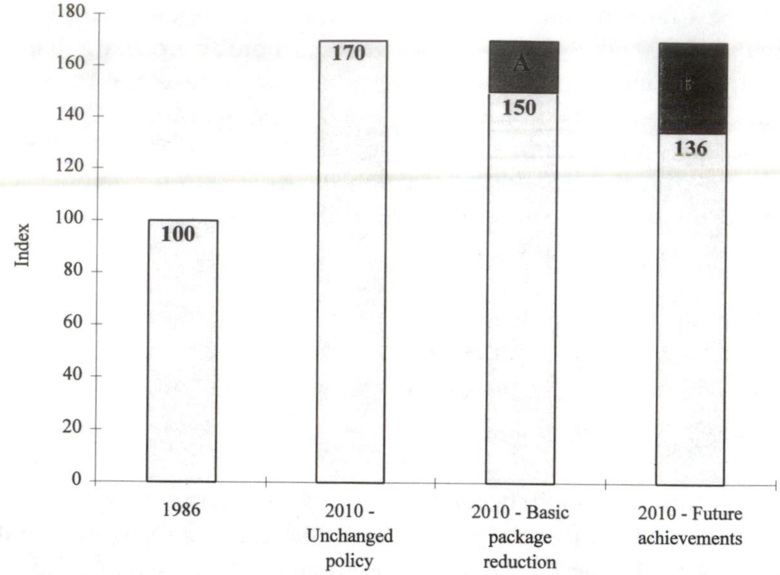

A Expected auto use decrease due to tax increase, parking restrictions, tolls, improved transit service, bicycles, and carpools

B Auto use decrease as a result of measures in **A** plus higher tax increase, extra tolls, and company-focused policy

FIGURE 4.4
Impact of different policies on future car use in the Netherlands
Source: Transport Structure Plan Project Team 1990

accommodate the increasing automobile traffic. The national government has greatly modernized the highway system but has resisted the pressure for immediate action to stimulate only one mode, because such a policy would not lead to a stable relationship between cities and car traffic. Instead, the government has developed a comprehensive strategy with the goal of "striking a balance between individual freedom, accessibility, and environmental amenity." The yardstick by which to measure the success of this strategy is the concept of the *sustainable society,* defined as "a society which meets the present generation's needs without jeopardizing future generations' ability to meet theirs" (Transport Structure Plan Project Team 1990).

This strategic plan analyzes the impact of alternative policies. As figure 4.4 shows, unrestrained growth in car use is projected to result in an increase in VKT of 70 percent by the year 2010. This growth is considered destructive to metropolitan areas and the country's environment. To alleviate the problem, two alternative strategies have been developed with different sets of policies to reduce growth in car use and induce travel by other modes, particularly transit. These strategies are considered far superior to unrestrained growth of 70 percent, because they would result in more manageable growth rates in VKT of 50 percent (Alternative A) or 35 percent (Alternative B).

Switzerland

Switzerland has a system of public referenda on many government actions, including such projects as construction of a major road or purchase of a fleet of buses. With such a system, it is important that the public understand not only the short-term need for improvements of individual facilities but also the long-range impact of alternative policies and actions.

Swiss citizens are very concerned with protection of the environment because of the country's unique natural beauty. This concern extends to urban areas, where non-automobile modes enjoy strong support. Unlike the public in U.S. metropolitan areas, which is not fully aware of the social and environmental advantages of transit over car travel, many Swiss people use transit out of concern for these issues. This concern is reflected in popular votes that are sometimes more restrictive on highway use than the government's position. For instance, the government was embarrassed in 1994 when a proposition was approved to impose higher tolls on trucks driving through the country than those the government had negotiated with its neighbors.

Switzerland is not, however, free of the basic conflicts of interest, decision-making problems, and difficulties in policy implementation that face all contemporary cities and societies. As mentioned, the country is ahead of most in resolving these issues. Yet, the recent trend toward stronger local autonomy has created obstacles to the implementation of major national transportation plans, such as the ambitious "Bahn 2000" plan, intended to further integrate the national railway system into a coordinated transit system. Economic recession in the mid-1990s brought pressure to delay or soften some environmental regulations. Finally, whereas the population often votes for restrictions on highway traffic, at the same time it usually rejects proposals for the introduction of tolls or other highway-user charges. Thus, one finds the basic dilemma that exists in most countries: Switzerland is making significant progress but also faces setbacks. Overall, however, the country has been much more successful than most of its peers in coping with urban and interurban transportation.

Among its numerous advanced technical and operational achievements, Switzerland presents an excellent example of the benefits of intermodal integration. Most Swiss cities offer integrated rail, trolleybus, and bus services, often with park-and-ride facilities for cars and bicycles. Railways and airlines are also integrated so that passengers can check their luggage at many railway stations for a flight from Zürich and not see the luggage until it appears on a carousel at JFK Airport in New York City or Narita Airport in Tokyo. That is one of the reasons the transit and railway share of access to Zürich's Kloten Airport, at about 50 percent, is higher than at most other world airports.

Great Britain

British cities, with rather narrow streets and considerable population densities, were among the first in Europe to experience chronic traffic congestion when cars came into wide use. Numerous studies of "the problem of cars and cities" were performed. Britain's academics are leading the research on road pricing and other economic aspects of urban transportation. Yet, Britain distinctly lags behind its peers in continental Europe in the quality of life in its cities and conurbations (Hall and Hass-Klau 1985). Obsolete, inefficient transit systems represent one of the components of this problem.

As mentioned in chapter 2, the report *Traffic in Towns* (Buchanan 1964) presented an important analysis of urban transportation and its relationship to the conurbation (Level I planning analysis). The report drew attention to the serious problem of the collision between the car and the urban environment and showed that there must be a comprehensive approach if this complex problem is to be prevented from seriously damaging cities—their economic efficiency, social life, and historical and cultural assets. The report, however, suffered from fundamental conceptual and technical errors. It analyzed hypothetical situations of cities served only by cars; although the report did not endorse such transportation solutions, it failed to state that such a unimodal system is inferior to a multimodal system. Transit should play a role, it said, but failed to recognize that, to achieve intermodal balance in major corridors, transit must be provided with independent rights-of-way. Nor were limits to car use addressed adequately.

In subsequent years, transit was given limited attention and funding. British cities—with the notable exceptions of *London, Glasgow, Newcastle,* and *Liverpool*—operated only buses in increasingly congested streets. While these systems required minimum investment, they also produced minimum levels of service that generally could not be competitive with car travel. Thus, transit progressively became less attractive to passengers and more expensive to operate.

In this situation, where there was an obvious failure of the government to develop and implement a constructive urban transportation policy, much criticism was directed at transit agencies for their inefficiency, declining ridership, and increasing costs. Thus, critics focused on the consequences, rather than the causes, of these problems—that is, failed governmental policies during the preceding decades.

The critics argued that deregulation and "free market conditions" would bring a solution. They did not explain how deregulation would avoid the problems from several decades ago that had led to regulation and the public takeover of numerous, competing private transit companies. The fact that the free market cannot function well where there are numerous uncompensated externalities—nor where competing systems (transit, paratransit, and car) have very different ratios of investment to operating costs—were not discussed.

In 1984, the British Department of Transport published a White Paper on transit entitled "Buses" (Department of Transport 1984). As the title indicates, this analysis was concerned neither with transportation as a function nor even with the entire transit system, but with only one of its modes; thus, focusing on the internal economics of transit agencies, it was limited to Planning Levels IV and III. Transportation policies in conurbations and the question of the car-transit relationship—that is, Planning Levels I and II, respectively—were hardly mentioned. The report recommended deregulation of bus services, with the exception of London (because of its unique conditions). Despite extensive testimony by numerous transportation professionals who overwhelmingly opposed the proposed legislation, Parliament adopted the law that led to the deregulation of buses and their separation from rail transit. Only the routes for which there would be no private bidders (that is, the least remunerative ones) would continue to be operated by public agencies and be given a subsidy.

Transit deregulation in Great Britain was highly controversial. It was preceded and followed by extensive debates and studies (Pickup et al. 1991). Briefly stated, its promoters claimed that application of the free market principles to bus transit would result in use of nonunionized labor with lower wages; this would reduce operating costs and allow the provision of more frequent and diversified services, including the use of minibuses. The more abundant services and lower fares induced by competition would generate additional ridership and higher revenues. It was also claimed that private enterprise would lead to technical innovations (Department of Transport 1984).

Opponents claimed that most of the problems that led to regulation about a century ago, and the integration of transit systems 40 to 60 years ago, would reappear. Private operators, oriented toward maximum profit at the expense of public service aspects, would concentrate on major routes while neglecting less utilized ones. Disintegration of networks would lead to confusion, payment of two to three fares for a single trip, and thus loss of passengers. The quality of workers who are paid low wages by competing operators would be questionable, as would vehicle maintenance. The most serious problem was claimed to be the disintegration of coordinated multimodal networks that had been created by extensive efforts over several decades. Short-term, profit-oriented operators would not be interested in technical innovations because they usually involve investments with indirect or long-term payoffs. The absence of integrated transit systems would lower planning and policy decisions from Levels I and II to Levels III and IV.

Several years after deregulation was implemented, its major results can be summarized as follows (Fawkner 1995; Pickup et al. 1991).

- Minibuses have been introduced in many areas, increasing the frequency of service.
- Most of the competition is concentrated on lucrative routes, while many previous routes have been closed.
- Total transit ridership has decreased substantially; in metropolitan areas there was a loss of 30 percent between 1986 and 1994.
- The number of bus-kms operated has increased: in metropolitan areas the increase was 21 percent; with lower ridership, utilization of vehicles has dropped drastically.
- Operating costs (and subsidies) were initially decreased as much as 20 percent, mostly due to lower wages, but then they began to rise again at a similar rate as before deregulation.
- Technical and operational innovations have been decreased or eliminated.

It is important to distinguish two fundamental concepts in transit reorganization: (1) *privatization*, or contracting out services while retaining control of fares and services, so that a transit system remains functionally intact (commonly used in U.S. cities); and (2) *deregulation*, which eliminates virtually all controls except for safety, so that the transit system is functionally disintegrated: different lines operate independently, schedules do not allow convenient transfers, and fares must be paid for each line separately.

The significant differences between these two basic types of changes were clearly demonstrated in British cities. In most cities, transit was deregulated—that is, not only privatized, but all controls of fares, schedules, and coordination among services were eliminated. Passengers were offered no joint fares, no coordinated transfers, not even information about services

TABLE 4.1
Results of Deregulation versus Contracting

Expectation	*Effects of Deregulation*	*Effects of Contracting*
Encourage service innovations	MIXED Increased use of mini-buses only important service innovation	MIXED Some service innovations from more enterprising operators
Encourage cost reductions	YES 25% reduction or more	YES 25% reduction
Reduce fares	NO Fares up 30%	NO Fares up 6%
Provide a service that corresponds better to the needs of the customer	NO Worsened regularity and poor information have offset the benefit of a substantial increase in bus-kms	YES Large improvement in quality
Arrest decline in bus travel and reduce reliance on the private car	MIXED Bus ridership down 30%, although in a few areas (usually where one operator has a monopoly) there have been large increases	YES Ridership maintained

Source: Fawkner 1995

offered by different operators. In London, however, bus services were contracted out (privatized) but not deregulated. Thus, control and coordination of services protecting the interests of passengers was retained. A summarized comparison of expected results and actual changes under deregulation and under contracting (tendering) only is presented in table 4.1. It clearly shows that, while the effects of privatization alone were mixed, *deregulation clearly has been damaging to the passengers and to the role of transit.* The only significant positive result of deregulation—cost reduction—has been achieved at the expense of quality of service, which caused serious passenger losses.

Briefly stated, for those who consider transit a commercial enterprise that should have minimal subsidy, deregulation has been successful. At making a profit, it has been marginal. However, if transit is to function as an integrated component of an urban system, and if it has as its major objective maximizing the number of passengers, deregulation in Great Britain clearly has been a failure.

As the situation with transit deregulation stabilized in the early 1990s, it became obvious that the basic problems in urban transportation had actually been aggravated: transit lost more riders because it had become even less acceptable as an alternative to car travel. This resulted in a worsening of street congestion. With transit use dominated by the captive riders, segregation between car and transit users increased, negatively affecting social conditions in conurbations. This development diminished the chance to achieve a reasonable balance among modes.

Significantly, the adoption of a bus deregulation law was followed by the government's program of a major increase in funding for construction of new motorways (Pickup et al. 1991). This indicates that the claims that deregulation would increase transit ridership was largely a cover-up used by highway interests seeking to further decrease the role of transit in British cities. Dogmatic obsession with the "free market" as a panacea lent ideological support to this action.

There were warning signs that, in urban transportation, the concept of free market is utopian because of three factors related to the basic competing modes—highways and transit. First, they have very different compositions of capital and variable costs. Second, the combination of government and private ownership among infrastructure and vehicles differs between the two modes. And third, the two modes have numerous positive and negative externalities that are not fully reflected either in their costs or in their user charges. Such a complex situation requires a major government role, rather than application of free market conditions. Yet, despite these strong arguments and warnings, dogmatic views of the universal supremacy of the free market prevailed.

Criticism of deregulation has always been strong and has been increasingly supported by facts as time has progressed. In 1994, Britain's Royal Commission on the Environment produced a report recommending a fundamental reversal in the national urban transportation policies, shifting to much greater reliance on and further development of rail transit systems, combined with measures to suppress use of cars in conurbations. Parliament is also considering bills that would reduce rather than continue to increase the country's reliance on the private car.

Despite an obvious lack of interest by the central government in improving urban transit, many British cities are showing a strong drive for such measures. *Manchester* opened, in the early 1990s, an innovative integration of rail transit modes: two radial regional rail lines were connected into one diametrical line running through the center city. One of six regional rail lines terminating in a stub-end railway station has been extended to the city center, where it operates as LRT on streets, mostly on

ROW category B. Having crossed the center, the line goes into another railway terminal, where it turns into a regional rail line again and proceeds to another suburban corridor. The two connected lines, offering better center city distribution and connectivity with other rail and bus transit lines, have experienced a 40 percent increase in ridership. *Sheffield* has opened a new LRT network, while *Croydon, Birmingham, Nottingham, Leeds,* and numerous other cities are building or planning new rail systems.

London, by far the largest conurbation in Britain, has been the subject of numerous planning analyses and studies of methods for balancing transit and car travel. The main constraint to car use has been rather strict control of parking supply. During the 1970s the requirement of a minimum number of parking spaces to be provided by each new building was changed to specification of a maximum number of spaces. This restriction of supply, with consequent increased cost of parking, has been effective in limiting car use. (The same type of parking–supply limitation has been used successfully in *Boston, Hamburg,* and *Portland,* Oregon.)

In the past three decades, several studies of road pricing have been conducted in Great Britain, with most applications being considered for London. The most important goal of road pricing is to make car users pay a greater share of the costs they impose on other car users through their road occupancy and other externalities. At the same time, road pricing has been considered an effective tool in reducing peak demand and congestion. Finally, road pricing could also be used to achieve a more desirable modal split, or travel distribution, among modes of transport. The latest study, conducted in the early 1990s, produced a specific plan for introduction in London. Although road pricing would follow the basic principle that users pay a more equitable share of their costs, which was applied to the extreme to transit systems in Great Britain, the government rejected the plan for road pricing "for political reasons."

Norway

Norwegians consider the private car a less essential mode of transport in cities than transit, bicycling, or walking. Various measures are therefore used to increase the out-of-pocket costs of driving and discourage discretionary travel by car. Whereas Great Britain and the United States lead in theoretical studies and analyses of road pricing and other mechanisms to charge for externalities of car uses, Norway has been a leader in implementing such measures. Car ownership is discouraged by a tax of more than 100 percent on the purchase price. Excessive driving is discouraged by the high price of gasoline. In 1994, this tax was increased by 20 percent, including a special "environmental tax" of 10 percent.

Oslo, the capital of Norway, has a population of only 500,000; Greater Oslo contains approximately 800,000 people. Yet, the city has a wider range of public transportation modes than many cities of much larger size. In addition to buses and tramways, there is an extensive metro and a regional rail network. Despite these extensive transit services, traffic congestion was a serious problem in the center city and on major arterials, largely because of through traffic that had no convenient bypass route. This condition affected both the livability of the city and the competitiveness and operating costs of transit.

To counter this trend, the city introduced a coordinated strategy of transit incentives and auto disincentives. Among numerous measures are the separation of tramways and buses from automobile traffic and the provision of preferential treatments for them at intersections. Several new tunnels and modifications of rolling stock have allowed integration of previously separate rapid transit and regional LRT systems. A circumferential metro line is being planned to serve the "ring" area around the city and to further integrate the rail network. Single fares are high ($2.50), but with monthly passes, the average fare for a regular rider is only about $1.

As an auto-use-disincentive measure, parking rates in the center city were set at $1.75 for the first hour and higher for following hours. In a bold step, the city introduced road tolls of $2 for cars entering the city. The tolls are collected at toll booths, manually or by smart cards in passing, on all streets entering the central area. The revenues are used mostly for highway improvements, although some go to transit also. Pedestrian streets and zones have been expanded, further encouraging transit use. Finally, a highway tunnel was built under the center city to take through traffic from surface streets.

As a result of these measures to balance public and private travel, there has been remarkable success in maintaining high transit use in the central city and attracting new transit riders, even in lower-density, high-income suburbs. Despite its northern climate, Oslo has extremely lively streets, and its attractive central area is a good example of what is referred to as a "livable city."

In 1996, the local governments of Oslo and the surrounding county took a joint initiative to the national government to request introduction of a $2.5 billion transit investment program for the period 1998–2007. The program, which includes major improvements and extensions of the infrastructure, is expected to be financed by the national and local governments, as well as by highway tolls from the ring around Oslo.

An interesting innovation in traffic regulation has been in operation since the early 1990s in *Trondheim*: a toll ring system around the central city. Tolls varying from 60 cents to $1.50 are charged from 6 A.M. to 5 P.M., with the highest being during peak hours. The revenues are used for improvements of the transportation system, including streets, transit, bicycle, and pedestrian facilities.

This system represents an amalgamation of several state-of-the-art concepts and devices. It incorporates user charges for transportation system improvements, applies peak-hour pricing to reduce peaks, and uses revenues to achieve a multimodal balanced transportation system. Toll collection is highly efficient: the latest electronic scanning devices are used, requiring minimum labor and not involving the stopping of vehicles.

Sweden

Stockholm has a long tradition of integrated land use and transportation planning. Instead of allowing unplanned suburban sprawl, which requires an expensive public infrastructure, generates full automobile dependency, and isolates some population groups (particularly teenagers and the elderly who do not drive), a number of suburban towns have been built around rapid transit stations. Typically, a shopping center and office and apartment buildings are located adjacent to the station. Medium- and low-density residential areas surround this core.

Typified by *Vallingby* and *Farsta*, these new towns and many activity centers are classical examples of coordination between land use and transportation. The large traffic generators are located within an easy walking distance from metro and bus feeder stations. Parking is provided on the town periphery, while its core is an extensive pedestrian area with many attractions—a modern version of old, lively, human-oriented towns.

Since the opening of its first line in 1950, Stockholm's rapid transit—T-Bana—has grown into a large network serving the central city and a number of corridors and suburban centers. Bus lines complementing T-Bana are extensive, and their quality is continuously being improved. Preferential treatment by traffic engineering measures ensures their reliability. Low-floor buses increase comfort. In addition to continuous gradual improvements of traffic and transit, a new plan for financing transportation infrastructure in the greater Stockholm area was adopted in the mid-1990s. Known as the "Dennis Agreement," this plan, signed by three levels of government and three leading political parties, will provide about $6 billion for transportation investments in the region: streets, freeways, railway lines and terminals, and transit facilities will get nearly half this amount. Tracks and signal systems on regional rail lines will be upgraded. T-Bana fleet will gradually be replaced by a new type of transit car. In response to the increasing activities in suburbs, a new circumferential light rail line around the central city is being built to serve the growing number of intra-suburban trips and to connect several metro lines.

Suburban travel is performed mostly, but not exclusively, by car. Consistent policies encouraging walking, transit, and bicycling have made these modes convenient for many trips. The policy of direct favoring of alternatives to the car, however, is particularly strong for travel in the central city. Transit and pedestrian improvements are complemented by limited, high-priced parking and auto disincentives. To operate in the central area, trucks must display a "green certificate." Public awareness of the social and environmental costs of car use, already extremely high, is maintained by the authorities. For example, a monument to the environment—showing the current condition of air pollution, noise, and other elements—was recently erected in the center of Stockholm.

The present plan, to be implemented by 2005, is to increase transit ridership by 15 percent. Car trips are expected to increase slightly. A plan to introduce road tolls in an effort to decrease car usage is being discussed, but so far it lacks the needed political support.

Gothenburg, Sweden's second largest city, with a population of 435,000, is the center of a metropolitan area of approximately 730,000 people. Its historic center was threatened by increased car traffic. In the late 1960s, a traffic plan was prepared that introduced the concept of traffic cells, which were successful in *Bremen*. The historic center city was divided into five cells, or areas separated from each other by streets that vehicular traffic cannot cross. Cars and trucks can enter each cell, but they cannot travel from one cell to another. LRT lines traveling along the streets separating the cells benefited from the increased speed and reliable service. Cross traffic was shifted to the ring road around the center. Parking garages were provided along the ring road, primarily for short-term parking for shoppers and business vendors.

This design for the center city, implemented in 1970, is shown in figure 4.5. Its introduction had a major impact on travel patterns, traffic conditions, and livability of the city center. From 1970 to 1990, while the number of cars owned in the city increased 58 percent and traffic outside the city limits (suburban areas) increased 100 percent, at the cordon around the central business district—the area organized in cells—traffic decreased 48 percent. In addition, the introduction of cells stimulated transit use and pedestrian movements in the central area. The number of pedestrian accidents decreased by about 45 percent during the same period (Bourgoin and Pierron 1987; Domstad 1991).

The concept of traffic cells has proved successful in both Bremen and Gothenburg, but its application is limited to areas with sufficient capacity

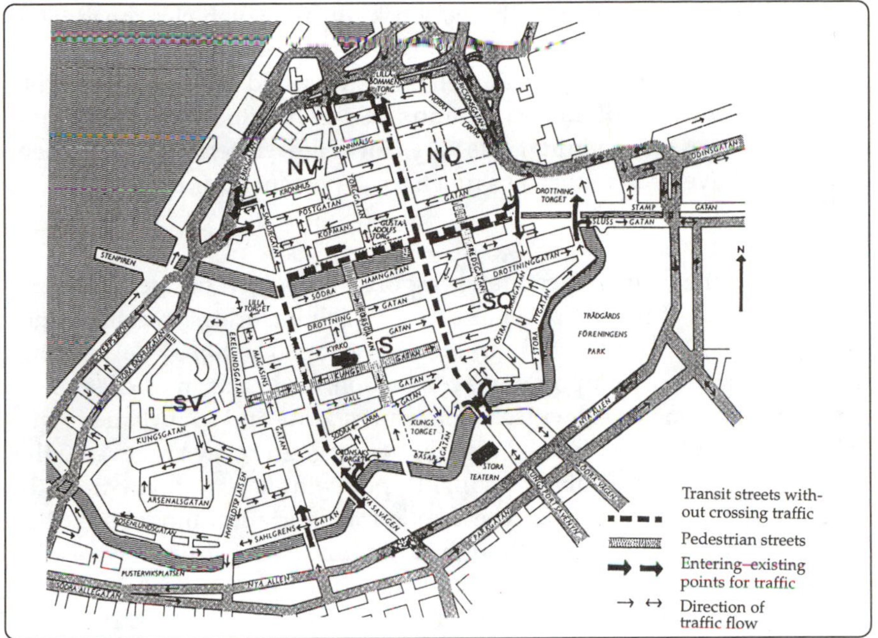

FIGURE 4.5
Gothenburg city center with five "traffic cells": NV, NO, SO, S, and SV

on the circumferential avenues or streets to accommodate the redirected traffic around the central zone without creating congestion or other unpleasant consequences for the ring area. Since the introduction of the initial five cells in Gothenburg, various traffic-calming measures have been applied to other areas after extensive negotiations with the residents and businesses affected.

Gothenburg is also known for its extensive network of LRT lines, which have separated rights-of-way along 89 percent of their length. Several lines were built at the time suburban residential complexes were developed. Utilizing specially reserved ROW and simple LRT standards, these lines required relatively low investments but provided fast service (on several outlying sections, average travel speeds, including stops, exceed 30 km/hour). They serve moderately priced housing on the fringe of the city. Their terminals in suburbs are often at shopping centers, with convenient pedestrian and bicycle access and transfers to buses with coordinated schedules and joint fares. The fare structure strongly encourages monthly subscribers.

The Transport Act of 1988 introduced the possibility of competitive bidding for bus routes. In the following competition, several new operators, as well as the transit agency, won different bids, so that now there are several competing operators, and bidding is conducted every few years.

The city continues to control the network, types of vehicles, headways, and fares. In recent years, this partial privatization, which retained integrated services for passengers as well as restructured rail lines, has led to substantial reduction of transit operating costs. The effects of these organizational changes on operating costs vary, but in the western part of Gothenburg, costs have been reduced as much as 45 percent (Domstad 1996).

Finland

Helsinki, the country's capital, is a port city located on the Baltic Sea. The population of the metropolitan area, which includes three surrounding cities, is 850,000. Like cities in other developed nations, Helsinki has suffered from increased pollution, congestion, and other maladies as car use has steadily increased with economic prosperity and suburban growth. In 1990, the city council formed a committee to study ways to reverse this increase in car use and divert people to public transportation before the situation became unbearable. The public transportation modal split had been declining for decades, although at the time of the study it was still a respectable 32 percent of all trips for the metropolitan area, with 22 percent of trips made by bicycle or on foot (Vepsäläinen and Pursula 1992). Within the city proper, the share of non-car trips was even higher. In the heart of the city, the peninsular geography, combined with a commitment to preserve the city's traditional atmosphere, were additional reasons for restraining car use.

The city council's consultants listed numerous possible measures for improving the transportation system, from extensions of the rapid transit and LRT lines to "Transit First" and various traffic engineering and management measures. A panel of experts then selected, evaluated, and ranked measures by their effectiveness in both the generation of transit trips and the reduction of car trips. Finally, a list of fourteen ranked measures was adopted by the City of Helsinki. In addition, the Helsinki Metropolitan Area Council used the comprehensive 1988 Metropolitan Area Transportation Study in the development of a transportation improvement program to be implemented as a joint effort of state road and rail administrations and all four cities of the metropolitan area.

This program foresees improvements to the highway system but avoids major investments in expansion of highway capacity. The bulk of the investment (60 percent) from inception until the year 2020 will go into transit projects: toward speeding up operations and improving the network. One significant improvement is introduction of a new high-performance, tangential bus line to better serve the trips not destined for the city center. This line is to be upgraded to LRT when demand requires. Another improvement is the construction of a regional rail link to the airport.

Virtually all the selected measures are planned for implementation in various forms. One exception is that there are no concrete plans to implement tolls or road pricing. Although ranked first in effectiveness, introduction of such a new concept is expected to require special operational and political preparations. The ambitious goal of this program is to maintain the modal split for transit at an impressive 40 percent of all motorized trips (YTV 1994).

East Asia

Several peer countries in East Asia—Singapore, Hong Kong, and Japan—have urban conditions different from those found in Europe and North America. Their transportation is even more constrained by limited space, which has led these countries to apply some innovative methods to solve urban transportation problems.

Singapore is a city-state that is among the world leaders in many aspects of urban transportation policy. In the mid-1970s, the city adopted a comprehensive multimodal plan for achieving and maintaining a desirable balance among modes in the city, as well as greater efficiency of each individual mode. The most interesting and innovative element of these policies was the introduction of tolls for cars entering the central city during the morning and evening peak hours, known as the Area Licensing Scheme (ALS). This system—combined with strict parking regulations, improvements to bus transit services, and construction of a rapid transit system—regulates modal split and prevents street congestion with all its social and economic costs. People are encouraged to use transit. Those who drive during the peaks have to pay for the privilege, but they have better driving conditions than in any comparable city without such controls.

The ALS is used as a permanent management tool that ensures the efficient operation of streets in the entire central city. As driving gradually increases over time and congestion builds up, tolls and parking rates are increased so as to decrease traffic volume to levels that do not exceed the available capacities of the street network. Further expansion of the metro and possible introduction of LRT are being considered.

Hong Kong, another city-state in the same region, became part of China in 1997. It is the second most densely populated urban area in the world, exceeded only by its neighbor, Macao. Given that it also has a prosperous economy with one of the largest ports in the world, it was inevitable that it would have serious congestion, even with an excellent, high-capacity rapid transit network. Due to limited space, the scope for adding more surface facilities for roads is constrained. Thus, the city faced the need to control travel demand earlier and more urgently than many other prosperous cities.

Hong Kong was already an expensive place in which to own and operate a motor vehicle, but it was in the interest of efficient allocation of space in the most congested areas that it tried an early experiment in electronic road pricing (ERP). From 1983 to 1985, electronic license plates on 2,500 vehicles were read each time a vehicle so equipped crossed one of several zonal boundaries. The vehicle's owner was charged according to the time of day and corresponding level of demand. Technically, the program was a success, but it was politically unpopular, ostensibly due to concern about the invasion of privacy (Dawson and Catling 1986; Hau 1995).

Since termination of the experiment in 1985, traffic has continued to grow steadily. The Second Comprehensive Transport Study appeared in 1989 and was updated in 1993. Several large transportation projects are under construction: motorways into New Territories and a new airport being built on Lantau Island, together with a special rail line and motorway connecting it with the Hong Kong ground transportation network. Recent analysis shows, however, that even with these large rail and road investments to increase supply already underway, further transportation demand management measures are also essential to keep average road speeds from dropping to low levels. These measures include increases in the already high annual vehicle license fee, increases in the fuel tax, improved control of goods vehicles, and the introduction of "area licensing." The last will be introduced eventually as a form of congestion pricing similar to the earlier experiment, but this time it will be done with "smart cards" that deduct charges anonymously, thus protecting privacy.

Japan, an island nation, has a serious problem of extremely populated cities with limited available land and narrow streets. To handle large passenger volumes, most cities have extensive, efficient rail transit systems. Traffic engineering is generally good, and many cities have numerous well-designed pedestrian facilities on the surface, in underground mezzanines, or in large plazas. However, integration of various rail and bus systems, as well as transit and highways (Planning Levels III and II), is not very advanced.

To accelerate economic growth after World War II, the Japanese government adopted a policy of constraining consumption, encouraging savings, and reducing labor costs. This policy strongly influenced the form and organization of Japan's urban transportation. To prevent dependence on private cars, transit systems, particularly rail, have been strongly promoted. In many cities, rail networks provide good area coverage in central areas, as well as extensive regional rail networks.

In suburbs, nonmotorized access has been encouraged (Hook 1994). It is estimated that in the past twenty years, some $10 billion has been invested in bicycle systems in Japan. The bicycle has become a major mode for access to rail stations, particularly for commuting trips. About 9,000 bicycle parking facilities have been built in the country, of which 3,250 are in *Tokyo*, where they are used by about one million people per day. The Bicycle Laws of 1977 and 1980 provided substantial public funding and tax incentives for governments and for private businesses to build bicycle facilities.

The result of these developments can be seen in a comparison of expenditures on transport in Japan as compared to the United States. Whereas in Japan the expenditures for passenger car and taxi transport amount to 2.4 percent of the gross national product (GNP), in the United States that figure is 9.5 percent. Although railway transport expenditures in Japan are much higher than in the United States, they still amount to only 1.4 percent of GNP.

Comparing at the individual level, Hook (1994) points out that the total annual travel cost for an employee in Japan who commutes by bicycle and train is less than $1,000. In the United States, a commuter in a multicar family spends about $5,000 per year for the purchase and operation of a car that is used primarily for commuting. In addition, public (tax) expenditures per car amount to $2,400 per year. The difference of about $6,400 between the total commuting cost in Japan and in the United States means that the labor cost for production in Japan for workers using other than car modes can be that much lower. This may amount to a considerable competitive advantage for that country.

The Japanese academic community and transportation professionals have intensive, advanced discussions about interactions between transportation and the urban environment (Planning Level I) and measures to alleviate the city–car collision. How to implement auto-use disincentives to reduce chronic congestion remains a major question, however. The high cost of owning a car—its high operating costs, particularly for parking—represents the main factor influencing intermodal balance. The high cost of driving also allows high transit fares and reduces subsidies to all modes of transportation.

Australia

Australia, like the United States, appears to have unlimited space available for growth of its metropolitan areas. As a nation, however, Australia is historically and culturally tied to Great Britain, which is reflected in its social and economic development policies. During the early decades of this century, Australia's large cities developed strong cores, while suburbs grew around stations of extensive suburban railway networks.

In recent decades, the problems arising from extensive suburban growth and highway congestion that appeared in the United States have started to demand attention in Australia as well. Although many trends are similar—increasing affluence, auto ownership, dispersal of activities and trips, and so on—there are interesting differences also. For example, unlike the population distribution in U.S. cities, lower-income neighborhoods in Australia tend to be located in the suburbs while the central cities have retained large numbers of middle- and higher-income residents. Similar to their U.S. counterparts, Australian cities have large, diverse immigrant groups, yet the extent and depth of poverty, slums, and crime in Australia is considerably lower than in the United States. Most important, however, are the differences in attitude and policy. This will be shown in the examples of the two largest cities, Melbourne and Sydney.

In 1990, *Melbourne* was selected by the International Study of the Population Crisis Committee as one of the most livable cities in the world. Eager to retain this designation, the city developed in 1994–95 the "Melbourne Metropolitan Strategy," which was intended to guide further development. The document defining this strategy emphasizes *livability*, which "depends on the attractiveness of an area as a place in which to live, work, invest, and do business." It points out that livability depends on urban form and public services such as health, safety, and transport. Diversity of activities and types of housing is one of its important features. Unlike the preceding plans, this one concentrates on outputs, rather than processes, of planning.

The trends common to all developed countries—growth of suburbs and car ownership—bring pressures for construction of additional freeways, including a beltway. Opponents of the beltway claim that the tradeoff in livability and environmental impacts would be too high. The "Strategy" document points out that a transport system is a component giving form and character to the metropolitan area, and that it must be planned as an integrated, multimodal system. The highway network is essential for suburban travel, whereas for radial and inner-city travel, use of transit should be encouraged.

Melbourne is known for its extensive tramway (streetcar) system. It survived the wave of conversion of trams to buses that occurred in other cities several decades ago. Now it is very popular because of the strong image it gives transit—distinctive lines and environmentally friendly features. Recently the tram network in the center city was adjusted to allow operation of a circle line that facilitates mobility and increases the image of this lively area for workers, shoppers, residents, and tourists. The importance of Melbourne's extensive suburban railway system supplemented by bus feeders is also increasing, especially with the growth of suburbs.

Several pedestrian areas have been created to provide a good pedestrian environment in central Melbourne. With covered plazas and walkways, these areas are within and around major activity centers. Melbourne's planning department is also active in introducing new layouts for suburban residential areas, which allow mixed zoning and make many pedestrian and transit trips feasible as essential elements of livability. In such neighborhoods, social contacts are much more intensive than in conventional car-based suburbs.

The other large Australian city, *Sydney*, also has an extensive regional rail system, which played a major role in shaping the region, especially several decades ago. Similar to its peers in other developed countries, however, in recent years, more than 90 percent of population growth has taken place in suburban areas, some of which were inadequately planned. This has led to a growing dependence on cars, which, in turn, overloads the highway system and results in a reduction of the role of transit.

Extrapolation of recent trends into the future shows that if present conditions and policies do not change, the increasing dispersal of activities and growing highway traffic will cause serious economic problems and environmental damage in the region. This would endanger Sydney's important role as the capital of the State of New South Wales (NSW), as well as its international competitiveness.

To prevent this problem, the NSW government in 1993 initiated a comprehensive study entitled "Integrated Transport Strategy for Greater Sydney" (ITS). The ITS (NSW DOT 1993) presents the government's vision with respect to accommodating the future growth of Greater Sydney. It defines comprehensive goals for the region and discusses the role of transportation in achieving them. The basic objectives of the ITS are shown in figure 4.6.

A basic goal of the ITS is to implement "urban containment," defined as "managing space by the sensible grouping of related activities and more focused use of public and private resources." Central Sydney and five other centers will be strengthened by concentrating employment and residences. The transportation system can then be organized to provide efficient accessibility in these areas.

To achieve an efficient, environmentally friendly transportation system, ITS sets as one of its primary objectives making optimal use of different urban transport modes. To utilize the specific advantages of each one, a balance between private and public transport must be achieved and maintained. It is recommended that utilization of highways be further improved through modern methods of traffic management. Growth in car use should be moderated by limiting supply and altering parking rates, by introducing other charges, as well as by improving transit and encouraging pedestrian traffic in the city and the suburbs.

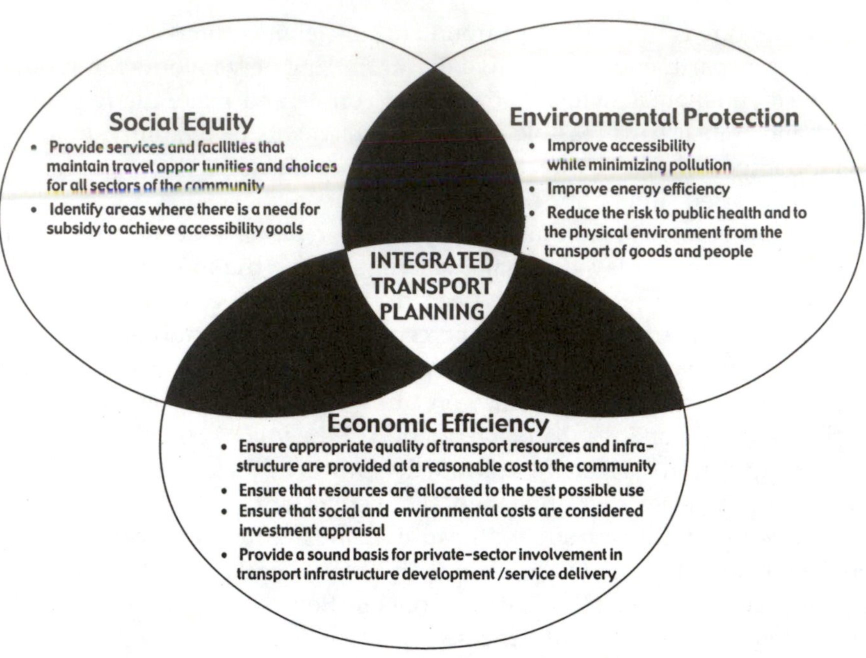

FIGURE 4.6
Sydney: concept of integrated transport policy

Major emphasis is placed on improved passenger information, intermodal coordination, and convenient transfers (including timed transfers in transit networks, park-and-ride, and provision of bicycle lockers at stations and ferry terminals). Most important, improvements of transportation systems are only a part of a comprehensive plan that should improve efficient distribution of land uses and result in a lower volume of vehicle-km traveled.

Canada

The division of responsibilities between the national government of Canada and the provinces has had important implications for the development of Canadian cities relative to the United States. The provinces and municipalities are responsible for all urban transportation planning and all financing assistance, both capital and operating. By comparison, in the United States, the federal government provides considerable capital and some operating assistance for transit. However, considering the relationship of cities and transportation systems (Planning Levels I and II), lack of national support in Canada appears to be more than offset by the absence of policies that favor car dependency.

In Canada, one cannot deduct mortgage interest or local property taxes on single-family owner-occupied houses; thus, abandoning the city and relocating in low-density suburbs is less attractive than in the United States (Pucher 1994). Moreover, Canadian cities have fewer freeways penetrating the heart of the city and fewer ring roads, no doubt in large part because there is no financing of freeway construction by the national government. Facing the full cost of freeway construction led to more careful decisions than was the case with metropolitan areas in the United States, which can acquire such facilities at 10 percent of their construction cost, while the federal government pays 90 percent.

With respect to efficiency and livability, *Toronto* stands out as one of the leading cities in North America. The foundation for this success was laid in 1953, when political leaders from the entire region agreed that the fast-growing metropolitan area required coordinated planning. To overcome the boundaries of dozens of townships and counties, Metropolitan Toronto was formed as the first regional government in Canada.

The Metro government has performed planning based on a comprehensive examination of the region's goals and alternative sets of policies. Unlike many U.S. metropolitan areas, the provincial agency reviews all plans for compliance with the official Metro's land-use plan. Coordination of land use with the transportation system is one of the basic considerations, and its success can be seen in the concentrations of high-rise buildings around metro stations. Toronto's city and regional transit systems are among the best in North America, and the city's human character is demonstrated by intensive social activities in the CBD, as well as in a number of activity centers throughout the Metro area.

As growth spread outward, four other regional governments were established. Together with Metro Toronto, these five units now comprise the Greater Toronto Area (GTA); each coordinates development in its territory. A study is underway to create a super-regional government that would coordinate developments in the GTA.

In recent years, unplanned developments have begun to take place outside the GTA. This phenomenon has been stimulated by lower business taxes and housing costs in those areas—short-term benefits that lead to long-term problems. Transportation conditions also contribute to this trend; economic slowdown forces transit fare increases, while the average cost of auto driving is dropping. It appears that such developments call for a reevaluation of governmental structure and transportation policies to cope with this trend (Perl and Pucher 1995).

Montreal, faced in the 1960s with the problem of a declining central area with lower accessibility due to chronic street congestion, decided to build a limited network of regional expressways and freeways, while the central city developed a metro network that would become the main passenger carrier. Its stations have been integrated with buildings and plazas. The largest metro-connected complex, Place Ville Marie, is an attractive pedestrian-oriented area on the surface and an extensive mezzanine with a shopping area. It connects several metro stations, the main railway station, and a number of hotels and office buildings. This development symbolizes the modern Montreal, with an emphasis on a livable urban environment that attracts business, shopping, and tourism from the entire region. The one freeway that enters the central city is covered to reduce its negative visual and noise impacts.

Edmonton developed a transportation plan in the mid-1970s with a saturation-type freeway network that included a loop around the CBD. Its proponents pointed to Los Angeles as an example of the "future city" that should be emulated. This brought strong criticism, eventual rejection of the plan, and development of a balanced plan with limited freeway construction and upgraded bus and rail transit. In 1978, Edmonton became the first North American city to open an LRT line; it also pioneered in reorganizing its bus network into a timed-transfer system.

Vancouver experienced similar rejection of freeways near the downtown area in favor of intermodal solutions. As the Lion's Gate Bridge to North Vancouver became overloaded, its widening through the environmentally sensitive Stanley Park area was rejected in favor of the Sea-Bus, a new, efficient ferry connection across Burrard Inlet. Another successful innovation was the Skytrain, a fully automated rail line built through the center city in 1986. These services are integrated with bus and trolleybus lines. A new LRT line and regional rail services are also planned to serve this city, which places a major emphasis on its livability and environmental protection.

The argument is often heard in the United States that availability of land, preference of a large population segment for single-family homes, high car ownership, and low gasoline prices inevitably lead to car-based cities; these make walking unattractive and prevent the effective use of transit. Canadian cities refute this argument. Canada exports oil, whereas the United States imports it. Land in Canada is abundant, and the levels of affluence and car ownership are similar to those in the United States. However, policies affecting urban transportation in Canada differ in a number of aspects from those applied in the United States. In addition to the lack of tax exemptions for single-family home ownership, subsidies for car use are more limited, and the planning of highways, transit, and pedestrian facilities is better coordinated (Pucher 1994). Much stricter gun control and lower crime rates also contribute to the different attitudes toward cities. The results of these policies can be seen in the fact that, today, Canadian cities are distinctly more livable than most of their U.S. counterparts.

COMPARISON OF CONDITIONS, TRENDS, AND ATTITUDES

A brief review of the conditions in peer countries that are relevant to urban transportation is presented here. It will lead to an overall international comparison of trends and policies in urban transportation.

Auto Ownership

The auto ownership rate (cars per thousand persons) has been rising in all countries in recent decades as a result of increasing economic affluence. In most peer countries this rise has shown a tendency to level off at certain saturation levels. These levels are influenced primarily by the economic status of the population and the functional need for cars. Functional need depends on the physical characteristics of living, particularly in metropolitan areas, as well as the availability of alternative modes of travel.

As figure 4.7 shows, auto ownership rates in developed countries are fairly uniform: 12 of the 17 countries shown have between 373 and 481 cars per 1,000 persons (or 2.1 to 2.7 persons per car). Canada, with 521 cars, is somewhat higher, and the United States ranks highest, with 566 cars per 1,000 persons (1.92 and 1.77 persons per car, respectively).

Two other indicators reflect the use and role of cars in different countries. Average distance traveled by car per year, plotted in figure 4.8, also shows a much greater use of cars in the United States than in its peer countries. This average distance traveled compounds the difference shown in auto ownership: not only do Americans have many more cars, but the cars are driven much greater distances than in peer countries.

Since the average per capita income in several European countries is comparable to that in the United States, and Europe has lower percentages of population below the poverty level, economic conditions cannot explain this phenomenon. Extensive car use in the United States can be explained by the country's larger size, by the longer distances between cities, and by the greater spatial spread of metropolitan areas compared to other peer countries (with the exception of Australia and Canada). Greater dependence on the car and lower availability of alternative modes of travel, except for air travel for longer trips, most likely contribute to this difference.

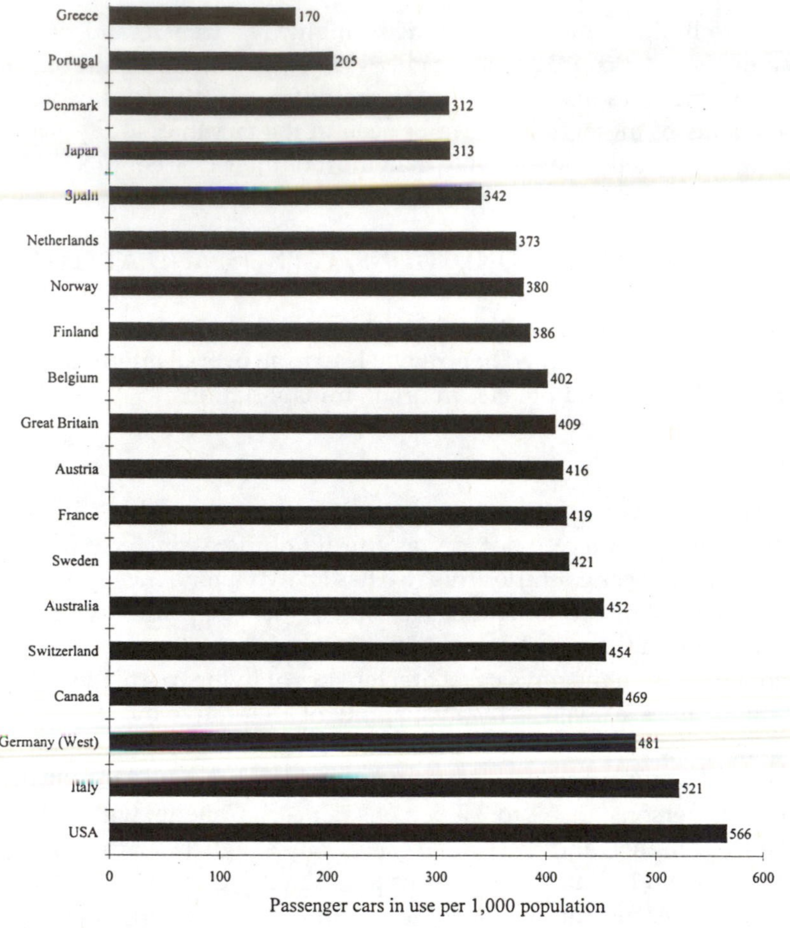

FIGURE 4.7
Passenger car ownership per capita (1992)
Source: International Marketing Data and Statistics 1996; European Marketing Data and Statistics 1995

The last factor, lack of alternatives to car travel, is corroborated for urban travel by the diagram in figure 4.9, showing percentage of trips in metropolitan areas made by car. The diagram shows that the United States has a significantly greater dependence on cars than any of its peers. Actually, the percentage of urban trips by car in Italy, Austria, and Sweden (34 to 40) is less than half that for the United States (84) (Pucher 1995). The figure for the United States may be somewhat exaggerated because many surveys of urban travel do not include walking trips, which are not at all negligible in such metropolitan areas as New York, San Francisco, and New

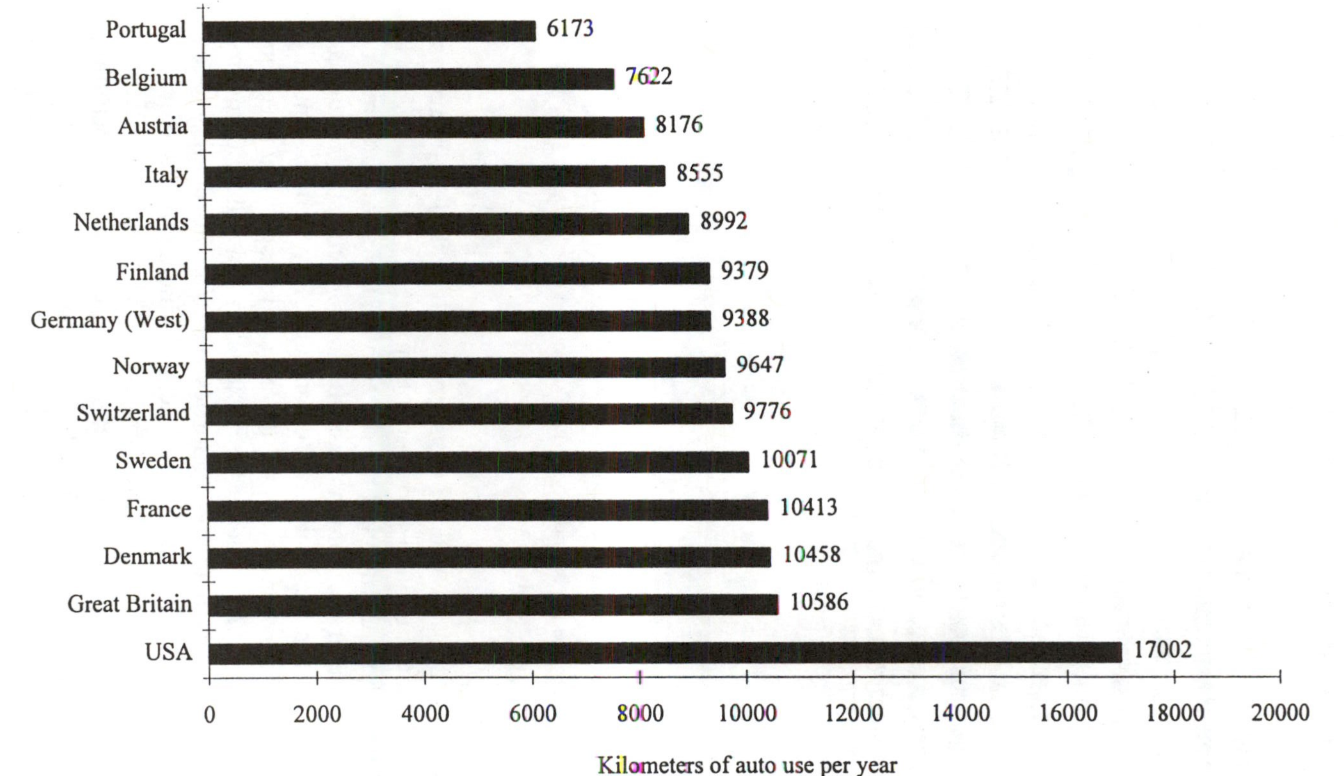

FIGURE 4.8
Average annual distance driven by car (1990)
Source: Based on data collected by and reported in Pucher 1995

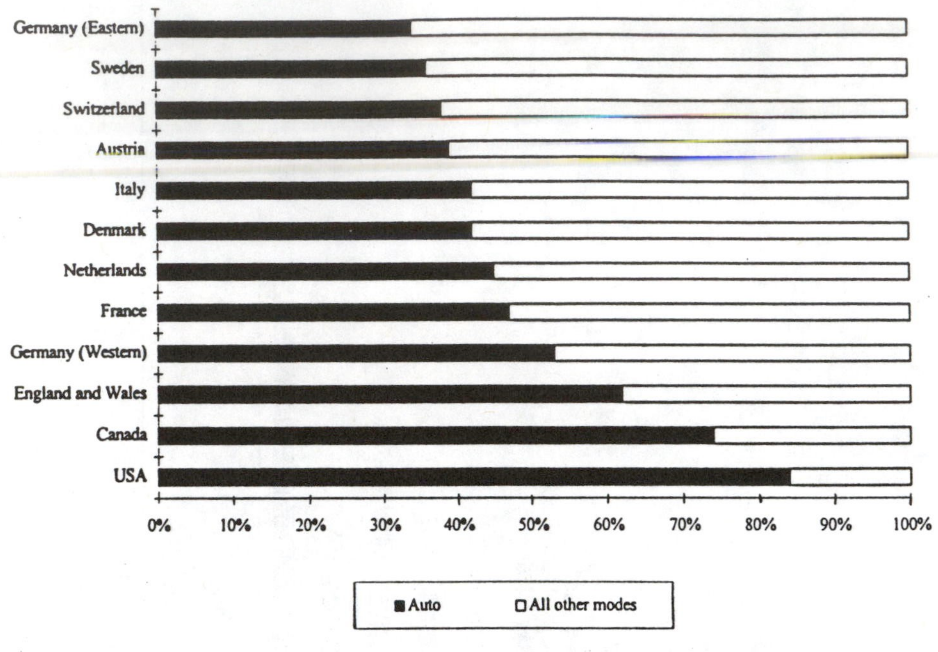

FIGURE 4.9
Percentage of passenger trips in urban areas made by car (1990)
Source: Based on data collected by and reported in Pucher 1995

Orleans. In peer countries, walking trips are usually included in surveys, and they often amount to 30 to 40 percent of trips.

Spatial spreading of cities and the development of sprawling metropolitan areas are other phenomena resulting from increasing affluence. Spatial spreading is made possible by personal mobility (provided mostly by the car), as well as by the increasing use of truck transport, which offers ubiquitous deliveries and benefits from extremely low direct monetary costs. This trend occurs in all peer countries, but to a considerably lesser degree than in the United States. Several factors influence the trend of suburban sprawl and largely explain this difference—for instance, availability and cost of land, public preferences, and government policies (including planning regulations and taxation of different types of housing).

The experiences of various countries show that among the above-mentioned factors, government policies again play a major role, and they differ greatly among countries and cities. In countries such as Switzerland and Sweden, regulations discourage single-family homes, while in the United States they are subsidized by tax exemptions of interest on loans and by other tax benefits.

The reasons for restraining single-family housing include the high cost of utilities and municipal services and the high consumption of land, energy, and other resources involved in this housing compared to higher-density residential developments. This is clearly recognized in planning studies and policy statements in most peer countries, including Germany, Finland, Australia, and Canada. Plans for a number of metropolitan areas state that projections of continuing sprawl over the next one or two decades show that such a trend is neither economically feasible nor environmentally sustainable.

Metropolization of Cities

In all peer countries, metropolization, or the reorganization of city governments and their functions to respond to spatial growth of traditional cities into expansive metropolitan areas, has become necessary to allow for the planning of coordinated regional transportation (Levels I and II). The solutions to this problem vary greatly in form and efficiency of results. In the Netherlands, Germany, Switzerland, Sweden, and Finland, metropolitan organizations undertake planning and have considerable powers to implement plans. Metropolitan Toronto is a good example: continuing growth of the area now appears to require further reorganization to cope with the latest trends.

In the United States, creation of metropolitan planning organizations (MPOs) has been required by federal law. In many states, however, these organizations are ineffective because they have no jurisdiction over local governments, and their advisory activities often have little impact on the land use and transportation planning of individual local governments, whether county, city, or township.

Traffic Congestion

Traffic congestion is common in most cities, though its severity and the solutions applied vary greatly. In most cases, experience has shown that attempts to accommodate unlimited VKT by increasing road capacity stimulate car dependence and encourage longer trips. Major construction is also opposed because of its negative environmental impacts. Therefore, construction of ever wider streets and new freeways is not deemed an effective solution unless it is a part of a coordinated multimodal plan.

Better utilization of existing street and freeway networks, however, is continuously being pursued. Peer countries such as Germany, Switzerland, and the Netherlands have sophisticated designs of urban streets and traffic engineering. In recent years, traffic management and a number of intelligent transportation system (ITS) projects have been developed through international cooperation. It is expected that these innovations will bring only a limited increase in capacity but significant increases in the reliability and safety of highway travel.

Traffic-calming Measures

Reducing traffic speeds by special street design or conversions of streets into pedestrian malls always causes public debates. Typically, in most cities, some store owners initially oppose introduction of traffic-calming measures or the elimination of vehicular traffic on their streets because they believe that vehicular access is the basic ingredient for their businesses. The vast majority of such projects, however, have demonstrated that the attractive, pedestrian-friendly environment that is created easily outweighs the problems resulting from "taming" or eliminating vehicular traffic.

The widespread success of these projects in European countries has increased public support for such measures as pedestrianization, rerouting of vehicular traffic, and parking controls. The pedestrian zones in most European towns have been a major factor in increasing their livability and preventing relocations of commercial activities into suburban malls (Monheim 1994; Topp 1995).

Organizational Integration of Transit Systems

Transit system integration to provide convenient transit travel has been achieved in most metropolitan areas of the United States and its peer countries. In U.S. cities, integration has been largely achieved and maintained even where new transit operators have been introduced in recent years through partial privatization. Cities with several transit operators that could not be merged—such as Hamburg, Munich, and Zürich—founded transit federations, umbrella organizations that ensure that passengers have integrated services regardless of who the public or private providers of service may be.

A major exception to this integration trend is Great Britain, where deregulation resulted in the disintegration of services with resulting confusion and loss of passengers. Great Britain today is the only country that prohibits multimodal transit agencies. If an agency operates a rail system, it is prohibited from owning or operating buses. Even individual bus operators are prohibited from offering information about services provided by other operators.

Multimodal operation and physical integration (Levels III and II) are recognized by many peer countries as basic requirements for efficient urban transportation. Since the late 1950s, Germany, Switzerland, the Netherlands, the Scandinavian countries, and other peer countries have built intermodal transit and intercity terminals and have integrated networks. In the United States, promotion of intermodal systems is required by ISTEA, but implementation of such systems is less advanced than in some peer countries.

The basic conflict between short-term individual choice of travel and social optimum distribution of travel among modes is, of course, found in all cities. Peer countries are applying various policies and measures aimed at approaching the social optimum. These policies and measures vary by their characteristics and effectiveness but, in most of the industrialized countries, they are better defined and more diversified than those pursued in the United States at all levels, from national to local.

Understanding of urban transportation relationships is considerably better in other peer countries than in the United States. Not only academics and professionals, but also political leaders and the general population, are well aware that there is a serious "collision between cities and cars"—that driving cars in cities, while valued by individuals and society, imposes much higher social and environmental costs than travel by transit or other modes. Most important, there is a broad awareness that the unlimited use of cars in cities is incompatible with human-oriented, livable cities. In most peer countries, political leaders, particularly mayors of cities and legislative representatives, are generally promoters of transit improvements ranging from giving priority to transit vehicles on streets to investments in rail transit systems.

In the United States, understanding of these complex urban issues is limited. Whereas environmental awareness increased strongly during the 1960s and 1970s, weakening government support and pressure from highway-related lobbies and suburban land developers have led to a denial of the problems caused by excessive reliance on private car use in metropolitan areas since the 1980s. Large segments of the U.S. population believe that highway users "pay their costs"; meanwhile, the detrimental impacts on quality of life of such conditions as extensive subsidized parking, inadequate transit services, unattractive walking facilities in cities, and the absence of even basic walkways in many suburban areas and new developments are not fully understood.

Special-interest lobbies and some of the media oppose even minor increases in gasoline or parking taxes, thus preventing any corrections to the

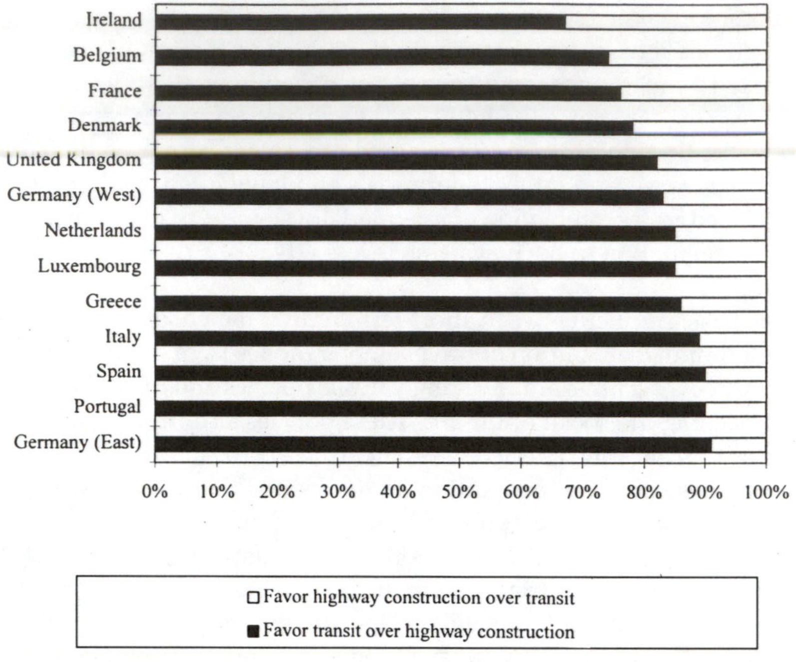

FIGURE 4.10
Public support for transit versus highway oriented policies
Source: Union Internationale des Transports Publics (UITP) 1995

present gross undercharging of car drivers for the services they use. Widespread "free" parking, which represents a subsidy to car drivers by users of other modes and by the general public, is a major obstacle to achieving a reasonable balance among modes in urban transportation. Yet, this and other long-term negative consequences of underpriced driving are overshadowed by its short-term popularity.

Investments in, and improvements of, transit systems have widespread public support in all the peer countries of Europe, as well as in Australia, Canada, and East Asia. Rail transit is broadly recognized as a high-quality system needed to attract car drivers, improve the urban environment, and give the entire metropolitan area the image of permanence and reliable transport service. The graph in figure 4.10 shows the results of a survey of population attitudes toward transit versus highway improvements in urban areas, conducted in several European countries by Socialdata and reported in UITP (1995). Support is consistently much higher for transit-oriented policies than for increasing highway capacity: it ranges from 67 to 91 percent.

In the United States, many businesses, civic leaders, and much of the general population consider rail systems built since the early 1970s, such as San Francisco's BART, Washington's Metro, San Diego's Trolley, and St. Louis's Metrolink, successful in improving travel, reviving central cities, and increasing mobility in the region. Yet, every metropolitan area that plans rail transit is targeted for intensive criticism by lobbies opposing any changes in the present trend toward total car domination. Critics, however, typically offer no realistic alternative solutions for the serious problems of highway congestion and urban deterioration.

As a result of transit-oriented policies in peer countries, most metropolitan areas with more than 500,000 inhabitants have, in recent decades, extended existing rail systems or built new ones. They have also introduced bus lanes and many operational and control measures that favor transit over other vehicles, which have become known as "Transit First" measures. Most U.S. cities lag far behind their foreign peers in this respect. Although more than 20 U.S. cities have, since 1970, built new rail transit lines—light rail, metros, or regional rail—this country remains the only developed nation with several large cities that have no transit system with ROW category B or A, and no transit services truly competitive with car travel.

Political leaders underestimate public support for transit and for rational urban transportation policies in general. Interestingly, concern has frequently been expressed by politicians about voter attitudes toward measures that involve major transit investments, as well as those that introduce certain restrictions on car uses in urbanized areas. In the European Union survey, the opinions of politicians about public attitudes on these issues were analyzed. The survey results, presented in figure 4.11, show that public support for transit actually is greatly underestimated by decision-makers: they believe that the support is much lower (27 to 59 percent in different countries) than it actually is (67 to 91 percent). Based on these data and the answers to some additional questions, the conclusion from the survey is that in all Western European countries, support for transit improvements and protection of the urban environment brings many more votes in political elections than championing "car user rights."

Support for transit improvements in U.S. metropolitan areas is not as strong as it is in peer countries, for several reasons. First, with the advanced sprawl development already in place, transit cannot play as important a role as it does in most cities of peer countries, due to differences in suburban densities and ways of life. Second, support for transit is not as strong because of the lower economic and ethnic homogeneity of the population in urban areas. Third, a large segment of the population, along with many

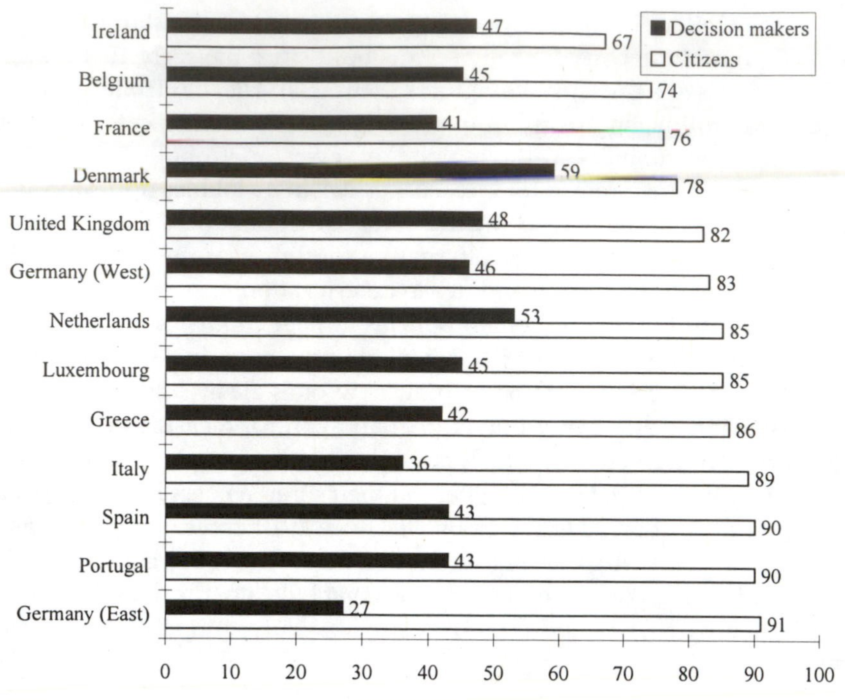

FIGURE 4.11
Decision makers' perception versus surveyed public opinion favoring transit-oriented policies
Source: Union Internationale des Transports Publics (UITP) 1995

political leaders and decision makers, has never seen or experienced the modern, efficient transit services that exist in many peer countries.

Yet, developments in recent decades in many areas of the United States indicate that, similar to the situation in peer countries, public support for more human-oriented urban developments and, specifically, for major improvements of transit, is much stronger than political decision makers believe. In most metropolitan areas, public interest and grassroots organizations exist that argue against total car orientation and support policies for more livable cities and balanced intermodal transportation systems. Dozens of these organizations—from the "Committee for Better Transit" and "Transportation Alternatives" in New York City, and "Modern Transit Society" in California, to the highly professional national organizations—"1,000 Friends of Oregon" and "Surface Transportation Policy Project"—promote policies very much in line with policies found in peer countries. These organizations generally oppose continuing promotion of the automobile over all other forms of travel and work toward policies that lead to more diversified, efficient, and livable cities.

These groups favor transit improvements, traffic-calming in selected areas, introduction of pedestrian malls and bicycle facilities, and emphasis on the livability of metropolitan areas. It is well known that citizen groups have played a critical role in numerous major transportation decisions, such as elimination of a number of freeways from transportation plans in *San Francisco, Boston,* and *Edmonton,* Canada; in planning and construction of LRT in *Sacramento, Portland,* and *San Jose;* and in the modernization of trolleybuses in *Dayton,* Ohio—to cite only a few examples.

These citizen activist organizations, with negligible funding, must fight entrenched interest groups, as well as some government agencies interested in the continuation of long-standing trends. Such interests and some transportation planning and traffic operating agencies continue to exert pressure for extreme pro-highway policies and for avoidance of the legal requirements of ISTEA and other relevant laws. For example, in 1996, while citizen organizations in New York City proposed traffic-calming and badly needed improvements of bus and pedestrian facilities, the city's mayor proposed closing the Department of Transportation, which plans, operates, and coordinates all surface modes!

Despite these pressures, many citizen organizations are playing decisive roles in introducing balanced transportation policies and more livable urban environments or in implementing significant transit improvements. For example, the repeal of plans for a saturation-type network of freeways in Sacramento, Portland, and Edmonton, as well as construction of LRT lines and rejuvenation of entire transit systems in these cities, was the result of dedicated, persistent work by citizen organizations.

THE UNITED STATES AND ITS PEERS: DIVERGING DIRECTIONS

The complexity of urban transportation has increased greatly in recent decades. In most countries, understanding the interrelationships of cities and transportation and the policies applied to urban transportation has often lagged behind development and thus has failed to prevent major problems and crises—from street congestion and problems of transit financing to urban decay and decreased livability of metropolitan areas.

The dominant problem in urban transportation today—the role and impact of the private car—has been faced by all developed countries; it is interesting to review their responses to it. In virtually all peer countries,

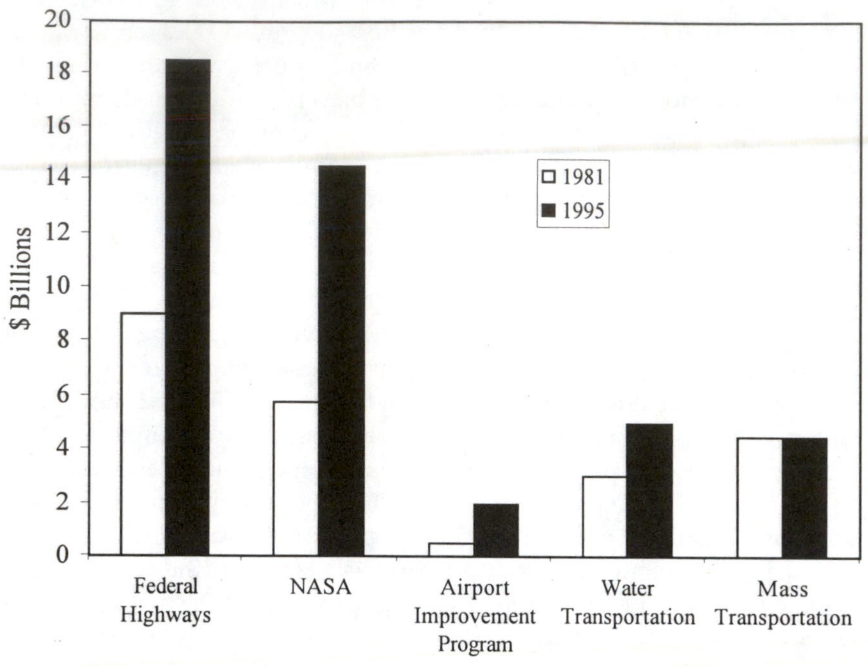

FIGURE 4.12
Nominal outlays for highways, transit, and related programs in the United States, 1981 and 1995
Source: Peyser Associates, Inc.

most political leaders, transportation professionals, and, to a considerable extent, the general public, have shown awareness of the basic problems: how to achieve an efficient relationship between transportation and cities, and how to implement a reasonable balance among modes. Also, the basic policies that should provide disincentives to car use and incentives to its alternatives are generally accepted in nearly all developed countries. The leading nations in this understanding are Switzerland, Germany, the Netherlands, and the Scandinavian countries.

The United States deviates significantly from this consensus. Following a period when its basic policies were similar to those of its peers (1967–1980), the United States is now, together with Great Britain, unique among developed countries in its pursuit of policies and measures that represent car-use incentives and even some transit-use disincentives. As figure 4.12 shows, between 1980 and 1995, federal expenditures for highways in the United States doubled, while transit expenditures did not increase at all. Because these funds are not adjusted for inflation, in real terms, transit funds have actually decreased. Thus, the imbalance between highways and transit that was reduced somewhat during the 1970s has, once again, intensified.

It should be noted that the Intermodal Surface Transportation Efficiency Act (ISTEA) of 1991, which was developed on the basis of a comprehensive collection of opinions and hearings across the country, contains the policies and a way of thinking similar to those of peer countries. ISTEA emphasizes the need to reduce highway congestion, not by highway construction, but by traffic management and reduction of VKT. It prohibits the use of federal funds for direct promotion of greater SOV use and mandates much stronger development of alternatives to the automobile. The law states that metropolitan areas must utilize the diverse capabilities of different modes; it points out that this should be achieved through careful intermodal integration. Moreover, the law emphasizes the need for better coordination between transportation and land-use planning. Thus, ISTEA actually requires that in urban transportation, Planning Levels II and I be given far greater attention than has been the case up to now. As discussed in chapter 3, however, ISTEA has been bypassed through various manipulations of concepts and is in danger of being decimated by organizational and legal challenges.

Implementation of policies for achieving a reasonable balance between transport modes varies among countries. Virtually all countries apply transit and pedestrian incentives; but, again, Germany, the Scandinavian countries, Switzerland, and the Netherlands lead in investing in high-quality, competitive transit systems. France, Italy, and several other countries are somewhat less vigorous in implementing these measures, while in Great Britain and the United States, such incentives have been applied in only a few cities.

Auto-use disincentives are considerably more difficult to implement because they affect some people negatively and therefore face political opposition. Thus, the basic measure to introduce realistic pricing for urban car use—road pricing—remains extremely limited. Singapore has successfully used it, followed by *Oslo* and, with similar measures, Stockholm and Bergen. Toll roads are used in several countries, mostly for intercity travel; most freeways in France and Japan and a few in the United States are toll roads. Germany is far behind in that respect; its extensive system of autobahns is still without tolls or speed limits, a condition that stimulates excessive and aggressive driving.

Short of road pricing, several countries have used capacity limitations and pricing of parking as effective means to limit car use in cities. The best examples are London, Singapore, Portland, and Boston; most other major European cities—such as Stockholm, Paris, and Vienna, as well as Japanese cities—also use elements of this approach. A high tax on gasoline is

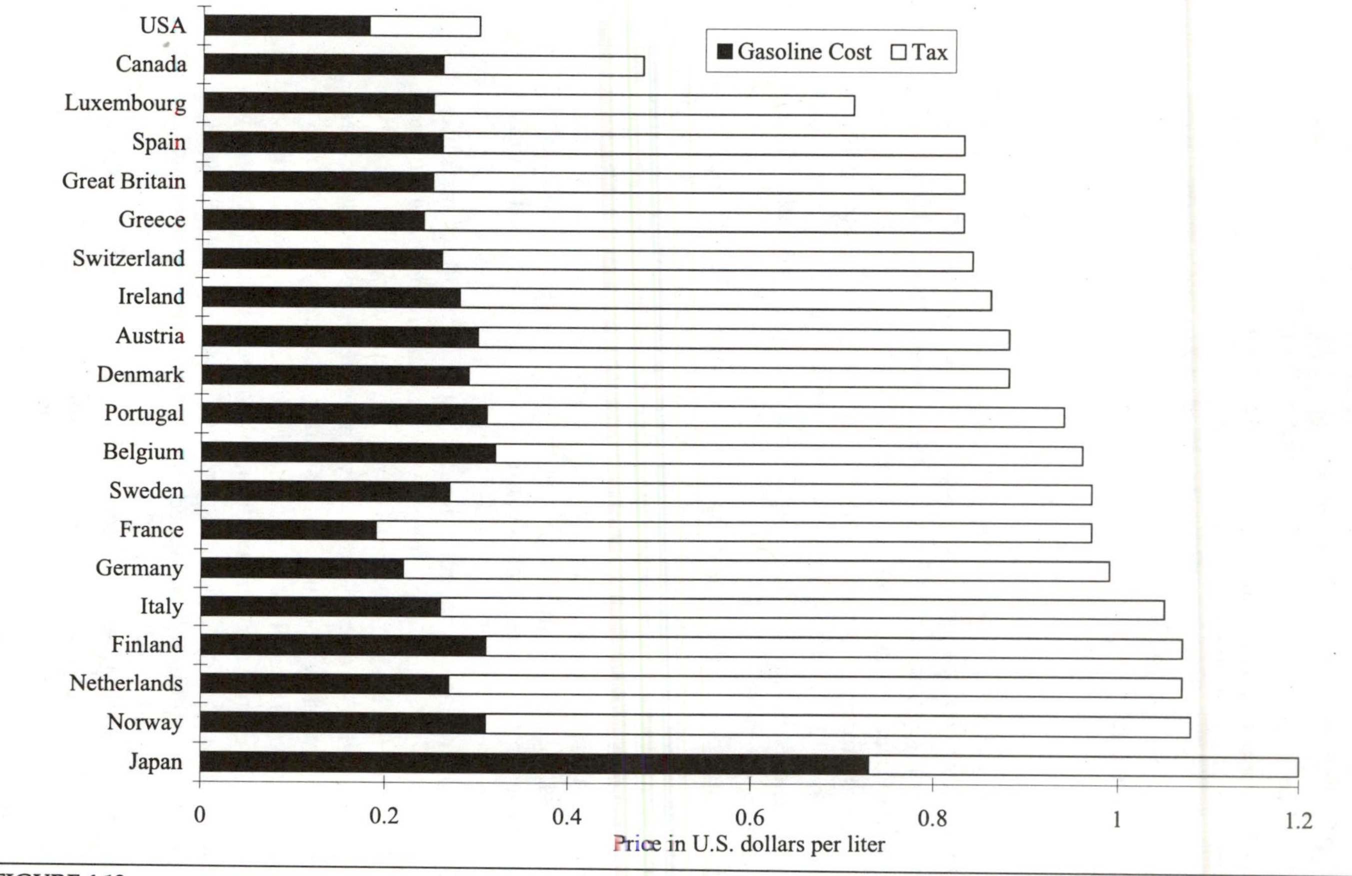

FIGURE 4.13
Price of gasoline and its composition in different countries, 1990
Source: OECD 1992

another method widely applied by peer countries. The tax has a double purpose: to collect revenue for transportation systems financing and for general funds, and to discourage excessive driving by increasing the out-of-pocket cost of car use.

As discussed in chapter 3, the United States began assistance to transit late, well after most cities had already built extensive freeway networks. Yet, considerable progress was made during the 1970s. The trend was sharply reversed in 1981, with the election of a new president and Congress. The attitude of the federal government toward transit became less supportive—in many cases even negative—and the "highway mentality," similar to that of the 1950s, gradually destroyed some of the transit-priority measures introduced earlier. Conversion of busways into HOV facilities, and the reopening of pedestrian malls for vehicular traffic in Seattle and Chicago, are good examples of this regressive trend. Consequently, although transit support in the United States, already limited, is being further reduced at the federal level, most of the recently introduced measures relating to car use in metropolitan areas are actually renewed incentives rather than disincentives (see chapter 3).

The drastic difference in policies toward car use and highway development can best be illustrated by two diagrams reflecting financial policies in peer countries. Comparison of gasoline prices in figure 4.13 shows that American drivers pay gasoline prices two to nearly four times lower than those of drivers in peer countries. The tax portion of that price accounts for most of the difference: gasoline taxes in France, Italy, and the Netherlands are up to seven times higher than in the United States.

Figure 4.14 shows the ratios of revenues from highway user taxes to the government expenditures for highways in West European countries and the United States. Conspicuously, in most countries, highway-related taxes (on gasoline, tires, and accessories) are much greater (up to five times higher) than highway expenditures. Thus, revenues from highway user taxes are applied not only to compensate for highway investments and operations, but also for general government budget expenditures. As mentioned in chapter 3, in the United States there is a legal prohibition against many highway user taxes being applied to any expenditures that are not highway related. One of the exceptions, a small gasoline tax surcharge of 4.3 cents per gallon (1 cent per liter), which Congress allocated to "deficit reduction," is frequently criticized on the basis of the obsolete concept that car use should not be subject to general taxes.

Figure 4.14 shows that in the United States, governments at different levels contribute, i.e., society absorbs, up to 40 percent of the total costs of highway transportation. (See also chapter 2, table 2.1.) Consequently, U.S. policy necessitates a diversion of general funds of governments at different

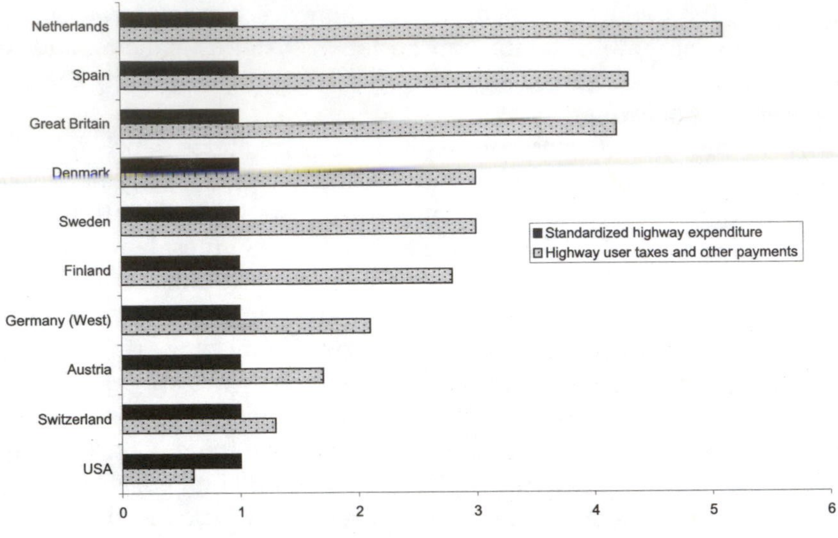

FIGURE 4.14
Ratios of revenues from highway user taxes to government highway expenditures in different countries
Source: Based on data collected by and reported in Pucher 1995

levels to cover direct costs of highway transportation, in contrast to European countries, where tax revenues considerably exceed the direct cost of operating and maintaining highways.

A recent report of the Worldwatch Institute (Roodman 1997) discusses the impact of gasoline price on its consumption. Although the use of cars in different countries is influenced by various local conditions and policies, price is clearly one of the strongest influences, particularly because it is an out-of-pocket cost to which users are most sensitive. The diagram in figure 4.15 shows gasoline consumption per capita in selected industrialized countries versus the cost per liter of gasoline in those countries. It is a classic example of elasticity of demand: the higher the price, the lower the gasoline consumption.

In addition to the impact of price on volume of driving (VKT), its impact on the types of vehicles people use is obvious by a comparison of vehicle fleets in different countries. Medium and compact cars are the dominant types in most European countries with high gasoline prices. In the United States, where fuel efficiency was required by governmental regulations and was successfully achieved, this goal has been diluted by the enormous growth of gas-guzzling vans and sports utility vehicles (SUVs), which are not subject

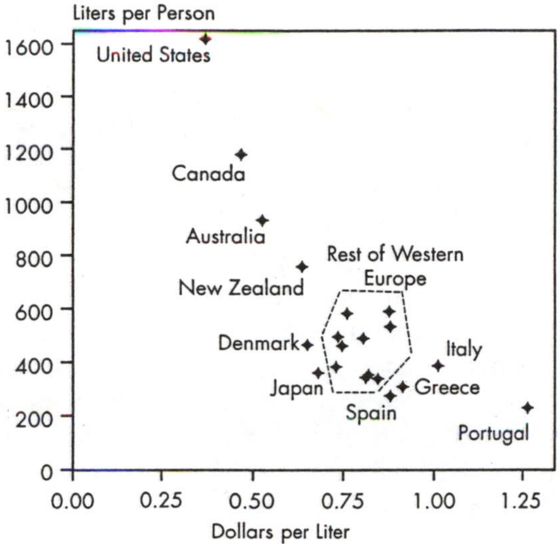

FIGURE 4.15
Gasoline price versus use in selected industrialized countries, 1994

Source: Roodman, David M. 1997. *Getting the Signals Right: Tax Reform to Protect the Environment and Economy*. Worldwatch Paper No. 134. Reprinted with permission of Worldwatch Institute, Washington, D.C.

to the same government energy-efficiency regulations. Their popularity is strongly encouraged, of course, not only by aggressive advertising but also by extremely low gasoline prices in the United States.

In summary, after a short period of policies reasonably paralleling those of other advanced countries, the United States currently pursues a number of urban transportation policies directly contrary to those of its peers. This divergence, in turn, leads to divergence in the quality of cities—their efficiency, livability, and international competitiveness. As two selected illustrations of this divergence in the next section indicate, the United States is presently losing the international competition.

POLICY IMPLEMENTATION AND RESULTS

With the United States and its peers on divergent courses in urban transportation, it might be asked: Which direction is correct? The best way to answer this question is to compare the results of recent policies and the condition of metropolitan areas among peer countries. This is done through two case studies that compare specific transportation-related aspects in U.S. cities with those of their foreign peers.

CASE STUDY I

The Retail Cores of Hannover, Germany, and Seattle, Washington

There is an interesting contrast between the development of the central business districts (CBDs) of Hannover, Germany, and Seattle, Washington, over the past two decades. It is a microcosm of the trends and attitudes in many cities in Germany and the United States.

Hannover, the center of a metropolitan area with roughly 750,000 people, adopted a policy to maintain the economic viability of the central city, improve its links with the surrounding suburban areas, and maintain livability by enhancing human orientation in urban design. Toward this end, former streetcar lines were converted into an LRT system with tunnel sections under the CBD, while several previous streets within the retail area were converted into a pedestrian zone. Coupled with this large transportation project, seven department stores, both new and renovated, were included.

Skeptics have criticized this development as overdesign, but the area has proved to be very popular, keeping its dominant role among retail areas of the region. The development is recognized as the centerpiece of a modernized, very livable Hannover metropolitan area.

Seattle is at the center of a metropolitan area of about 1.5 million people. It has a large, growing CBD where more than 140,000 people work on weekdays. However, it has a low modal split for transit, relying entirely on buses with very limited separation from other traffic. Only regional lines are served by dual-mode (diesel/electric) buses, which utilize an exclusive transit tunnel under the CBD. Streets are often congested, trapping both cars and transit vehicles. Meanwhile, large suburban shopping malls proliferate, mostly at major freeway interchanges. The result is a steady decline in the attractiveness of the city center for shopping.

A little more than a decade ago, there were four major department stores; in 1995, only two were left. The owners of one of the remaining stores threatened to leave unless an adjacent pedestrian mall was reopened to automobiles and the city built an additional parking garage. (This street had been closed only a couple of years before to create the Westlake Mall.) The street was later reopened to vehicular traffic, and a large parking garage was built by the city at a cost of about $45,000 per parking space.

Hannover and Seattle differ greatly in their history, policies, topography, and population attitudes. Thus, any comprehensive comparison would have to be complex. What the two cities have in common, however, is the desire to create economically sound, livable urban areas. The point of this

PHOTO 4.4
Pedestrian area with transit in the center of Hannover.
(ÜSTRA, Hannover)

simple comparison of conditions in central cities and their related transportation developments is to show the differences in some relevant policies and attitudes. National policy in Germany favors strengthening a city's viability, whereas in the United States, suburban areas are given largely a free hand in land development. The resulting sprawl leads to deterioration of the central city, with all its unique values and its livability. Although many factors influence this condition, transportation policies are a major contributor to this problem. Inefficient transit prompts stores in the central city to compete with suburbs in parking availability, instead of utilizing the central city's potential superiority to offer a much more efficient intermodal system that incorporates attractive transit, walking, and a human atmosphere—with only limited car access.

In addition to land-use policies, these two cities differ greatly in their transportation expertise. Hannover has worked for several decades to modernize all modes in a coordinated manner. Many streets and arterials have been redesigned and equipped with modern traffic engineering devices; streetcars have been upgraded into one of the world's best-designed LRT systems; and portions of the center city core area have been pedestrianized.

Although Seattle realized the need for transit improvements, it suffered from poor planning and considerable confusion over decision making. Two rapid-transit plans failed to get voter approval during the 1960s and 1970s, before planners included the LRT as an alternative. A multimodal plan developed in 1995 was also rejected after extensive attacks by a variety of groups, including promoters of the monorail (which has operated one line with two stations since 1962), highway interests, suburban developers, and even promoters of some unrealistic "new modes." A revised plan was finally approved in 1997, and some progress may be expected; but the confusion brought on by controversy over modes continues. A proposal to build a network of monorails was also approved by the voters, but it is totally disconnected from the overall transit plan, so that officials now do not know how to handle two uncoordinated yet competing mandates!

Hannover is now in a situation where its central city is the preferred destination for many businesses and shoppers. Through overreliance on the car and lack of restraint of mall development in outlying areas, Seattle's Puget Sound region has evolved to the point where the most attractive option is to drive to an outlying mall and shun the more congested, insufficiently attractive central areas. To compete with sprawling suburbs, the city must make concessions to retain commerce and continue in a spiral of accommodation of ever more parking. The older city, forced to compete with the suburbs, is becoming more car-adaptive rather than utilizing the unique advantages of a city with intermodal access and diversified, human-oriented activities.

CASE STUDY II

The Accessibility of New York City versus Its Peers

In the present strong trend toward a world economy, intensive international trade, tourism, scientific cooperation, and so on, the competition of world cities is increasing and becoming crucial for their future viability and prosperity. New York City is in severe competition with its peers—Paris, Tokyo, London, Berlin, and Hong Kong—as well as Frankfurt and Zürich, which are much smaller but are competitors as strong centers for banking, trade, and company headquarters. This brief comparison will focus on only one aspect of competitiveness: accessibility of these cities from other cities by ground and air public transport, i.e., by railroads and airlines. This is an extremely important aspect, because large cities—particularly their business activities, government meetings, cultural and tourist events, and so on—rely primarily on public transport rather than private car travel.

New York City relies on air transport for all international and most national common carrier access. It is served by three large airports—JFK, LaGuardia, and Newark—all of which are among the world's busiest airports (measured by number of flights and volume of passengers handled). The problem, however, is that all three airports are served only by highways. Hundreds of thousands of cars, vans, and buses entering them every day depend on the condition of access highways and other roads in the region, many of which are chronically congested. Without rail service on a separate ROW, travel into Manhattan from either international airport, JFK or Newark, can take between 45 minutes and two hours, depending on the day and hour. For intercity rail service, Amtrak service goes from the city of New York in only two directions—Philadelphia–Washington and New Haven–Boston. These services are available at only one location—Pennsylvania Station in Manhattan, which has extremely constrained platforms, escalators, and waiting areas. However, in 1995, Congress reduced funding for both operations and investments in upgrading this single rail facility for the country's largest city. As a consequence of such limited service, the number of intercity passengers in New York represents a tiny fraction of passengers who use rail services in any of New York's peer cities. Present policies and developments will increase reliance on the private cars, taxis, vans, and buses—all of which depend on the condition of highways.

Paris is served by two international airports, Charles De Gaulle and Orly. Both are linked to the city by rail lines. The city has superb railway connections with the entire country from half a dozen major and numerous small stations. Service to De Gaulle includes the world-renowned TGV lines toward the south and west (Paris) and north (London) via the Channel Tunnel. A third airport, now planned, will be located at a major railway junction on the TGV Atlantic line.

Tokyo has two high-speed rail lines to its major airport, Narita, and an exclusive monorail line to its older airport, Haneda. Rail lines, including high-speed Shinkansen, provide services to all major cities on Japan's main island from a number of stations in the Tokyo metropolitan area with frequencies similar to those of urban transit. In most respects, rail service in Tokyo is more extensive than rail service in any other world city.

London has rail connections to all three of its airports—Heathrow, Gatwick, and Stanstead. In addition to the Piccadilly line, which connects the entire Underground network with the airport by frequent transit service, Heathrow is connected by a new high-speed regional rail link to Paddington Station. The city is also served by nine regional and intercity railway terminals, most of which are connected by the Circle Line of the Underground for distribution in the city.

Berlin has one of the densest networks of long-distance (national), regional rail (S-Bahn), and metro (U-Bahn) networks in Europe, with intermodal terminals and extensive transfer conveniences and joint fares. Its two airports are served by rail lines.

Hong Kong has a long-distance railway in only one direction because of its unique geographic situation (peninsula and island). Its recently built metro network serves major corridors, but not the old airport directly. Because airport capacity is insufficient, a new one has been built on an island, with an entirely new rail line dedicated to its connection with the city.

Frankfurt Airport, one of the busiest airline hubs in Europe, has a railway station, used by regional and long-distance trains, in its basement. Special airline-operated trains run from the airport to Cologne and several other cities. The city has superb railway connections, including high-speed intercity express (ICE) lines to cities throughout Western Europe.

Zürich's Kloten Airport, another major European hub, also has a railway station on its ground level, which is served by both regional and intercity trains. Several other railway stations throughout the metropolitan area have frequent intercity services.

This comparison of accessibility among peer cities around the world demonstrates that New York City is significantly inferior to its competitors. Particularly distressing are the policies pursued by the U.S. federal government and Congress, which, since 1980, have resulted in decreasing financial support for transit in constant dollars (see figure 4.12). These reductions have aggravated the city's disadvantage, thus further hurting its competitiveness with its world peers.

In concluding this comparison of the urban transportation systems in the United States with those of its peer countries, it is appropriate to quote an observation made by a member of a group of U.S. transportation professionals after a tour of European cities: "In European communities public transportation is not viewed as a 'social service' for people who are unable to afford private means of transportation. Instead, it is regarded as a solution to protect and preserve the environment, to reduce automobile use and traffic congestion, and to improve mobility of the overall population" (Wynne 1995). It is in this understanding of the concept of quality of life, or livability of cities and communities, that the United States must learn from its peers if it is to avoid a worsening of the problems its metropolitan areas face.

References

Bourgoin, M., and M. Pierron. 1987. *Fighting congestion in city centers.* 47th International Congress of Union Internationale des Transports Publics (UITP), Lausanne, Switzerland. Brussels, Belgium: UITP.

Brandl, P. G., and K. W. Axhausen. 1998. Karlsruhe 1975–1995: a case study of light rail transit development. *TR Record* 1623: 155–164. Washington, DC: Transportation Research Board.

Buchanan, Colin, et al. 1964. *Traffic in towns.* London, UK: Her Majesty's Stationery Office (HMSO).

Dawson, J. A. L., and I. Catling. 1986. Electronic road pricing in Hong Kong. *Transportation Research* 20A: 129–134.

Department of Transport. 1984. *Buses.* London, UK: Her Majesty's Stationery Office (HMSO).

Domstad, Ragnar. 1991. Development of light rail in Gothenburg. Paper presented at conference, "The Tram in Middle-Size European Cities," Padua, Italy.

_____. 1996. *Tendering for bus services in Gothenburg.* Gothenburg, Sweden: Gothenburg City Traffic Authority.

European Marketing Data and Statistics. 1995. Vol. 30. London, UK: Euromonitor Publications.

Fawkner, J. 1995. Bus deregulation in Britain: Profit or loss? *Public Transport International* 6: 18-23. Brussels, Belgium: UITP.

Hall, Peter, and Carmen Hass-Klau. 1985. *Can rail save the city? The impacts of rail transit and pedestrianization on British and German cities.* Aldershot, UK: Gower Press.

Hollatz and Tamms. 1965. *Die Kommunalen Verkehrsprobleme in der Bundesrepublik Deutschland.* Essen, Germany: Vulkan-Verlag.

Homburger, Wolfgang S., and Vukan R. Vuchic. 1972. Transit Federation—a solution for service integration. *Revue de l'UITP* 2: 73–100. Brussels, Belgium: Union Internationale des Transports Publics (UITP).

Hook, Walter. 1994. Role of nonmotorized transportation and public transport in Japan's economic success. *TR Record* 1441: 108–115. Washington, DC: Transportation Research Board.

International Marketing Data and Statistics. 1996. Vol. 20. London, UK: Euromonitor Publications.

Lehner, Friedrich. 1961. Public transport within the framework of urban general traffic plans. Report I. 34th International Congress of Union Internationale des Transports Publics (UITP), Copenhagen, Denmark. Brussels, Belgium: UITP.

______. 1969. Regional organisation of transport and urban development. Report Ia. 38th International Congress of Union Internationale des Transports Publics (UITP), London, UK. Brussels, Belgium: UITP.

Matsoukis, E.C., and H. A. van Gent. 1995. A comparative study of the environmental impacts of transport policies in the Netherlands and Greece. *IATSS Research* 19, 1.

Monheim, Rolf. 1994. From pedestrian zones to traffic calmed city centers. In Harry Dimitrious, ed., *Moving away from the motor vehicle: the German and Hong Kong experience*. Hong Kong: Centre of Urban Planning and Environmental Management, The University of Hong Kong.

New South Wales Department of Transport. 1993. *Integrated transport strategy for Greater Sydney*. First release for public discussion. Sydney, Australia: New South Wales Department of Transport.

Organisation for Economic Co-operation and Development (OECD). 1992. *Energy prices and taxes*. No. 3. Paris, France: International Energy Agency.

Perl, Anthony, and John Pucher. 1995. Transit in trouble: the policy challenge posed by Canada's changing urban mobility. *Canadian Public Policy* 23, 3 (September).

Pickup, Laurie, et al. 1991. *Bus deregulation in the metropolitan areas*. Aldershot, UK: Avebury/Gower.

Pucher, John. 1988. Urban travel behavior as the outcome of public policy: the example of modal split in Western Europe and North America. *Journal of the American Planning Association* 54, 4 (Autumn): 509–520.

______. 1994. Public transport developments: Canada vs. the United States. *Transportation Quarterly* 48, 1: 65–78.

______. 1995. Urban passenger transport in the United States and Europe: a comparative analysis of public policies. *Transport Reviews* 15, 2 (April–June): 89–107; and 15, 3 (July–September): 261–283.

Roodman, David M. 1997. *Getting the signals right: tax reform to protect the environment and economy*. Worldwatch Paper 134. Washington, DC: Worldwatch Institute. May.

Socialdata. 1991. Verkehr in Stuttgart: Kennziffern der Mobilät. Verkehrs- und Tarifverbund Stuttgart, Germany. p. 10.

Topp, Harmut H. 1995. A critical review of current illusions in traffic management and control. *Transport Policy* 2, 1: 33-42.

Transport Structure Plan Project Team. 1990. *Second transport structure plan, Part D: government decision. Transport in a sustainable society*. Joint policy statement by several Ministers of the Government, submitted to Parliament, the Netherlands.

Union Internationale des Transports Publics (UITP). 1995. *Public transport: the challenge*. 51st International Congress of Union Internationale des Transports Publics (UITP), Paris, France. Brussels, Belgium: UITP.

Vepsäläinen, S., and M. Pursula. 1992. Developing transport policy to raise the market share of public transport in Helsinki. *Proceedings* of Seminar C, European Transport Highways and Planning, 20th Summer Annual Meeting. University of Manchester and Institute of Science and Technology, UK.

Verband öffentlicher Verkehrsbetriebe (VÖV), Deutscher Städtetag, Deutsche Bundesbahn. *Gemeinde-Verkehrs-Finanzierung für Busse und Bahnen 1967–1986*. Köln, Germany.

Wynne, George G. 1995. Transit managers gain perspective on European systems. *Passenger Transport* (July 3): 7.

YTV (Helsinki Metropolitan Area Council), Ministry of Transport and Communications. 1994. Helsinki metropolitan area Transportation System 2020. Helsinki Metropolitan Area Series A.1994:3. Helsinki, Finland: YTV.

5

Common Misconceptions in Urban Transportation

Policies affecting urban transportation—and, particularly, decisions about the roles different modes should play—are the subjects of extensive debate in most cities around the world. Controversy focuses on such issues as "cars versus transit," "bus versus rail," "LRT versus metro," and "freeway construction versus improved street utilization."

The debate about basic modes—cars, bus, and rail—is especially intensive for several reasons. First, many people have a strong emotional attachment or aversion to particular modes. Each major mode—car, bus, and rail—has its enthusiastic supporters as well as devout critics. Second, powerful lobbies support arguments favoring specific modes and criticizing other modes. These two pressures often have greater influence than the opinion of transportation experts who promote the planning of systems at Level II—that is, the development of balanced transportation systems. The third factor in these modal debates is the underlying differences in preference for the types of cities with which the various modes of transportation are compatible: that is, car-based cities, in which highways and parking facilities dominate the form and character of land uses; or cities based on a balanced intermodal system that emphasizes people as the basic element of urban spaces. Cities in the latter group utilize human-scale design of public areas, making travel without cars not only feasible but attractive. This system is given priority in central cities and other major activity centers.

Extremists on both sides of this debate, pro-highway or anti-highway, present obstacles to the solution of current transportation problems. In the United States, more than in its peer countries, the pro-highway lobby has traditionally been extremely powerful. Most transportation plans aimed at reducing dependence on the automobile face strong attacks by those who continue to claim that the car is virtually the only desirable form of transport for the future. Since transit, particularly rail, is the strongest symbol of balanced transportation and human orientation of metropolitan areas, it often serves as a lightning rod for criticism by promoters of car-dominated cities. In nearly all cities that have planned rail systems or major bus improvements, from Washington and Atlanta in the 1970s to Honolulu and St. Louis in the 1990s, strong campaigns have been mounted against these projects.

Every major public investment deserves careful scrutiny and a constructive search for the most efficient plan and design. Highways, rail transit, airports, and other infrastructure projects must be carefully designed to ensure maximum efficiency and benefits to users, as well as to the city and society in general. In most U.S. cities, however, transit, especially rail projects, is criticized as "too expensive," or "not needed." Many of the attacks are factually incorrect and emotional, with a clear bias against one mode or another. This is demonstrated by the fact that critics of transit subsidies as "outlays of taxpayers' money" seldom question order-of-magnitude greater spending of taxpayers' money for highway construction, which is usually referred to as "investment." In a similar euphemism, providing "free" (that is, fully subsidized) parking facilities in central cities and suburban areas often is referred to as "customer service." A similar pro-highway bias has been demonstrated by theoreticians who have produced unrealistic, hypothetical models of transportation systems and used them to make the simplistic claim that one mode is "better" than another.

This chapter quotes common overgeneralizations and misconceptions about planning, cities, highways, and transit and gives a brief explanation of the facts. The emphasis is on transit, because most misunderstandings involve bus and rail projects.

URBAN PLANNING AND DEVELOPMENT

The traditional suspicion of some Americans toward cities sometimes extends to criticism of urban planning in general. There are also arguments that defend the development of urban sprawl and the characteristics of related transportation systems. Several typical claims follow.

"Planning is contrary to the principles of our free society." The planning of cities and metropolitan areas and their transportation systems is a normal function of a rational society. It is necessary to achieve long-range, socially desirable goals that cannot be reached through decisions based on the short-term desires of individuals or groups. Although implementation of plans for a development or a city does mean the imposition of some restrictions and requirements on individuals and their behavior, implementation also brings efficient development, a livable city, and stronger social interactions. Rational planning can actually prevent harmful or wasteful conditions and lead to new options. Just as well-organized private companies must plan for their future, a basic duty of government is to plan public systems and services, such as transportation. Every step in the evolution of human civilization is characterized by a higher level of planning and social organization.

In his recent book calling for the planning and protection of Pennsylvania's land and communities, Hylton (1995) points out the sharp contrast often seen between the long-range planning implemented by private individuals and corporations and that of public agencies: "Successful people and successful corporations set goals and make plans to achieve them. The Commonwealth of Pennsylvania has no plan. In Pennsylvania, government spends billions of tax dollars annually and employs more than 650,000 people without having a clear notion of what it wants to achieve. . . ."

Planning and its implementation do not in any way conflict with a free society. By far the best planning of cities and transportation systems is conducted in some of the most democratic countries in the world, such as Switzerland, the Netherlands, and the Scandinavian countries.

"Suburban growth shows that people prefer single-family housing over apartments and urban living." Many factors present obstacles to the creation of attractive urban developments: lack of ability to implement coordinated land use/transportation plans; urban designs that neglect human needs at both a macro and a micro scale; racial relations, and so on. All these factors limit the choice of housing and distort market conditions. For example, in many cities, housing in the central city consists mostly of two extremes—luxury apartments and slums. Many potential residents, especially those with children, feel compelled to live in suburban areas because of better schools, less crime, and lower taxes. In the long run, these conditions aggravate the problems of economic and racial segregation and the deterioration of central cities—the trends which, in turn, have a strong negative impact on the entire metropolitan area.

Cheaper land and lower taxes are strong stimuli to the development of housing and businesses in suburban areas. Many such advantages, however, are based on short-term direct costs to developers and buyers. In the long run, suburban sprawl causes excessive land consumption, high public infrastructure costs, and numerous negative environmental consequences for which developers do not pay. Eventually, excessive investment in continuous spatial spreading leads to a shortage of public funds for maintenance and thus to the deterioration of older sections of metropolitan areas. The results are economic depression, social problems, and, eventually, negative impacts on the entire metropolitan area's economic prosperity and quality of life (Adler 1995; Bank of America et al. 1995; Burrington 1994; Whitman 1998). In the longer perspective, weakening of central cities leads to the loss of the numerous economies of agglomeration that have been major reasons for the existence of cities since their beginning (Persky et al. 1991).

"The free market should determine land uses and the form of metropolitan areas." The free market is an excellent mechanism for much of the economy, but it is incorrect to claim that all functions in the economy and society can be resolved by the free-market mechanism. City and regional transportation planning at all levels, from local to federal, is a function that belongs to the government domain because the free market cannot handle it alone. This is because the free market tends to reflect short-term commercial aspects while ignoring externalities—costs and damages imposed on nonparticipants in economic transactions. Planning for public systems and facilities must include long-term benefits and costs, as well as numerous nonquantifiable aspects such as social and environmental impacts and the quality of life.

"Whatever is done, trends in urban developments and travel habits cannot be changed." Known as the "inevitability hypothesis," this view is used by opponents of all change as a second line of defense. When criticism of present trends cannot be refuted, the validity of the criticism is granted, but it is then dismissed as irrelevant on the grounds that nothing can be done to change existing trends, or that it is "too late" to make such changes. Just how valid is this argument?

It is true that many past and present practices in the choice of housing, locations of businesses, dependence on car travel, neglect of pedestrians, and so on, are imbedded in "the system," that is, in existing laws, economic relationships, and human habits. Yet, there is no justification for this fatalistic attitude. Many examples can be found of traditional practices and deeply ingrained habits that were changed when serious problems developed or when a better solution was found. For example, if somebody had suggested in 1970 that smoking should be prohibited in entire buildings, airports, and convention centers, that person would have been accused of "not understanding human nature and the political realities." Similarly, would anyone in 1960 have expected that millions of Americans would "rediscover" bicycle riding, or that 40,000 people would run in a single marathon?

Concerns about air pollution, environmental deterioration, and excessive energy consumption arose rapidly and became important factors in determining policy and behavior. Therefore, the view that past and present trends in urban transportation cannot be changed, and that policies can have no significant impact on trends, is not valid. It has been disproved on numerous occasions and in many metropolitan areas during recent decades. American society and the U.S. system of government have shown repeatedly that when a change is obviously needed, laws, trends, and habits can be changed.

"Do we still need cities?" This question, which stimulated the writing of the book *Does America Need Cities?* (Persky et al. 1991), reflects confused thinking about the role of cities and frustration with a failure to maintain livable metropolitan areas. There is no question that our civilization is urban-based. This is shown by the fact that a vast majority of the population has moved, and continues to move, to metropolitan areas. The question, then, is, "What form should our cities and metropolitan areas have?" It is clear that future cities will not be the same as high-density monocentric cities such as the Chicago or Baltimore of 1900. It is also clear, however, that their successors—metropolitan areas—will continue to be centers of activity. There are no major new settlements in the form of "suburbs" growing in rural areas far from any established cities; there are no "suburbs" without "urbs." Thus, there is no doubt that cities will continue to exist in the future. But they should be better designed to achieve coordination between their diverse activities and the transportation function, rather than being totally directed by excessive reliance on a single mode of transport. The incompatibility of total reliance on the car with the livability of cities must be resolved, rather than ignored in the belief that urban problems will disappear if we give up on cities.

"Highway congestion will be reduced with the forthcoming telecommunications revolution." This is another misguided, escapist myth. The introduction of the telephone decades ago, and its widespread use since then, has

had no visible impact on the volume of personal travel. Similarly, the explosion of personal computers, faxes, e-mail, and other powerful communication tools since the 1970s has been paralleled by continuous growth in the volume of travel and VKT. The reason is that the volume of communications and transactions is increasing so rapidly that they require increased travel in addition to the exploding volume of transactions performed by telecommunications. Recent studies by Salomon and Moktarian (1997) confirm this explanation.

"Our low-density cities are not suited to transit." It is true that the efficiency of transit decreases with density. The ability to provide good transit, however, depends not only on density but on the overall transportation network and organization of activities as well. If street networks and land use are designed without any regard for pedestrians and transit, bus service cannot be efficient even in areas with a considerable number of activities. There are, however, many suburban areas with low densities, such as Calgary, the San Francisco Bay Area, and Washington, D.C., in which not only bus but also rail systems operate efficiently because they have extensive suburban feeder systems (bicycles, cars, and buses) and convenient distribution in the central city via walking, buses, and other modes.

The car will certainly remain the basic mode of transportation in low-density areas, but its efficiency can be increased if it is supplemented by walkways, bicycle-path networks, and transit services. Moreover, there is a growing movement in many states and other countries to use the design concept of "transit oriented development," or TOD. Not only does this design result in higher use of transit, bicycles, and walking in suburban areas, but it creates a more diversified social life and much richer opportunities for activities by residents—particularly children, youth, and the elderly. TOD also is much more in line with the goals of sustainable communities than is the concept of unlimited suburban sprawl (Project for Public Spaces 1997).

TRANSPORT AND ECONOMIC ASPECTS

Economic aspects and impacts of transportation systems, particularly highways and rail transit, often need clarification. Several common but confusing statements are analyzed here.

"Auto users pay for their travel." Often used by politicians in opposing gasoline or other taxes on car and truck use that would go to general government funds, this statement is incorrect. The concept that car users "pay

their costs" comes primarily from the fact that the Highway Trust Fund, which is financed primarily by highway user taxes, pays most of the investments in certain categories of highways. Used by highway-related organizations, it has become a widespread myth.

As was shown in chapter 2, auto users are subsidized in numerous ways—from "free parking" privileges to tax exemptions for various car uses. Moreover, car drivers are not charged for many costs and negative impacts they impose on other travelers and society as a whole in the short or the long run. Estimates of these costs are on the order of hundreds of billions of dollars annually, far exceeding the subsidies given to all other modes of transportation combined. For example, Lee (1995) estimates that in 1991 highway costs exceeded the payments made by highway users by $330 billion.

"Car travel is private, paid by users, while transit is a public, subsidized system." This statement is highly misleading. Most transit systems are publicly owned and subsidized; but the auto-highway system, too, is largely publicly owned. Virtually all streets and highways and most other facilities—such as bridges, terminals, many parking garages, and vehicles—are publicly owned and operated. This public portion of the system has obtained far more public funds, especially in the United States, than any other transportation system. As mentioned in the preceding point, highway transportation is extensively subsidized by the government and society at large; thus, it is not a private system paid by its users, but, similar to transit, a partially subsidized public system used mostly by operators of private vehicles.

The high subsidy of car travel is actually one of the reasons governments must subsidize transit. Introduction of more realistic charges for auto use would result not only in reduced government subsidies for highways but also in an opportunity to reduce transit subsidies. Increasing charges for driving, such as a higher gasoline tax, increase of parking charges, or introduction of road pricing, would also bring significant benefits in the form of reduced negative impacts of auto use, particularly in urban areas.

"Transit share of travel is decreasing; therefore, public assistance to it should be decreased." This is a misguided observation and illogical conclusion. A decrease in the travel share of transit in most U.S. cities is a logical consequence of the country's housing, taxation, investment, and other policies affecting urban areas, as well as the subsidies to highways and car travel, which are greater than subsidies to all other modes combined, as discussed in chapter 3. The policy implications of this trend should be based on the

goals set for urban transportation. Because the goal is to develop intermodal systems and decrease reliance on highway travel only, the decreasing share of transit travel is the reason to increase rather than decrease transit investments.

"Construction of highways creates jobs." Although this statement is correct, it is not a valid argument for building highways if they are not justified for other reasons. All public projects create jobs, so the selection among them should not be based on construction benefits alone. Aschauer (1991) performed a study of the macroeconomic impact of transit versus highway investments and found that transit has more than twice the potential to increase worker productivity, and that its benefits are more than twice the net benefits of highway investments.

"Investments in rail transit increase employment in construction." The comment about the preceding statement applies here as well. It is the permanent value and the benefits to be accrued over many years that may or may not justify construction of a rail project or any other public project. Construction jobs, however desirable, are of relatively small significance because they are temporary. Similarly, the problems of disruptions due to the construction of a metro (or highway), however serious, are a temporary phenomenon, not a permanent impact of such facilities.

"Increase of gasoline taxes would hurt low-income people." True, an increase in the cost of any product hurts low-income people. A simple analysis, however, clearly shows that an increase in the tax on gasoline would have a much lower economic impact on car users than is commonly alleged. The federal gasoline tax, or average among states, amounts to only 12 percent of the price of gasoline (14 cents out of $1.20 per gallon, or 4 cents out of 32 cents per liter). Assuming fuel efficiency of only 20 miles per gallon (8.5 km/liter), the cost of gasoline in 1997 was 6 cents per mile (3.8 cents per km), of which 0.72 cents, or 12 percent, is federal tax. *This represents only 2 percent of the total cost of operating a motor vehicle.*

Suppose that, by U.S. standards, a very large tax increase is implemented. It is tripled – that is, increased by 28 cents per gallon (7.4 cents per liter). Here, three different impacts are of interest: economic impact on travelers, revenue obtained from the tax increase, and impact on user travel decisions (and thus on VKTs, the basic measure of externalities and impacts of car use).

Economic impact, particularly relevant for low-income people, depends on the user's total expenditure. For this example, assume that a person driving 10,000 miles (16,000 km) per year pays a total of $3,400 for owning and operating his or her car (an amount in the low range of the American Automobile Association's estimates of driving costs, assuming our user operates an economical vehicle rather than a luxury car). This amount—the total user cost—would increase to $3,540, or by less than 4 percent, if the federal gasoline tax were tripled.

The revenue from the 28 cents per gallon (7.4 cents per liter) increase would be about $31 billion per year. Such a large fund could be used for better operation, maintenance, and modernization of *all* transportation systems—highways, streets, transit, and Amtrak; for mitigation of environmental damage; or for reducing highway subsidies.

The present cost of gasoline per vehicle-mile (km) is virtually negligible: it is so low that most drivers do not consider it at all in deciding how far to drive, at least for short trips. The additional tax of 28 cents per gallon would result in an out-of-pocket increase from 6 to 7.5 cents per mile (3.7 to 4.7 cents per km). Although it represents 25 percent, this increase would still be an extremely small amount. Because (in the vast majority of cases) the user's value of a trip far exceeds this amount, one could expect users to continue making all essential trips. At most, some of the numerous discretionary trips—those that could be combined, replaced, or forgone without significant inconvenience to the user—would decrease. This would be a most desirable result, because there would be a decrease of VKT with no significant economic impact on users. Such a decrease in VKT actually has been the goal of most trip-reduction programs applied to reduce highway congestion, pollution, and related problems.

The preceding analysis shows that the argument of hardship on low-income people cannot be used legitimately against a gasoline tax increase. Such an increase would produce significant revenues and would have a negligible economic impact on users but would begin to make drivers aware that transportation costs are proportional to the distance traveled.

It should be noted that large groups of low-income people, in both metropolitan and in rural areas, are among those who do not own cars and who rely on public transportation. In recent years, they have been hurt far more than car drivers by price increases. From 1980 to 1992 the average bus fare increased from 39 to 88 cents, or by 126 percent in constant dollars. During the same period, the price of gasoline *decreased* by 2 percent, dropping from 122 to 119 cents per gallon, or 31 to 30 cents per liter (Urban Transportation Monitor 1993). The trends of lowered gasoline prices and increased transit fares are distinctly adverse to those people with the lowest income. Increasing gasoline taxes would at least partially alleviate this anomaly, especially if the revenue is used to improve alternatives to car travel.

"Rail transit does not reduce traffic congestion." There have been cases in which the streets or major roads in a city center or around a suburban station have experienced renewed traffic congestion a few years after a metro system was opened in the city. This, however, cannot by any means be considered an argument that metro construction is ineffective, or that investment in its construction is not justified. First, transportation service in congested areas where there is a metro is considerably better than in congested areas with no alternative means of travel: all metro passengers travel free of congestion, and those who travel on congested streets have the option of switching to the uncongested mode. Moreover, the metro usually has reserve capacity, so that an increase in economic and social activities is not as constrained as it is in congested, car-dependent areas.

There are many examples of such benefits from rail transit. Today, Washington, D.C., offers fast and reliable travel via the Metro at all times, whereas in 1975, without the Metro, travel during peak hours was unreliable, taxi service was difficult to get, and there was no congestion-free alternative. Similarly, in the San Francisco Bay Area, one can travel during many peak hours faster from San Francisco to Oakland or Berkeley by BART than by any highway mode. Prior to BART's opening, all travel options were subject to traffic conditions on the Bay Bridge and its access roads.

It is important here to note that street congestion recurs after a metro system has been built only when the activities in the areas served by rail transit have intensified so much that the number of generated trips has increased by as many as the rapid transit now carries. The claim that building a new metro system does not eliminate street or freeway congestion, therefore, may be true in some cases, but at the same time, it indicates that rapid transit has a major positive impact on the activities and vitality of a city.

There also have been claims that rail transit failed to produce either of the preceding two impacts. Webber (1977) claimed that San Francisco's BART neither had a significant impact on the development of downtown San Francisco nor reduced highway congestion. These two claims are mutually contradictory. If a rapid transit system carries, for example, 100,000 people per day into a downtown, these people must either have been diverted from highway vehicles, thus reducing congestion, or the activities in the area must have intensified, thus indicating a strong, positive impact of rapid transit on economic activities and land uses.

"Rail transit does not intensify land uses." In most cases, rail transit stimulates intensification of land use. The impacts of rapid transit on land use, however, depend considerably on supporting policies. In some cases, impacts

have been small, especially where communities surrounding rail transit stations have prohibited intensified development (for example, in some suburban townships in the San Francisco Bay Area). But, with good planning and/or strong market demand, metro stations have led to major investments in joint developments and intensified land use around metro stations. Some examples are Eaton Center in Toronto; the San Francisco Financial District; Crystal City, Ballston, and Pentagon City in the Washington, D.C., suburbs (KMPG 1994); and Montreal, Hong Kong, and Stockholm.

"Rail transit reverses the trend of sprawl and inefficient land use developments." This is a case of overgeneralization in the opposite direction. Rail transit has the *potential* to strongly influence the shape of developments. However, rail transit alone cannot do this if various policies favor dispersed buildings. Policies and planning that integrate land use and transportation can achieve this objective if the power to implement exists or if market conditions are favorable. Nevertheless, planning of rail transit does stimulate interest in planning not only by government agencies but also by businesses and the population at large. Thus, rail transit usually becomes a strong catalyst for various civic and private initiatives, innovations, and investments. Recent public/private cooperation in the development of a former rail yard in Alexandria, Virginia, is a good example of the impact of rail transit.

MOBILITY AND ACCESSIBILITY

Many aspects of car and transit travel often are poorly understood or are overgeneralized, resulting in incorrect conclusions. Some examples follow.

"People want maximum privacy, which the automobile offers." Most people like to have privacy, but this desire should not be taken to the extreme. Total privacy means *no* contact with other people; yet, humans are social beings, and people move to urban areas in large part to interact with other people. Metropolitan areas that rely almost exclusively on auto travel have a more limited social life than those areas with a combination of modes. Mixed land uses, human-oriented design of residential and commercial developments, and pedestrian areas, in contrast, stimulate social life (Holtzclaw 1995).

As for privacy in traveling, the automobile offers both independence in the vehicle and pleasant or unpleasant indirect interactions with other drivers. Travel by transit or walking on the streets can also vary from an adverse experience to a very positive social contact, or to an event that is unique to human-oriented cities. Paradoxically, some critics of transit who disparage its "lack of privacy" and low service frequency promote car- and vanpooling as better alternatives to SOVs than transit. Actually, car- and vanpooling generally offer less privacy than transit, and their frequency of service usually is limited to one round-trip per day—far inferior to any transit frequency. Vanpooling, therefore, is most efficient for trips that are not served by good transit.

"Car-based transportation provides freedom of choice and maximum mobility." Incorrect. Cities that have multimodal transportation systems provide mobility for *all* people, rather than only for car users. They also offer alternative options for all travelers, some of which may be independent of highway congestion. Finally, *mobility,* measured by vehicle-km or person-km traveled (usually very high in car-based cities), is not as important a measure as is *accessibility,* that is, the ability to travel between different activities. For example, travelers in Phoenix and Detroit, two cities that rely almost entirely on cars, provide high mobility for car users. Their population, however, has much less choice about trips than do the populations of, say, San Francisco or Montreal, which offer not only car but transit and pedestrian travel as well. Thus, cities with integrated, multimodal transportation systems provide greater and more efficient accessibility than do car-based cities.

The one-third of the population without a driver's license is particularly vulnerable. This group has extremely low levels of mobility and independence in unimodal, car-based cities. It should also be mentioned that the ability to travel in an area conveniently, without dependence on a private car, is an important component of a city's livability.

"Every citizen has a right to drive." Not unconditionally. Any society faces a conflict between the interests of the individual and those of the rest of the community. Certain individual rights are established and upheld by the legal system or by social norms; others are accommodated as privileges, subject to conditions that set limits on the adverse affects and risks to other citizens. Driving an automobile has consistently been interpreted by the courts in the United States as a privilege, not a right, because it can easily be shown that driving affects the community in many ways. Furthermore, exercising the privilege of driving depends on the willingness of society as a whole to subsidize this privilege.

"Cars are very harmful to cities." A gross overgeneralization. Cars are a fundamental component of our civilization and life, both individual and social. Cities totally without cars would be neither economically nor socially viable. It is the excessive and exclusive use of cars that leads to negative impacts and problems. The solution to the "collision of cities and cars" problem is to develop balanced intermodal systems and limit car use to the level where its benefits are utilized but its negative side effects are kept to a minimum. While the volume of car travel should be decreased, efficiency of its use should be increased.

"Americans will not use transit, because they will never leave their cars." Again, an overgeneralization. Although cars do have a certain emotional attraction for many, Americans, like most people, make rational decisions when selecting a mode of transportation. They avoid transit when it provides poor service or when it is infrequent, slow, unreliable, and/or expensive, as is the case in many U.S. cities. However, major improvements in bus service, such as those introduced in Honolulu and Portland in the 1970s, resulted in ridership increases of 30 percent or more. High-quality rail transit, such as the San Francisco BART and Washington Metro, or LRT systems in Calgary and San Diego, have created demands for park-and-ride in suburbs because many car users prefer to leave their cars and use transit when it offers efficient service.

"Transit is used only by those who have no other choice." This is generally true in small cities as well as car-oriented metropolitan areas with extensive highway systems and subsidized car use but only low-quality transit services—generally buses on streets. This statement is incorrect, however, for metropolitan areas with high-quality express buses or rail transit that can, and does, attract many car owners. This is the case with regional buses in Seattle, Denver, and New York, and with most of the more than 50 rail transit systems (LRT, metro, and regional rail) operating in North America. It is also clearly true of most cities around the world with extensive rail transit systems, from Melbourne and Osaka to Paris and Oslo.

"Rail systems are segregated because they serve affluent communities." Paradoxically, this criticism of rail transportation is often made by the same people who make the preceding, diametrically opposite, criticism. It is fallacious to relate population mix to a specific transit technology, because ridership composition depends on the population of the served area as well as the service area and fares. The Metrolink commuter rail system in Los Angeles has been accused of being for upper-middle–class suburban

residents; but the fact is that minorities make up 40 percent of the system's ridership (Stanger et al. 1995).

Although some recently built rail systems—such as BART, the Washington Metro, and the Los Angeles Metrolink—serve predominantly affluent suburbs, their changing ridership on different sections and at different times shows that high-quality transit systems with reasonable fares can attract a variety of social and ethnic groups (Stanger et al. 1995). Actually, in all these cases, rail transit is the only quality transportation available to low-income people and those without cars.

Interestingly, no question of ethnic or economic equity has been raised about public investments in, and subsidies to, highways, which in all alignments exclude non–car owners, who belong predominantly to low-income groups. The only way these groups can use freeways is if they ride transit or paratransit; but many freeways are not used by any bus transit or paratransit services.

"Park-and-ride involves 'cold starts' and therefore does not actually reduce energy consumption and air pollution." Park-and-ride, typically in suburban areas, replaces long car commutes by transit, which reduces VKT in the most congested corridors of a region. The least economical and most damaging driving—peak-hour, peak-direction commuting—is thus replaced by more efficient transit. There are clear benefits from avoiding the negative impacts of VKT on congestion, the environment, and non-human–oriented land uses. As for the number of "cold starts" of cars, commuter behavior must be analyzed as a whole. Many commuters combine their travel with various errands, such as stopping at a bank, a bookstore, or for lunch. Transit commuters typically walk for these purposes, whereas commuting by car involves special stops along the way. Because each stop results in restarting the car, park-and-ride actually eliminates several such cold starts in the central city, where they are the most harmful. In addition, energy consumption is reduced by far more than average consumption per VKT, due to inefficient urban driving.

HIGHWAY TRANSPORTATION

Many aspects of policies toward car use, highway congestion, and positive and negative impacts of constructing highways in metropolitan areas are more complex than is perceived by the public. Again, numerous simplistic statements only confuse, rather than inform, the public.

"Nobody can change Americans' 'love affair' with the automobile." This statement combines two fallacies. First, not only Americans, but all people like cars, not only because of their convenience but because of the feeling of independence and social prestige they offer, as well as the excitement of driving. The functional part of this "love affair," however, depends greatly on the conditions under which cars are driven. In the United States, extensive direct and indirect subsidies of car driving (discussed in chapter 2) influence car use to a much greater extent than the emotional bias toward it. Lack of an attractive alternative is another major reason for the fact that in most cases the car is not an emotional but a logical—often the only—choice for individuals.

The second fallacy is the implication that the preference for car use is unchangeable. There is ample proof that both transit incentives and auto-use disincentives can influence modal choice significantly, not only in Singapore and Munich, but also in San Francisco, Washington, D.C., and Portland. Congested park-and-ride lots and garages around rail transit stations in suburbs of these cities demonstrate this.

"The car reflects the American way of life." Yes, many features of life based on extensive car use are more typical of the United States than they are of most other countries. This has numerous advantages, which must be retained. Metropolitan areas can be improved, however, if their car-based mobility is complemented by other modes of travel in areas where they are more efficient and have fewer negative impacts than the private car. With its diverse population and dynamic economy, the "American way of life" is extremely diverse. It represents different things to different people, including driving cars for some, and riding trains, buses, or bicycles for others. Moreover, in spite of an extremely high rate of car ownership, many Americans have rediscovered the pleasures of walking when they have attractive pedestrian-oriented areas, be they the streets of New York or New Orleans, attractive enclosed shopping malls, or the Santa Monica coastal area. The problem is that most U.S. cities and suburbs have seriously neglected the need for diversity and the importance of humans as the basic element of both the macro design of metropolitan areas the micro design of individual developments.

If it is accepted that diverse, lively, attractive cities such as Boston, New York, Baltimore, and San Diego are a part of the "American way of life," then an intermodal transportation system represents another American tradition. These examples, and many others around the world, demonstrate that *large cities cannot be livable without multimodal transportation.* High-quality transit and good treatment of pedestrians are a sine qua non of livable cities. This is also true of American traditions and the American way of life.

"Congestion should be reduced by building more highways." The policy of responding to highway congestion by providing more capacity is merely a temporary solution which, if followed to its extreme, may be counterproductive in the long run. With car travel grossly underpriced, particularly with respect to out-of-pocket costs, any increase of highway capacity tends to generate additional travel—new and longer trips with lower car occupancies. For this reason, in the long run, the policy of increasing street and highway capacity in response to traffic congestion results in the generation of additional VKT and, sometimes, in congestion that spreads throughout the network.

In mature metropolitan areas, this "highway widening syndrome," or the construction of more and wider highways, has been rejected as a viable way to solve traffic problems or to reduce congestion. Actually, in certain areas of many cities the opposite solution to congestion has been used: traffic-calming, and, in most congested streets in the center city, conversion of streets into pedestrian malls. ISTEA mandates traffic management rather than an increase of highway capacity as a way to mitigate congestion and increase the efficiency of urban transport.

A recent study in Great Britain (SACTRA 1994) again proved the historically experienced phenomenon that increasing the capacity of a highway results in the generation of 10 to 20 percent more trips within a short period of time. In highly congested areas, growth as high as 40 percent was observed. The study has contributed to cancellation of dozens of highway construction plans in that country, with the government stating that "building new roads is the last resort" (see also Goodwin 1996).

"Advances in 'clean cars' will solve the main problem of cars in cities." Because the passage of the Clean Air Act in the United States and similar laws in other countries have legally imposed certain actions to reduce air pollution from various sources, more attention has been drawn to air pollution than to several other problems caused by the use of cars in cities. Thus Johnson (1993), Sperling (1995), Transportation Research Board (1997), and a major article in *The Economist* (1996) focus on "clean cars" as if they were the main solution to urban transportation problems while downplaying other issues. They ignore the crucial roles of transit and other modes in reducing VKT and improving the livability of cities; consequently, they fail to provide a realistic solution to problems other than air pollution that are created by excessive car use.

The statement quoted above represents an extreme oversimplification of a complex urban transportation problem. Air pollution caused by highway transportation is a major, but by no means the only, component of the collision of cities and cars. Even if perfectly clean cars were invented in the immediate future, street and highway congestion, accident losses, excessive land and energy consumption, negative long-term impacts on quality of life, and other problems would remain.

"ITS technology will greatly increase highway capacity and resolve the congestion problem." Incorrect. First, the degree of potential increase in highway capacity through ITS technology remains highly controversial, with estimates ranging from 8 to 400 percent. Second, even if a major increase in capacity on freeways were to occur, there is little discussion as to the impact that increase would have on surface streets. Finally, the positive and negative impacts of such a capacity increase on the total transportation system and on metropolitan areas has received inadequate attention. Meanwhile, enthusiasm for technology is suppressing attention to the much more important aspects of the transportation system (Lowe 1993).

"Construction of new HOV lanes leads to a diversion from SOVs to HOVs." This erroneous statement has led New York City's Committee for Better Transit to allege that "HOV = HOAX." Surveys show that, in most cases, the opposite is true: construction of new HOV lanes actually results in diversion of travel from HOVs to SOVs. The reason is simple. For individuals, traveling alone in a personal car—an SOV—is in many cases preferable to carpooling. Therefore, diversion of travel from SOVs to carpooling and other HOVs is best effected through a tandem action of HOV incentives and SOV disincentives. The *conversion* of existing lanes to HOV lanes is such an action. However, when *additional* HOV lanes are built, HOVs that already travel in existing lanes transfer to them; this reduces congestion in the general-purpose lanes and makes them more attractive for SOVs. Given the additional highway capacity and a choice, many travelers opt to leave carpooling and use SOVs for their own convenience. This is true not only for some of the trips previously made in HOVs but also for new trips (Leman et al. 1994; Vuchic et al. 1994).

To summarize, the "convert-a-lane" concept is an HOV-incentive/SOV-disincentive measure that is very effective in achieving diversion of travel from SOVs to HOVs. The "add-a-lane" concept—construction of additional highway capacity in the form of HOV lanes—represents an HOV-incentive/SOV-incentive measure, so that in most cases SOVs remain more rather than less attractive relative to HOVs. This has been corroborated by data showing increased SOV volume after the introduction of HOV lanes—for example, on Interstates 5 and 405 in the Seattle area (PSRC 1995).

"Construction of new HOV lanes is beneficial to bus transit." In most cases, the opposite is true. While buses improve their speed and reliability due to lower congestion in HOV lanes, usually they lose more riders than they gain because reduced congestion in general-purpose lanes also makes driving SOVs more attractive. The result of additional HOV lanes is always an increase in VKT and, in many cases, a decrease in transit ridership (Leman et al. 1994).

"Parking pricing should be determined by free-market forces." This is true only where transportation has no major externalities. In metropolitan areas, however, parking in CBDs, commercial areas, and other major traffic generators is an important component of the transportation system and should be treated as such. The level and structure of parking rates should be established to reflect realistically the social and environmental costs that the use of cars in cities imposes on society. Parking charges can also be used as an effective tool to decrease peak-hour travel, to influence modal split, or to shift travel in the street network in implementing transportation system management.

"People think of ample parking as a component of urban livability." Where this opinion is dominant (Shoup 1997), it shows a lack of understanding by the public of the conflict between individual and social interests and the impacts of cars on cities. Personal attraction to abundant (and, if possible, "free") parking conflicts with implementation of a balanced intermodal transportation system—that is, it works *against* the goal of achieving a social optimum in intermodal distribution. Moreover, abundant parking is in conflict with the human orientation of urban areas. This is exemplified by most medium-sized U.S. cities, such as Syracuse (New York) and Dayton (Ohio), where parking garages are a dominant land use in the CBD. Garages and lots greatly decrease the area's attraction for pedestrians and human activities in general.

PEDESTRIANS, BICYCLES, AND NEIGHBORHOOD LIVABILITY

Pedestrian and bicycle modes of travel suffer mostly from neglect in the planning, design, and operation of streets and highways (Whitman 1998).

Some misconceptions contribute to the failure to realize the need for greater use of these modes and to understand their potential contribution to achieving efficient, livable cities. Traffic engineers working on the design of suburban shopping centers, arterials, and even neighborhood streets, often find not only neglect but negative attitudes toward pedestrians on the part of developers and some planners. For example, at several important intersections in suburban areas of Pennsylvania, the "pedestrian problem" supposedly is "solved" by signs that read "Pedestrians prohibited."

A culmination of anti-pedestrian attitude occurred in 1997, when New York's Mayor Rudy Giuliani closed several of the busiest pedestrian crossings in midtown Manhattan, supposedly to "remove obstacles to vehicles." The measure forced some pedestrians walking along an east–west street to cross three roadways instead of one at an intersection. Under pressure from truck and car lobbies, this measure was pushed through without consulting the city's transportation authorities. It was condemned by virtually all professionals in the city and across the country.

In the past, bicycle users faced a similar attitude in Philadelphia, New York, and many other cities. Only during the 1990s did policies and actions toward these modes begin to change from largely restrictive to positive and encouraging ones.

Several typical misconceptions about these modes are discussed.

"Elimination of pedestrians from streets increases safety." False. The opposite is true. A street design that neglects pedestrians may create less safe walking conditions than streets with adequate sidewalks, crossings, and signals, especially when vehicular traffic is heavy and there are few pedestrians. Moreover, streets with few pedestrians and thus less "street life" have higher crime incidence than streets with lively activities. This, of course, is only one factor in street safety; others are the social and economic factors that often have the dominant role in safety and security.

"There is no need for pedestrian facilities in auto-oriented suburbs." Wrong. This myopic view often turns into a self-fulfilling prophecy. Absence of pedestrians in suburban areas is to a large extent a consequence of the lack of safe and convenient walkways, street crossings, or protected, pedestrian-friendly areas around schools, hospitals, theaters, or stores. This is an unfortunate result of the car-only orientation in land-use planning and design. Actually, when pedestrian facilities exist, they are used by school children, those going to nearby destinations, and people walking or jogging for recreation. This is the case not only in older suburbs built prior to the car-dominance era but also in recently built pedestrian zones, transit-oriented

developments, and other pedestrian-oriented areas, regardless of the extent of car ownership. Pedestrian movements and activities continue to be a vital element of the life of every city and a basic element of its livability.

"Bicycles are specialized recreational vehicles, not a significant mode of transportation." Wrong again. This view, dominant a few decades ago, has been drastically revised since the 1970s, following a dramatic increase in bicycle ownership and use. Towns and cities that have developed bicycle facilities have often had positive results in increasing bicycle use. Although in North America the bicycle will never approach the role it plays in such countries as Denmark or Germany, many towns, cities, and suburban areas can facilitate and encourage its use and thus bring significant benefits to riders and the community.

Particularly high potential for bicycle use exists around schools and campuses, in areas with concentrated employment, and for commuters to rail transit stations in suburban areas. Excellent examples in the United States of how good planning, ordinances, and police actions can be used to stimulate use of bicycles are two university towns: Davis, California, and Boulder, Colorado. In these cities, bike lanes, exclusive paths, and auxiliary facilities make the bicycle an extremely attractive, practical, and environment-friendly mode for a diverse group of urban travelers.

"Bicyclists are a nuisance and a danger to pedestrians." This can be true, at least in cities where the police exert no control over bicyclists' behavior. Upgrading and encouragement of bicycle use must include not only improved conditions for bicyclists but also enforcement of bicycle travel laws and regulations, which exist in all states but which are ignored in many cities.

BUS TRANSIT

Buses—the most widespread mode of transit— are often viewed as a group of vehicles that can be deployed in multiple services with a modest investment, little preparation, and frequent change of routes. The system aspect of bus service—the need to upgrade buses from operation in mixed traffic to preferential or exclusive facilities—is often neglected. Many statements tend to overestimate some features of buses (such as "flexibility") or underestimate the need to upgrade them through preferential treatments and facilities (Vuchic et al. 1994). Examples of these misconceptions are given here.

"Buses are cheaper and offer better service than rail." It is true that buses require far less investment than rail transit modes if they run on the streets. However, buses cannot attract many passengers who have cars available because they travel more slowly than cars and may be unreliable. If, however, their level of service is greatly improved through the construction of busways, the cost advantage of buses is diminished while most of the disadvantages (in comparison to rail) – lower capacity, service quality, and labor productivity – remain.

Under certain conditions, bus systems utilizing traffic priorities and exclusive busways may require lower investment than rail, as well as offer excellent service. The best examples of such systems are those of Ottawa and Curitiba. The conditions in both cities that made such upgrading possible include rational planning, effective plan implementation, strong transit priority policies, and continuous police control and enforcement. In the United States, however, these conditions do not exist. Actually, the trend in the United States has been to reduce bus priorities and virtually destroy the concept of busways by converting them into HOV lanes. Bus services in HOV facilities tend to be commuter services (rather than regular transit services) that have no distinct image and do not offer the superior service of the Ottawa system.

It should be reiterated here that, in general, it does not make sense to compare modes solely with respect to costs while ignoring levels of service and consequent passenger attraction. The fact that streetcars are cheaper than metros is never used as a basis for claiming that they are a "better" transit system. Saying that buses are cheaper than rail – implying that as a mode they are superior – is similar to saying that bicycles or motorcycles are better than cars because they involve lower costs!

"Conversion of busways into HOV facilities increases highway capacity without adversely affecting bus service." Not true. Highway capacity is increased, but the benefits are accrued by high-occupancy cars as well as by SOVs, while buses experience significant losses. First, their performance is negatively affected by additional traffic in their lanes, instead of buses with professional drivers only. Second, buses lose riders because their competitiors – vans and SOVs – have become more attractive (the latter often "steal" passengers at bus stops to qualify as HOVs for entry into the HOV facility!). Third, buses lose riders because their image as an exclusive, high-performance transit facility is diminished. In the long run, these conversions have practically eliminated the concept of exclusive busways in the United States. Pittsburgh remains the only city with a sizeable network of busways.

"HOV lanes are more effective than rail in improving transit." A confusion of concepts. Buses on HOV lanes do involve lower investments than rail, but they provide only commuter, rather than regular, transit services. Also, they follow freeway corridors, which generally are not close to passenger destinations: land uses along freeways seldom have pedestrian-oriented traffic generators. Therefore, bus lines on HOV facilities tend to have few or no stops along the way. Their role can be significant for commuting to one or a few points, but they cannot provide line and network-wide services, as buses on busways and rail systems do.

Bus transit in HOV facilities has virtually no potential to be a catalyst for land-use intensification or aesthetic improvements of local communities.

"People will not transfer; transit must provide direct service, and buses can do that better than rail." An incorrect generalization. Passenger resistance to transfers between transit lines varies greatly with the type of service. People strongly resist transferring between two infrequent and unreliable bus lines on a street corner without a shelter or bench. The most successful transit systems, in contrast, are those that consist of frequent, high-quality service on trunk lines coordinated with feeders in suburbs and integrated stations in the center city. Transfers are then convenient, resulting in more attractive travel than on transit networks that consist of numerous infrequent lines. Consequently, transit can better compete with car travel not by copying its door-to-door routing (which it can never match) but by providing opportunities for flexible travel throughout an integrated network with convenient, rapid transfers. It is preferable that stations and other transfer facilities be designed to incorporate amenities and various services, stores, banks, and restaurants.

The superiority of the transit network type with fewer, frequent lines relying on transfers over the network with numerous, infrequent lines is demonstrated by the fact that cities with the highest transit-riding habit (annual trips per capita), such as Boston, Paris, Toronto and Zürich, generally have transit systems with the highest transfer ratios. Similarly, bus networks that consist of numerous routes in suburbs funneling into a trunk busway or HOV facility for fast travel, and then distribution on several streets in the CBD, have far lower ridership than metro lines that rely on many transfers from feeders but more than compensate for this inconvenience with frequent, reliable, and comfortable rail lines.

These two types of networks and methods of operation are not necessarily identified with either bus or rail. The inferiority of multiple infrequent routes, compared to few frequent lines, is not inherently a liability of buses. Competently designed transit networks often consist of trunk lines with frequent service and separate feeders, even when both sections are served by buses, as is true of the network in Curitiba, the Denver Downtown Shuttle, and Portland's timed-transfer system.

"Buses are flexible; rail lines do not go where people go." Several theoretical studies have been written in the United States in recent decades arguing that buses, because of their smaller unit size and their ability to travel on any highway or street, can provide better coverage and more diversified service than rail—and at a lower cost. However, actual studies selecting modes for individual cities—for example, Washington, Atlanta, Portland, and Vancouver—as well as studies comparing actual rail and bus systems (Vuchic and Stanger 1973; Vuchic and Olanipekun 1988) show the following:

- The ability of buses to operate on highways and streets, while an advantage, also is a major disadvantage when they are compared to rail. It is much more difficult to provide a separate right-of-way (ROW)—B or A—for buses than for rail transit. Without a separate ROW, buses can never provide service that is competitive with cars with respect to speed and reliability.
- Capital investment is much lower for buses on streets than it is for rail on a separate ROW. If buses are upgraded, however, the investment for separate rights-of-way and large stations becomes much greater, similar to that required for rail systems. Operating costs for buses on heavily traveled lines are much higher than for rail systems due to their labor-intensiveness.
- Even though buses can cover many different routes, the most effective bus service usually consists of trunks and feeders (similar to rail) because trunk line service provides much greater frequency, reliability, and economy than a large number of "flexible" lines with infrequent service and inconvenient transfers.
- A study of bus and rail service in similar areas shows that buses are much less attractive to passengers than rail transit. In the New Jersey suburbs of Philadelphia, a single 22-km (14-mile) rail line (PATCO) attracts 40,000 weekday riders. In the same suburbs, 17 bus lines with 28 branches, with a network of 904 km (563 miles), attract only 30,000 weekday riders.

"Buses can reach a capacity of 24,000 persons per hour." Not on a regular line with stops. Buses can carry more than 10,000 persons per hour only when they have multiple exclusive lanes in each direction for organizing "bus platoons," large stations with overtaking lanes, and special supervision.

Volumes exceeding 20,000 persons per hour have been achieved only on highway sections without stops, such as the approach to the Lincoln Tunnel in New Jersey and a multistory Port Authority Terminal in Manhattan with more than 180 bus berths.

RAIL TRANSIT

As the highest-quality transit mode, one that interacts strongly with the functioning and livability of metropolitan areas, rail transit is a particular subject of criticism by those who emotionally oppose transit and defend present policies that favor car use. Some proponents of rail transit, however, also use overgeneralizations. Following are statements used in the debates in cities that have planned and constructed rail transit.

"Rail is a nineteenth-century technology." This belief, espoused by Melvin Webber and Adib Kanafani of the University of California, Kenneth Ogden of Monash University, and other opponents of rail systems, lacks merit. The best response to such a statement, when it was used to criticize the multimodal transit plan for Seattle, was given by Matoff (1995): "This is a meaningless argument. Cars are a nineteenth century technology. Highways are a second century A.D. technology. Universities are a twelfth century invention. Would anyone advocate that we don't need our highways or universities because they are old concepts?"

Modern rail systems utilize more state-of-the-art computer and electronic technology than is the case with any other surface transportation mode. They bear less resemblance to the old-time trolley car than modern automobiles do to a Model-T Ford. The high-speed rail system is as much a system of the future as is the freeway or ITS technology.

"Rail transit is suited only for large, high-density cities; it cannot serve auto-based cities in North America." This statement runs counter to numerous real-world experiences. An overwhelming majority of citizens and civic leaders consider rail transit systems built in recent decades—such as San Francisco's BART, the Montreal and Washington Metros, Philadelphia's PATCO, and LRT systems in San Diego, Calgary, Portland, Sacramento, and Baltimore—to be extremely successful. With the exception of emotional rail critics, the public in many low-density cities have supported the construction of new rail systems. Actually, the planning of many of these rail systems (for example, Portland, Sacramento and Buffalo) was initiated by citizens' groups and later adopted by metropolitan planning agencies.

With respect to population density, one of the most successful rapid transit lines in the United States is the PATCO line, which serves Philadelphia suburbs with populations of only 1,350 persons per square km (3,500 per square mile). This is a much lower density than those of many parts of Los Angeles, symbol of the low-density metropolis. The trend has been to adjust line characteristics to suburban conditions, and in recent years more cities in North America have built LRT and regional rail than rapid transit systems. The new rail systems are designed for low-cost operation and heavy reliance on access by car in low-density suburbs. For example, LRT lines in Calgary, San Diego, Sacramento, and Baltimore, and regional rail in Los Angeles, serve similar low-density areas with better financial results than do many older rail systems or new bus systems.

"Rail lines are fixed; they cannot be adjusted to changing demand." Correct. This is actually one of the main assets of rail transit: people prefer permanent, reliable service to service that changes on short notice. The permanence of rail facilities attracts development and gives this mode the potential for interdependence with various land uses—thus allowing a city to select from a much greater variety of development patterns than if only highways and bus transit were available. Moreover, heavily traveled corridors in which rail transit is built almost never have a decrease in travel that would require relocation of a line. In fact, over time, rail transit tends to build up activities around its stations, thus increasing the need for high-quality transit service.

"Rail transit is superior to other transit modes." This generalization must be carefully qualified. Rail transit does have higher capacity, comfort, reliability, and image than other modes; but this makes it superior to other modes only when these features are needed and are justified by high demand, constrained area, topographic conditions, desired impacts, and so on. Buses, paratransit, and other members of the family of transit modes are superior to rail under the conditions to which their features are best suited. In "overlapping areas"—that is, on the lines where rail and bus would provide comparable levels of service measured by such quantitative elements as speed, frequency, and reliability—rail generally attracts significantly higher ridership through its stronger image, permanence, comfort, ease of orientation, and other qualitative characteristics.

This is demonstrated by the fact that nearly all cities worldwide in which transit plays a major role have rail transit. Only a few cities have managed to apply similar high-quality planning and organization to achieve comparable features by using buses: Ottawa, Curitiba, Wiesbaden (Germany), and Copenhagen are examples. In many cities that have extensive metro and bus services, however, a substantial portion of riders use the metro only because of its easier orientation and stronger image. It is well known that the vast majority of visitors to Paris, London, New York, Seoul, and Tokyo use rapid transit extensively but avoid bus services, which are more difficult to understand. In fact, with the construction of rail systems in such cities as Washington, San Diego, and St. Louis, the overall image and usage of transit was greatly enhanced.

"Federal financing leads to overbuilding of rail transit." No, rail transit has not been overbuilt, because investments in it in the United States have never been abundant. Some facilities have been overdesigned but, by most standards, transit systems in U.S. cities are far less developed than those in all peer countries and fall far below the needs for establishing a balance between private and public transportation. Further, elaborate procedures for the selection of locally preferred transit projects are now in effect which, before ISTEA, were rarely applied to highway projects. The federal share of transit capital investments has always been significantly lower than that for interstate highways. Most transit projects are now usually negotiated for local contributions, and most receive federal capital assistance of 50 percent or less, whereas the Interstate Highway System was built with a 90 percent federal share and had much higher investment funds. Overdesign of interstate highways and their interchanges is fairly common, from sections of I-95 in Philadelphia to the Century Freeway in Los Angeles.

"Construction projects for rail systems always exceed their budgets." No more than other long-range investment projects that are subject to inflation and various construction standards, such as dams, highways, and power plants. Many rail projects have been constructed on schedule and on budget. Consideration must also be given to which budget figure is analyzed. Often, the initial rail line project is expanded to include street reconstruction, adjacent public areas, and so forth, increasing the value of the project to the city and therefore having an intentionally increased budget.

"Rail transit does not save energy." This is a major distortion of facts. First, the energy efficiency of different modes cannot be analyzed without consideration of where and under what conditions they operate. Wherever conditions for effective utilization of rail transit exist, this mode is more energy-efficient than most modes it replaces, particularly SOVs. Second, the most important factor is usually the long-run impact: rail transit promotes greater density of development, which results both in shorter trips and in significantly lower consumption of energy for all other purposes than exists in low-density developments (Holtzclaw 1994; Newman

and Kenworthy 1989; Pushkarev and Zupan 1980). Among the findings of these studies is the fact that general energy consumption per household is significantly lower in cities with multimodal systems than in low-density, car-based cities. A third relevant factor is that electric propulsion of rail systems reduces dependence on imported oil—a very important factor in many countries.

"New rail systems attract people from buses, not from cars." While a certain number of rail passengers come from buses that have been replaced by the new line, there is also a substantial increase in transit trips throughout the city, as well as on feeder bus lines to train stations. For example, records of the Washington Metropolitan Area Transit Authority show that total transit ridership in Washington, D.C., increased from 125 million per year in 1976, when the first Metro line was opened, to 240 million in 1989. This absolute increase in number of transit trips comes either from former users of cars or from new trips, which represent increased mobility. Finally, attraction of bus passengers to rail is not a negative phenomenon; it represents a significant and equitable social benefit because it improves the mobility of bus travelers, who typically impose the lowest social costs by their travel.

EMOTIONAL ANTI-RAIL TRANSIT CAMPAIGNS

Determining the role of different modes in urban transportation, as a very complex problem, reveals certain differences of opinion among transportation experts as well as amateurs, particularly those with specialized backgrounds in only one mode. Many highway and traffic engineers, transit experts, and bicycle specialists tend to favor *their* modes and thus have a limited understanding of other modes. Views about the roles of different modes are less one-sided and controversial among professionals with a broad transportation background who understand complex, multimodal urban transportation systems.

However, the frequent controversies over modes, such as "highway versus transit" and "rail versus bus," are not created so much by experienced transportation experts as by the extreme views of emotionally biased persons and lobbyists for individual modes or technological systems.

Particularly intense in most U.S. cities is the controversy concerning rail transit, which exerts a strong emotional pull on much of the population. One group—known as "rail enthusiasts"—admit that they are emotionally attracted to this technology and call themselves "rail fans" (short for "fanatics"). Rail technology, however, can trigger the opposite emotions: certain groups make concerted efforts to prevent the planning or construction of rail systems. In Great Britain, for example, the mission of an association called the "Railway Conversion League" was to eliminate intercity railways by paving them and turning them into highways. In the United States, many of these anti-rail fans claim that they have scientific proof that rail transit is inferior to other modes—that it is inefficient and should not be built in any city. Thus, while the professionals may debate under what conditions buses should operate on busways, or where LRT or regional rail would operate most favorably, or whether a line in Los Angeles or Vancouver should be a metro or an LRT, anti-rail fans claim categorically that rail transit is inferior to highway modes under all conditions and should never be built.

How does one recognize the anti-rail fans? Some of their typical claims and tactics follow.

- They consistently criticize plans for the construction of *any* rail transit mode—LRT, metro, or regional rail—claiming that no rail transit should exist in any American city. They admit only that old systems such the New York subway may be an "exception."
- They often base their "proof" that rail transit is inferior on theoretical models of hypothetical cities.
- They support the naïve claim that buses involve lower costs and can better serve low-density cities by operating on more extensive networks and with higher frequency than rail. With fewer transfers (which passengers supposedly do not tolerate), buses can attract more riders.
- Some free-market proponents, such as Alan Walters and Alan Armstrong Wright, formerly with the World Bank, claim that instead of rail, it would be more efficient to use not regular buses but jitneys of the type found in Manila, Damascus, and Bogota, on the grounds that they are "flexible" and require no subsidies.
- Anti-rail fans' arguments in favor of upgraded bus service are aimed primarily at preventing implementation of rail projects; when real improvements of buses, such as priorities, busways, and special terminals are proposed, they provide no support for them. Moreover, they usually favor conversion of busways to HOV facilities.

- They believe that the role of transit is to serve commuters between suburbs and downtown. Other trips are ignored because they can be better served by cars. The problem of lack of mobility for non–car owners is generally ignored.
- They strongly criticize government assistance to transit but usually do not mention much greater subsidies to highways and other modes. They ignore or downplay the negative impacts of auto traffic: congestion, air pollution, and decline in the quality of urban life.
- Arguing that present trends should not be changed, they fail to project how these trends will affect metropolitan areas and how future problems that are likely to arise will be solved.
- Finally, they ignore the trend toward construction of rail transit in cities worldwide simply by saying that conditions in the United States are different from those in any other country.

A large part of the anti-rail fans' arguments is produced by academics who deal in theory, have no training in the field of urban transportation systems, and do not cooperate with professional transit planners and operators. It is currently fashionable among some academics to criticize transit, as demonstrated by a stream of publications with extreme views and naïve support for their arguments. Examples illustrating this follow.

Confusion in comparing modes. Anthony Downs (1992) compares HOV *facilities* with rail transit *systems.* The former are sections of radial transit lines that typically serve commuters during peak hours, while the latter are systems offering all-day service between many points along their lines. Comparing such different concepts without mentioning the fundamental differences in the performance, roles, and markets is conceptually faulty, and the results can only be deceptive.

Melvin Webber (1977), following the model of Meyer, Kain, and Wohl (1965), claimed that buses on freeways and streets, operating as expresses and locals and serving many branch routes, could provide better service at much lower cost than San Francisco's BART. The bus system he hypothesized, however, is similar to that of the 1950s, when people in the Bay Area voted for BART because bus service could not meet the region's need for a high-performance transit system that would be competitive with car travel.

Rubin and Moore (1996) compare buses on streets with a metro system as if the two modes offered the same service and attracted the same number of riders. This classic example of comparing "apples and oranges" represents a fundamental conceptual fallacy. Not only transit experts, but also passengers using the two modes, as well as the general population, know how much they differ.

Hypothetical models of cities and transport systems. These models are easy to manipulate by changing assumptions to show any results an analyst wishes to reach. Deen (1973) noted that studies of this type have produced results that varied up to 1,000 percent from each other. Also, it has repeatedly been shown that using cost as the only criterion in comparing modes offering different types of service is fundamentally incorrect. (If consistently performed, such comparisons would yield the bicycle and motorcycle as optimal modes of urban transportation.) Finally, one cannot analyze the commuting of 30,000 persons from one corridor by car into the center city without considering the physical problem of accommodating the required twenty-lane freeway, along with its ramps, and the necessary 25,000 parking spaces—not to mention the livability aspects of such a city.

Unrealistic theoretical studies. The extent of the divorce of these transit critics from the real world is exemplified by Kain (1988) in an article about the choice of transit modes, published more than twenty years after his book with Meyer and Wohl (1965). During these two decades, transit-planning projects in dozens of cities in North America and around the world found rail transit to be the preferred mode. Passengers, political leaders, and citizens have expressed high praise for the rail systems of Atlanta, San Diego, Washington, D.C., and other cities. People have voted for new taxes for rail transit in many metropolitan areas, showing that the value of high-quality transit encompasses much more than considerations of cost. Clearly, this is contrary to theoretical modeling that finds that rail has no place in urban transportation.

Yet, Kain continues to defend the 1965 study. As "proof" of the correctness of this view, he quotes several subsequent studies that utilized the same [incorrect] methodology that he and his colleagues used in 1965—and, predictably, reached similar, though numerically divergent, results. He does not mention the fact that none of the studies of real-world systems produced results even remotely resembling his theoretical studies. As before, Kain is critical of all rail projects and considers their construction a mistake in all cases.

In his 1988 article, Kain first provides an explanation of why LRT was not included in the Meyer-Kain-Wohl (1965) study: the authors, he claims, found that LRT was under all conditions dominated by bus or by rapid transit. In other words, there is no place for LRT in urban transportation. The correct explanation is that LRT was unknown in the United States at the time of the study; if it had been, an assertion of its "dominance" by other modes would have been invalid, as subsequent developments have clearly shown.

Kain then admits that he still does not understand why LRT systems are being built. He attempts to define the differences between LRT and rapid transit as follows. Rapid transit has a third-rail power supply, whereas LRT uses an overhead wire. Therefore, he concludes, rapid transit must have a fully separated ROW, while LRT can use at-grade crossings. This is a confusion of system technology with functional characteristics. In reality, the basic system feature is ROW category (see chapter 2), and the method of power supply is a result of it, rather than power supply dictating the ROW! Moreover, it is not true that all rapid transit systems have a third-rail supply. Among others, rapid transit systems in Hong Kong, Tokyo, Cleveland—and even one line in Boston, Kain's hometown—have an overhead power supply; yet, they do not have grade crossings. LRT systems have an overhead power supply because they operate on ROW B and ROW C, rather than having crossings because of overhead wires.

This anti-rail propaganda seems to know no limits. In a recent publication, Rubin and Moore (1996) go so far as to claim that rail transit is not fast, that it does not have high capacity, and that it does not attract riders. These claims do not represent a different point of view; instead, they are distortions of numbers and physical facts about transportation systems.

Divorce from the real world. Although some theoreticians in various fields are not in direct contact with the real world, in the field of urban transportation, the gap between groups of theoreticians and actual transit systems is enormous. As shown, many academics perform theoretical research on unrealistic system concepts in hypothetical cities. Personal Rapid Transit (PRT) motions are analyzed on networks of aerial guideways in cities where they could not physically be accommodated; or, simplistic economic analyses of corridors where private cars carry 40,000 persons per hour are made without considering the physical aspects of accommodating a 30-lane freeway and parking facilities with 32,000 spaces. Members of these groups then mutually quote each other—but do not quote publications of transit professionals or real-world studies (Simon 1991). Thus, they manage to create an aura of "consensus." They have produced anti-rail statements such as "Rail is a nineteenth-century technology," "Americans will never leave their cars for transit," and many others which professionals dealing with urban transportation systems easily refute on the basis of real-world experience. The weakness of these rail critics' arguments is obvious from the lack of a realistic alternative to rail transit in their writings. Many of the bus systems they propose as solutions superior to rail would be physically impossible to operate.

The materials produced by anti-rail fans are used by lobbies interested in preventing any changes in the present situation of highway domination. Regardless of the numerous fallacies used in the anti-rail campaigns, and the obvious lack of practical validity of their proposals, the publications of these writers, who are presented as "transit experts," are distributed widely to public officials in many cities that are planning transit improvements, and to state legislatures, the U.S. Congress, and the media.

The role of ideology. Attacks on rail transit are strongly supported by most libertarians and by conservative organizations such as the Cato Institute and the Reason Foundation. Weyrich and Lind (1996), themselves among the country's leading conservatives, argue that this political stand of the conservatives represents an inherent paradox. Weyrich and Lind analyze systematically a number of anti-rail arguments and point out that while many arguments have some truth, they become false when taken to the extreme. For example, the car does bring freedom, but not when a great many people use it in a high-density area. Additionally, while the car enhances mobility, it also disperses families and society, while transit and pedestrian areas enhance society and the family. Most important, they point out that "The dominance of the automobile is not a free-market outcome, but the result of massive government intervention on behalf of the automobile. . . . Without government intervention, public transit might have a substantially higher market share than it now enjoys" (Weyrich and Lind 1996).

Weyrich and Lind further point out that, by one-sided subsidies to highways over several decades, "[government] intervention was especially severe in terms of its [negative] effects on rail transit, which is better able than bus to offer a quality of service competitive with automobiles." They contradict the notion of Americans having a "love affair" with the automobile, noting that

> [T]he current dominance by the automobile in the U.S. would not have arisen without public policies that both directly and indirectly encouraged Americans to use the automobile. Large subsidies to suburbanization and auto use over many decades in the United States have made auto use very appealing if not irresistible. Since the same policies contributed to the decline of mass transit, that alternative was eliminated for most Americans anyway.

Although succinct, the Weyrich and Lind study is much broader in its scope, historic and future perspective, and systems view of urban transportation than the one-sided anti-transit writings it challenges and proves inconsistent in approach, economic analysis, and philosophy. The authors call for an informed dialogue between conservatives and transit authorities.

Returning to the general controversy in urban transportation, it is time to broaden the view and discussion. Instead of the emotional attacks on rail transit by anti-rail fans and special interest groups, there is a need to see transportation systems and their relationship to cities as a totality. It is also time that academics in this country accept the challenge to step out of their ivory tower with respect to urban transportation and get in touch with the real world. Instead of studies aimed at proving that present-day trends are inevitable and that nothing can be done to change them, these theoreticians should increase their efforts to contribute to innovations and improvements in cities. Inventing and implementing new solutions is more difficult than arguing against changes; creative, rather than negative, thinking, however, is a basic duty of academics.

NON-CONVENTIONAL TRANSIT MODES

Non-conventional transit modes often attract attention because of their innovative image and exotic features. It takes considerable understanding of transportation systems to distinguish their advantageous features from the features that make them inferior to conventional modes or even, in one case (personal rapid transit, or PRT), functionally infeasible. There are entire modes that are conceptually unsound but that attract the attention of the public. Promotional efforts by some inventors, as well as the naïve views of inexperienced theoreticians, often cause confusion and costly delays when cities intend to develop new transit systems. Selected misleading statements are briefly reviewed here.

"Monorails, AGT, and PRT are modes of the future." The popular view that the solution to present-day urban transportation problems lies in new technology is for the most part incorrect, because these problems have been created by incorrect policies rather than by inadequate technology. The potential of these non-conventional modes is briefly described.

Monorails have been known and enjoyed popularity as a concept ever since their introduction in science fiction as early as 1900. Today, there are several dozen monorail systems worldwide, of which about a dozen are regular transit lines; most are in Japan. Monorail has some attractive features, among them, public appeal; but it is usually much less efficient and practical than a rail system.

Automated Guided Transit (AGT) systems, also popularly known as "people movers," are increasingly being used for short-haul transportation, particularly in airports, major activity centers, university campuses, fairgrounds, and so on. Since 1980, several have been installed and used as small-scale rapid transit systems (for example, automated rail systems in Vancouver, London-Docklands, and Detroit, and automated rubber-tired systems in Kobe, Osaka, Lille, Miami, Taipei, and Toulouse). Although their use is likely to increase, there probably will be no rapid proliferation of these systems because of their considerable investment costs.

Personal Rapid Transit (PRT) is claimed by its promoters (J. Edward Anderson, President of Taxi 2000 Corporation, and Jerry Schneider of the University of Washington, among others) to combine the advantages of rapid transit and private cars. Actually, this is an imaginary system based on an operationally and economically infeasible concept (elaborate infrastructure, yet low capacity) and has no realistic potential for application in urban transportation.

PEER COUNTRIES AND THE UNITED STATES

As was shown in chapter 4, the differences in urban transportation policies and actions between the United States and its peer countries are rather dramatic. The result, with respect to the livability of metropolitan areas, is generally not favorable for the United States. Yet, some U.S. Department of Transportation (DOT) officials have stated that there are no fundamental differences between the United States and its peers in transportation policy. This obviously incorrect claim is supported by explanations that defy reality.

"There is no fundamental difference between Europe and the United States in urban transportation conditions and trends. In spite of all efforts to balance modes, European countries continue to follow the same trends." Anyone who visits other industrialized countries can see that this statement is false. Yet, this conclusion about transportation policies and developments in the peer countries of the United States was used by a delegation of highly placed U.S. DOT officials who visited several European countries in 1994 to explain divergent U.S. attitudes and policies. Although the basic trends of auto ownership, growth of suburbs, and so on, are similar in all developed countries, the fact is that the rate of change, as well as the level at which the rate stabilizes, is quite different. Even more significant is the fact that the attitudes and policies in peer countries are similar to those defined in ISTEA but contrary to those followed in practices prevalent in the United States.

TABLE 5.1
Impacts of Policies Balancing Transportation Modes: Examples of Munich and Stuttgart
(in percent)

Modes	Munich			Stuttgart		
	1976	*1992*	*Percent Change*	*1976*	*1990*	*Percent Change*
Pedestrian	31	24	-7	34	28	-6
Bicycle	6	15	+9	2	6	+4
Car	42	36	-6	48	43	-5
Transit	19	25	+6	16	23	+7
Travel distance, km/person/day	21	22	+1	not available	not available	-

Source: Socialdata, 1991, 1992

As an illustration of the differences in trends, the results of the policies aimed at balancing transport modes in peer countries are far different from the results of practices that stimulate car use in U.S. metropolitan areas. Table 5.1 shows that from the mid-1970s to the early 1990s, Munich reduced the share of car travel by 6 percent, while transit share increased by the same percentage. In Stuttgart, car use decreased by 5 percent while transit use increased by 7 percent. Similar successes in reaching a desirable balance have been recorded in Oslo, Zurich, and several other European cities.

During October 1982, the introduction of zonal fares to replace sectional fares in London, along with a fare reduction of 32 percent, resulted in a ridership increase of 30 percent. In March 1983, a 96-percent increase in fares resulted in a major ridership loss. Similarly, in 1985, the advent of the "Capital Card," which introduced intermodal transfers, quickly boosted ridership on both the regional rail Network Southeast and the Underground (Mackett 1995).

These examples show that urban transportation policies can have a major impact on modal split, travel patterns, and, ultimately, the livability of cities. Claims that nothing can change the pressure for car use in cities have been discredited by the experiences of various countries, as well as by some North American cities. Portland, Oregon, for example, has applied coordinated, mutually supporting policies to land use and transportation planning in an effort to strengthen its central area. The increased livability of cities such as Edmonton, Calgary, and Vancouver can be traced back to new planning concepts and an emphasis on the modernization of transit systems, as well as their intermodal integration.

"Political realities do not allow the introduction of auto-use disincentive measures." This argument, expressed by Anthony Downs (1992), Martin Wachs (1993), and several others, is a euphemism, an excuse for avoiding actions that would result in changes to present practices. Naturally, any measures that impose a change in human behavior are resisted by some among those directly affected. Popular support, however, can be achieved when people become aware of the system aspects, rather than considering only their individual interests. When people realize that there is a serious crisis in the transportation system, and that only major changes in the behavior of travelers can lead to improvements, they will support the necessary changes. It must also be borne in mind that car-use disincentives are much easier for the public to accept if there are complementary incentives to use alternative modes (Hope 1996).

The United States's peer countries have a much greater awareness of issues related to the quality of life and to long-range social goals with respect to metropolitan areas. Better education of the public about these issues in the United States is a sine qua non for reaching a constructive consensus on the goals and policies of urban transportation.

References

Adler, Jerry. 1995. Bye-bye, suburban dream. *Newsweek* (May 15). pp. 40–45.

Aschauer, David Alan. 1991. *Transportation spending and economic growth – the effects of transit and highway expenditures.* Washington, DC: American Public Transit Association.

Bank of America et al. 1995. *Beyond sprawl: new patterns of growth to fit the new California.* San Francisco, CA: Bank of America.

Burrington, Stephen H. 1994. *Road kill: how solo driving runs down the economy.* Conservation Law Foundation (CLF), Boston, MA. May.

Deen, Thomas. 1973. Discussion of the article by Miller et al., "Cost comparison of busway and railway rapid transit." *HR Record* 459: 10–12.

Downs, Anthony. 1992. *Stuck in traffic: coping with peak-hour traffic congestion.* Washington, DC: Brookings Institution.

(The) *Economist*. 1996. Taming the beast—living with the car. June 22. pp. 3–18.

Goodwin, Philip B. 1996. *Extra traffic induced by road construction: empirical evidence, economic effects, and policy implications*. Roundtable 104, European Conference of Ministers of Transport, Paris, France. November.

Holtzclaw, John. 1994. *Using residential patterns and transit to decrease auto dependence and costs*. San Francisco, CA: Natural Resources Defense Council. June.

_____. 1995. Convenient cities. Presentation at Green Fleets Project Workshop #3, Chicago, IL. September.

Hope, Richard (interviewer). 1996. Kinnock charts path to rail's comeback. *Railway Gazette International* (February): 74–76.

Hylton, Thomas. 1995. *Save our land, save our towns*. Harrisburg, PA: PB Books.

Johnson, Elmer W. 1993. *Avoiding the collision of cities and cars: urban transportation policy for the twenty-first century*. Chicago, IL: American Academy of Arts and Sciences and the Aspen Institute.

Kain, John F. 1988. Choosing the wrong technology: or how to spend billions and reduce transit use. *Journal of Advanced Transportation* 21, 3: 197–213.

KPMG Peat Marwick. 1994. Executive summary. The impact of Metrorail on the Commonwealth of Virginia. Prepared for the Northern Virginia Transportation Commission.

Lee, Douglass B. 1995. Full cost pricing of highways. Paper presented at the 74th annual meeting of the Transportation Research Board (TRB), Washington, DC.

Leman, C. K.; P. L. Shiller; and K. Pauly. 1994. *Rethinking HOV: high-occupancy vehicle facilities and the public interest*. Annapolis, MD: Chesapeake Bay Foundation.

Lowe, Marcia D. 1993. Smart cars: a really dumb idea. *Seattle Times*. December 16.

Mackett, Roger L. 1995. Railways in London. *Transport Review* 15, 1: 43–58.

Matoff, Thomas. 1995. Without rail transit, Puget Sounders aren't moving ahead. *Seattle Post-Intelligencer*. September 12.

Meyer, J.; J. Kain; and M. Wohl. 1965. *The urban transportation problem*. Cambridge, MA: Harvard University Press.

Newman, P., and J. Kenworthy. 1989. Gasoline consumption and cities: a comparison of U.S. cities with a global survey. *Journal of the American Planning Association* 55: 23–37.

Persky, J.; E. Sclar; and W. Wiewel. 1991. *Does America need cities?* Washington, DC: Economic Policy Institute.

Project for Public Spaces, Inc. 1997. *The role of transit in creating livable metropolitan communities.* TCRP Report 22. Washington, DC: Transportation Research Board (TRB).

Puget Sound Regional Council (PSRC). 1995. *Trends.* Seattle, WA: PSRC. October.

Pushkarev, B. S., and J. M. Zupan. 1980. *Urban rail in America.* Bloomington, IN: Indiana University Press.

Rubin, T., and J. E. Moore. 1996. *Ten transit myths.* Los Angeles, CA: Reason Foundation.

SACTRA. 1994. *Trunk roads and the generation of traffic.* London, UK: Department of Transport, Her Majesty's Stationery Office (HMSO).

Salomon, Ilan, and Patricia L. Moktarian. 1997. Why don't you telecommute? *Access* 10 (Spring): 27–29. Berkeley, CA: University of California Transportation Center.

Shoup, Donald C. 1997. The high cost of free parking. *Access* 10 (Spring): 2–9. Berkeley, CA: University of California Transportation Center.

Simon, Jesse. 1991. Let's make forecast and actual comparisons fair. *TR News* 156: 6–9 (September–October).

Socialdata. 1991. Verkehr in Stuttgart: Kennziffern der Mobilät. Verkehrs- und Tarifverbund Stuttgart, Germany. p. 10.

_____. 1992. München setzt auf den Umweltverbund. Munich, Germany.

Sperling, Daniel. 1995. *Future drive: electric vehicles and sustainable transportation.* Washington, DC: Island Press.

Stanger, Richard, et al. 1995. Report on the status of the Metrolink system with emphasis on the MTA's costs and benefits. Southern California Regional Rail Authority, Los Angeles, California.

Transportation Research Board. 1997. *Toward a sustainable future.* Special Report 251. Washington, DC: Transportation Research Board (TRB).

Urban Transportation Monitor (UTM). 1993. Numerous statistical data and information items. Burke, VA: Lawley Publications. October.

Vuchic, Vukan R., and Shinya Kikuchi. 1994. *The bus transit system: its underutilized potential.* Final Report No. DOT-T-94-20. Washington, DC: Federal Transit Administration.

Vuchic, Vukan R., and O. Olanipekun. 1988. Lindenwold Rail Line and New Jersey Transit buses: a comparison. *TR Record* 1266: 123–128. Washington, DC: Transportation Research Board.

Vuchic, Vukan R., and R. M. Stanger. 1973. Lindenwold Rail Line and Shirley Busway—a comparison. *HR Record* 459: 13–28. Washington, DC: HRB.

Wachs, Martin. 1993. Learning from Los Angeles: transport, urban form, and air quality. *Transportation* 20: 329–354.

Webber, Melvin. 1977. *The BART experience: What have we learned?* Monograph No. 26. Berkeley, CA: University of California, Institute of Urban and Regional Development.

Weyrich, Paul M., and William S. Lind. 1996. *Conservatives and mass transit: Is it time for a new look?* Washington, DC: Free Congress Foundation and American Public Transit Association.

Whitman, Christine T. 1998. Inauguration speech, Trenton, New Jersey, January 20.

6

Transportation Policies for Livable Cities

The relationship between a transportation system as a service function and all other activities (economic, social, quality of life, recreation, and so on) is very complex and seldom adequately understood. In the four levels of urban transportation planning and operation, two levels—individual projects and modal systems (Levels IV and III)—are usually completed competently and efficiently. However, coordination among modes, as well as relationships between transportation and other activities (Levels II and I), is seldom satisfactory. In addition to insufficient understanding of the interactions between transportation and different land-use activities, coordination at these higher systems levels is complicated by different governmental jurisdictions and financing sources, as well as by differences in the professional backgrounds of experts. Moreover, different emotional proclivities among modally oriented transportation professionals often prevent efficient planning at Levels II and I.

A review of different metropolitan areas illustrates this situation. Remarkable designs and efficient systems involving individual modes are found in many cities: freeway systems in Los Angeles and Houston, a pedestrian walkway system in Minneapolis, the Metro in Washington, and a bus system in Ottawa—are all well designed and operated. Only cities that have had strong activities at Levels II and I, however, have achieved balanced multimodal transportation systems and integrated them with other activities. This is demonstrated by the fact that all cities known for their livability and efficient transportation services have a high degree of intermodal coordination. They tend to have coordinated financing of different modes, as well as land-use planning that integrates transportation not only in plans, but in their effective implementation. Examples are Portland (Oregon), Toronto, and Stockholm.

For a long time, the complex role and impacts of transportation on cities, particularly since the wide use of private cars began, was not understood. For example, street and highway congestion was believed to indicate that additional capacity was required; it appeared logical that streets should be widened and new highways built. It took years of experience, successes, and failures to learn that capacity increase is desirable only when it causes no excessive negative impacts. Looking at the entire system's impact on the city (Level I), provision of greater highway system capacity generates ever-increasing sprawl of low-density land uses, which leads to ever-greater volumes of vehicular travel, especially in situations where driving and parking are subsidized in various ways. Continuous expansion of highway and parking capacity is therefore neither desirable nor feasible. The question of how much capacity to add so that damage to the urban area and the environment is not excessive is very complex and should be given careful attention in each metropolitan area.

Another example of learning through experience occurred with the introduction by many cities of a requirement that with construction of any new building, a certain number of parking spaces must be provided. Again, this is a farsighted policy when applied appropriately. But it took several decades for planners to realize that increasing parking is counterproductive when applied to large cities that need to discourage the use of cars. For this reason, in some cities this regulation was not only abandoned, but reversed. London, for example, changed from requiring a certain minimum number of parking spaces (a policy to increase the parking supply), to prescribing the maximum number of parking spaces that may be provided with any new construction (a policy to prevent an increase of the parking supply). Numerous other cities (for example, Boston, Hamburg, and Ottawa) have for many years had limitations on the parking capacity in their central areas; they consider this regulation to be the most effective tool for achieving a desirable intermodal balance and for control of the flow of cars into the central urban area.

Partial solutions or pressures from individual industries to apply their particular products to urban transportation systems and the developments they influence also often lead to activities at the project and mode level (Planning Levels IV and III), without consideration for the overall system aspects and impacts on the city (Levels II and I). For example, the extensive Intelligent Transportation System (ITS) program lacks adequate policy consideration. If freeway capacity is increased, what is the impact of such a change on local streets, on other transport modes, and, most important, on the livability, sustainability, and environment of cities? In many cases, these neglected larger system questions are more important than individual projects and technology developments.

In spite of the many complex questions and unresolved issues, a considerable base of knowledge and experience has been developed regarding transportation and cities. Knowledge and experiences do vary from city to city and country to country (see the review of international developments in chapter 4).

To find solutions to current problems, it is necessary to pay much greater attention to Levels II and I of urban transportation—that is, to take a broader look and treat transportation as a functional system that consists of different modes, interacts with different activities, and influences the character of cities. The process of evaluating transportation in a city or area, of defining the goals and requirements for its improvement and achievement of a livable environment, is discussed in this chapter.

TRANSPORTATION AND THE FUNCTIONING OF CITIES

It is true of all civilized societies that behavior which individuals would choose for their own personal benefit and desires does not always coincide with the societal interest. The condition that exists when all users make their own choices, known as individual equilibrium, or IE, usually is different from the social optimum, or SO. The conflict between the two must be reconciled by laws, regulations, pricing, or various other policy measures. This is the case, for example, with the behavior of individuals in public places, with limits on noise production in streets, and with design codes for buildings. Interestingly, this conflict has been resolved in many areas more effectively than it has been in transportation. The Clean Air Act and motor vehicle inspection requirements are two examples of advanced measures for promoting the social optimum.

In transportation, the problem of reconciling individual interests with those of society has been solved reasonably well at the level of traffic flow on streets, but not with respect to intermodal distribution. Traffic rules, which require individuals who are traveling to behave in a way that leads to the efficient and safe movement of multiple vehicles and persons, have long been used. Such measures include one-way streets, signal-controlled intersections, and regulation of pedestrian crossings. With respect to the

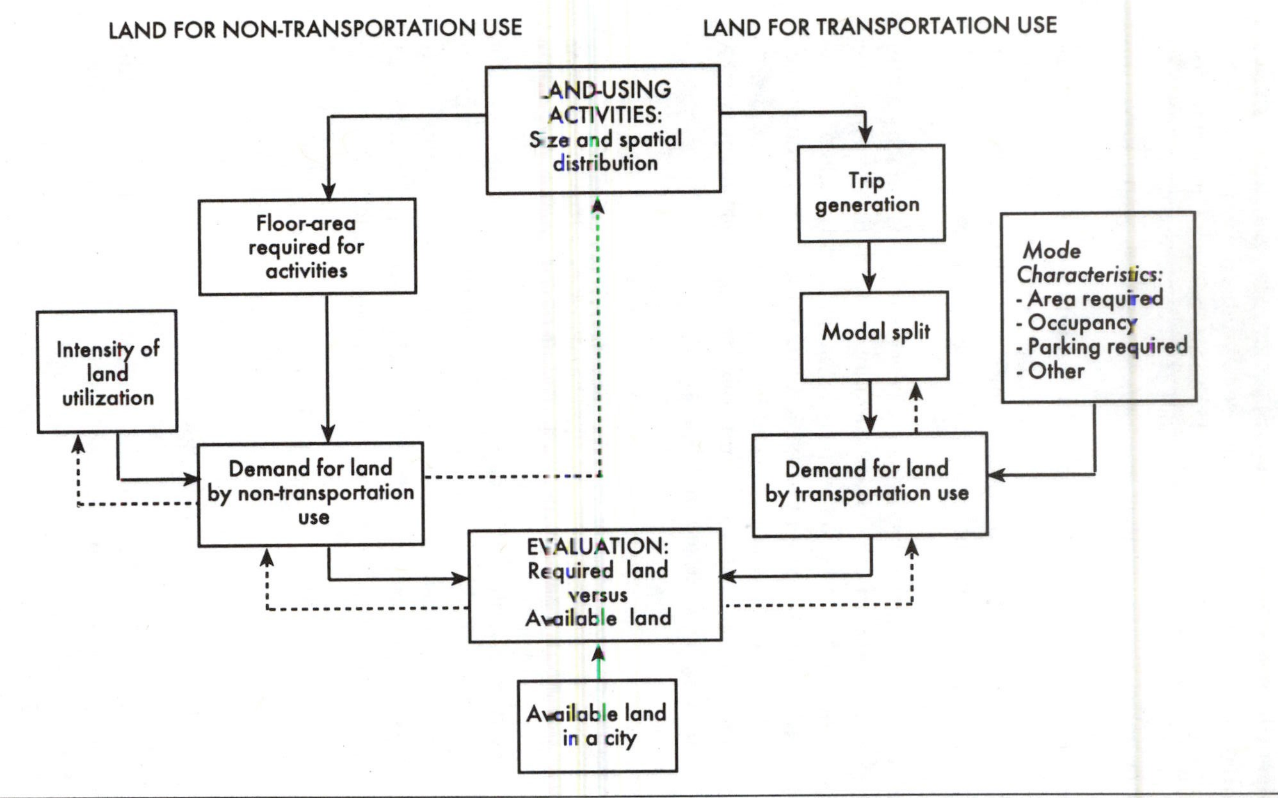

FIGURE 6.1
Distribution of urban land between transportation and other activities

Source: Shin 1997

use of different modes for travel, however, most regulations are still rudimentary. Travelers have no restrictions in choosing among modes, and they pay nowhere near the social costs they incur. For example, an individual can use a bicycle, motorcycle, small or large car, or even a truck or bus in a high-density area. Although the social costs of these modes vary greatly (and may be high), users pay no charges for driving or using street space. People do pay slightly varying charges for parking, though in most cases the parking structure and rates are determined by direct, free-market conditions that reflect neither short- nor long-term social costs or environmental impacts. This condition is exacerbated by the fact that public financing goes much more to the modes that are the least efficient and that impose the highest consumption of resources without paying corresponding charges.

Viewed in perspective, the basic problem of travel by car in urban areas is that it uses many times more space per unit of travel (person-km or person-miles) than other transportation modes. Moreover, parking, which is required at trip destinations, consumes areas greater than many activities, such as office work, themselves require. Thus, the two functions—activities (such as work, trade, services, housing, and recreation) and transportation—compete for the same available area in a city. A simple but conceptually important model, presented as a flowchart in figure 6.1 (Shin 1997), shows that the area occupied by each of the two functions depends on a number of factors. Land occupancy by various activities depends on the volume of activities, their nature (how much area each activity requires), and the intensity of land utilization—basically, how many floors the respective buildings have. The land occupied by transportation depends upon the volume of travel, the modal split, and the physical characteristics of each mode.

If the land occupied by the two functions is less than the total land available in a city (or certain area within a city), there is no problem in the performance of activities or the operation of the transportation system. If, however, the two need to occupy more land than is available, both the activities and transportation suffer from congestion and its resulting inefficiencies. This situation has occurred in many cities experiencing growth in population or activities, or where activities remained the same but the modal split changed; that is, travel shifted significantly from transit and walking to private car. As the demand for travel by car increases, transportation begins to suppress other activities, or even to displace them, thus causing their relocation to other areas. This chain of events results in the conversion of cities from centers of concentrated activity to dehumanized areas characterized by concentration of vehicles.

The increasing use of the private car is generally blamed as the central cause of transportation problems in the cities of industrialized countries. Actually, the car plays a basic role in personal transportation; without it, contemporary society could not function. The problem is its excessive use in densely populated areas where it is inherently inefficient, plus a failure to provide adequate levels of service by other modes of personal travel, primarily transit and pedestrian systems, which are more efficient than car travel in high-density areas. In short, transit and pedestrians make areas more efficient and more livable than does the private car.

The challenge of urban transportation, then, is to devise methods for implementing a transportation system that will reduce the present excessive dependence on the private car while providing more efficient transportation service that supports, rather than impedes, development of livable cities.

As shown in chapter 5, there is considerable controversy with respect to urban transportation policies and their goals. Special interest groups that benefit from car dominance and the resulting land developments on the outskirts of urbanized areas promote the continuation of laissez-faire policies. In many countries, particularly the United States, current transportation policies support the use of cars much more strongly than the use of other modes. When the problematic conditions resulting from current practices come into question, the promoters of these policies fall back on fatalism, admitting that a multimodal system would be superior to total car dominance, but claiming that "people will not sell their cars," and it is too late to make drastic changes anyway. This fatalism is strongly rejected by transportation and urban planners who promote balanced transportation and the advancement of livable, instead of fully car-dependent, cities. They support their claim that changes in policies and urban developments are possible by citing numerous examples of the successful implementation of rational policies and new concepts in urban design (UITP 1991; Girnau 1995; Project for Public Spaces 1997).

In the next section, the role of transportation is reviewed in order to develop specific goals and requirements for transportation systems in livable cities.

GOALS, REQUIREMENTS, AND COMPOSITION OF URBAN TRANSPORTATION SYSTEMS

Because of the strong interrelationship between transportation and cities, the basic goals of urban transportation systems should refer to the desired characteristics and type of city or urbanized area. Inefficient transportation—particularly the chronic traffic congestion of streets and highways, and the deteriorating conditions for transit users and for pedestrians—has contributed to the deterioration of urbanized areas, even during periods of population growth and spatial expansion. Central cities in particular have suffered; but suburban areas also increasingly face serious problems: traffic congestion exacerbated by residents' inability to make any trip without a car, the isolation of many population groups, and the resultant environmental deterioration.

In reaction to this trend and to the broadening crisis, the concept of the livable city has been developed and is increasingly mentioned as a goal for urban areas. As stated in a report by the Project for Public Spaces (1997), "Indeed, the avid interest in livability today seems to have emerged because people are increasingly recognizing the unlivable aspects of the places where they live, work, and spend recreational time."

The adjective *livable* for a city connotes a desirable quality of life for its citizens—including social activities, attractive public places, provision of a certain level of privacy, as well as a sense of community. In this discussion, the term *livable* is defined even more broadly, as encompassing the city's economic soundness, social health, and environmental viability. Such a broad definition is used because all these elements are interdependent. A city may be physically beautiful, but if it suffers from high unemployment, it probably will also suffer from crime and other social problems. Consequently, within the overall goal of achieving a livable city, three major sets of objectives can be defined as characteristics of such a city:

- *Human-oriented and environmentally friendly,* with features that make it attractive and make living in it convenient, safe, and pleasant; a high degree of sustainability is a component of this characteristic
- *Economically viable and efficient*
- *Socially sound*—that is, without social, economic, or ethnic barriers, or wide variations in income, crime, and unrest; there should be a sense of togetherness and pride in the city and region

A livable city is difficult to define precisely, but one can recognize elements that contribute to making an urbanized area livable. By the same token, one can quickly recognize the city that is nonfunctional, that is riddled with problems, that has no social life and few cultural functions.

Due to its numerous impacts on a city's functioning, as well as its social and environmental aspects, transportation is a basic element of livable cities. An *efficient transportation system* is necessary to meet each one of the three goals for urban livability. The definition of an efficient transportation system is also difficult to make concisely, because efficiency depends on each city's local conditions. In most cases, however, to be considered efficient, a transportation system must satisfy the following general requirements:

- Provide *service to all areas* where there is a need for transportation
- Be *available to all groups of people:* in the city and suburbs, to all age categories, all economic groups, to most categories of disabled persons, etc.
- Provide *local access to long-distance terminals* such as airports, railroad stations, and bus terminals, and interchanges with intercity freeways
- *Satisfy travel volume requirements, particularly to areas of major activity concentration*
- Have *satisfactory performance (e.g., speed, safety, reliability, comfort)*
- Involve *reasonable costs* and be *properly priced*
- Provide for efficient *movement of goods and deliveries throughout urban areas*
- Provide facilities and services that are *efficiently incorporated with a human-oriented urban environment,* accommodating the specific needs of residential, business, and shopping areas, historic objects, attractive sights, street life, etc.
- Stimulate *creation of desirable urban developments and forms*
- Have *low negative side effects*

Achieving an efficient system depends on several factors, including network form and its relationship to the form of city and land-use distribution, as well as macro and micro system design. It is clear from the list above, however, that no single mode can satisfy all requirements, particularly in large cities. For example, cities such as Los Angeles, Detroit, and Houston tried for decades to rely solely on cars/highways, and they faced diminished livability both in the central business district and in many suburban areas. Their metropolitan areas, relying almost exclusively on car and truck transport, faced growing problems arising from an escalation of highway congestion with no alternative modes of travel. Therefore, in planning an efficient transportation system for large cities, the most important decision is the selection of modes and their relative roles. For this purpose, some basic terms and concepts should be defined.

- A *unimodal transportation system* consists of one primary mode; all others play minor or negligible roles.
- A *multimodal system* is a set of transportation modes that operate in one city or metropolitan area. These modes may or may not be integrated.
- An *intermodal system* is a multimodal transportation system in which modes are integrated so that their efficiency is increased and passengers can easily make intermodal trips. Integration usually includes coordination of networks (streets and freeways, feeder and trunk lines, transfer points, complementary area coverage) and schedules, availability of joint fares, information about all modes, system image, and so on.
- A *balanced transportation system* is an intermodal system designed and operated so that each mode performs its role where it is most efficient. In other words, different modes are coordinated so that passengers can easily make intermodal trips, but each mode performs the role for which it is physically and operationally best suited. Thus, overall passenger convenience, as well as the technical/economic efficiency of the transportation system, is maximized. A balanced system thus represents the highest form of urban transportation.

The question then is, which combination of transportation modes can best satisfy the above-defined requirements in a given city?

POLICIES FOR ACHIEVING BALANCED TRANSPORTATION SYSTEMS

The desirable combination of modes for a specific city depends on its size and character. Generally, in a small city, the selection of modes should not be a major problem. Private transportation—consisting of walking, bicycles, and cars—can satisfy most needs without undue cost or negative side effects. The requirement for service availability to all population groups, however, necessitates some paratransit or transit services. These services

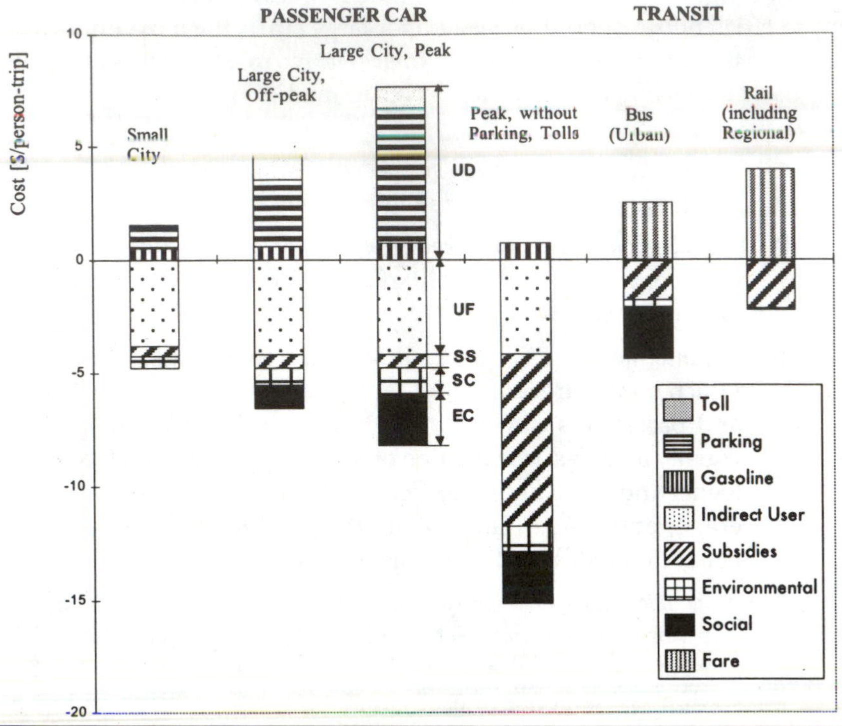

FIGURE 6.2
Total costs of urban travel by different modes and conditions

Note: Negative signs are used to distinguish indirect from direct costs; they do not imply negative values.

are especially important in cities with low car ownership or with a large non-driving population. When car ownership is high, small towns are the only place where a unimodal system—basically car/pedestrian/highway—may be adequate and efficient.

In medium-sized and large cities, the need for higher-capacity transit systems increases, while the requirements for large areas and the negative side effects of automobiles create serious problems. Thus, there is a need to implement a balanced transportation system. For this purpose, it is necessary to achieve a desired modal split, that is, to move the distribution of travel between modes from one of individual equilibrium toward one of social optimum.

For further analysis of intermodal relationships, referring mainly to large and medium-sized cities, the structure of costs or disutilities of travel by different modes will be utilized. The costs are illustrated as bars in figure

6.2. This diagram is based on the discussion in chapter 2, where costs are classified as user costs, subsidies, and unpaid costs (which consist of social and environmental costs). To highlight the costs that most influence modal choice, however, user costs are divided into direct and fixed costs, so that the following five categories are shown for six types of trips:

- *User direct costs* (UD), paid out-of-pocket, showing here gasoline, sometimes parking and tolls, and in the case of transit, fares
- *User fixed costs* (UF), paid by car owners independently of individual trips
- *Subsidies* (SS)
- *Social costs* (SC), including congestion costs
- *Environmental costs* (EC), including various impacts and externalities

Again, user direct costs are plotted above the horizontal line, to highlight them as the cost category most directly affecting user modal choice. The other four categories, which users tend not to consider strongly in choosing their modes of travel, are plotted below the line.

The diagram clearly shows the two cost aspects that stimulate the use of cars: 1) the extremely low share of direct costs in total user costs; and 2) the higher unpaid costs in large cities. The most flagrant case of unaccountable users, with respect to costs, is found for peak-hour driving in a large city when there are no tolls and parking is subsidized (the fourth bar). The paradox of car travel, which is very cheap for users but very expensive for society, is clearly illustrated by this case. To correct this unaccountability of car users, policies should be aimed at shifting some cost components from below the line—user fixed costs and unpaid costs—to the categories above the line, i.e., user direct costs.

Transit costs, plotted as the last two bars in figure 6.2, show only the fare above the horizontal line, whereas subsidies consist mainly of government contributions. The social and environmental costs per trip generally are much lower than the corresponding costs of car travel. The diagram shows a major problem in achieving a balanced intermodal distribution: even with subsidies, transit is often more expensive than car travel on an out-of-pocket basis because of the structure of car costs, particularly when parking is "free," i.e., when it belongs in the subsidies (shown by the fourth bar). Paid parking (the second and third bars) changes considerably the relative competitiveness of car and transit. Extremely low gasoline prices contribute greatly to the problem of user cost structure. This problem has been increasing in the United States in recent years because gasoline prices have actually decreased in constant dollars, while other user costs, especially vehicle depreciation and insurance, have been increasing.

In many countries, including the United States, policies aimed at making transit travelers pay a greater share of their costs have been introduced in recent years. Implementation of these policies has, in many cases, shifted some of the subsidy costs to fares—that is, from below the horizontal line to above it. Such a change would increase cost accountability for urban travel if a similar shift of costs were introduced for car travel. This could be done by increasing gasoline taxes, eliminating parking subsidies, placing a surcharge on parking rates, and so forth. However, if reduced transit subsidies are introduced while the direct costs of car travel remain low, an increase in transit fares is counterproductive because it would lead to a shift of modal split in favor of the car—i.e., to the less cost-accountable mode.

The fundamental issue of policies toward intermodal distribution of travel will be examined systematically here. Two aspects of transportation policies deserve careful attention, because they are critical to determining the intermodal composition of transportation in a city. First, what funding levels and degrees of mobility and accessibility should be provided? Second, what intermodal composition should the urban transportation system have?

The first aspect—the funding/mobility package—is the basic policy issue with regard to urban personal transportation or travel versus other activities in a city. Generally, low-cost, convenient travel has a stimulating effect on economic, social, and other activities, and for this reason it is often encouraged and subsidized. The transport of goods in urban areas, although less complex than personal transportation in its interactions with other activities, is sometimes subsidized because of its economic and developmental impacts. When subsidies are excessive, however, transportation tends to be overused at the expense of all other resources, such as energy, land, and user time. An additional problem is encountered when transportation causes major negative side effects for which users of the transportation system do not pay, as is the case with car use in urban areas.

The consequences of excessive subsidies become clear when the extreme solution is imagined: fully subsidized (often referred to as "free") transportation. With "free" transportation—that is, transportation with no user charges—the monetary cost of travel ceases to be a component in the cost of performing business, shopping, selecting recreational activity, and so on. The same effect, but with even more drastic consequences, would occur in freight transportation. For example, the construction industry would tend to purchase the cheapest gravel or coal in the country, regardless of its location, because transportation cost would be eliminated from its price. Thus, for a company, the transportation of goods over great distances may be economically attractive. However, the transportation provider, or society, would be paying for such uneconomical and inefficient transport of people or goods.

The present underpricing of car travel in urban areas and the extremely low share of user direct costs make car travel virtually free when it comes to making short-term decisions; thus, driving is stimulated to an excessive level. This condition also makes subsidies to transit necessary. Therefore, the question of the degree of subsidies and user payments in urban travel is an important one, although its complexity is often underestimated.

The second aspect, intermodal distribution of travel, is, to a greater extent than is commonly believed, a result of policies. Increasingly, analyses of urban transportation show that the emotional "love affair with the car" is, in the long run, a much smaller factor than policies that have strongly favored car travel and neglected its alternatives. For this reason, it is useful to consider a systematic and exhaustive analysis of policies toward different urban transport systems or modes.

To make the basic concept of intermodal relationships clear, several simplifications will be made. First, the discussion will again focus on two major modes: car/highway and transit systems. In a broader sense, this discussion can be extended to include other modes. Second, policies toward these two modes must be understood in the proper context. They do not imply, for example, that car-use disincentives would mean that all uses of cars would be discouraged by increasing their costs or making them inconvenient. Policies toward cars and transit for the most part refer to the categories of travel in which the two are interchangeable—that is, most users would be able to select either one, and policies would influence that choice. Third, the analysis will be based on a conceptual model of user disutilities. The bar charts used will be similar to those representing costs by different modes in figure 6.2, but here they will be broader, including the total costs, inconvenience, time, and other elements of travel. In other words, the bar charts in figure 6.4 will represent the inverse of the level and quality of service that users experience: the higher the bar, the less attractive the travel by that mode.

For the generalized, simplified model used here, policies of incentives and disincentives toward each of the two modes, car and transit, will first be analyzed. Thus, there is a matrix of four policies, shown as a sketch in figure 6.3 and, for convenience, designated by mode (car/transit) and by policy type (incentive/disincentive) as CI, CD, TI, and TD. These four

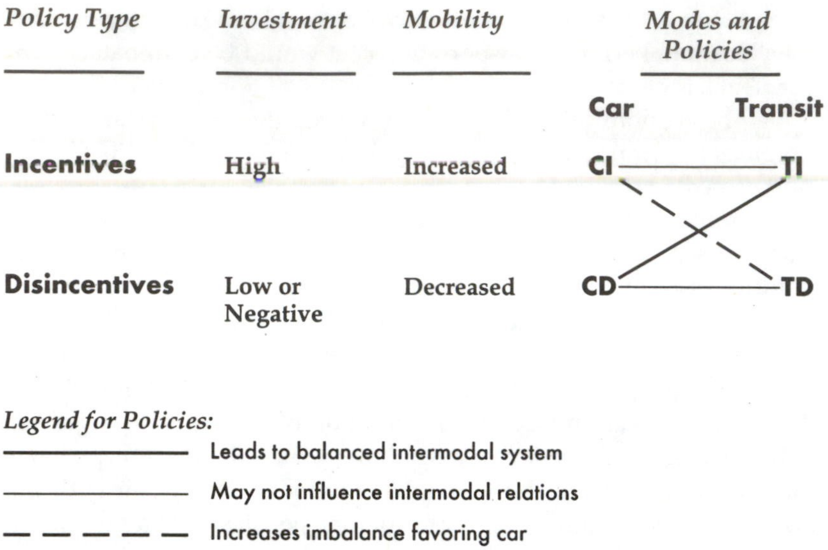

Policy Type	*Investment*	*Mobility*	*Modes and Policies*	
			Car	**Transit**
Incentives	High	Increased	**CI**	**TI**
Disincentives	Low or Negative	Decreased	**CD**	**TD**

Legend for Policies:

——— Leads to balanced intermodal system

——— May not influence intermodal relations

— — — — — Increases imbalance favoring car

FIGURE 6.3
Policies toward modes and their impacts on intermodal balance

policies will be defined here, then their combinations in implementation, shown by different lines in the figure, will be discussed.

CI – Car-use Incentives. These are policies and measures that make car travel faster and more convenient and parking easily available and cheaper. They are desirable and effective in areas with no space constraints. In urban areas, however, particularly in large cities, their application must be planned as a component of a total transportation development policy that is related to the functioning and character of the city (Level I). Excessive application of car incentives has been the primary cause of the present problems in many urbanized areas—reconstruction of cities with loss of their human orientation, underpriced car travel, extremely high total costs of transportation, and excessive negative impacts of cars on urbanized area environments.

CD – Car-use Disincentives. This set of actions consists of measures designed to make travel by car less attractive. These measures can be classified as *physical* (design or redesign of streets, which reduces or eliminates vehicular traffic); *regulatory/organizational* (prohibition of traffic from certain facilities); and *economic/pricing* (charges for driving or parking). Highways, freeways, streets, and parking facilities must again be considered integral components of car and truck transport. In the United States, these measures are often referred to collectively as Travel Demand Management, or TDM; in Europe, they are also known as "push measures" (for pushing people away from car uses) (Girnau 1995). In a broader sense, and in the long run, land-use planning that reduces car reliance and taxation on the purchase of vehicles, among other measures, belong in this category.

Effective implementation of car-use disincentives reduces the amount of vehicular traffic, or VKT (VMT), bringing savings and benefits. When faced with the lower attractiveness of car travel, users may consolidate tasks into multipurpose trips; other trips may be shared by travelers, resulting in carpooling, which increases average car occupancy. Some trips are switched to transit or other modes, when these are available; finally, many discretionary trips are made to closer locations or are not made at all. The cost of disincentives varies. Some require investments in construction or regulatory measures; others—such as increased parking charges and gas taxes—result in additional revenues. Thus, in some cases, government expenditures may in fact decrease.

TI – Transit-use Incentives. These "pull" measures consist of a variety of actions that make the use of transit modes more convenient, attractive, and economical. Short-term strategies in this category include regulatory changes giving transit vehicles preferential treatment, fare incentives and contributions to transit passes by employers or stores, improvements in transit information and marketing, and so on. Long-term incentives usually require comprehensive planning and greater investment, but they achieve a permanent high-quality bus or rail transit system that has a strong image and attracts all economic, ethnic, and age classes of users.

TD – Transit-use Disincentives. These disincentives may consist of deterioration, decrease, or discontinuance of transit services. In most urban areas, they represent an irrational policy under present conditions, except where there is a significant decline in population or activities. Yet, TD policy is actually indirectly implemented when there is a lack of government funds, or it is directly imposed by highway and parking construction projects that do not consider the negative impacts of such projects on public transportation, bicycles, and pedestrians.

The diagrams in figure 6.4 show the costs or disutilities of travel by car and by transit as bars. As the basic case, an existing condition where the automobile has a lower direct disutility than transit is shown. At the present time, this is a typical situation for cities with extensive highway/street networks and inadequate high-quality transit, such as Detroit, Miami, Rome,

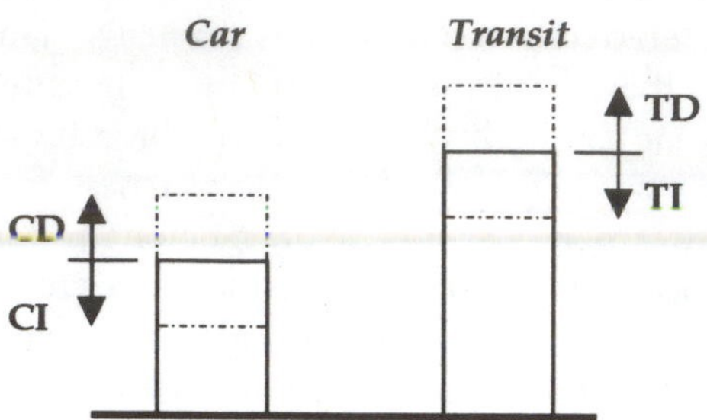

The basic case with impacts of the four policies on disutilities of the two modes

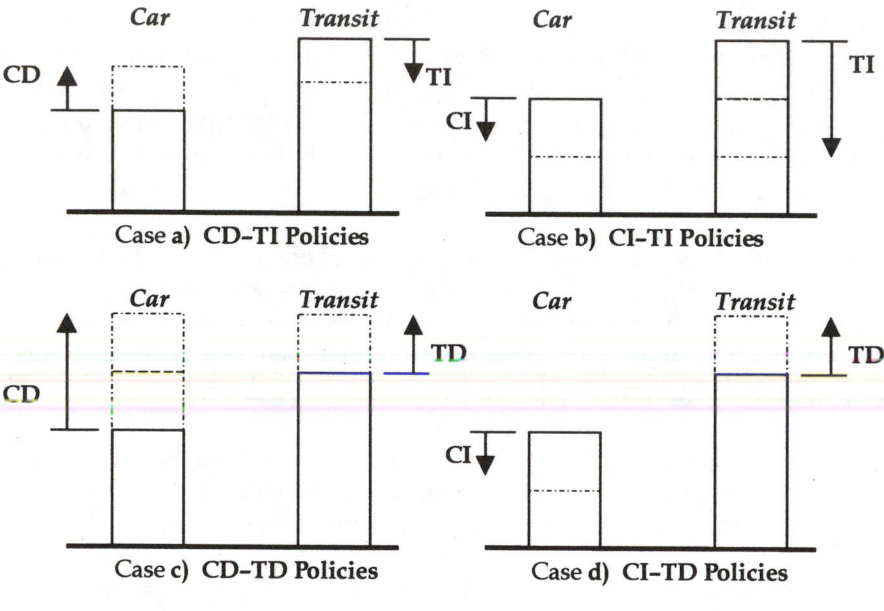

FIGURE 6.4
Impacts of different sets of policies on four sets of relative disutilities of different modes

or Bogota. This basic case is used as a model for illustrating different policies toward transportation modes. The impacts of policies CI and CD are shown by dashed lines. CI would decrease disutilities and thus make the car even more attractive than it is at present. CD would make the car less attractive and, in the case shown, make it closer to transit with respect to disutilities. Similar changes can be seen as a result of policies toward transit;

TI would make transit travel more attractive and more competitive with car travel, while TD would lead to a more unbalanced condition in favor of cars.

The four diagrams in figure 6.4 show the combinations of policies toward the car and transit. Case ***a***—a combination of CD and TI policies—shows that a balance between the two modes can be achieved with moderate disutility changes in each mode, because the two measures work "toward" each other. A conceptual balance is achieved by a smaller effort on each mode than would be required if measures were applied to only one of the modes, as illustrated in the basic case.

Most cities with integrated policies toward the two modes pursue this CD–TI combination. For example, in the early 1970s, Munich built rapid and regional rail transit lines through the center city, while simultaneously converting several major streets into pedestrian malls and rerouting car traffic around the central business district. Toronto and Portland have also applied a combination of these two policies. In all cases, the result has been an improved balance between transit and car travel.

In Case ***b***, CI–TI policies are pursued, resulting in investments in both modes and greater attractiveness of both transit travel and driving. The relationship of the two modes remains unbalanced, however, which continues to be true unless an extremely large investment is made in transit to "catch up" with the lowered disutility of driving. The overall situation results in greater subsidies for travel by both modes.

Examples of this situation are found in numerous cities, particularly in North America. The metro systems of Washington, D.C., and Atlanta could have been built at lower cost and yet attracted the same ridership had there not been extensive construction of freeways and subsidized parking in the central areas of these cities. Similarly, Baltimore and Philadelphia built multistory parking garages directly above their rail transit stations. The large, multifunctional business district in Paris—La Defense—has excellent metro, regional rail, and intercity railway access, yet it also provides an underground garage with 26,000 parking spaces.

In some cities, highway interest groups are so strong that any investment in transit is accepted only if a corresponding investment is made in highways. Good examples of such wasteful competing investments are those cases where the construction of LRT lines was conditioned by investment in the widening of a parallel freeway! In this situation—which occurred, for example, in San Jose and Salt Lake City—investments are made in two directly competing systems. In south San Jose, an entire new freeway has been constructed with an LRT line in the median. Thus, not only is very attractive competition provided, but the LRT alignment is in the least attractive position for pedestrians, and land-use intensification around the stations is hampered by the freeway and its interchanges. Although transportation systems in such cities or corridors are multimodal, they are neither integrated nor balanced.

Case ***c*** represents CD–TD policies where the attractiveness of both modes is decreased. There is decreased funding for both modes, while the balance between modes depends on the relative impacts of disincentives on both. There are few examples of this situation as a rational, basic policy, but the condition does occur when funding is inadequate and is therefore decreased for both transit and highway travel.

Finally, Case ***d***, or CI–TD, represents disincentives to transit and incentives to car travel. This combination of policies is contrary to the goal of achieving balanced transportation, since it leads to the "vicious cycle of urban transportation," the spiral of events described in chapter 1 and shown in figure 1.1. It leads to unimodal, car-based systems which are particularly undesirable and even infeasible in large cities. Their total transportation costs are much greater than those of intermodal systems, their services are inferior, and there is an increase of all the negative impacts of exclusive reliance on highway travel, such as chronic congestion, air pollution, and reduced livability of the city.

Similar to most disincentive measures, TD is seldom announced as an established policy. It is, however, often followed de facto, usually in countries and cities with no comprehensive plans or clearly defined intermodal transportation goals and policies. Some examples will illustrate such situations.

As described in chapter 3, during the period of the Interstate Highway System construction, when there was no federal aid to transit (from the mid-1950s to 1970), most U.S. cities actually followed CI–TD policies. In many cities, these policies have resumed since 1980 when cuts in the funding of transit systems were introduced, while car use has enjoyed increasing subsidies (lower gasoline prices, building codes that provide for parking, parking tax exemption as an employee benefit, etc.). CI–TD policies have also been pursued in Great Britain, especially since the deregulation of transit in 1985. Government assistance to transit decreased, while highway investments increased. With the change of the ruling government in 1997, transportation policies were reevaluated and revised.

Most paradoxical and damaging is the application of de facto CI–TD policies in some developing countries. With cities growing much more rapidly than those in developed countries, with low car ownership and large masses of population depending on transit services, these cities desperately need durable, economical, high-capacity transit systems on rights-of-way separated from street congestion. The technology used may be buses on busways, LRT, metro, or regional rail; but availability of category B or A is absolutely critical for cities with populations exceeding one million.

Some rapidly growing cities in developing countries—such as Caracas, Kuala Lumpur, Manila, Mexico City, Sao Paulo, and Tunis—have made significant progress in building high-capacity rail and bus transit networks. Most of them, however, still depend heavily on modes totally inadequate for the capacity needs of such agglomerations: buses, minibuses, and jitneys operating in chaotic traffic conditions. In most large cities of developing countries—such as Bogota, Bangkok, and Lagos—progress is extremely difficult due to lack of comprehensive plans and policies, and inadequate financing, organization, and professional expertise.

Even more serious is the pressure to build more highways and parking, while transit is shifted to private bus and jitney services. Typically, these are fast but unreliable, chaotic, and unsafe, so that their users have a great incentive to purchase a car, which, in turn, increases street congestion. Despite the obvious need for high-capacity transit systems on separate rights-of-way, their construction has often been prevented by the World Bank's financing policies, which are biased toward low-capacity street modes and against transit on separate rights-of-way. In several cases, dogmatic pressures for deregulated competition have led to the loss of transit rights-of-way. For example, an excellent, exclusive busway in Lima, Peru, became practically inoperable when the buses and minibuses of many different owners were allowed to use it without control by the transit agency.

While in these conditions it would clearly be rational to apply TI as the basic policy, in actuality most efforts go into highway construction without any infrastructure for transit. A strong influence toward such CI–TD policies is often exerted by the World Bank, which applies double standards for investments in highways and in transit. Its economic analysis methodology for highway investments does not include revenues, because these are typically collected through gasoline taxes and are thus considered available and growing. For transit projects, however, strict financial, rather than economic, analysis is performed, even though transit has substantial intangible social and other benefits, and its fares are usually not based on market principles alone but are influenced by social and other considerations. Hook (1994) gives a detailed, thorough analysis of the biases built into the methodology used by the World Bank (and other international institutions) to evaluate highway and transit investments, favoring highways.

This analysis of the four policies toward car and transit modes, and their combinations, shows that the TI–CD coordinated policy is the most

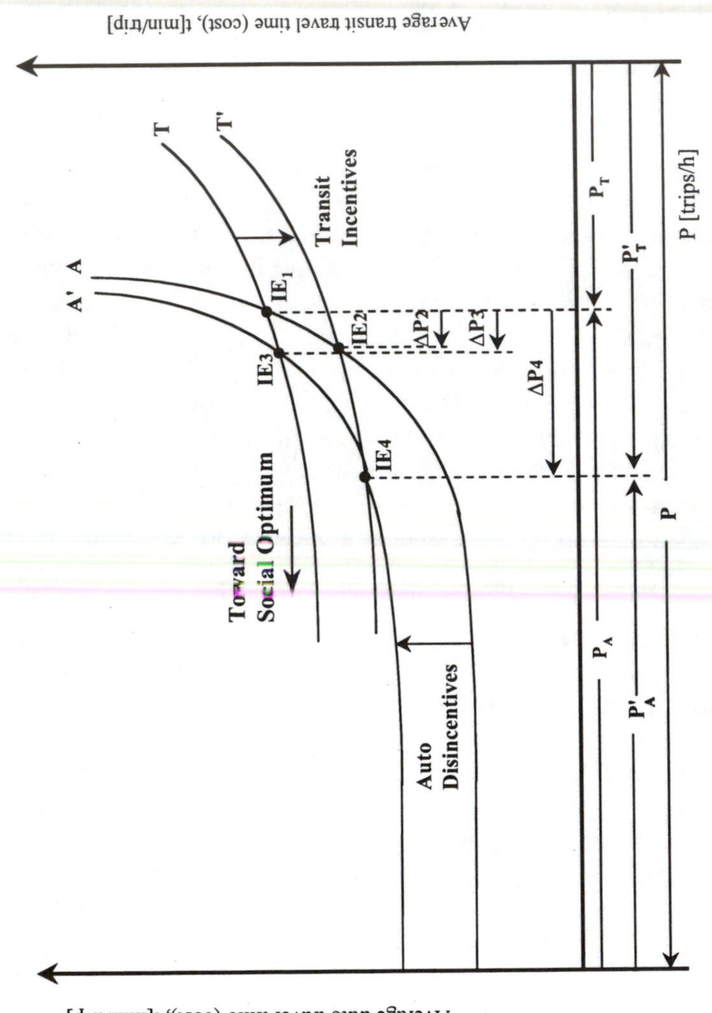

FIGURE 6.5
Impact of auto disincentives and transit incentives on intermodal shift of travel and individual equilibrium points

rational and cost-effective policy for achieving both a balanced transportation system and livable metropolitan areas. This can also be seen when the results of these policies are plotted on the diagram of intermodal distribution of travel for a specific corridor or for an area, such as a CBD; this is shown in figure 6.5, which is based on figure 2.8. The diagram is plotted for a situation where disutilities of travel by car and transit are shown by curves A and T, respectively. As in figure 2.8, the reverse plotting, from right to left, is used for the T curve, so that the horizontal dimension of the diagram represents the total number of travelers distributed between the two modes. The initial intermodal distribution, or modal split determined by individual choice, represents the individual equilibrium point, IE_1.

Application of TI measures leads to a diversion of ΔP_2 trips from cars to transit, so that the equilibrium shifts to the IE_2 point. Alternatively, application of CD measures alone would lead to a switch of ΔP_3 trips to transit and bring the curves to the IE_3 point. Combined TI and CD policies would cause a shift of ΔP_4 trips from car to transit and lead to the IE_4 point. This combination of policies would thus lead further toward SO than would either policy individually. Such coordinated TI and CD policies, sometimes popularly designated "push–pull measures," are broadened to include incentives to other modes, such as pedestrians, bicycles, and vanpools.

It should be pointed out again that the preceding analyses of costs, disutilities, and intermodal trip distributions are conceptual. Similar to the supply–demand diagrams in economics, they are difficult to plot and interpret numerically, but they are useful for presenting the respective concepts clearly. The travel cost bars shown in figure 6.2 are based on realistic values for specific sets of conditions; the disutility bars in figure 6.4 are conceptual only. The diagram in figure 6.5 is also conceptual. It does not imply, for example, that CD measures are always more effective than TI measures in changing the modal split; that may vary with conditions that influence the shapes of the two curves. The diagram does, however, show realistically the greater effectiveness of the combinations of TI and CD measures than of either of the two alone.

The intermodal policy TI-CD is most effective for several reasons. First, the two policies can be mutually supporting. Revenues collected from CD measures can be used to partially support the TI policy and improvements of all alternatives to cars, particularly to SOVs. Second, a policy of car disincentives is more acceptable to the population when it is accompanied by better alternatives. Third, the combination of these policies avoids expenditures for mutually competing systems. Fourth, coordinated policies may, as a "package," be "mobility neutral"; that is, the mobility reduction due to car disincentives can be compensated by mobility increases in other modes. Fifth, when combined, these policies increase awareness of the complexity of the urban transportation system and the need to coordinate modes. The review of developments in different countries in chapter 4 shows that cities with coordinated intermodal policies generally have greater public understanding and thus enjoy stronger support of transportation policies than cities relying mostly on one mode.

PRINCIPLES FOR PLANNING AND IMPLEMENTING BALANCED TRANSPORTATION SYSTEMS

This section presents a summary review of the role of transportation and its relationship to other activities in cities. It then briefly discusses some basic principles for planning and implementing policies that lead to a balanced transportation system. Building on this, chapter 7 presents specific measures for implementation of such a system.

Transportation of persons and goods, as an integral component of most functions and activities in cities, should be provided in the required quantity, with satisfactory quality, and at a realistic cost and price. The demand for travel implied by the "required quantity," however, depends to a great extent on the costs and prices (charges) of transportation. In a narrow sense, costs consist of the expenses involved in providing the service. In urban transportation, however, indirect costs are, in many situations, very high; if major distortions in cities are to be avoided, these indirect costs must be included in planning transportation and pricing services. For example, the provision of parking in high-density central cities often can be financed from user payments (Level IV); however, at Level I (consideration of the negative impacts of excessive parking facilities on the attractiveness and livability of cities), unrestrained construction of parking may not be feasible or even desirable.

The relationship of the costs and prices of transportation services is another important element affecting the role and composition of the transportation system. Again, if transportation were simply a commercial function, pricing based primarily on costs might be efficient. However, in urban transportation, such pricing is in most cases neither physically possible nor desirable from a systems point of view. Due to the dynamic influence of personal travel on a city's functioning and livability, pricing is often subsidized, directly or indirectly, by the government, by the private sector, and by society at large. In addition to the stimulation of activities, financial subsidies are often necessary and desirable when they support the provision of socially important services, or when they lead to a greater use of more environmentally friendly modes. Thus, for different modes in individual areas or functions in cities, the functional aspects and benefits of transportation, as well as its negative side effects, should be considered in determining subsidies or penalties.

Subsidies to transit systems are discussed and debated frequently. In fact, not only are subsidies common for all modes, but in many urban and suburban situations they are higher on a per-trip basis for cars than for transit travel, although usually they are not recognized as subsidies. "Free" parking, mentioned frequently in this book, is just one of the many forms of subsidies to car travel.

Economic efficiency requires that subsidies be determined on the basis of a rational intermodal transportation policy, rather than independently for individual modes and facilities. Such a policy should be aimed at achieving an optimal transportation system (Level II) and an efficient and livable city and metropolitan area (Level I). This policy would reduce subsidies for competing transportation systems and facilities, which would lead to excessive and ineffective spending.

The method of financing different modes and facilities has a direct impact on the level of transportation planning. As discussed in chapter 3, separate financing of different modes has some advantages, including simpler accounting and higher public satisfaction, since earmarked funding is usually more acceptable than use of general funds. In the layman's view, user charges by mode of transportation appear to be logical and equitable. For example, taxes collected from car usage, such as a gas tax, seem to be properly used exclusively for highways if that mode is considered alone (Level III), and not as a component of an intermodal system (Level II).

At Level II, however, urban transportation is understood to be a function that should be performed by several modes in a coordinated manner. From such a broad perspective, it becomes clear that at least some transportation funding, including user tax revenues, should be used for the entire system, rather than separately and disjointedly for different modes.

There are several reasons for intermodal coordination of financing. Because many urban trips are intermodal, it is logical that projects be planned and funded jointly. Coordinated financing encourages system integration and the creation of balanced transportation systems. Further, the interests of users of different modes are often interconnected. Thus, it is in the interest of auto drivers that some travelers switch from cars to transit and thus reduce congestion and social costs for all travelers. Similarly, it makes sense to use general transportation funds for intermodal facilities, such as access roads or driveways to major metro stations, or for pedestrian areas that generate transit travel. This is the rationale for funding of transit systems that include projects for improvements of entire station areas, or for the construction of extensive transit-pedestrian malls. Clearly, both modally dedicated and intermodal transportation funding have advantages and disadvantages. Local conditions, as well as the level and type of state and national programs, may influence the selection between them.

Another important observation about transportation as a function in a city (Levels II and I) is that the goal of transportation planning should be to allow maximum accessibility, or the maximum number of trips, between various locations of activities. This does not necessarily coincide with the maximum amount of person-km of travel (PKT). The location of activities, or urban form, has a major influence on the amount of travel required for a given number of activities. A common problem in metropolitan areas is that land use frequently is planned without adequate consideration of its transportation consequences, particularly the need to travel, or the number, length, and characteristics of required trips. Excessive travel distances by all modes—particularly car dependency and its negative consequences—are largely a result of the excessive spatial spread of developments that are functionally strongly related and generate travel. With good land-use planning, a large share of such trips could be performed by walking or by transit; short-sighted planning often disperses activities because it does not adequately consider the need for efficient transportation and human-oriented urbanized areas.

With respect to usage of modes in a city, it should be borne in mind that a unimodal, car-based system is functionally, economically, and environmentally inferior to a balanced intermodal system. While car travel can generally satisfy most travel needs in a small town, the need for other modes, such as transit, paratransit, bicycles, and pedestrians, grows with city size. With the increasing economic and environmental feasibility of using other modes, deployment of those modes leads to the creation of superior intermodal transportation systems, especially when they are functionally balanced.

Mode composition, therefore, is a very important aspect of transportation in large cities and metropolitan areas. With the agglomeration of activities in large cities, the system characteristics of different modes—particularly their performance, costs, space consumption, and side effects—become very important. Generally, concentrated activities make high-capacity modes spatially necessary, as well as physically and economically superior to lower-capacity modes.

Table 6.1 shows the relative area occupancies for different modes and types of trips using urban streets and freeways. The table gives car, van, bus, and LRT/streetcar modes with different vehicle loadings. Relative area occupancies for different vehicles are accounted for through the passenger

TABLE 6.1
Occupancy of Street Area per Person Traveling by Different Modes and Vehicle Loadings

Mode	*Load Factor [%]*	*Capacity*	*Number of Passengers*	*Passenger Car Unit (PCU) Coefficient*	*Occupancy Rate [PCU-km/prs-km]*
Car—Chauffeuring	10	5	0.5	1.0	2.00
Car—SOV	20	5	1	1.0	1.00
Car	40	5	2	1.0	0.50
Car	100	5	5	1.0	0.20
Van	50	12	6	1.5	0.25
Van	80	12	9	1.5	0.17
Bus	50	60	30	2.0	0.07
Bus	80	60	48	2.0	0.04
Articulated Bus	50	100	50	3.0	0.06
Articulated Bus	80	100	80	3.0	0.04
LRT/Streetcar (1 car, ROW C)	50	160	80	4.0	0.05
LRT/Streetcar (1 car, ROW C)	80	160	128	4.0	0.03

car unit (PCU) coefficient—the ratio between area occupied by a given vehicle and that occupied by the passenger car. (The numbers used are approximate averages.) The numbers in the last column are the computed relative area occupancies for a passenger carried by each mode as compared to the passenger car with a single occupant, or SOV.

The table shows that the only mode less efficient than the SOV with respect to area occupancy is chauffeuring a single passenger, because actual occupancy by a passenger is one in one direction, and zero on the return trip. Except for taxi trips of this kind, paratransit modes are more efficient than private cars, and transit modes are considerably more efficient than paratransit. Among transit modes, the efficiency increases from regular buses to articulated buses, and then to LRT. The figures for the LRT mode are, however, not always comparable with those of buses because they operate under different conditions. Since LRT typically has a separate ROW, its impact on street congestion is even lower than the numbers in the table indicate. On the other hand, the ROW used for LRT in such cases does occupy land permanently, and its efficiency must be computed separately. Metro and regional rail modes are not included in the table at all, because they have fully grade-separated rights-of-way, so that they usually do not use any street or freeway areas in central cities or along corridors they serve.

Because most of the externalities—such as noise, air pollution, parking area requirements, and negative impacts on the livability of an area—are proportional to the area requirements of individual modes, the numbers in the table show that the passenger car, particularly when operated as an SOV (as well as when used for chauffeuring), is by far the least efficient mode of urban passenger transport. That is why many cities apply measures to discourage the use of private cars. The Employer Trip Reduction Program and various other measures in U.S. cities are aimed at decreasing the vehicle-km/passenger-km ratio and increasing transportation system efficiency. This relative efficiency of transit modes—and their public-service feature—provides the rationale for giving the highest priority to transit, then paratransit, followed by private cars, which can be further classified by their occupancy.

The main problem of urban transportation is pointed out by this analysis: the single-occupancy vehicle (SOV), often the most attractive mode for individuals, is by far the least efficient mode, and thus, from a systems point of view, is the main problem. When its use is reduced by CD and TI measures, car-free travel becomes more attractive than car travel for most trips. This condition is most obvious in the cases of very large cities, such as New York, Paris, and Tokyo. However, many cities much smaller than these have pursued coordinated intermodal planning in recent decades and have made transit travel and walking superior to car driving for a large portion of urban travel. Examples are Hamburg, Montreal, New Orleans, Oslo, Prague, and San Francisco.

This aspect of mode efficiency should be considered not only in the planning of modes, but also in their operation, where a primitive concept—that all vehicles be treated equally in traffic regulation—is aimed at maximizing the capacity of facilities in terms of vehicles instead of persons. The present equal treatment of cars with an average occupancy of 1.2 to 1.6 persons with the treatment of buses that may carry 25 to 50 persons, as well as widespread neglect of bicycles, is inefficient and inequitable; there is no rationale for it.

The objective of transportation is to move people, not vehicles. Thus, it is clear that the unit in passenger transportation must be a person, rather than a vehicle. Whenever this obvious fact is recognized and applied in traffic operations, the efficiency of a transportation system is increased significantly. This is demonstrated by such cities as Copenhagen, Hannover, and Zürich, where extensive priorities for transit vehicles have been introduced: buses in the first city, buses and LRT in the second, and all three main surface modes—buses, trolleybuses, and LRT—in the third. A competitive transit system and intermodal balance are obtained at a much lower cost than on a system in which the limited capacity of streets and arterials is absorbed by large volumes of vehicles with extremely low average occupancy.

In planning, financing, and operating urban transportation, Planning Level II (achievement of the desired characteristics of an efficient transportation system) should be used for guidance. In addition, an efficient functional relationship between transportation and other activities must be achieved (Level I). The first and most important principle is that transportation services by all desired modes must be available wherever there are land uses that generate a certain level of travel demand. This implies that all intensive land uses should be located where they can be served efficiently, not only by local access streets, but also by transit; they must also be accessible to pedestrians. Consequently, land-use plans must be coordinated with networks of all desired transportation modes. This prevents problems that occur when land-use developments aggravate existing highway congestion but their locations and microdesign do not allow efficient transit services or convenient pedestrian access.

Street and freeway networks. The extent of street and freeway networks, together with parking capacity in individual areas, should depend on the type of city and the roles given to various transportation modes. This approach (Level I) should replace planning at Level IV, which has been conducted in many cities where plans were based on the "demand" estimated by assuming unrestricted car use, which is encouraged commercially and socially, as well as subsidized. How extensive should the street and freeway networks be? Logically, preferences among cities vary considerably; while some cities may decide that they want to develop a more human-oriented environment and apply CD policies, others may prefer to rely on car use and apply CI policies. Whatever the preference, it is important that the goal for the form and character of the city be discussed and a conscious decision made. That decision should lead to determination of the transportation system's basic form.

Transit. As the most effective mode and, for many trips, the only feasible alternative to the car, transit must be included in the basic decision about the form and character of the city and its metropolitan area. In small

PHOTO 6.1
Soundwalls are increasingly being built to reduce negative impacts of major freeways on their surroundings. *(U.S. Department of Transportation, Federal Highway Administration)*

cities, transit can attract some choice riders if it is well organized, convenient, and if it provides good information to the public. It may have terminals and transfer stations, but no special rights-of-way are required or economically justified. In medium and large cities, the main planning decision for transit is selection of the roles for two different mode categories:

street transit, which requires no major infrastructure and improvements; and *independent transit,* usually rail modes on ROW category B (LRT) or category A (metro). The role of transit, and thus intermodal balance, depends primarily on the extensiveness of the network of independent transit lines. Physical separation of transit ROW is far more important for transit performance, image, and competitiveness with the car than any other features, including priorities in traffic, peak-hour or all-day HOV facilities, or various demand-responsive services.

Consequently, rational long-range transportation planning for new towns and developments should provide independent ROW for transit lines on a network that would later serve most sections of the city. This would ensure a balanced, intermodal transportation system at a much lower cost than later construction of tunnels and elevated structures in built-up areas after the cities have grown and come to recognize the need for high-performance transit. Its construction involves large investments; yet, in many cases, this investment is justified because it provides improved functioning, ensures livability of the city, and prevents paralysis by highway construction. Such an investment also greatly reduces the need for parking and for construction of extensive freeways in high-density areas, which would be disruptive and involve larger investments than construction of high-performance transit.

Paratransit, vanpooling, and carpooling. Paratransit and other modes "between the private car and transit" should also be given priority over cars because of their higher efficiency (see table 6.1). These modes, however, are seldom provided a special infrastructure, because they operate on streets in mixed traffic. Their use can be encouraged by various organizational and pricing incentives, such as free parking or toll exemption for vanpool vehicles; entry of taxis into areas, streets, or lanes from which private cars are prohibited; organizational assistance for car- and vanpooling; and other incentives.

Bicycles. In some cities, bicycles can play a significant role in transportation. Factors that contribute to their use include mostly flat terrain, moderate climate, high-density areas with many trips of short to medium length, and a large segment of young population (teenagers, university students, and sports-minded people). Planning for bicycle travel—including bikeways, specially designated paths on streets or sidewalks, and bicycle parking facilities—can also play a major role in encouraging the use of bicycles. For example, many Dutch, German, Scandinavian, and Chinese cities have introduced measures to facilitate and encourage bicycle travel, and this

PHOTO 6.2
Many cities design intermodal systems to encourage use of bicycles and transit (Munich). *(Vukan R. Vuchic)*

has resulted in extensive use of bicycles by all population groups, even in less-than-ideal climates and topographic conditions. To assume a significant and desirable role in cities, however, the behavior of cyclists must be regulated. Disregard of traffic laws by cyclists in this and other countries is ultimately harmful to the interests of bicycle users and undermines the potentially significant role of this mode in urban areas.

Pedestrians. Because they represent an essential element of a livable city, pedestrians should be given an important role in transportation planning and street operations through protection, convenience, and preferential treatment, particularly where vehicular traffic is heavy. They should not be neglected because, to varying degrees, pedestrians represent all urban travelers. All transit (even car travel) begins and ends with walking. In multifunctional, diversified, human-oriented city centers, walking may be used for up to 40 percent of all local trips, even in cities with a very high rate of car ownership. If pedestrians are neglected and a substantial number of walking trips are replaced by car trips, congestion increases rapidly and can be alleviated only if streets, freeways, and parking are increased significantly. This, in turn, makes the city less "walkable" and induces more driving, thus continuing the vicious cycle that leads to reduced livability. To prevent this outcome, the planning process must give careful attention to the role of pedestrians in both macro design (land use) and micro design of urban developments.

The role of land use in urban personal travel depends to a great extent on the treatment pedestrians are given on the streets in relation to vehicular traffic. In most developed countries where they enjoy full protection and convenience in their movements, pedestrians typically also meet the obligation to obey traffic laws. At the other extreme, in some cities there is still an atavistic condition under which motor vehicles, being physically more powerful, have all rights, while pedestrians and bicycles must yield. In such situations, pedestrians and bicyclists do not enjoy safe and comfortable crossing of streets. This condition has a highly negative impact, not only on pedestrians and vehicles, but on the city's livability.

Interestingly, regulations and attitudes involving pedestrians vary greatly, not only among countries, but among states and individual cities as well. For example, pedestrians are regulated and treated better in California than in most East Coast cities. This is a paradox, because the older cities on the East Coast were designed to a human scale and have much stronger pedestrian traditions than the newer California cities with their extensive car-dominated streets and arterials. In recent years, however, there have been movements in Boston, New York, and other eastern U.S. cities to revive their human character and reduce the dominance of motor vehicles in both urban cores and residential areas.

In summary, careful planning, design, and operation of transportation systems and facilities is needed to achieve efficient, livable cities and metropolitan areas in which transportation plays its important functional role without excessive negative impacts. Several basic decisions required to achieve this goal have been outlined. First, the role given to transportation must be decided on and implemented through policies, investments, charges for use, and subsidies. Second, another, usually concurrent, decision concerns the selection of the composition of transportation modes. The main question usually considered is the relationship of the car and the transit system. In reality, the problem is broader, involving all modes, from transit and paratransit to bicycles and pedestrians. This should be followed by decisions about the extent and form of the freeway network and the composition of transit, particularly rail transit with separate rights-of-way.

Finally, there must be attention not only to the macro design—the shape of the city and its transportation networks—but also to the micro design of individual areas and facilities. The latter often has a major influence on the roles of different modes and, particularly, on pedestrians. The human scale of design aimed at convenience for users is crucial for enhancing, instead of losing, the human element and livability of cities and suburbs.

References

Girnau, Günter, ed. 1995. Urban traffic management and public transport. *Public transport: the challenge.* Brussels, Belgium: Union Internationale des Transports Publics.

Hook, Walter. 1994. *Counting on cars, counting out people.* Paper No. I-0194. New York: Institute for Transportation and Development Policy.

Project for Public Spaces, Inc. 1997. *The role of transit in creating livable metropolitan communities.* TCRP Report 22. Washington, DC: Transportation Research Board.

Shin, Yong Eun. 1997. *Analysis of city/transportation system relationship via land consumption.* Ph.D. dissertation, University of Pennsylvania, Philadelphia, Pennsylvania.

Union Internationale des Transports Publics (UITP). 1991. *Green light for towns.* Brussels, Belgium: UITP.

7

Implementing the Solutions: Measures for Achieving Intermodal Balance

Extensive efforts to achieve balanced transportation in urban areas are well documented in the transportation literature. Numerous reports describe and analyze different measures; designs of facilities, neighborhoods, and major developments; manuals for implementation of measures; and so on. Among the comprehensive items in the technical literature are, for example, the publications by 1,000 Friends of Oregon (1997), Dunlay and Soyk (1978), Gordon (1997), Institute of Transportation Engineers—ITE (1997), Metropolitan Transit Development Board—MTDB (1993), Pennsylvania Environmental Council—PEC (1997), Project for Public Spaces (1997), Pucher and Hirschman (1993), and Union Internationale des Transports Publics—UITP (1991).

This chapter presents a succinct review of selected measures that can be used to achieve an efficient urban transportation system. The discussion here refers primarily to medium-sized and large cities in which a unimodal system produces many problems and limitations; thus, the basic goal is to achieve a balanced intermodal transportation system. Some basic measures, such as providing pedestrian and bicycle facilities, naturally apply to all cities and towns, urban and suburban areas.

Planning Levels I and II (defined in chapter 2) posit two tasks in planning new cities or improving existing ones. The first task is to select the combination of transportation modes and to define their roles. This will contribute to the development of the city by helping to establish the desired type of city and quality of life. As an example, the city may be conceived of as spatially spread, with low-density residential areas, car-based shopping malls, and commercial strip developments. In that case, the role of the pedestrian will be minimal, requiring only basic paths and standard safety elements at intersections. Another city, however, may be designed to have major activity centers, a traditional downtown, or new multiactivity, pedestrian-oriented business or residential developments. For this case, elaborate pedestrian facilities should be planned and the entire transportation system—that is, selection of other modes—should be designed accordingly, with strong emphasis on transit.

The second task is to create and maintain coordination and balance among the selected modes. For example, in many cities bus transit on streets cannot compete with private cars; therefore, separate transit rights-of-way, category B or A, must be built to establish a stable intermodal balance. In some cases, bus lanes are sufficient; in others, rail modes may be more effective. The optimal roles of these two modes and their coordination must then be planned. In most cases, however, the central question in Level II planning, as well as in introducing regulatory measures, is how to establish and maintain a desired relationship between private cars and transit, or private cars and all other modes (sometimes referred to as "alternative modes"—alternative to the car, particularly the SOV). This central problem of urban transportation today—intermodal balance—is extremely complex, not only because of the conflict between individual and social interests, but also because of different cost and pricing structures, separate jurisdictions over different modes and facilities, influences of special interests, and, often, differences in mind-sets of professionals working on different modes (as discussed in chapter 5).

There are many ways to categorize transportation planning and regulatory measures. Following are several common and logical methods of classification.

- *Type of measures*—Policies; regulatory requirements; economic/financial, organizational, legal, and physical measures;
- *Time period*—Measures may be short-term, medium-term, or long-term;
- *Jurisdiction*—Programs, actions, and financing can be performed by private companies and public agencies, as well as under jurisdictions and financing by local, state, and federal governments;

- *Objectives and goals to be achieved*—Improvements and incentives for transit and other non-car modes and car-use disincentives. Because achieving a better balance between cars and other modes is the central issue in most cities, this classification is often used for implementation of balanced transportation policies. Popular names for the two policies toward transit (and other non-car modes) and cars are, respectively, incentives and disincentives or, more popularly, "pull and push" and "carrot and stick."

The sequence in this chapter progresses from a brief overview of transportation in the basic procedures of urban planning (Level I) to measures toward individual modes: car, transit, paratransit, bicycles, and pedestrians. In each section, various measures available for implementation in different situations are presented. Each measure and its characteristics are described, and conditions under which the measures can be applied are defined. In the last section, measures that have been discussed are classified by type, effects, and implementation time.

There are, of course, considerable differences between situations where new systems are planned or existing ones are improved; between developed and developing countries; between older European cities, "middle-aged" cities in North America (such as Philadelphia and New York), and recently matured cities such as Houston and Los Angeles. The discussion here attempts as much as possible to encompass this diversity by presenting elements and considerations that can be used in all cases; the discussion, however, may result in different outcomes because of different conditions and local preferences of the population and/or political decision makers.

TRANSPORTATION IN URBAN PLANNING

In designing new developments or improvements to existing urban areas, planners must evaluate the role and characteristics of the transportation system in light of the goals adopted for the character of the city and metropolitan area. Lifestyle and functions required for individuals—as well as social, commercial, recreational, and other activities—lead to formulation of the transportation services needed and to the transportation modes that can deliver them.

To achieve an intermodal system that can utilize the benefits of diversity provided by a combination of modes, each mode must be planned separately and then integrated with other modes through an iterative planning and design process. It is important, however, that the street/freeway system, which in the context of the total transportation system actually is a subsystem, initially be planned as a system and network. Similarly, a transit subsystem must be planned as a system, then integrated with the street/freeway subsystem. This is especially true when the transit system has a special infrastructure: separate rights-of-way (rail), stations, even special lanes on streets and freeways (buses). If transit consists only of street modes (buses, streetcars or tramways), coordination of the car/street and transit subsystems will be mostly at the operational level, rather than in planning infrastructure—that is, street and freeway networks.

Transportation systems and the composition of modes vary not only among cities, but also for different sectors within metropolitan areas. In central cities, the street network is ubiquitous because it must provide access to all lots; but in addition to the access function, it must serve the traffic-carrying function. In revising an existing street network, an important goal is usually to convert a street network with numerous streets of equal significance into a network of local streets and arterials. That way, through traffic is discouraged or eliminated from local streets, while the arterials are upgraded through design and traffic engineering measures to handle large traffic volumes and, secondarily, to provide access to the abutting land and buildings.

Construction of freeways (motorways) into central cities is a critical decision for a city's character and livability. During the freeway construction era, many large North American cities, such as Houston, Boston, and Philadelphia (Automotive Safety Foundation 1964), designed three freeway rings, or "beltways," as parts of a saturation-type freeway network for the entire metropolitan area. This was based on the belief that all travel in the future would be by private car, supplemented by buses during peak hours and for "transit-captive" riders only at other times. Unlimited travel by car was considered a basic need of metropolitan areas, more important than historic buildings, amenities, environment, or quality of urban life. Eight-lane freeways were planned across lower Manhattan, through the historic part of Philadelphia, and around San Francisco, extending the infamous Embarcadero freeway to Golden Gate Bridge. Even Honolulu's world-renowned Waikiki Beach was slated for a freeway corridor.

With increasing concern over the environment, however, these plans were reevaluated in the 1970s and many "rings" were omitted from plans—for example, in Boston, Philadelphia, San Francisco, and New York. Yet, "inner rings" tightly encircling CBDs were built, for example, in Columbus and Hartford. In Houston, Dallas, and San Antonio, such inner rings around CBDs were supplemented by outer beltways and radials connecting the two circular freeways. The freeway networks in Los Angeles and Detroit form more elaborate grids, providing a saturation-type pattern for the entire metropolitan area and allowing multidirectional travel.

These extensive networks bring and distribute large volumes of vehicular traffic into the heart of the city or throughout the region. Although convenient for drivers, these designs, especially radial ones, have three harmful consequences. First, because they require the destruction of buildings, parks, and residential areas, they have a harmful physical and environmental impact on the central city as well as other highly concentrated areas through which they pass. Second, they create physical barriers between areas, often becoming economic and social dividers in the process. Third, they overload street networks with heavy traffic volume and require high parking capacities, further disrupting the urban texture and destroying the city's human character.

The outer freeway ring, or beltway, is usually much more successful because it serves the major functions of circumferential travel, connections among outer radials, and diversion of through trips from inner radial facilities and the central urban area. Because of lower densities (at least initially), an outer-ring freeway usually has a much less damaging impact on its surroundings than inner rings have on the central core. The outer ring is an important bypass for small cities, as well as for large metropolitan areas (for example, the famous Baltimore and Washington Beltways).

The function of beltways – to serve as bypasses and connectors between other freeways – is very useful. The problem is that present-day living habits based on cheap driving, virtually total reliance on cars and trucks, and the absence of controls on land use all lead to intensive growth of traffic generators around beltways, resulting in chronic overloading and congestion of these facilities. Because there are no attractive alternatives to travel in such entirely car-based suburban areas, this problem has no feasible solution. Widening of beltways and other freeways, implemented or planned in some cities, only temporarily relieves congestion. A sarcastic but valid comment on this problem is that attempting to solve congestion by widening freeways is like trying to cure obesity by loosening one's belt: the additional capacity only generates further development and more traffic, so that the same problem reappears at an even larger scale. Obviously, the basic causes of uncoordinated land development, as well as the "free driving syndrome," are the problems that require correction – control of traffic volume, which will assist in achieving efficient functioning of the beltways.

The character of the city is influenced by two basic decisions about the network of streets and freeways:

- What is the relationship between the street/arterial network and the freeway network?
- What is the role of cars versus transit in travel to, from, and within the central city?

Different decisions about the role of street, arterial, and freeway networks can and do have highly different impacts on cities. Construction of several radial freeways converging on an inner freeway ring results in a car-dominated city with extensive parking garages and lots. Conversely, central cities without freeways are more compact, and concentrated volumes of travel must be handled by high-performance transit, usually one or several rail transit modes.

The balance between car and transit use in central cities is strongly influenced by the character of the area (its physical design, organization of space, and types of development) and by the relative convenience and attractiveness of the two systems. The desired balance between these systems can also be influenced and adjusted by various car-disincentive measures, among which a limitation on parking capacity and its pricing is often most easily introduced and maintained.

The extent and the form of freeway networks depends on the demand for travel by car, as well as on the physical limitations of the area and its individual corridors. Generally, freeways should be placed around major activity centers and corridors. Because of the large area they consume, freeways should not go through centers of activity. In addition, the impact of large traffic volumes can be ameliorated if freeway traffic is distributed from interchanges through arterials and streets, rather than brought directly into high-density activity areas. It is important that each network—street, arterial, and freeway—be designed to meet its set of requirements; however, all three must be considered together. They should be complementary, and their contact points, intersections and interchanges, should have balanced capacities.

Transit must also be planned with respect to the two basic functions it serves. Local, mostly short-distance travel usually is served by street transit, which utilizes streets and arterials and requires little separate infrastructure. A high-performance or high-speed network serves trips of all lengths, but predominantly medium to long ones. It has "high performance" because it operates on independent rights-of-way, that is, B or A. These lines must be incorporated with urban land uses; unlike freeways, they optimally should go through the cores of high-density activity areas, since rail lines rely on pedestrian access and directly support activities in station vicinities. In addition, these lines should be coordinated with local transit and have joint stations where passenger transfers take place.

PHOTO 7.1
In Chicago, excessive reliance on cars led to construction of six roadways with 18 lanes in a major corridor, incompatible with high-rise apartment buildings.

In planning new developments, towns, and cities, it is important to develop not only arterial street networks but also transit rights-of-way. The latter may be a right-of-way eight-meters (25-feet) wide, usually partially separated (category B), or an entirely controlled right-of-way (category A) for a semirapid or rapid transit system, respectively. This ensures that an independent, congestion-free transit system will be provided. At the planning stage, these rights-of-way involve low investment costs. If they are not provided, however, transit will indirectly be given a secondary role, because it cannot compete with car travel. Provision of an independent transit system may be necessary later, but then it will involve much higher costs than if the land was reserved for it at the beginning.

The presence of independent, high-performance transit is very important for transportation system reliability. Large travel volumes can load any facility —street, freeway, bus, or metro line—to its capacity. However, high-volume operation creates different conditions on different systems. Congestion on streets and freeways causes frequent breakdowns, drastically reducing capacity and further exacerbating congestion. The operation of independent transit systems (such as metros) at their capacity does

PHOTO 7.2
Attractive landscaping along roadsides and interchanges in Seattle. *(Washington State Department of Highways)*

cause decreased comfort for passengers, but such systems continue to operate at their maximum capacity level without losses due to congestion. LRT lines in San Francisco and Manila can carry some 15,000 persons per hour, and metro lines in Moscow, New York, and Tokyo can carry 50,000 or even 80,000 persons per hour at a steady rate for any duration of time. Reducing uncontrolled congestion and breakdown of flow on freeways to a fraction of capacity is one of the objectives of ITS (Intelligent Transportation Systems) technology and other control techniques, as well as one of the objectives in introducing road pricing.

Not only is coordination of land use and transportation necessary and possible in the initial planning of new developments and areas, it must be done for any development of significant size. The basic requirements must be that the new development is accessible by car, transit, and walking and that the traffic the development generates can be served by the projected street network and transit services. Most cities with coordinated land-use and transportation planning—such as Portland, Toronto, Frankfurt, and Stockholm—perform this type of analysis and give approval for development only when accessibility and transportation service requirements are satisfied. In most other North American cities and many cities overseas, however, this coordination is not performed, which is the main reason for subsequent paralysis of the urban areas by traffic congestion and inadequate transit services.

Neglecting to consider transit access is a very common problem, and its consequences are greatly underestimated. The widespread construction of large suburban shopping, office, residential, and other developments leads to transportation problems that cannot be resolved physically or financially. Sprawl in medium- and high-density developments is even more serious than the "traditional" sprawl of single-family housing, for several reasons. In addition to extensive land consumption, high energy consumption, and heavy environmental load, low-occupancy cars become the only physically feasible mode of access. The result is high generation of VKT , a need for extensive highway construction (which the population needs for travel, but which is rejected for environmental reasons), inability to provide either transit or paratransit without extremely high subsidies, extensive chauffeuring of passengers (businesspersons, children, the elderly), and not surprisingly, minimal use of walking and bicycling.

The last aspect, use of walking and bicycling, is an extremely important, albeit overlooked, component of transportation planning. Whereas inadequate land-use planning is caused by a lack of adequate controls on land use as well as by political and commercial pressures, failure to provide for convenient walking and bicycling is usually a result of professional lapses and misguided thinking (for instance, that walking "happens" and needs no major attention in planning and design). Sound planning, therefore, must include not only land use/transportation at the macro scale but also at the design level of individual buildings, developments, streets, and other transportation facilities. Requirements and standards for pedestrian and bicycle transportation must be included in every plan for the design or redesign of facilities and urban developments.

Excellent materials on the topic of transportation in comprehensive urban planning are found in the following references: 1,000 Friends of Oregon (1997), Felz (1989), ITE (1997), Ministry of the Environment of Finland (1996), MTDB (1993), Newman, Kenworthy, and Robinson (1992), Project for Public Spaces (1997), and Union Internationale des Transports Publics (1991).

FINDING THE OPTIMAL ROLE FOR THE CAR

With its unique ability to provide superb personal mobility, the car is a fundamental element of our civilization. Its availability and use are a major asset and element of our living standard. Its utility to users depends on the value of mobility in absolute terms, as well as relative to other expenditures such as housing, education, and recreation. In urban areas, the use of the car is less efficient than in rural areas because of the large space requirements and environmental costs car travel involves. Travel by large numbers of people in the same corridor or area is accomplished more efficiently by higher-capacity modes, primarily transit. The role of the car in cities should therefore be balanced with the optimal roles of transit and other modes.

The optimal design, regulation, and efficient operation of highway and street traffic, particularly in metropolitan areas, is a broad area of engineering that has been developed, elaborated, and broadened since its beginnings in 1930. Major fields and programs that have been developed and applied to handle traffic and its interaction with other activities and the city are reviewed here.

Traffic engineering. Traffic engineering is the field of engineering that deals with the efficient and safe operation of traffic on streets, highways, and their surroundings. A large field and profession, it plays a crucial role in traffic planning, design, and operation of the street, highway, and transit systems of every metropolitan area.

Transportation System Management (TSM). TSM was developed in the late 1960s as a logical broadening of traffic engineering to incorporate not only highway but all modes of transportation; to utilize not only specific engineering techniques, but also regulatory and economic elements such as pricing; to consider not only traffic flow but also transportation function and its interaction with the environment and the city in general.

Traditional traffic engineers who broadened their domain of work in this manner gradually assumed the title of "transportation engineer." This evolution is reflected in the change of the leading professional association in this field from the Institute of Traffic Engineers to the Institute of Transportation Engineers (ITE).

Travel Demand Management (TDM). TDM is a set of measures, including legally mandated programs, that was developed to provide solutions to the problem of increasing highway congestion by reducing the volume of travel rather than by traditional approaches that focused mostly on increasing

PHOTO 7.3
Freeway ramp control is an efficient method to improve utilization of freeways. *(U.S. Department of Transportation, Federal Highway Administration)*

the supply side—highway and parking capacities. TDM encompasses a broad and diverse set of activities, such as limitations on parking supply and encouragement of taxi ride-sharing, legal and business-sponsored inducement of increased average car occupancy for employees or visitors, so-called Employer Trip Reduction (ETR) programs, telecommuting, and, in the long run, land-use developments that reduce the need for vehicular trips or their excessive lengths. Several of these measures, especially car-use pricing and parking-control measures, are discussed in the following sections.

Intelligent Transportation Systems (ITS). In recent years, ITS has been by far the most important technological development in most developed countries. Its primary purpose is to utilize modern technology—mainly electronics, computers, and communications—to increase the safety, capacity, and convenience of travel, primarily in metropolitan areas. Initiated as a system for highway traffic operations and control, ITS has been broadened to transit and other modes, although the emphasis remains heavily focused on highways. ITS has the potential to be used for intermodal coordination and control of interactions between transportation and other activities in cities, but at present the focus is on the technological aspects of traffic flow and safety rather than on intermodal system development. If this focus is not broadened, ITS may enable important safety and traffic flow improvements but also may exacerbate some of the problems of the collision between cities and cars by increasing, rather than decreasing, VKT and thus causing new problems in metropolitan areas.

Networks and traffic controls. The extent of street and freeway networks and the control of traffic volume are basic issues in urban transportation, but they often receive less attention than technical developments such as ITS or procedural processes such as demand-estimation techniques. Some recent publications with interesting material on this topic are Johnson (1993), Burrington (1994), Transportation Research Board Special Report 245 (1995), and World Bank (1996).

In developing countries where car ownership is increasing, considerable expansion of roads and parking facilities is needed, because the role of the car logically increases with a growing living standard. In most developed countries in which the expansion of streets and freeways has taken place (in many cases exceeding the scale compatible with livable cities), the problem is how to limit or reduce car use. The goal is to keep road facilities and VKT below the level at which vehicular travel begins to cause chronic congestion and becomes counterproductive.

These problems, at the heart of the collision of cities and cars, consist of several elements. First, street and highway congestion impedes the movement of *all* vehicles and thus paralyzes the normal functioning of the city. Second, transport of large volumes of passengers by car becomes much less efficient than their transport by higher-performance transit modes. Third, extensive use of cars creates numerous negative environmental impacts—from air pollution and noise to energy consumption, sprawl, and long-term influences that reduce the city's livability. Finally, excessive reliance on the car while neglecting its alternatives leads to social inequities and problems because it divides the population into highly mobile auto owners and virtually stranded non–car owners.

Reduction of car trips and VKT. The reduction of car trips and VKT is therefore the main objective in efforts to achieve a desirable balance between the private car and other modes and to reduce the negative impacts of excessive car use. Two sets of measures—*car-use disincentives* and *incentives to use alternative modes*—are complemented by long-term planning for reduction of the demand for car travel. The measures directly concerning the use of the car, particularly in its single-occupancy version, are reviewed here, grouped in three major categories. Incentives to use alternative modes are discussed later in this chapter.

- *Car-use pricing, or charges for driving and parking.* This group of measures represents mainly "market-based" tools—that is, the introduction of pricing measures that depend on conditions and that affect car users' behavior through monetary charges. The objective of these tools is to reduce the present "free driving syndrome."
- *Reduction of VKT through organizational measures.* These encompass technical and engineering measures that physically redirect or restrict car travel and parking.
- *Reduction of demand for car use through planning and design.* This represents a rational approach to coordinated planning, which results in a sustainable system of urban development and transportation that is physically compatible with it. Congestion, inadequate services, or destruction of developments to accommodate transportation infrastructure thus are prevented through this process of comprehensive planning (Levels I and II).

Car-Use Pricing

With the realization that urban transportation problems cannot be solved merely by building more roads, it has become clear that conditions could be vastly improved if travelers would to some extent face cost elements reflecting market conditions. During the 1980s and 1990s, political pressures increased to implement the policy that "the user should pay a greater share of travel costs." However, although such changes have been applied to most public carriers from urban transit to railways (particularly Amtrak) and airlines, this principle has only just begun to be used to introduce additional charges for car use. There have been only a few innovative methods of user charges, such as parking cashouts, and the construction of a few toll roads, while subsidies in many forms continue. The trend is toward a search for different forms of car-use charges, for both basic reasons: generation of revenue required for transportation infrastructure and reduction of highway congestion.

In most countries, transportation experts—planners, engineers, and economists—agree that more realistic pricing of car travel is fundamental to greater efficiency not only of car use, but of all urban transportation. Yet, the subsidies and indirect payments are widespread and large. Germany's huge Autobahn network remains free of user charges, subsidized parking is a common phenomenon in most countries, and extremely cheap gasoline inflicts high national costs in the United States. Measures for correcting this situation have been widely discussed over the years, but their implementation is proceeding very slowly. Pressure for their introduction is likely to increase, however, because the physical and economic problems of rapidly increasing VKT cannot be rationally solved without correcting the present system. The measures most likely to be introduced are discussed below.

Various methods for pricing the use of cars have been used. Some, such as road tolls and parking charges, are conventional, while others have been used successfully in a limited number of cities. These include area licensing schemes, "ecotaxes," and other programs. Finally, a number of pricing methods have been proposed but not yet implemented. In recent years, the need for increased user charges in highway and urban transportation has grown due to two trends—the need for additional funding of transportation systems, and the need to increase the efficiency of system operations by raising the direct costs of driving and compensating for currently unpaid social and environmental costs. These trends are likely to lead to the introduction of innovative pricing methods. The different types of charges for car use can be classified by their objectives, rationales, and methods in four main categories:

1. Restructuring of car user costs—increasing the share of direct costs;
2. Conversion of subsidies into user charges;
3. Impact charges—payments for presently unpaid costs; and
4. User charges to influence travel behavior.

These four categories generally correspond to the items of indirect costs shown under the horizontal line in figure 2.11 (chapter 2). Due to the need for "improved accounting" of the costs related to car use, these charges are aimed primarily at achieving two types of effects:

1. Shifting portions of the costs from below to above the horizontal line (objective 1) in order to ameliorate the "free driving syndrome," that is, make travelers' decisions about whether and how much to drive more rational than they are now (when they are based on a minute fraction of total costs); and
2. Making car users pay for the costs that are presently paid as subsidies (objective 2) or for externalities now absorbed by other travelers or by society (objective 3).

In most countries, subsidies to car travel are lower and operating costs are higher than in the United States, but out-of-pocket user costs are still small compared to the total costs. The problem of travelers' decisions is not as serious as it is in the United States, but it still exists. An increase in direct costs is therefore the main goal in pricing car use, and several countries (such as the Netherlands, Germany, and Norway) have increased them consistently. Increasing direct costs in some situations is more important for its impact on driver behavior and VKT than for the additional revenues it generates.

Most other user charges discussed below, such as reduction of parking subsidies, fuel tax increases, and road pricing (objective 2), are also aimed at increasing the direct costs of car driving by shifting other cost components from those below the line to those above the line in the cost diagram (objective 1). Although it is possible to shift only some of the costs from below to above the line, all such changes are desirable. Their purpose is to make the car user more aware of the total costs of travel. For this same reason, however, such costs are unpopular with users.

These charges vary greatly by their monetary amount and method of collection. Some, aimed primarily at restructuring costs (objective 1) may be, on the average, revenue-neutral—that is, individual costs may be shifted without necessarily increasing the total amount the car user pays. Most of the measures reduce subsidies (objective 2) or are impact-based (objective 3). Both types of measure reflect costs currently not paid directly by users but instead by employers, companies, stores, the community at large, or society. Finally, the last category represents charges introduced to achieve a certain impact (objective 4); thus, these charges may be unrelated to either the direct or the indirect costs of driving.

Most car-user charges relate to more than one of the four categories of objectives. For example, the parking cashout method is usually revenue-neutral for car users, but its form presents certain incentives to use alternative modes of travel. The introduction of tolls, road pricing, or a fuel tax increase represents a shift from subsidies to user charges: some fixed costs are changed to variable ones. They increase accountability and make car user behavior more rational, thus introducing some elements of market pricing. Reduced-rate or free parking for vanpools may be introduced as a package, with parking rates as car disincentives; but this actually represents an incentive for vanpool usage. Pricing measures will be described here starting with the most common ones and proceeding to those that have only been proposed but not yet tested. Objectives and impacts of each one are discussed.

Parking control and charges. In their various forms, parking controls and charges represent the most practical method for introducing or modifying user charges. The most logical parking charge measures described here have, to varying extents, all four major objectives: they increase direct costs, reduce subsidies, reflect impacts, and influence driving habits. Pennsylvania Environmental Council (1997) provides an excellent discussion of various aspects of parking, including supply, pricing, and control.

Reduced parking subsidy and supply. One of the most effective intermodal balance tools in cities that have applied it is the reduction of parking subsidies and supply. In most U.S. cities, however, parking is oversupplied and underpriced (Pennsylvania Environmental Council 1997; Regional Transportation Authority 1994; Shoup 1992, 1997; Topp 1993; Wormser 1997) and thus represents one of the largest subsidy items in urban transportation. Although it is an important component of the transportation system, parking usually is treated as an independent function, a basic element of the living standard, a marketing device—or, from the operator's point of view, an asset of private enterprise. Traffic engineering studies often define the "demand for parking" as a supply that is consumed when its price is either zero, or extremely low. Not surprisingly, a result of these attitudes is that more than 90 percent of parking in the United States is "free"—users do not pay for it directly.

Oversupplied and underpriced parking causes widespread economic inefficiencies, social inequalities, negative environmental impacts, and urban transportation problems. For example, Cervero (1988) estimates that about three-quarters of "suburban economic center parking" is in surface facilities. In many suburban areas, all parking is on the surface. As a result, a typical suburban shopping center dedicates 55 to 70 percent of its total area to parking and driveways, and an office park 50 to 60 percent. In addition to this land consumption, the cost of providing a parking space varies from $2,000 in suburban areas to $20,000 in urban areas—not counting maintenance, supervision, and so on. When the cost of these facilities is absorbed by the building owners and businesses, every customer or employee who comes by transit, bicycle, or walking actually subsidizes the parking of those who arrive by car. Not only is this inequitable, it stimulates the modal split toward the car rather than its alternatives. Richard Willson puts the problem succinctly:

> Parking is a vital but often ignored transportation policy issue. Parking policy decisions shape the form of cities, their density, travel patterns, and the quality of the environment. For example, they affect transit ridership because they are a key determinant of the cost and

> convenience of automobile commuting. Often parking policy decisions are made without regard to their broader consequences. (Willson 1992)

The significance of parking for the entire urban transportation policy, from reduction of congestion to modal split impacts, is confirmed by Ulberg et al. (1992), who found that transportation models reveal parking as the "most sensitive variable in modal split." This is confirmed by numerous experiences in various cities. Parking restriction is therefore considered the single most effective measure for reducing that demand.

Unlike road pricing, congestion pricing, and other measures that are not yet common and that require special arrangements for implementation, parking measures can be organized and introduced fairly easily. The main step to be taken is to adopt a policy toward the supply and pricing of parking. Several measures can be used to correct present inefficiencies and integrate parking into a coordinated transportation system.

The federal tax bias toward car use. The federal tax bias in favor of the car should be eliminated. Until 1991, all costs of employee parking were exempt from federal business taxes. Employers' contributions to transit passes were limited to a mere $15 per month. An employer contributing more than this amount would lose even this small exemption. The Intermodal Surface Transportation Efficiency Act (ISTEA) limited the parking exemption to $155 per month while increasing the transit and employee-provided vanpool exemption to $60. Although this is an improvement over the previous unlimited federal subsidy of employee parking, it nevertheless represents a subsidy for the car that is two and a half times that of its alternative—an illogical measure from a transportation policy point of view.

The first step in correcting this counterproductive federal government subsidy would be to eliminate the pro-car bias by making exemptions equal for all modes. This would be a "modally neutral" policy. For the policy of favoring alternatives to the car, all tax exemptions of parking costs should be eliminated, as is the case in most other developed countries.

Parking rates. Parking rates can have a major impact on modal split in a particular area. Two elements are important—(1) parking rate level and (2) structure. The rate level influences the relative attractiveness of car use in relation to other modes, as well as whether or not a trip will be made. Structure, on the other hand, can also influence trip and modal split fluctuations in time. For example, a flat parking rate (independent of parking duration) encourages car commuting while discouraging short-duration parking, which usually serves trips for shopping or business meetings. From the system efficiency point of view, this is counterproductive, because commuting by car is the least efficient mode compared to others, whereas shopping and business meetings often require use of a car. Graduated parking rates, sometimes even progressive ones (hourly charge increases with duration) can therefore be used effectively to reduce peak-hour congestion and all-day parking, which is highly undesirable, especially in urban centers. At the same time, it means easy and economical parking for many trips, such as visits, shopping, and meetings.

Parking validation schemes. These plans usually offer partial or full payment for shoppers or customers. Many merchants consider this an effective marketing tool. As is true of the practices discussed above, parking validation is both socially inequitable and counterproductive from a transportation systems point of view. The competitive advantage of this mechanism exists, however, only as long as other stores offer free parking as well. Therefore, the inequity can be removed by introducing the same or similar accessibility conditions to all stores in a given area. Another correction would be that every store that validates parking must also compensate passenger fares for customers who come by transit.

In some cases, where transit and other non-car modes are thought to be used by lower-income or an otherwise "less favored" population, merchants reject any suggestion of extending validation to non–car users. In such a situation, parking validation amounts to a veiled segregation measure that probably could be legally challenged.

Parking "cashout." Parking cashout is an arrangement whereby employers who provide their employees with either free or greatly discounted parking convert this benefit into a "travel allowance"—an amount equal to the market value of a parking space—which each employee can then choose to use for parking or for transit fare, or can take as cash, then ride a bicycle or walk. This logical arrangement, supported by the employer and thus by all employees, would correct the present subsidy given only to car owners. From a transportation system point of view, it would eliminate the bias toward the car as opposed to other modes, which is generally counterproductive.

With respect to those who park their cars, this measure represents a clear change of "accounting form," but no change in the amount they pay. The cashout, however, makes the parking subsidy visible and offers the parkers an attractive way to change their mode of travel. Thus, its objective is to increase accountability and indirectly encourage use of alternatives to cars.

Cashout programs were introduced in Southern California in response to the Clean Air Act requirements. In many cities, they were found to be effective and well received by employees, especially when the option of using transit and vanpools was available. Employers' expenses were not increased where they represented cashout equal to the amount they had already been paying for parking. Shoup estimated that cashout programs can reduce the use of SOVs by the very significant amount of about 20 percent.

Reduced fee or free parking for HOVs. This measure, applied successfully in many cities, corrects the bias toward SOVs by favoring HOVs, which require much less space per passenger and thus increase efficiency. The measure thus represents compensation for social and environmental costs as well as an incentive to use an alternative to the SOV.

Fuel taxes. Today, gasoline and diesel fuel taxes represent the largest source of revenue paid by car and truck drivers for the public portions of the highway transportation system. These taxes have several important inherent advantages, including three well-known ones: they are related to vehicle travel distance; as such, they are acceptable to users; and they are easy to collect.

Current low fuel taxes and the resulting low price of fuel in the United States cause serious problems, however (Pennsylvania Environmental Council 1997; Transport Structure Plan Project Team 1990; Vuchic 1993). First, the fuel tax is a constant charge for travel regardless of location, facility, and time. Revenue collected is used, however, for a certain category of highway investments at any location in the country. For example, drivers on the very expensive Century Freeway in Los Angeles pay the same fuel taxes, and thus the same contribution to the Highway Trust Fund, as those who drive on local country highways (which involve no investment and little maintenance). Second, fuel costs do not reflect differences in the impacts of driving on congestion (a social cost); nor do they reflect environmental externalities, except for a small difference in increased fuel consumption in driving on highways under congested conditions. Third, their amount is so low that the revenues collected cover only a portion of total costs of highway infrastructure and operations. As mentioned in chapter 2, several studies have shown that the shortfall in revenues is large even if the extensive externalities are not included. Fourth, the direct cost of car use, even with fuel taxes, is so low that it involves a high consumer surplus. This leads to overconsumption, that is, excessive driving—the main component of urban transportation problems. Finally, with oil imports accounting for about 50 percent of oil consumption in the United States and continuing to increase (Wald 1997), this country's dependence on foreign oil represents a major economic and political liability.

Most countries that import large quantities of oil have policies aimed at reducing its consumption. The United States has no such policies. It is the only developed country that subsidizes the highway system as a whole (see figure 4.14 in chapter 4). While low or moderately priced transportation provides extensive economic and social benefits, extreme underpricing of one mode makes it necessary to subsidize other modes that perform more efficiently than the car under certain conditions, but which cannot compete on an out-of-pocket basis.

Stated simply, the main reason for the present unrealistically low, inefficient fuel taxation is that cheap driving is popular at the individual level. People love a "free lunch." The only way they will accept paying for it is if they understand the whole picture: that they pay for that lunch in another way, regardless, or that "overeating" resulting from the free food, or excessive driving due to low costs in this case, causes many negative side effects. Public support for taxes that are well explained and justified has been observed frequently in recent decades both in the United States and abroad.

Raising fuel taxes should be analyzed with respect to the impacts of those taxes on personal transportation (cars) and freight transport (trucks) in urban areas. Truck transport differs from car travel in that it has fewer alternatives. Most urban freight is carried by trucks, whereas for personal travel cars can be replaced to a considerable extent by transit, bicycles, paratransit, and other modes. The common features, however, are that some of the objectives, such as reduction of negative environmental impacts and decrease of excessive transport distances due to underpricing at the margin, are common for both passenger and freight transport.

The introduction of the federal fuel tax in 1956, accompanied by an explanation that the new revenues would result in construction of the Interstate System, found full public support. Parenthetically, it should be mentioned that the 4 cent per gallon tax represented about 20 percent of the price of gasoline at that time; today that tax would be equivalent to an additional tax of about 25 cents per gallon. With respect to average incomes (accounting for inflation), today's equivalent would be even greater. Similarly, in many European countries increases corresponding to as much as 50 cents per gallon were introduced for the purpose of improving transportation, decreasing negative environmental impacts, or, in the case of Germany, generating funds for investment needed in the former East Germany after unification in 1990.

In recent years, sensational media, populist dogma against all taxes, and lobbies interested in perpetuating total dependence on cheap car travel have generated strong negative publicity about any increase in gasoline taxes. This has been carried to such an extreme that, in many areas, highways and streets are poorly maintained because of insufficient funding, while increases of gasoline taxes, which would be moderate by any standards, are rejected as a "hardship for motorists." The hardships caused by poor roads, inadequate pedestrian facilities, and the absence of alternative means of travel tend to be overlooked.

A major obstacle to any increase in fuel taxes is the obsolete concept that the only acceptable use of revenues from highway use is for construction or operation of highways. This concept was highlighted by the 1956 federal legislation and by numerous state laws to that effect. "Motorists should get what they pay for" is the slogan powerfully promoted by highway interests. Actually, as discussed in chapter 3, the user tax concept is valid and useful occasionally, but it is illogical and counterproductive at other times. It is useful when funding for a specific facility or class of highways is needed. It is harmful when it is broadly applied, because it is based on the concept that highway users are a separate class of people, which directly contradicts the principle of treating intermodal transportation as an integrated system. The concept also defines highway transport as a branch of the economy that should be exempt from general taxation. Such a rationale is invalid and is contradicted by the practices of nearly all peer countries that use the fuel tax as a significant source of general tax revenue.

Consequently, the argument that the gasoline tax cannot be increased for "political reasons," used by those defending current trends to argue that the present "free driving syndrome" can never be altered, is supported neither by valid arguments nor by historic evidence. A substantial increase in fuel taxes is needed, not only to raise funds for improving the transportation system, but also as an essential element in improving the efficiency of both the highway system and the entire intermodal system. A substantial tax increase would actually amount to a small total expenditure for users (see chapter 2); thus, it would not represent a serious hardship either for businesses or for low-income people.

The visibility of a gas tax has both positive and negative features. Its advantage is that it is precisely what is needed to produce an effect on the reduction of VKT. Its disadvantage is that its opponents skillfully use the tax's high profile to point out its impact on individual drivers—without explaining its positive side in achieving the desirable goal of VKT reduction. Introduction of taxes will therefore take political leadership and a responsible, professional explanation of facts in order to overcome the populist, dogmatic opposition to all taxes.

Toll roads. Toll roads, or direct user payments for the construction and maintenance of highways, have received increasing attention in recent years. Tolls have traditionally been used for major structures such as bridges and tunnels (for example, the Hudson River crossings in New York City and Bay crossings in San Francisco). They were also applied to the financing of major roadways such as the Pennsylvania and New Jersey Turnpikes, New Jersey's Garden State Parkway, and other major roadways. Highway development using this type of financing, common after World War II, was diminished by the establishment of the Interstate Highway System in 1956, which was financed mostly by fuel and other taxes. Although designated as "user charges," these taxes are collected for all driving and thus have only an indirect relationship to specific highways.

The massive federal Interstate Highway System was subject to the legal prohibition against the collection of tolls on federally supported highways. This concept, indirectly further promoted by the adoption of the term "freeway" for all access-controlled highways, was strictly pursued until 1991. In response to increased interest in toll financing, the ISTEA of 1991 allowed allocation of federal funds to toll roads under certain conditions. There have been few toll roads constructed since then, and their financial and functional success has been mixed. It is significant, however, that these highways—particularly the State Route 91 express lanes in California—have introduced and experimented with some innovative pricing concepts that are likely to be used increasingly not only for new facilities, but for regulating demand and controlling traffic flow on existing facilities through selective variable pricing.

This evolution of highway tolls reflects the changing conditions, attitudes, and policies that come with the growth and maturation of the highway system. The initial concept was to charge tolls simply to finance construction and maintenance of a specific facility—a road, bridge, or tunnel, for instance. With the growing problem of low operating costs and the need to control traffic volume in high-density areas during the 1960s, road pricing received considerable attention, particularly in Great Britain. The third objective of tolls or road pricing may be to influence modal split and thus lead to a balanced transportation system. Another objective may be to recover the environmental costs of driving, either to compensate for them or to decrease costs by discouraging driving. In many countries, interest in tolls and road pricing for these and other objectives has increased steadily. Comprehensive descriptions and analyses of road pricing are given by the Congressional Budget Office (1997) and the Pennsylvania Environmental Council (1997). Lewis (1995) also discusses the characteristics of road pricing and possible ways to implement it, as well as describing several cases of its applications in different countries.

Area Licensing Scheme. The Area Licensing Scheme (ALS) is a special form of road—or, more precisely, area—pricing aimed at discouraging the use of cars in a potentially congested area and ensuring efficient, congestion-free streets. In addition, the ALS is used to influence modal choice—to encourage conversion of car trips into transit trips to achieve the overall goal of more efficient urban transportation. In these applications, the amount of tolls, or road-pricing rates, is based on neither facility nor user costs, but on the transportation system goals that should be achieved and on elasticity of demand for travel by car.

Road pricing. As a general concept, road pricing is a form of user charge for driving that is more specific than a fuel tax because it can be related to the type of facility used. Its basic features are similar to those of the fuel tax: it is proportional to use and, as a user charge, it is more acceptable than a flat tax per vehicle. Road pricing can be applied at several levels and can be aimed at multiple objectives. In all cases, it increases direct user costs. In its most common form—tolls for highways, bridges, tunnels, and similar facilities—pricing is used for its initial purpose: to pay for the construction and maintenance of the facility. Thus, it eliminates subsidies by other users or from other government sources. The next most common objective of road pricing may be to reflect the indirect costs and externalities of car use. The purpose of these charges is twofold: to recover the imposed costs (and sometimes to finance their alleviation or compensation); and to discourage excessive travel, thus preventing generation of externalities.

The potential benefits of road-use pricing are very significant. Pricing represents the most effective—sometimes the only—tool for converting highways from uncontrolled facilities that break down whenever volume approaches capacity, to an efficiently operated system that is controlled so it does not reach a breakdown condition. This means that a change from individual equilibrium to social optimum can be achieved. The benefits of this upgraded control have been amply demonstrated by an ALS used to maintain efficient traffic conditions throughout the central urban area of Singapore since 1975. Recently, this was followed by implementation of similar systems in several Norwegian, French, and Swedish cities, and by the planning of charges for large areas in the Netherlands and Great Britain (Gomez-Ibanez and Small 1994). Whenever there is a change in conditions—such as an increase in traffic volume or a shift in hourly traffic fluctuations—the system is simply adjusted by raising the entry fee accordingly to retain the same efficient traffic conditions.

Road and area pricing goals may be set at different levels. At Level IV, for instance, pricing may be used to control traffic on a single facility. The recently opened private toll facility SR-91 in Southern California is a good

PHOTO 7.4
The Area Licensing Scheme, shown here in Singapore, is a simple and very effective method of preventing CBD congestion. *(Vukan R. Vuchic)*

example. The revenue collection and control of traffic conditions in a network, such as the tolls on the Hudson River tunnels and bridges in New York City, are goals mostly at Level III. Intermodal travel distribution, i.e., shifting travel from highway to transit and other modes—represents a Level II goal. The Singapore ALS has been conceived as such a measure (to some extent, the Hudson crossings tolls also reflect modal split considerations). Finally, the use of road pricing to reduce VKT to ameliorate the "collision between cities and cars" is a Level I policy tool. Interestingly, the ring of tolls around Oslo was set up primarily to generate revenues for highway and transit improvements (Level III), but the tolls actually have had both intermodal and city impact aspects (Levels II and I). The reduction of VKT to meet clean air standards, legally required in the United States and a few other countries, also represents Level I and, to some extent, even national goals.

If road pricing is so important and potentially so effective, why does it remain mostly in theoretical studies and academic papers (where there is a considerable consensus about its desirability across the ideological spectrum, from liberals to conservatives)? Traditionally, there have been only two obstacles (albeit serious ones) to its implementation:

1. *The physical difficulty of collecting charges* that could apply to entire areas and change with locations or times. Stopping all traffic for toll collection in a dense urban area has often been considered physically and operationally infeasible.
2. *Opposition by the driving public,* which has an aversion to out-of-pocket payments. This opposition creates a disadvantage for the areas served by tolled facilities versus those with free services.

The first obstacle may appear more difficult than it actually is. Singapore has shown that a large central area can be cordoned off by a ring of "gates," which actually consist only of overhead signs. Drivers make payments prior to approaching these locations, so that entry does not require them to stop. Moreover, the invention of "smart cards" has made feasible efficient collection of charges in any amount, variable by location, time, and vehicle. Implementation of the system for charge collection and control does, of course, require careful planning and the installation of extensive electronic or other control systems; but the entire concept can be applied on most streets in urban and suburban areas.

The second obstacle, public opposition, remains serious, although some inroads have been made. Similar to the problem of introducing a fuel tax, the introduction of new charges is strongly opposed because "free driving" is considered by many to be a basic feature of our society and living standard. The difficult task facing professionals and, ultimately, political leaders is to demonstrate to the public that, in many cases, charges for driving can create conditions that may give travelers the choice between low-cost congested facilities and tolled but uncongested ones. In many situations, the case is even stronger. As the late Nobelist transportation economist William Vickrey (1969) discussed in his writings, certain types of user charges may create conditions in which drivers on *all* highways on alternative routes or in an area (Level III) would be better off than when there are *no* charges. The same point is shown in chapter 2 for Level II: a shift of travel from highway to transit generally results in lower disutility to both modes.

The task of gaining public acceptance may be somewhat easier for road pricing than for fuel taxes because it applies to specific areas. If drivers are burdened by major highway congestion day after day, gradual introduction of road pricing in a few places may be a precursor to maturing public understanding, which will eventually prevail and allow the introduction of a more intelligent highway of multimodal transportation systems than the presently popular "free" but inefficient ones.

Peak-period road pricing. Increasing prices during peak traffic periods is another measure that combines multiple objectives. Its main purpose is to reduce peak-period congestion by influencing the time distribution of travel (a "flattening of peaks") to achieve more efficient traffic flow. This effect is achieved by charges that directly reflect the social costs of driving. Additionally, peak-hour pricing usually results in a shift of modal split from SOVs to their alternatives that have the greatest advantage in efficiency during peak periods.

Distributing travel from peak to other periods is socially beneficial when it shifts discretionary travel or trips of people who do not have firm schedules. However, many schemes of telecommuting—one weekday at home, or even flexible hours—that are introduced to reduce highway traffic volume may have social and economic costs (inefficiency of work), and thus represent negative impacts of traffic congestion. In many cases, reduction of dependence on SOVs by improved transit, paratransit, bicycling, and carpools can alleviate traffic congestion with less sacrifice of economic efficiency and convenience than suppression of travel to and from work and its concomitant decline in efficiency. Detailed discussions of peak-period pricing appear in Komanoff (1997) and Transport Structure Plan Project Team (1990).

Congestion pricing. Congestion pricing has the same basic objective as peak-period pricing. The main difference between the two is that congestion pricing is applied not for fixed time periods but as a direct function of traffic volume on a highway or in an area. This concept has some theoretical validity, in that it would result in a "flexible optimization" of traffic volume. In practice, however, there are two problems with such flexibility. First, the equipment and control of such a pricing system would be more complicated than pricing during fixed time periods. Second, and more important, is that drivers want to know what the charges are before they enter a facility. Unexpected changes—surprises—would not be acceptable. This has been proven by the negative reactions to this type of pricing when it was tested on the new SR-91 toll facility in California. Moreover, if drivers cannot predict the price they have to pay, the impact of such pricing on their behavior would be diminished. Thus, the main objective of the pricing system would be defeated.

A review of congestion pricing applications in different countries is presented by Gomez-Ibanez and Small (1994). The same topic is discussed by Komanoff (1997), Lewis (1995), and Pennsylvania Environmental Council (1997), among others.

Ecotaxes. These are surtaxes imposed in some countries with the specific goal of reducing car use for environmental protection (see Pennsylvania Environmental Council 1997). An entire category of "polluters should pay" taxes are being widely discussed and implemented in specific cases in the countries of the European Union, as well as in some of the U.S. states. They are representative of the taxes imposed to reflect and reduce the negative impacts and externalities of car use and other activities affecting the man-made and natural environment.

Registration fees. Fees contingent on car-km (miles) driven would make the present fixed registration cost more proportional to the extent of car use and thus shift a portion of fixed costs into variable user costs. Basically, this is a sound concept, but its application is limited to states that have substantial car registration fees. In some states, with registration well below $100 per year, this measure would not be felt unless registration were substantially increased. Various aspects of registration fees are discussed by Komanoff (1997) and Pennsylvania Environmental Council (1997).

Insurance at the pump. Also known as "pay as you drive" (PAYD), this measure would consist of a fuel price increment that would provide for basic, no-fault auto insurance coverage. It would require certain legislation by state governments, which would collect the premiums and invite auto insurers to bid for blocks of business (Gordon 1997; Litman 1997; Pennsylvania Environmental Council 1997).

PAYD has two positive features. First, it represents a visible increase in car operating cost without necessarily increasing drivers' total costs. Second, it represents automatic payment of basic car insurance—a major step toward solving the problem of uninsured vehicles and motorists. Among its disadvantages is the inability to apply rates according to drivers' safety records or risk categories, although this would not be a problem if PAYD were used to replace only the basic categories, such as liability and fire, rather than all the insurance for a car. The questions of how to include trucks in this scheme, and what the impact of PAYD on trucks would be, need careful analysis. Opposition from the stakeholders in the present system, such as lawyers and insurance companies and their agents, may be an obstacle to the introduction of this type of insurance mechanism.

Disincentives to car ownership. Disincentives to car ownership can be effected on a national basis through taxation of car purchases and high registration fees. In some countries, usually those with no domestic car-manufacturing industry, governments pursue this policy to reduce imports as well as to reduce VKT, with all the attendant problems generated by heavy highway travel. Most countries, however, find policies that directly discourage travel more effective in reducing VKT than those that limit car ownership.

On the other hand, many countries encourage car ownership to strengthen their automobile industry. This policy seldom takes into account the problems that accompany a rapid increase in car ownership. Such is the case in many developing countries, including, recently, the People's Republic of China. There is little doubt that encouraging car ownership results in urban transportation problems with negative consequences that may easily outweigh any benefits from the development of a nation's automobile industry.

Car-use pricing presents a major dilemma for contemporary societies because it involves the collision of two powerful forces. On one side of the equation is the common sentiment that roads are a basic element of the public infrastructure that should be free for use. On the other side is the fact that highway and street systems, particularly in urban areas, are so extensive that they have major impacts on the environment and society and cannot function efficiently without large-scale investment and the control of traffic flow. The investments, efficiency of flow, and control of impacts can be effected through pricing much more efficiently than by any other means. The problem lies in explaining to the traveling public and to residents that "free driving" is neither physically nor operationally feasible in urban areas—the focal points of our civilization. Consequently, populations must be made aware that car-use pricing is, in many situations and forms, necessary for greater highway system efficiency, for achieving a superior intermodal system, and for the existence of livable cities.

Reduction of VKT through Organizational, Planning, and Design Measures

The measures directly or indirectly aimed at reducing VKT and increasing the livability of cities include a range—from administrative, mostly palliative prohibitions or limitations on car use to long-term area or transportation system designs that generate fewer and shorter car trips.

Even/odd license numbers. This driving restriction is a purely regulatory, usually temporary measure to enforce reduction of VKT. The concept is simple: a decree is made that on alternate days only cars with, respectively, even or odd license numbers may be driven. Thus, half the cars are simply prohibited from driving in the city. This measure effectively achieves a significant reduction in the volume of vehicular travel and induces car users to travel by some mode other than car, or to carpool. The negative side of the measure is that it can impose serious problems on those people who do not have or cannot use any other mode of travel.

Driving restriction by license number has been used effectively on occasion in a number of metropolitan areas that faced emergency conditions and where reduction of VKT was urgently needed. It was first introduced during the energy crisis of the 1970s as a fuel conservation measure. Seoul, Korea, used it as a traffic-reduction measure during the 1988 Olympic Games, and some large employers have continued to apply this restriction to reduce the enormous pressures of street congestion in that city. Mexico City and Paris have applied this measure to reduce the volume of exhaust during periods of severe air pollution.

Parking supply standards. These standards represent a powerful tool in controlling the use of cars in cities and suburbs, and thus in controlling overall modal split. The standards, therefore, have a double impact on the livability of areas. Ample and low-cost or "free" parking induces reliance on the car and physically deteriorates the human character of areas by dedication of large spaces and structures to parking. A restricted parking supply and consequent higher parking rates, on the other hand, encourage alternatives to the car and allow most of the urban land to be used for more human-oriented activities.

Parking policies and standards, usually implemented by ordinances, have undergone an interesting evolution (Wormser 1997). When increased use of cars caused congestion on urban streets, cities mandated that new construction provide a certain minimum number of off-street parking spaces to prevent further congestion. This measure, however, led to difficulties when standards were very high or when developers provided more than the minimum number of required spaces. The problem became especially serious in cities where the idea that ample parking is always "good for business" prevailed. Many cities built so many parking lots and garages that even their CBDs became dominated by parking facilities—such was the case in Dayton, Houston, and Syracuse, for example. In addition to the physical damage to an area's human character, such ample parking makes use of any other mode very inefficient.

Recognizing the negative impacts of excessive parking in CBDs and other major activity centers, cities began to reverse the regulations. Instead of requiring a minimum number of parking spaces for each new development, they introduced a maximum number of spaces that could be provided. Thus, a ceiling on the supply of parking was introduced to meet two major objectives: (1) to increase the use of transit and other modes, and (2) to prevent an excessive concentration of vehicles in an area that should be human-oriented. Many cities, including Hamburg, London, Boston, and

PHOTO 7.5
Boulder, Colorado, street design provides for cars, bicycles, and pedestrians. *(Mario Semmler)*

Portland (Oregon), have a maximum number of parking spaces allowed in their central areas.

The parking problem in suburban areas is somewhat different. Town ordinances often prescribe not only the minimum number of spaces required for any new development, but even the dimensions of parking stalls. Typically, the required number is quite high and the dimensions, based on the standard large car of the 1960s, are larger than necessary for today's car sizes. These requirements result in high costs, excessive land consumption, and reduced pressure for the development of alternatives to car use. For example, many suburban residential and commercial areas are designed without sidewalks, forcing people to use cars even for short trips.

Because parking supply and pricing are among the most powerful factors influencing modal split and the livability of an area, all regulations, planning, and control measures that affect parking should be carefully considered and incorporated into a coordinated intermodal transportation policy (Vuchic 1978; Bayliss 1998).

Traffic calming. The livability of cities or discrete sectors within urban areas can be enhanced by the control of speed and reduction of vehicular

PHOTO 7.6
In Newark, Delaware, traffic taming is employed for a pedestrian crossing on a state highway that traverses the town center. *(Vukan R. Vuchic)*

traffic volume. In most existing cities, street networks cannot be redesigned to change traffic flows, but there are a number of organizational measures that can be taken to achieve these goals.

Also known as "traffic taming," traffic calming is a comprehensive set of techniques for control of vehicular traffic. It is usually applied in residential streets and areas to enhance their safety and livability by protecting pedestrian activities and children's play. Traffic-calming techniques reduce noise and pollution while permitting through traffic at controlled speeds. Zein et al. (1997) report that the implementation of legal, visual, and physical traffic-calming measures in four sections of the Greater Vancouver area resulted in an 18 to 60 percent reduction of accidents. In some countries, such as Germany and the Netherlands, the concept of traffic calming is well known and legally defined. A "calmed" street has a low speed limit, and drivers expect to find various speed-control devices. These range from signs and pavement markings to street realignment—curves in the roadway, narrow locations, and physical "bottlenecks" (islands in the middle of the roads, speed bumps, large flower or bush containers, widened sidewalks with benches, and frequent crosswalks).

Initially, during the 1960s, traffic calming was used in the form of adjustments to existing streets for modification of traffic lanes and sidewalks without major reconstruction. Later, streets were reconstructed to incorporate new design and regulatory concepts. What would have been considered obstacles and safety hazards to vehicles during the 1960s have since been recognized as efficient elements of traffic calming technique in the 1990s. Street alignments, designs, visual effects, and objects in calmed streets actually are "obstacles" to vehicles, aimed at forcing them to travel at low or moderate speeds. The safety hazard is eliminated by making drivers aware of these elements. Driving with caution results in lower speed and increased safety. Initially implemented in European countries, this concept has in recent years spread to metropolitan areas of North America.

Appleyard (1976, 1981) provides an excellent discussion of livability in urban areas. Comprehensive treatment of contemporary residential streets—including the planning process, street layout and design, traffic control with emphasis on calming, and implementation procedures—is provided by Homburger et al. (1989). Newman, Kenworthy, and Robinson (1992) and Union Internationale des Transports Publics (1991) discuss traffic reduction and calming in central city sections. Reviews of extensive experience with traffic calming, pedestrian malls, zones, networks, and so on have been presented by Monheim (1994), 1000 Friends of Oregon (1995), and Topp (1990, 1993), among others.

A particular advantage of well-planned, -designed, and -implemented traffic-calming techniques is that the design, infrastructure, and stationary objects in traffic-calmed streets and areas perform most of the control, greatly reducing the need for policing and other labor-intensive measures.

Taming of traffic is the common objective of a broad movement in many countries to reconcile transportation needs with the livability of areas, particularly residential ones. Traffic calming, most widely used in Western Europe, is the most advanced method for a comprehensive and permanent solution of this problem. In the United States, with extensive freeway networks through residential areas, sound barriers have become common as a means of reconciling traffic and livability; but this device solves only the noise and visual problem—local traffic requires additional control measures. In some cities of North America, and even more frequently in Latin America, the security aspect is so important that walls and gates around neighborhoods are in wide use. By controlling entry of each individual vehicle by permanently employed guards, traffic volume is automatically reduced and one element of traffic calming is achieved. However, vehicle speed and behavior inside the residential area are not necessarily controlled by this arrangement.

Layout and design. The layout and design of existing streets should sometimes be evaluated. Standard design practices should be questioned and new concepts explored to meet the higher levels of emerging livability requirements. A study of neighborhood design and traffic considerations performed by a committee of the Institute of Transportation Engineers (1997) found that many standards for residential neighborhoods in the United States have followed 1950s guidelines, which were based on the presumed need for evacuation in the event of a nuclear attack! Street design is also discussed by Burden (1997) and 1000 Friends of Oregon (1995).

In conventional street design, wide, straight streets were considered desirable to provide ample curb parking and to serve "future needs." Experience later showed that streets three or four lanes wide (10–13 meters, or 30–40 feet) actually induce faster travel, as a natural driver behavior. Control of speed by policing such facilities is difficult because it appears "artificial." Narrower streets and traffic calming are increasingly being recognized as superior for neighborhood attractiveness and easier traffic control.

Auto-restricted zones (ARZ). ARZ is a broad set of traffic-calming measures—including regulatory, design, and sometimes pricing measures—used with the goal of drastically reducing vehicular traffic, strengthening the pedestrian character of an area, and protecting and intensifying human activities in a physically defined zone. Usually, this is applied to urban areas that have a residential or local-activity character, though sometimes it is also used for shopping and business zones (in the latter cases, the required parking facilities must be provided on the perimeter of the ARZ). In some locations, this technique can be used in an area that is functionally and visually delineated by major arterials, parks, hills, or bodies or water. With imaginative design and regulatory interventions, ARZ can also be applied to areas consisting of open street networks, such as a rectangular grid. This is achieved by strongly discouraging through traffic and reducing the speed and volume of area-destined vehicles.

It is important that the movement of transit vehicles, usually buses, through ARZs be planned so that they are not made inefficient by traffic diversions and limitations. On the contrary, by exempting buses or rail vehicles from traffic restrictions, transit becomes relatively more attractive than car travel within ARZs. This can be done by providing surface rail transit tracks through diversion barriers, or by "traps"—wide-wheel path surfaces with a sand ditch in the middle that buses can negotiate but cars cannot (used, for example, in suburban areas of Calgary, Canada).

The reduction of vehicular traffic is achieved by measures that may strongly discourage parking and make travel through the zone slow and inconvenient. Regulatory measures may include prohibition of certain movements; making streets one-way so that through trips must make turns; and parking restrictions such as limitation of parking spaces, limited parking duration, or entry and parking allowed only with permits for residents or certain special-user categories. This technique has been used in many neighborhoods of North American cities since the 1970s, when the concept was introduced with support from the Urban Mass Transportation Administration (UMTA) and was documented by five reports on the topic (Herald 1977). Under a variety of designations, the ARZ concept is used extensively in the central areas of European cities such as Rome, Florence, and Salzburg.

Design measures include a variety of street designs, curb layouts, and objects that direct or prohibit traffic movements. For example, simple diagonal barriers at intersections can be constructed to force turns and prevent straight travel through the zone. Street designs that include curves, "bottlenecks" by extruding curbs, islands in the middle of the street, speed humps and speed bumps, small traffic circles at intersections, and even mid-block cul-de-sacs with turnarounds all create restrictions and "inconveniences" to fast and through traffic and make the remaining traffic much more compatible with the pedestrian character of an area.

The livability of ARZs is enhanced by good transit services, easy access for taxis, design of streets with pedestrian furniture, mini-plazas, covered arcades along storefronts, trees, flowers, and other elements that physically and visually attract and encourage shoppers, residents, and children's activities.

Traffic cells. Already mentioned in chapter 4, traffic cells are also based on the concept of reducing vehicular traffic, achieved by the prohibition of all traffic except transit vehicles among the cells. With the goal of increasing livability, traffic cells usually are applied to the urban core zone, often the central business district. Circumferential arterials around this central zone are improved, and parking facilities are provided along its periphery. The zone is then divided into several "cells"—areas that vehicles can enter from the circumferential arterial, but from which they cannot travel to other cells. Transit vehicles follow the dividing lines between the cells, so that they are not intersected by vehicular traffic. Traffic cells applied in Bremen, Gothenburg, and several other cities have proved effective in achieving a drastic reduction of private car traffic, greater use of transit, and increased commercial and civic activities, which are stimulated by the pedestrian-friendly environment.

Woonerf. The *woonerf* is a concept developed in the Netherlands for designing residential neighborhoods of any density. It provides for vehicular traffic access and limited parking designed in such a way that it co-exists with bicyclists, pedestrians, and even children at play. It is, in a way, a traffic-calmed neighborhood. The woonerf's desirable relationship between people and vehicles is thus not retrofitted but is integrated from the beginning, and thus is more efficient. The woonerf concept is applicable to the design of new residential developments.

Traditional neighborhood development (TND). Traditional neighborhood development (TND) (Institute of Transportation Engineers 1997) and transit-oriented development (TOD) (Porter 1997; Project for Public Spaces 1997) are designs for residential neighborhoods and communities that provide mixed land uses and nearby location of residential buildings with stores, neighborhood schools, and various services. Many trips that residents make are thus within walking distance, children can use bicycles, and transit stops are placed at the core of the developments. The design of these communities provides travel and other functions that are superior in terms of convenience and involve lower costs than those required by low-density, single-family housing suburbs.

This type of community design has long been used in countries that practice comprehensive physical planning, such as Switzerland and the Scandinavian countries. In recent years, these designs have been used increasingly even in the United States, Australia, and Canada, which traditionally have emphasized strict separation of land uses and the maximum residential lot sizes that owners can afford. Expansive land consumption, high-cost municipal services, total dependence on cars, and lack of mobility among non–car drivers are problems that have led to a fundamental change in planning concepts in many areas. A review of policies and actions supporting TODs in U.S. cities may be found in TCRP 20 (Porter 1997).

INCREASING THE ROLE OF TRANSIT

The important (and stable) role that transit should play in increasing the livability of all medium-sized and large cities can be achieved through a number of measures. Appropriate measures range from intermodal urban transportation policies and their implementation via regulatory measures to the construction of high-performance systems. These incentives, or measures for increasing the use of transit, should be based on a rational, comprehensive transportation policy that encompasses a clear definition of the role of transit in the city and its relationship to other modes. The policy should include numerous measures and actions, which can be classified by duration as short-, medium-, and long-term transit incentives. The major categories are listed below and briefly described.

SHORT-TERM TRANSIT INCENTIVES:

- Introduction of priorities for transit vehicles in traffic
- Introduction or strengthening of intermodal integration of transit modes, as well as between transit and other modes
- Contributions to, or full payment of, transit fares by employers, businesses, and retail stores, usually related to greater use of transit passes

MEDIUM-TERM TRANSIT MEASURES:

- Introduction of advanced methods of fare collection, such as self-service and smart cards for all transportation payments—tolls, transit fares, parking, and so on
- Use of ITS techniques to implement transit priorities, integrate modes, increase reliability of services, and improve transit information

LONG-TERM TRANSIT MEASURES:

- Provide adequate, stable, and predictable financing for transit; this may be from an integrated transportation fund, a special, dedicated tax, or some other revenue source
- Plan and build a transit network as a high-performance system competitive with the car
- Incorporate transit in the planning of all major developments, to create intermodal services that enhance livability

Each of these transit improvements and incentives is briefly discussed below.

The role of transit in the city must be clearly defined. As described in chapter 2, in small cities social aspects dominate the services transit must provide. The system typically consists of buses and minibuses on streets, complemented by taxi and other paratransit services. In larger cities, the advantage of transit—transporting large volumes of passengers more efficiently—becomes increasingly important. To utilize this advantage to its fullest, transit must be competitive with the car, especially in terms of speed and reliability. This can be achieved only by giving transit vehicles priority in traffic or by providing separate rights-of-way (category B or A). Transit planning and operation differ considerably for the two types of systems—street-running and independent. Therefore, defining the role of transit is necessary for an overall approach to planning and operating transit systems.

Short-term Transit Incentives

Priority for transit vehicles. Common practice in several western European countries, priority for transit vehicles is seldom used in North America and other parts of the world. The traditional traffic-engineering practice of basing traffic control on the number of vehicles was valid when each mode was treated separately. With the adoption of a comprehensive transportation policy, this practice has been replaced by the fundamental, logical principle that a person, not a vehicle, should be the basic unit in regulating traffic. If a street's productivity is measured in persons transported per unit of time, all traffic control must be modified to favor high-occupancy vehicles in a way that is proportional to occupancy in each vehicle category. This approach leads logically to the introduction of transit priority in traffic.

"Transit First." The popular name for giving transit priority treatment is "Transit First," a set of primarily low-investment cost measures that allow transit vehicles to travel faster and to experience fewer delays along their routes. Transit vehicles are separated at intersections or along streets by transit, or "diamond," lanes or by curb-protected rights-of-way. At signals, they either get a green light before other traffic or have a "full override" (an immediate green light) as they approach an intersection. Transit stops are located conveniently for pedestrians, transit vehicles can make turns or travel through certain blocks where other vehicles are prohibited, and so on.

In broader terms, these physical and operational measures can be complemented by pricing, publicity, and other image-building information to provide an overall package of actions stimulating transit use. The benefit of the Transit First measures lies not only in the better services they provide, but in the distinct image and competitive advantage they give transit over other traffic. Detailed descriptions of Transit First measures are presented in Dunlay and Soyk (1978), Horn et al. (1995), Ministry of the Environment of Finland et al. (1996), Metropolitan Transit Development Board (1993), and Union Internationale des Transports Publics (1991).

Intermodal integration. Intermodal integration is paramount in increasing the quality of transit services and attracting ridership. Competing with the ubiquitous travel capability of the car, transit must also provide service that is "seamless," involving a minimum of interruption. To achieve this, transit must consist of an integrated network of one or several modes provided by one or more public agencies or private companies. When a passenger wants to travel by transit, he or she should be able to view transit as a unified system rather than several different systems or modes that require special knowledge about which lines to use, how to transfer, and how to pay fares. Provision of services by different agencies should not represent a problem for passengers; transfers between different modes should be designed and organized so that passengers believe it is well worth the effort of transferring to use two different modes, each one superior to other alternatives for a given trip. For example, transferring from a suburban bus to a rail line is acceptable if the travel on rail is sufficiently superior to the bus travel to outweigh the effort required to transfer.

Organizational integration. Transit services must be provided either by one agency or by an umbrella organization that unifies all functions affecting passengers. This is achieved by having agencies and private companies make special arrangements for joint terminals, fares, and so on. The best known is the highly effective concept of the transit federation, which is used in a number of central European cities (Homburger and Vuchic 1972). The transit federation plans and coordinates all modes and services, collects fare revenue, and redistributes it to the partners on the basis of an agreed-upon formula reflecting the costs of performed work.

Operational integration. In operationally integrated service, different lines and modes are coordinated by network layout and schedules designed for the most efficient and convenient transfers at stations or terminals. Fares are paid only once for each trip, regardless of the modes used. Information about services is also fully integrated.

Physical integration. In physically integrated systems, the location and design of stations and the control of vehicle movements are planned and designed so that passenger transfers are safe, fast, and convenient.

Integrated transit systems are much more capable of attracting passengers and competing with other transport modes than are separate modes. It is therefore important to provide integration even if there are several transit service providers. Deregulation usually destroys service integration. This is admitted even by its promoters (Hibbs 1986), and it is a major reason for the decline in ridership that deregulation brings (Fawkner 1995; Pickup 1991; Vuchic 1986). Privatization may, but does not necessarily, lead to problems of disintegration. If a central coordinator is retained, it is entirely possible to achieve cost savings while retaining integrated services, even when services are provided by several public agencies and private companies. This has been shown in a number of U.S. cities that privatized some of their services (Morlok 1987), as well as by the excellent integration of transit and intercity rail services in Switzerland, which includes a number of national and local operators in both the public and private sectors.

PHOTO 7.7
Pedestrian zone served directly by transit in Jena, Germany. *(Mario Semmler)*

Fare policy. The level and structure of fares, as well as innovative collection methods, can have a significant impact on the attraction of travel by transit (Pucher and Hirschman 1993; Transport Structure Plan Project Team 1990). The level and structure of transit fares should represent an optimal compromise between the need to maximize revenues and the dominant goal of transit services—to attract as many trips as possible. How high fares can be while still attracting potential riders depends on local conditions in a city—physical size, population density, social conditions, and so on. Quality and pricing of competing services is another major factor. The low direct cost of driving often dictates moderate fares, which, in turn, make subsidies necessary. If parking and other aspects of car use are also subsidized, the need for transit subsidies is even greater.

To enable transit to compete with low, direct car-user costs, there has been a trend toward increased use of transit passes—weekly, monthly, and in some cities, even annual. With a pass, the urban traveler selecting a mode of travel faces a decision between more comparable expenditures: transit travel, similar to driving with many subsidies, does not involve a direct payment for each trip. To compensate for the indirect subsidies of car travel (such as parking or use of a company car), employers in many cities have begun to contribute to the cost of transit passes. This contribution may be in the form of "parking cashout" schemes, or supplying transit passes through monthly payroll at a discounted rate.

Medium-term Transit Incentives

Technical and operational innovations often allow significant improvements of transit services. These include innovations such as smart cards for fare payment, ITS measures, "cleaner" buses, low-floor buses and LRT vehicles, and improved monitoring of operations. Most belong in the category of medium-term improvements.

Introduction of "smart cards." Smart cards are credit or charge cards that can be used for transit or, even more effectively, for all transportation charges, including gasoline, tolls, and parking. Often, they have a significant impact on attracting ridership. This technological innovation will also help in making transit charges comparable to charges for driving. It will make feasible various innovations in charge differentiation, such as peak-hour pricing and commuter discounts, in addition to making it easier to implement and change these charges as required.

Intelligent Transportation System (ITS). ITS technology and programs are heavily funded by governments and industry in many advanced countries. Although strongly oriented to highway traffic, ITS includes a number of features that can benefit transit. In addition to the safety devices and increased reliability of traffic flow, which benefit all vehicles, ITS can provide significant improvements in the precise tracking of transit vehicles. This facilitates the operation of control centers that follow bus travel and intervene when delays occur, detours are needed, or other unusual events must be handled.

ITS technology will bring major transit improvements in the area of communications. For example, with simultaneous tracking, vehicle positions can be checked against scheduled times and locations. Comprehensive information about schedules, as well as continuous reports about the conditions of each line, can be made available to potential travelers calling in by telephone or personal computer.

Although ITS has the potential to play a significant role in controlling intermodal relations and to move modal split toward the social optimum, this potential is not, at present, receiving sufficient attention in ITS development. The enormous efforts to develop ITS are limited to Levels IV and III: individual components and entire modes, mostly highways and some transit. The complex problems at the transportation systems Level III, for which ITS has potential, have not yet been afforded much attention.

Long-term Improvements to Upgrade Transit

Adequate and stable financing. Availability of needed funds is a basic condition for implementing the permanent provision of attractive services that can respond to increasing demands for high-quality, high-volume public transportation. As with most transportation modes, methods of financing transit systems differ for capital expenditures and operating expenditures (Pucher and Hirschman 1993; Transport Structure Plan Project Team 1990).

Capital expenditures include purchases of vehicles and construction of facilities and infrastructure for high-performance systems, such as rights-of-way and stations for rail systems and exclusive busways. These expenditures usually exceed the financial capacity of local governments; thus, state and federal governments must participate with significant, often dominant contributions. Allocation of funds should always be subject to careful review of the justification for the planned transit lines or facilities and of the efficiency of their design.

Operating assistance for transit should be a result of intermodal policies that dictate how favorable the policy is toward attracting travelers to transit and what level of cost recovery through fares is required. While efficiency of transit system operation is a major factor in the coverage of operating costs through fares, the degree of subsidy or charges for car use also has a major impact on the required level of cost recovery.

Private contributions to transit investment and operating costs can play a positive role in expanding transit systems or providing attractive services. For example, "benefit-sharing programs" have been organized in Washington, D.C., through which businesses near or around future metro stations have paid for extensions of mezzanines or other access facilities to their buildings. Additionally, employers and storeowners may sponsor shuttle bus services from rail lines to their buildings or neighborhoods. This public–private cooperation is useful, even though private contributions usually represent only a fraction of the total costs of system construction and operation. Similar to highways and other passenger transportation facilities, transit investments come mostly from public funds.

High-performance transit. High-performance transit must be provided in all medium-sized and large cities to achieve a balanced transportation system and avoid total car dependence (Vuchic 1981; Newman, Kenworthy, and Robinson 1992; Pucher and Hirschman 1993). The basic feature of high-performance transit—its physical separation from general traffic (ROW category B or A)—provides service that is reliable, high-speed, and independent of congestion, and that has a strong image, so that it becomes competitive with car travel. Transit modes in this category are usually rail systems—LRT, metro, or regional rail—but buses on busways, AGT systems, and monorails may also be included.

Because of separate rights-of way, all these systems require substantial investment; but their construction represents a fundamental change in the character of the transit system, as well as an upgrading of its role in the city. This has been demonstrated in dozens of cities that have constructed new rail and busway systems in recent years—from Ottawa and Curitiba with busways, to San Diego and Calgary with LRT, to Munich, Washington (D.C.), and San Francisco with their metro and regional rail systems.

Consequently, the only way cities with solely bus services on streets can enhance their human orientation, livability, and sustainability is to make a major effort to develop a partially or fully independent transit system. Ideally, such a system will have a network that provides reasonable coverage of the city and region, such as is available in Chicago, Toronto, and Hamburg. For cities that are belatedly developing such a system, it is important that a general plan be conceived and consistently implemented in stages.

The task of constructing a high-performance transit network appears daunting for cities that have only buses on streets; recent developments, however, show that a consistent policy and program for implementation of a balanced system is achievable. For example, some 15 to 25 years ago, Atlanta, Washington, San Diego, and Calgary started by building single rail lines. Today, they have sizable high-performance rail transit networks and are far ahead of their peers who stayed with buses only, such as Seattle and Houston, in offering the diversified mobility of a balanced system.

From the considerable variety of modes available to cities wishing to upgrade their transit systems, the most common selections are among the following.

Buses on busways. Busways, including guided buses (O-Bahn), are effective in networks with numerous branches. Some branches may be either busways or regular streets with exclusive bus or general-purpose lanes. Exemplified by the systems of Ottawa or Curitiba, these systems can serve a network of diametrical lines covering the city and suburbs, rather than only commuter runs into and out of the CBD.

Although buses on busways may require investments similar to those for LRT with similar ROWs on trunk lines, their advantage lies in the continuity of lines into numerous branches where streets are used—thus obviating the need for investment. In other words, buses on busways can provide a more extensive network for a given investment than any other mode with a separate ROW. Moreover, the introduction of busways is simpler because no new technology is needed, with the possible exception of somewhat differently designed buses to better fit the operating conditions of the upgraded network. Some shortcomings of this mode are high operating costs (a large number of drivers without the economy of high-capacity units such as trains on rail systems have), lack of a distinct system image, and vulnerability to a compromise with their reserved ROW—often leading to conversion of busways into HOV facilities, which diminishes services into a commuter system with little competitive advantage over cars, vans, or other alternative modes.

Light Rail Transit. LRT is the most diversified rail transit mode, due to its ability to utilize different alignments and types of ROW and to provide a broad range of capacity, performance, and types of service. It is the fastest-growing high-performance mode in North America and many other countries because it fits the need for upgrading transit in many cities served only by buses. These cities need transit service superior to that provided by buses, but with a larger network and much lower investment than metro systems require. Typically, when a city builds a major LRT line, it is the major trunk line. Its upgrade to a rail mode allows the restructuring of the entire bus transit network into a system that attracts a large share of transit riders, including many new riders. LRT usually has a major impact on the downtown of the core city, as well as on the outlying towns and subcenters it serves. This has been the case, for example, in Newcastle (England), Grenoble (France), and in many North American cities, such as San Diego, Buffalo, Portland, Sacramento, Calgary, and St. Louis.

Investment costs for LRT vary greatly by type of ROW and local conditions. They are usually higher than the cost of busways, except for special cases, such as the trolleybus tunnel in Seattle. (The reason is that tunnels for highway vehicles must be much larger and are more expensive to build and operate than those for rail systems.) LRT is superior to buses in riding comfort, vehicle performance, system image, and other qualities that the electric traction of LRT offers: quiet operation, absence of air pollution, the ability to operate in tunnels. In pedestrian malls and other people-oriented areas, LRT is accepted much more readily than diesel-powered buses. LRT is also free of the political pressure to share its ROW with other vehicles.

Extensive technical materials on all aspects of LRT—including system description and evaluation, technical and operational topics, and case studies—are available in the Proceedings of seven National Conferences on Light Rail Transit, such as the Transportation Research Board's Conference Proceedings 8, vols. 1 and 2 (TRB 1995–1997).

PHOTO 7.8
Diversity of light rail transit: high-speed line in Portland, Oregon, has a CBD distribution on streets. *(John Schumann)*

Metro or rapid transit system. The highest-performance, highest-investment transit mode is a metro or rapid transit system. It is the optimal choice in corridors with high passenger volumes, with potential for strong coordination of transit with intensive land uses, as well as major intermodal transfer points in suburban areas. Expectations of future growth often favor the use of metro instead of LRT. Also, if most of the ROW must be fully separated, usually in tunnels, metro may be more logical to use than LRT because of similar costs for such alignments but metro's higher performance.

In U.S. cities, the role of metros has increased with the growth of suburbs, which has created a need for transit systems "between" metro and regional rail. San Francisco's BART, Washington's Metro, and Atlanta's MARTA are examples of this new breed of systems that serve networks resembling regional rail, but that have controlled stations and operate with frequency as high as metros. In planning such systems, joint planning of metro lines and stations with developments in CBDs and major activity centers throughout the region is important.

Regional rail. Regional rail lines are playing an increasing role in many metropolitan areas. Typically, radial railroad lines on which these services are operated serve areas with high car ownership. However, regional rail can attract riders because these suburban areas have a growing population, and regional rail can compete with car travel with its high level of service: a separate ROW allows high speed and reliability, and the large cars are very comfortable.

The traditional commuter rail service, consisting of long trains operating mostly during commuting periods at long headways (intervals), is not the only type of operation that should be considered. With the growth of regions and the increasing diversity of travel directions, there is a need for all-day service at 20- to 30-minute headways. To offer this service economically, traditional long trains with large crews that collect fares manually must be upgraded to self-service fare collection (also known as "proof of payment" collection), as well as central control of doors and other functions, which allows operation with one- or two-person crews. For electrified lines, self-powered cars in one- to two-car trains can then be operated at a cost considerably lower than present costs. For non-electrified lines, several European manufacturers have recently built newly designed, efficient, single-powered rail diesel cars, or RDCs. These cars can provide services at far lower cost than trains consisting of a locomotive towing four to eight cars.

In considering the possibilities for providing service to suburban areas that have railroad lines with underutilized capacity, transportation planners in many cities have used recent innovations to create an attractive form of regional rail. With self-service fare collection and self-powered cars, it is increasingly becoming possible to provide all-day, transit-type service that attracts not only traditional center city commuters but also "reverse commuters" working in suburban areas, as well as off-peak travelers.

This development actually represents the creation of a new mode that incorporates LRT elements with the former commuter rail lines and offers service combining the advantages of both: low operating cost and short service headways of LRT with high speed and reliability of service on long regional rail lines. The most advanced examples of this mode are in Karlsruhe (Germany) and Manchester (England), which have extended regional rail lines into urban streets and introduced no-transfer operation of LRT-type vehicles and trains from suburban railway lines into the core of the center city. This direct service has resulted in strong passenger attraction; ridership growth on the order of 30 to 40 percent is typical for most lines. In Karlsruhe, about 40 percent of new riders were attracted from their automobiles. This successful innovation in creating an integrated regional transit system has drawn international attention. Saarbrücken (Germany) has opened a new LRT/regional rail system, as have a number of other cities in France, Austria, and Switzerland. Other countries are exploring or planning similar systems (Brandl and Axhausen 1998).

Automated Guided Transit (AGT). AGT is a viable option for lines that have short station spacings, go through areas with space for aerial ROWs, and that have considerable volumes of travel. In such cases, AGT, typically utilizing medium-sized rubber-tired or rail vehicles, can offer more frequent service at lower cost than conventional metro. Automatic operation of cars or trains is now an option that should be considered in planning metro lines. If planned for full automation at the outset, the additional cost for this technology may be offset by the ability to offer frequent services at all times, to adjust the service according to unexpected demand, and other advantages of operating trains without crews. Reference materials on AGT are presented in the Proceedings of ASCE Conferences on AGT (American Society of Civil Engineers [ASCE] 1997).

Promoting transit use in the city. Promoting transit use through coordinated land use and transportation planning is a sine qua non for permanent avoidance of aggravated urban transportation problems in the future, and for the creation of a livable city. The great variety of policy, planning, and design measures needed to ensure the creation of urbanized areas that can rely on an efficient, balanced intermodal system can be classified into two major categories: (1) macro-scale planning, involving urban form and its relationship to the networks of different modes; and (2) micro-scale design, which makes housing, commercial, business, and other developments pedestrian-friendly and which physically provides for easy and convenient use of transit. Numerous obstacles at both levels are found in many cities, especially those built during the era of car–highway orientation. Such mistakes should be avoided in planning and designing future developments.

Macro-scale planning. Planning land use and transportation networks must be based on the principle that adequate, efficient accessibility is a basic requirement for every development (Ministry of the Environment of Finland et al. 1996). This is a requirement similar to that of providing water, electricity, and other utilities; fire protection; and other amenities needed for buildings and complexes to function. In urban areas, accessibility should consist of car, transit, and other modes of service, their relative roles varying with the type of development and local conditions.

To provide highly efficient access while allowing diverse development with respect to functions, densities, and environmental conditions, a transit network must be designed to serve all major activity centers. These include city and suburban town centers, commercial and business buildings, shopping malls, high- and medium-density residential areas, and so on. These developments should be built only at locations that have adequate access not only by street and road networks, but also by high-performance transit. Thus, land use must be coordinated with a present or planned transit network.

At the same time, the operational requirements of the network must be considered, particularly if it is a rail system. These include the requirement that lines be reasonably direct along major passenger-demand corridors. Network density and direction of lines should be planned so that they maximize area coverage and provide convenient transfer points among lines. The operational feasibility of line interconnections and the number of branches to suburban areas must also be considered.

Major activity centers or town centers in suburban areas can often be planned as the locations of intermodal centers—transfer points between rail transit and bus, park-and-ride, and other feeders. Moreover, a large bus stop operated as a timed-transfer facility among many routes can be integrated as a "focal point" in a major retail, business, or residential development.

Many towns built during the first half of this century were designed to be fully integrated with transit. For example, a string of towns in the Philadelphia suburbs became known as the "Main Line" because the area was developed around the stations of the main railroad line to Pittsburgh and Chicago. In recent decades, however, land-use planning has created serious problems by enforcing extensive zoning that allows only low-density residential developments and separates different land uses. This type of development, together with a disregard for access by any mode except car and truck, has resulted in total dependency on the car for all travel.

Having recognized the inefficiency of such development for transportation, town planners and developers have increasingly shown interest in changing these planning concepts. The emerging concepts of TNDs and TODs are based on diversity in housing density and mixed land use. These developments provide opportunities for making trips for many purposes—such as school, shopping, and neighborhood social activities—by walking, bicycling, and transit. Cul-de-sacs are replaced by streets that allow through travel at moderate speeds (traffic is "tamed"), and a network of pedestrian paths connects all major trip-generators and areas for pedestrians, children at play, and others engaged in outdoor activities.

The present total car dependency in many suburban and urban areas, which results in a continuous increase in VKT on one side, and lack of mobility for some groups on the other, can be stabilized or reduced in the long run only by improved coordination of land-use planning with transit services. Based on the definition of access as a basic requirement for the functioning of diverse activities, every plan for a new development should be evaluated with respect to its accessibility. This must include not only car access but also intermodal access, which serves all potential users and is compatible with the present and future transportation system. The evaluation must therefore be based on an analysis of trip generation, modal split, and assignment, and must include street capacity and the quality of transit services.

Micro-scale planning and design. This planning and design includes access roadways, parking areas, transit stops or stations, pedestrian paths, and other traffic facilities for immediate access and local circulation within major activity centers or residential areas (Metropolitan Transit Development Board 1993). These elements often have a major impact on modal split because of access trips, as well as on trips within activity centers.

Because vehicular traffic is the major mode of travel, roadways and parking usually receive most of the attention, while other modes tend to be neglected. This is a serious mistake. When the factors that impact pedestrians and bicyclists—such as traffic exposure, trip distances, directness of paths, and weather protection—are ignored in planning a development, many potential walking, bicycling, and transit trips are shifted to cars. Such a change of modal split will require a much larger area and higher-cost facilities, and increase traffic congestion with its associated negative consequences.

To reduce car dependency by encouraging the use of alternative modes, the design of a development must not only protect pedestrians but make walking, transit, and bicycle use convenient and attractive. This is achieved by developing layouts with buildings that are clustered or connected by attractive walkways and with bus or rail stations in the "center of gravity" of the development—that is, with easy access to all trip-generating buildings and areas. The circulation layout should separate modes as much as possible and provide convenient circulation roadways for cars and trucks, for bicycles, and preferably, an independent, clearly designated network of pedestrian walkways. If transit access is by bus, routing should allow buses to come to the building core so that passengers can wait in a weather-protected area rather than at the fringes of the parking lot. If rail transit is available, its station should be connected directly to the pedestrian area and the walkway network.

ENCOURAGING THE USE OF OTHER MODES

While car and transit modes dominate urban passenger travel, other modes may have superior performance for certain categories of travel. The efficiency of commuting traffic can be increased by car- and vanpooling. Several types of specialized services are often provided most effectively by paratransit; bicycles offer the most economical type of vehicular travel and are especially convenient for trips in neighborhoods, small towns, or high-density areas. Finally, walking represents the basic, unique mode, one that complements all other modes and which performs many short trips more efficiently and attractively than vehicles.

A rational systems view of urban transportation clearly shows the advantages of intermodal systems over those using one mode only. However, whereas highway and transit modes are provided by special agencies that plan, finance, build, and maintain these systems, this is not the case for all modes. The most paradoxical situation is that of pedestrians, who are somewhat considered when highways and transit are planned but whose needs are too often overshadowed by vehicular modes. Moreover, pedestrians—and walking—are seldom analyzed adequately as an integrated system or mode.

Acknowledging this problem, many states and cities have begun to pay more attention to intermodal systems. The strongest boost to "intermodalism" in the United States was adoption of the Intermodal Surface Transportation Efficiency Act (ISTEA) in 1991. Although ISTEA represented a major step forward, its results remain limited by the numerous historical obstacles to its implementation.

The modes other than cars and transit that can significantly enhance the efficiency of urban transportation and the livability of cities are briefly reviewed here.

Carpooling and vanpooling. Carpooling and vanpooling offer considerable advantages over SOVs for commuting trips. The cost, area occupied, pollution, and other negative impacts of travel on the environment and the city in general are cut dramatically when trips are shifted from SOVs to these modes. A two-person pool cuts these costs per person by approximately 50 percent; a ten-person vanpool reduces the unit costs to 15 to 20 percent of SOV costs.

Carpooling and vanpooling are mostly limited to commuting because they require coincidence of time and trip origins and destinations; they also involve some inconvenience in comparison to SOV travel. It is desirable to facilitate and encourage the use of these modes of travel whenever there is the potential to shift trips from SOV to pooling. Measures for this purpose include the exchange of information about commuting schedules among potential carpooolers, discount or waiver of tolls and parking charges, employer organization of vanpool financial arrangements, and others.

Paratransit. In certain categories of travel, paratransit can replace private cars, particularly SOVs, and offer considerably greater efficiency. Among the numerous forms of paratransit, the most common are taxi, jitney, and dial-a-ride, each of which has a different potential role in urban transportation.

- *Taxis.* Providing unique service as personalized public carriers, taxis play a significant role in large cities, where they are often more convenient to use than private cars because of ubiquitous service and the absence of parking problems. Instead of merely allowing taxis to operate on a commercial basis, their use can be encouraged by various regulatory and physical measures. For example, organizing taxi stations and radio control help assure the user that a ride will be available when it is needed. Taxis may be allowed to use certain lanes and streets where cars are prohibited. Modification of regulations can be made to allow shared rides by unrelated users or flagging down of partially occupied taxis under certain conditions (a practice used in Washington, D.C.). Finally, taxi service can be coordinated with transit in several ways. At major terminals, as well as at suburban stations, taxis can wait for specific train or bus arrivals. In some cases, joint fares for transit and taxi distribution can be organized, along with replacement of buses by taxis or vans on lightly traveled routes during late evening hours and on weekends.
- *Jitneys.* Jitneys, privately operated minibuses under various degrees of coordination by a dispatcher, are used extensively in developing countries where labor costs are low and transit services do not offer adequate service. Jitneys are seldom used in developed countries because regular transit services on fixed lines and schedules are the preferred mode of travel.
- *Dial-a-ride.* This and various other route-deviation concepts for bus and minibus services have had limited success in various cities in the past 20 years. However, recently developed computer-based communications and control systems and ITS techniques make these services considerably more promising. In addition to specialized services for the disabled and the elderly, for special schools, and so on, dial-a-ride is likely to be used increasingly for

travel in suburban areas—for instance, as a feeder to regional transit and as transportation for reverse commuters.

- *Bicycles and other non-motorized vehicles (NMVs).* NMVs play a significant role in some cities, where conditions, habits, and policies favor their use. The bicycle, the most common NMV, has some unique advantages: very low cost, speed adequate for many short or medium-length urban trips, convenience of use and simple parking, partial independence from street congestion, pleasant experience and physical exercise, and environmental soundness. Major limitations and disadvantages of this mode are that many people cannot or will not ride a bicycle; bicycles are less safe than cars and are vulnerable to hilly terrain and inclement weather; and carrying objects is inconvenient.

Interestingly, bicycle use is not necessarily related to a single condition, such as a sizeable student population, a developing country, a low-income population, or a moderate climate. Bicycles are often used even in areas where some conditions are not favorable. A massive use of bicycles is actually found in diverse cities. For example, bicycles are used in Chinese or Indian cities with very low car ownership, as well as in cities with very high car ownership in the Netherlands and Denmark. Bicycles are well-suited to small and medium-sized towns, as well as to very large cities (several million bicycle trips are made daily in Tokyo, the world's largest city) (Hook 1994). In many North American cities, bicycles are ignored or are virtually nonexistent, while in San Francisco they are popular despite the hilly terrain. The city has established numbered bike routes, erected route markers similar to those for state highway routes, and published a map for bikers. In Madison, Wisconsin, bicycles are used extensively despite summer storms and severe winters; and in many university towns with good facilities and bicycle-friendly policies, such as Davis, California, the role of this mode is quite significant.

These and numerous other cases demonstrate that bicycles, when their use is facilitated and encouraged, can be used for a significant portion of trips in many towns and cities. Their popularity decreases to some extent with increasing affluence and motor vehicle ownership; but as traffic congestion increases, the potential of bicycles to offer an attractive alternative to the car may again increase. As a system, bicycles offer great benefits in terms of much lower costs and negative impacts as well as contribute to the livability of an area or city. A number of measures favoring bicycle use are briefly described.

- *Traffic laws and regulations.* Laws and regulations concerning bicycles exist in most countries and states, but they are often ignored by motorists as well as by many bicyclists. This leads to unpleasant and unsafe friction between, on one side, bicycles and cars, and on the other, bicycles and pedestrians. To achieve optimal use of bicycles, the public must be educated about the relationships between modes; the rights as well as the responsibilities of bicyclists must be defined by regulation; and those regulations must be enforced. Measures to change organizational and attitudinal aspects of the bicycle mode require no major funds, but they involve public attention and a concerted effort by traffic authorities and bicycle organizations.
- *Bicycle parking, storage, and lockers*. These are the basic physical elements needed to make extensive bicycle use feasible. Such facilities, which involve relatively low cost and limited area, can be provided by traffic authorities or by employers, retailers, and building owners. Especially important are bicycle facilities at transportation terminals, which make intermodal trips convenient and attractive. In suburban locations, bike-and-ride facilities at rail and bus transit stations are far less expensive and less damaging to their surroundings than park-and-ride areas because bicycles take only a fraction of the parking space required by cars.

  Minimal bicycle parking facilities provide special racks that allow easy locking. More elaborate ones, provided in many Western European and Japanese cities, have covered or enclosed parking, sometimes with mechanical devices for high-density storage of bicycles.
- *Bicycle lanes, paths, and bikeways.* Special lanes, paths, and bikeways are the main infrastructure element defining bicycle transportation as a distinct system. Bicycle lanes can be located on sidewalks (where there is sufficient width) or on streets. They are usually designated by painted lines or by distinctly textured pavement. Although "bike lanes" have only visual designation, they represent an important step in separating bicycles from motor vehicles and pedestrians.

This separation is important for safety, convenience, and greater speed, as well as for giving the bicycle its deserved legitimacy among other modes.

Bicycle paths are visually distinct paved facilities within rights-of-way of streets and suburban roads. Bikeways, physically separate facilities, may be within streets or may follow independent paths through parks, via shortcuts, with access to campuses, sports areas, and so forth. Exclusive bicycle facilities, whether paths or bikeways, usually require more area than bicycle lanes in roadways, and their construction requires greater investment. At intersections, they must be provided with designated crossings, usually paralleling pedestrian crosswalks, as well as special bicycle signals. With this infrastructure, bicycle transport becomes a much more attractive mode of urban travel. It is much safer and faster than bicycle travel in mixed traffic. Even more important, separate bicycle ways make bicycle travel more reliable than car travel because bicycle movement is independent of street traffic congestion.

- *Maps and other information.* Maps and other sources of information can be used as another means of encouraging bicycle travel in an area or city. Public education about bicycles should not only include traffic rules but should make the public aware of the social and personal benefits of bicycles compared to other modes for certain categories of trips. Therefore, this information should be provided not only for present and potential bicyclists but also for motor vehicle drivers and pedestrians.

  An international review of bicycle use as related to public transport was made and published by Replogle (1983). Litman (1994) analyzes bicycles as a component of urban transportation. Kuranami and Winston (1994) present a systematic review of issues, policies, and measures related to NMV, particularly bicycle systems. Although they focus on Asian cities, their material is so general that it can be applied to most other cities.

- *Pedestrian travel.* Walking is the most ubiquitous though often overlooked mode of travel and activity in all human settlements (Burden 1997; Project for Public Spaces 1997). It is important to understand the dual role of walking in cities: as a mode of transportation and as a basic element of social and economic activities and quality of life. The character of cities depends to a great extent on the treatment of pedestrians.

As a mode of transportation, walking is the most convenient mode for travel between close buildings or points, or within high-density areas. Walking is also a part of every vehicular trip, although its role in such trips varies considerably. A person walking to the garage at home can hardly be considered a "pedestrian." However, a driver who leaves a car in a major parking lot usually has to walk a considerable distance, and the environment of the walk may set the tone of the entire trip. If the environment is pleasant and the person can stop along the way to sightsee or run errands, that person may enjoy fairly long walks, and the entire area can be designed with garages separated from pedestrian zones. If walking is unpleasant, the pressure to provide garages throughout the city grows, and the entire urban environment eventually becomes car-dominated. The definitive study on pedestrian characteristics was published by Fruin (1971).

The importance of the quality of the pedestrian system and its facilities is particularly great for transit riders. Experience around the world shows that transit systems that provide good service and represent the preferred mode of travel for most urban trips always have strong interaction and mutual support with high-quality pedestrian facilities.

The other function of pedestrians is their presence in streets, plazas, and buildings—giving life to all public spaces and contributing greatly to the conditions that make a city livable. This function makes walking not only a mode of transportation but a basic element in the functioning of all urbanized areas.

Both pedestrian roles in cities can be endangered or destroyed if the planning, design, and operation of city streets focuses predominantly on vehicular traffic. A major problem in many cities and suburbs is the absence of pedestrian facilities. Sometimes pedestrians are neglected in urban design and street-layout standards. In many cities in developing countries, where pedestrian volumes are typically very large, sidewalks are poorly designed and maintained. Even

PHOTO 7.9
Careful design of details enhances livability of cities: Logan Circle in Philadelphia. *(Christopher Wallgren)*

in the large cities of countries with extensive infrastructure, such as Caracas and Mexico City, the condition of pedestrian traffic is far from satisfactory. Finally, in many areas of cities developed in recent decades with one-sided attention to vehicular traffic, streets and roads have been built with no accommodation for pedestrians. This design is widespread in U.S. suburban areas, even in the surroundings of large residential, shopping, and business developments.

In some residential areas of North America where the potential for crime exists, pedestrian movement is intentionally prevented to increase security. Thus, in some suburbs of Phoenix, Arizona, and in Mexico City, entire residential areas are surrounded by walls. Much less justified is the practice of highway departments in some states (e.g., Pennsylvania and New York) to prohibit certain pedestrian movements, such as on sidewalks and street crossings), claiming that it is necessary "for their safety." This philosophy amounts to a policy that tries to eliminate traffic accidents by prohibiting the use of motor vehicles!

Intermodal transportation and the creation of livable cities require a positive and supportive attitude toward pedestrians, giving great attention to them in the planning, design, and operation of streets and pedestrian facilities. These are not merely paths and sidewalks needed for the basic safety and protection from accidents. Pedestrian planning must include the enhancement of existing pedestrian systems or the provision of new ones. These consist of safe and attractive sidewalks, independent walkways, and, in recreational areas, campuses, or major developments, networks of paths that are both functionally efficient and visually appealing.

In central urban areas, pedestrian and transit malls have become popular areas for shopping and business. Many cities have gradually developed a number of pedestrian streets, plazas, and passages into a pedestrian zone, which has a continuous network and limited, well-controlled crossings with vehicular traffic. The same goal of making many trips more convenient for walking and transit rather than car travel is being pursued in the TOD concept—suburban developments with moderate densities and mixed land uses. A study by Parsons Brinckerhoff Quade and Douglas, Inc. (1993) shows that the share of non-car trips—including pedestrian, bicycle, and transit trips—originating in an area or zone can vary from 5 to 23 percent, depending on the Pedestrian Environment Factor (PEF). This factor consists of characteristics related to sidewalk continuity, street design and crossings, and topography.

As with other modes, the role of pedestrians and their relationship to transportation modes, primarily car and transit, varies greatly with the size and character of metropolitan areas, their climate, and, above all, their population habits. It is, however, always desirable to give full attention to pedestrians as a component of an intermodal system that is very important to the efficiency of that system. Even more important, regardless of the degree of motorization, pedestrian treatment greatly influences the livability of all public areas—downtowns, shopping malls, residential areas, and other developments. Thus, it influences the total image and competitiveness of a city with its peers.

References

Appleyard, Donald, with M. Sue Gerson and Mark Lintell. 1976. *Livable urban streets: managing auto traffic in neighborhoods.* Report prepared for Federal Highway Administration, U.S. Department of Transportation. Washington, DC: U.S. Government Printing Office.

______. 1981. *Livable streets.* Berkeley, CA: University of California Press.

American Society of Civil Engineers (ASCE). 1997. *Proceedings,* Sixth International Conference on Automated People Movers, Las Vegas, Nevada. Washington, DC: ASCE.

Automotive Safety Foundation. 1964. *Urban freeway development in twenty major cities.* Washington, DC.

Bayliss, David. 1998. Parking policies and traffic restraint in London. *Public Transport International* (March): 40–45.

Brandl, P. G., and K. W. Axhausen. 1998. Karlsruhe 1975–1995: a case study of light rail transit development. *TR Record* 1623: 155–164. Washington, DC: Transportation Research Board.

Burden, Dan. 1997. *Walkable communities.* Lansing, MI: Tri-County Regional Planning Commission. March.

Burrington, Stephen H. 1994. *Road kill: how solo driving runs down the economy.* Boston, MA: Conservation Law Foundation (CLF). May.

Cervero, Robert. 1988. *Suburban gridlock.* New Brunswick, NJ: Center for Urban Policy Research, Rutgers University.

Congressional Budget Office. 1997. Toll roads: a review of recent experience. CBO Memorandum. Washington, DC. February.

Dunlay, William J., and Thomas J. Soyk. 1978. *Auto-use disincentives.* Report No. PA-11-0016-B. Washington, DC: Urban Mass Transportation Administration.

Fawkner, J. 1995. Bus deregulation in Britain: profit or loss? *Public Transport International* 44 (November): 18–23.

Felz, Herbert. 1989. *Revitalizing city centers by public transport. Proceedings of* 48th UITP Congress, Budapest, Hungary. Brussels, Belgium: Union Internationale des Transports Publics (UITP).

Fruin, John J. 1971. *Pedestrian planning and design.* New York: Metropolitan Association of Urban Designers and Environmental Planners.

Gomez-Ibanez, Jose A., and Kenneth Small. 1994. Road pricing for congestion management: a survey of international practice. *NCHRP Synthesis of Highway Practice 210*. Washington, DC: National Cooperative Highway Research Program (NCHRP).

Gordon, Deborah. 1997. *Getting there: transportation policy alternatives for a new century*. Report prepared for the Energy Foundation, San Francisco, CA. May.

Herald, William S. 1977. *Auto-restricted zones: background and feasibility*. Report No. UMTA-VA-06-0042-78-1, Vol. I (also Vol. II-V). Washington, DC: Urban Mass Transportation Administration (UMTA). December.

Hibbs, John. 1986. The market alternative to integration. *City Transport* (May/July): 23–24.

Homburger, Wolfgang S., et al. 1989. *Residential street design and traffic control*. Institute of Transportation Engineers (ITE). Englewood Cliffs, NJ: Prentice-Hall.

______, and Vukan R. Vuchic. 1972. Transit Federation—a solution for service integration. *Revue de l'UITP* 2: 73–100. Brussels, Belgium: Union Internationale des Transports Publics (UITP).

Hook, Walter. 1994. Role of nonmotorized transportation and public transport in Japan's economic success. *TR Record* 1441: 108-115. Washington, DC: Transportation Research Board.

Horn, Burkhard; Katsuji Hashiba; and Veronique Feypell. 1995. *Fighting traffic congestion: an agenda for the future*. *IATSS Research* 19, 2: 6–15. Tokyo: International Association of Traffic and Safety Sciences (IATSS).

Institute of Transportation Engineers (ITE), Transportation Planning Council Committee 5P-8. 1997. *Traditional neighborhood development: street design guidelines*. Washington, DC: ITE. June.

Johnson, Elmer W. 1993. *Avoiding the collision of cities and cars: urban transportation policy for the twenty-first century*. Chicago, IL: American Academy of Arts and Sciences and the Aspen Institute.

Komanoff, Charles. 1997. *Environmental consequences of road pricing*. Report prepared by Komanoff Energy Associates, New York, for The Energy Foundation. April.

Kuranami, Chiaki, and Bruce P. Winston. 1994. Factors influencing ownership and use of nonmotorized vehicles in Asian cities. *TR Record* 1441: 116–123. Washington, DC: Transportation Research Board.

Lewis, Nigel C. 1993. *Road pricing: theory and practice*. London: Thomas Telford.

Litman, Todd. 1994. Bicycling and transportation demand management. *TR Record* 1441: 134–140. Washington, DC: Transportation Research Board.

______. 1997. Distance-based vehicle insurance as a TDM strategy. *Transportation Quarterly* 51: 119–37. Summer.

Metropolitan Transit Development Board (MTDB). 1993. *Designing for transit*: a manual for integrating public transportation and land development in the San Diego metropolitan area. San Diego, CA: MTDB. July.

Ministry of the Environment of Finland, et al. 1996. *Public transport in Finnish land use planning.* Helsinki: Ministry of the Environment.

Monheim, Rolf. 1994. From pedestrian zones to traffic-calmed city centers. In Harry Dimitriou, ed., *Moving away from the motor vehicle: the German and Hong Kong experience.* Hong Kong: Centre of Urban Planning and Environmental Management, University of Hong Kong.

Morlok, Edward K. 1987. Privatizing bus transit: cost savings from competitive contracting. *Journal of the Transportation Research Forum* XXVIII, 1: 72–81.

Newman, P.; J. Kenworthy; and L. Robinson. 1992. *Winning back the cities.* Australia: Pluto Press (Australian Consumers' Association).

1000 Friends of Oregon. 1995. *Implementation* 6. Portland, OR: 1000 Friends of Oregon.

______. 1997. *Making the connections: a summary of the LUTRAQ project.* Portland, OR: 1000 Friends of Oregon. February.

Parsons Brinckerhoff Quade and Douglas, Inc., with Cambridge Systematics, Inc., and Calthorpe Associates. 1993. *The Pedestrian Environment* 4A. Portland, OR: 1000 Friends of Oregon. December.

Pennsylvania Environmental Council (PEC). 1997. *Initial investigation of the feasibility of market-based transportation strategies for congestion mitigation in the 5-county Southeastern Pennsylvania region.* Delaware Valley Regional Planning Commission Project #61-800-60, Philadelphia, PA. January.

Pickup, Laurie, et al. 1991. *Bus deregulation in the metropolitan areas.* Aldershot, UK and Brookfield, VT: Avebury.

Porter, Douglas R. 1997. *Transit-focused development.* TCRP Synthesis 20. Washington, DC: Transportation Research Board.

Project for Public Spaces, Inc. 1997. *The role of transit in creating livable metropolitan communities.* TCRP Report 22. Washington, DC: Transportation Research Board.

Pucher, John, and I. Hirschman. 1993. Path to balanced transportation: expand public transportation services and require auto users to pay the full social, environmental costs of driving. *Public Transport International* 41, 3. Brussels, Belgium: Union Internationale des Transports Publics (UITP).

Regional Transportation Authority (RTA). 1994. *An assessment of travel pricing strategies.* (Chicago) Regional Transportation Authority, Planning and Market Development Department, Market Development Division, Chicago, IL.

Replogle, Michael A. 1983. *Bicycles and public transportation: new links to suburban transit market.* Washington, DC: The Bicycle Federation.

Shoup, Donald C. 1992. *Cashing out employer paid parking.* Report No. FTA-CA-110035-92-1. Federal Transit Administration, Office of Technical Assistance, Washington, DC.

______. 1997. The high cost of free parking. *Access* 10 (Spring): 2–9. Berkeley, CA: University of California Transportation Center. Spring.

Topp, Hartmut H. 1990. Traffic safety, usability and streetscape effects of new design principles for major urban roads. *Transportation* 16: 297–310.

______. 1993. Parking policies to reduce car traffic in German cities. *Transport Reviews* 13, 1: 83–95.

Transport Structure Plan Project Team. 1990. Second Transport Structure Plan, Part D. *Government decision, transport in a sustainable society.* Joint policy statement by several Ministers of the Government submitted to Parliament, The Netherlands.

Transportation Research Board (TRB). 1995. *Expanding metropolitan highways.* Special Report 245. Washington, DC: Transportation Research Board.

______. 1995–97. *Proceedings,* Seventh National Conference on Light Rail Transit, Baltimore, MD. Vols. 1 and 2. Washington, DC: Transportation Research Board.

Ulberg, Cy; Graciela Etchart; and Bethany Whitaker. 1992. *Local option commercial parking tax analysis.* Final report, Research Project GC8719, Task 30, Washington State Transportation Commission, Spokane, WA. January.

Union Internationale des Transports Publics (UITP). 1991. *Green light for towns.* Brussels, Belgium: UITP.

Vickrey, William. 1969. Congestion theory and transport investment. *American Economic Review* 59: 251–260. Reprinted in *Public economics,* selected papers of W. Vickrey, Cambridge University Press (1994).

Vuchic, Vukan R. 1978. *Parking policy as a transportation system management measure.* Report PA-11-0016. Washington, DC: Urban Mass Transportation Administration.

______. 1986. Deregulation: a return to the primitive. *City Transport* (May/July): 18-20.

______. 1993. Cheap gasoline: an American addiction. *Urban Transportation Monitor* (February).

Wald, Matthew L. 1997. U.S. increasing its dependence on oil imports. *New York Times* (August 11).

Willson, Richard W. 1992. *Suburban parking economics and policy: case studies of office worksites in Southern California.* Report No. FTA-CA-11-0036-92-1, Federal Transit Administration, Office of Technical Assistance, Washington, DC.

World Bank. 1996. *Sustainable transport.* Washington, DC: World Bank.

Wormser, Lisa. 1997. Don't even think of parking there. *Planning* 63 (June): 10-15.

Zein, Sandy R., et al. 1997. *Safety benefits of traffic calming.* Paper No. 971326, 76th Annual Meeting of the Transportation Research Board, Washington, DC. January.

8

Cities and Transportation: What Is the Future?

The causes of transportation problems in cities are far more complex than is commonly believed. Many popular, short-term solutions to problems, when used indiscriminately, can become counterproductive in the long run. Examples include the belief that building more highways will relieve congestion and air pollution; the expectation that construction of one rail transit line will reverse trends or change travel habits in an entire region; and the hope that free market principles can be successfully applied to urban transportation systems through deregulation of public services, despite the fact that these systems have major social and environmental (that is, nonmonetary) impacts.

This book has highlighted urban transportation conditions and problems and their impacts. It has shown which policies have led to improvements and which have caused transportation problems to worsen. The basic characteristics of transportation modes and their relationships and roles in different types of cities have been discussed, and developments in U.S. cities and their peers in other countries have been described and compared. This chapter reviews previous chapters and then, utilizing materials from chapter 7, focuses on finding directions for the future: How can the present problems be resolved so that transportation contributes to, rather than negatively affects, the livability of cities?

DIVERSITY AND CONFUSION IN FUNDAMENTAL POLICIES

The definitions of "livable city" and "quality of life" vary considerably from country to country and city to city. So, too, does the composition of different transportation modes, which influences these concepts. Thus, a variety of goals have been adopted in metropolitan areas, and numerous policies have been implemented. However, it can be said that most developed countries believe that, in medium-sized and large cities, accessibility for the entire population, efficient transportation, and protection of the environment are among the basic elements of livability. Consequently, they have been working to implement intermodal transportation systems. The thrust of their efforts is to reduce car use and improve its alternatives in order to achieve the required balance of transport modes.

In urban transportation, the United States has, with some notable exceptions, followed a distinctly different path (see chapter 4). During the 1950s and until 1965, U.S. policies at all three governmental levels—federal, state, and local—were focused mostly on Planning Levels IV and III: they concentrated on extensive, virtually unlimited construction of facilities for accommodating car travel in metropolitan areas, while all other modes were considered secondary supplements. Planning Levels II and I—transportation as an intermodal system and its interaction with the city—were hardly discussed.

In the late 1960s, however, the United States was a leader in developing an awareness of the environment. As a result, during the 1970s, the federal government was instrumental in turning attention to the quality of life in metropolitan areas and, consequently, stimulating transit development. During the 1980s, this policy was reversed, and highways regained dominance. Then, in 1991, the nation's most progressive transportation law, the ISTEA, was introduced. Its effects, albeit significant, have been limited due to extensive avoidance of its requirements by powerful forces intent on maintaining traditional dominance of highway transportation and neglecting all the alternatives. See, for example, the Environmental Defense Fund's comments on the Atlanta Interim 1998–2000 Transportation Improvement Program (Replogle 1997) and the critique of busway conversions into HOV facilities (Vuchic et al. 1994).

It is significant that the major transportation laws in the United States, which were based on systematic analyses of the country's needs, have strongly advocated a balanced transportation systems approach. The 1962 Transportation Act, which required the "3C's" ("Continuing, Comprehensive, Cooperative"); the TSM program emphasized in the late 1960s; federal efforts during the 1970s; the Intermodal Surface Transportation Efficiency

Act (ISTEA) in 1991; and ISTEA's successor, the Transportation Equity Act for the 21st Century (TEA-21)—have all supported the use of comprehensive planning, the balancing and integration of different modes, consideration of the environment, and enhanced livability of cities. These laws have had some significant results. Several cities that implemented them successfully, such as Portland (Oregon) and San Francisco proper, now have well-deserved reputations for human orientation and livability.

Thus, the spirit and requirements of several transportation acts in the United States resembled those of peer countries. Implementation of policies and financing pursued since about 1980, however, have differed from other countries. During the 1990s, major differences in transportation developments, as well as in types of metropolitan areas and their quality of life, have become even more apparent. Instead of implementing intermodal balance through coordinated car disincentive/transit incentive policies, the United States has generally renewed the 1960s policies of increasing highway capacities—although expansions were initially disguised as new HOV lanes rather than new general-purpose lanes. At the same time, funding for urban transit and Amtrak was frozen or reduced.

The creation and implementation of transportation policy has lagged behind environmental legislation. For example, the major efforts mounted to implement disincentives to SOV use through Employer Trip Reduction (ETR) and several similar programs aimed at reducing VKT and lowering air pollution were based on the Clean Air Act Amendments rather than on clearly defined transportation policies (Tehan 1999). However useful, these trip-reduction and other measures for increasing the efficiency of highway travel are undermined by a variety of subsidies to car travel. Because the out-of-pocket cost of driving is negligible and declining, any reduction of work-related trips is quickly replaced by new and longer trips whenever any congestion reduction is achieved. Thus, with the out-of-pocket cost of driving only four cents per car-km (six cents per car-mile), congestion remains the only major system deterrent to more driving.

With the reduction of federal funds for transit and Amtrak, incentives for travel by public transport are being further reduced and, predictably, weakened by continuing car-use incentives. The two policies have led to a greater need for subsidies of both highways and transit. Paradoxically, when reductions in transit and Amtrak subsidies result in decreased ridership, these systems are criticized as "inefficient." At the same time, much higher subsidies to highways and car use are largely hidden, and they are seldom criticized.

In recent years, simplistic proposals have been made for applying free market principles to public transit services; however, these proponents do not apply their "arguments" to public highways. The argument that users should pay a greater share of travel costs has been applied to transit and has resulted in major fare increases. Corresponding increases in charges for car use (gasoline tax, parking, tolls, and road pricing) are swept aside by the claim that they are not realistic because of "political realities." Because, on average, car users are in higher income groups than transit users, this policy leads to further increases of subsidies to high-income groups.

Congress has shown little interest in correcting the fundamental anomaly of favoring private over public transport with respect to Amtrak and travel in metropolitan areas, where these policies have particularly negative results; the overall trend of decreasing federal assistance to transit and Amtrak operations continues. With few exceptions, state and local governments have failed to compensate for these cuts. Thus, the imbalance among existing modes has been increased from both sides—by auto incentives and transit disincentives.

The lack of coordination of different national, state, and local policies affecting cities (Level I) has numerous negative consequences. For example, subsidies to car use in many different forms—such as "free" parking and tax exemptions for a number of trip categories, which indirectly necessitate subsidies to transit—stimulate travel to greater distances for all purposes. The multiplicity of suburban governments and an absence of effective implementation of regional plans create conditions for unlimited land development, usually with no consideration for transportation other than highway vehicles. Taxes that are higher in central cities than taxes in suburban counties and developments on agricultural land (without full compensation for externalities) also contribute to the problem. The resulting car dependence exacerbates many problems, hidden (indirect) as well as visible (direct).

The spatial mismatch of inner-city residents and employment centers that are located in low-density suburban areas is another casualty of uncontrolled land-use development and excessive dependence on the car. Once again, those who lack understanding of the transportation–urban form relationship point to the lack of mobility of low-income people to further criticize transit because it "cannot provide the service." In fact, this problem stems from an absence of rational planning, which coordinates land uses with transportation networks, rather than some "inherent weakness of transit."

Wachs (1993) goes so far as to suggest that low-income people from central cities should be subsidized to buy cars to get to their jobs. Thus, instead of solving the underlying problem, total dependence on the car would be intensified by government subsidies. Anti-transit bias, along with the belief that the car is the only solution to travel needs, again leads to this

"Let them eat cake" suggestion that would burden even low-income people with the expenses of car ownership, the most expensive mode of travel.

MOVING FROM TECHNOLOGICAL IMPROVEMENTS TO SYSTEMS SOLUTIONS

Given the serious problems resulting from the collision of cities and cars, the growth of areas that cannot be served by an efficient intermodal system, and the emergence of increasingly dehumanized cities, there is a great need for intellectual and political discussion about the future of cities. However, technological improvements continue to attract much greater funding and attention than more fundamental (and more difficult) solutions to problems of the city-transportation relationship at the systems level. Vast private and government funding is made available for research and development of technological systems or components that can at best improve some features of existing systems at Planning Levels IV and III. Professional and academic groups focus heavily on these developments. At the same time, there is an intellectual void about the fundamental problems of the efficiency of intermodal transportation systems and their contribution to the livability of cities—Planning Levels II and I, respectively.

This situation is especially stark in the United States. Many academics and professionals alike focus on single technological problems. ITS development attracts significant public and private funding, resulting in a great flurry of activities. As mentioned in chapter 1, the development of electric cars and other "clean engines" is discussed at Transportation Research Board forums and by some authors as the main solution to urban transportation problems. The fact that these technological developments, if successful, would at best ameliorate some aspects of urban problems but have no influence on congestion or mobility, is not mentioned. Even more academically narrow are proposals for unrealistic technical solutions (such as PRT) or for marginal variations of existing systems (monorail).

Current discussions about the environment, livability of cities, sustainability, and related issues in most countries around the world—as well as by international bodies such as OECD (Organisation for Economic Cooperation and Development), European Commission (1996), the World Bank (1996), and Union Internationale des Transports Publics (UITP) (1995)—focus on transportation as a key problem. The trend of increasing car use is recognized as the basic cause of the deterioration of living conditions and the intensification of environmental problems in cities. Most studies of this problem include extensive discussions of transit, non-motorized transport, and other alternatives to cars, emphasizing the need to increase the role of those modes in solutions to urban transportation problems.

Virtually the only exceptions to this broad consensus are a number of studies of these problems in the United States. Following numerous constructive studies and publications during the 1970s, in recent years there has been an obvious failure in many transportation circles to accept intermodalism. The simplistic view from the 1950s—that the car is the only significant mode of urban transportation, and that all its alternatives are negligible and not worth investing in—has regained its strength. Several recent studies of sustainable cities (Transportation Research Board 1997), expansion of metropolitan highways (Transportation Research Board 1995), and problems of highway congestion follow this line of thought. They hardly mention transit, bicycles, or pedestrians, which are vital components of the solution to congestion problems; in fact, they usually present no viable solutions at all. The underlying attitude of these studies is that cheap gasoline, subsidized parking, and unlimited driving cannot be changed; that road pricing is infeasible; and that transit and all other alternatives to the car cannot play any significant role.

The proponents of this type of thinking thus argue, directly or by rejection of any significant changes, for continuation of the present trends. They do not confront the conditions to which the extrapolation of present trends will lead. Failure to offer feasible solutions and the absence of any vision of livable cities are the hallmarks of many such publications.

UNDERSTANDING CITY-TRANSPORTATION RELATIONSHIPS

A brief summary of the preceding chapters relating to the complex relationship between cities and their transportation is presented here.

Throughout history, predominant forms of transportation have had distinct impacts on the form, density, and character of cities. As Schaeffer and Sclar (1975) described, pedestrian and horsecart transportation led to dense cities with intensive activities; streetcars opened up suburbs and formed major arterials. The strongest and most complex impact, however, came with the private car. While the car gave great mobility to its individual users, as a system, vehicular traffic allowed dispersion of activities which, in turn, increased the need for travel over greater distances. With the decentralization of cities, the very large area requirements of car travel has led to the allocation of large land surfaces to highways and parking. Yet, chronic highway congestion and many negative impacts on the environment and livability of urbanized areas have increased rather than decreased.

This conflict between cities and cars was initially understood to be a problem of physical congestion, which could be resolved by building more highways and parking facilities, by better traffic engineering, and other measures for increasing the capacity of the car/highway system. Several theoretical studies in the 1960s (Buchanan 1964; Leibbrand 1970; Smeed 1961) focused on the physical analysis of car space requirements and the possibilities for their accommodation in cities. Most U.S. planning projects focused on providing facilities to "meet the demand" for car and truck travel in metropolitan areas. "Demand" was considered a given, rather than a variable dependent on the cost of travel and capital investments provided—that is, on transportation policy decisions.

In several West European countries, as early as in the mid-1950s, transportation professionals had begun to point out that transportation policy has a major impact not only on the functioning of transportation systems, but also on the character of cities, their quality of life, and, ultimately, the type of society that inhabits them. The conflict between individual behavior and the optimum form of a transportation system—which appears within the highway/street networks, as well as between private and public modes (car and transit)—was recognized as a major problem to solve in achieving efficient urban transportation.

Pressure to satisfy the individual's desire for travel by car in the short run tends to divert attention from externalities and long-term impacts and to lead to solutions that increase reliance on the car. In the long run, full accommodation of car travel has severe negative impacts on entire metropolitan areas.

Realizing the strong impacts of urban transportation policies on cities and society, the extensive discussions of professionals and political leaders in most developed countries led to the introduction of policies for solving problems and attempting to achieve viable metropolitan areas. Prevailing experiences and consensus on the problems and possible solutions for cities and transportation that have been developed in the countries most advanced in this area are summarized here.

1. The basic policies in urban transportation can be classified into two general categories:

    a. *Follow laissez-faire policies toward individual travel behavior*, under which maximum effort is concentrated on accommodating private car travel, which is subsidized in many direct and indirect ways. This policy leads to *car-based cities* that stimulate a high degree of privacy, separation of social groups, and limited social activities.

b. *Influence transportation system development to reach desired social and economic goals.* When these goals are the *creation of human-based, livable cities,* which allow more diversity and economic vitality than car-based cities, it is necessary to develop a *balanced intermodal transportation system.* This can be achieved only if efforts are focused on utilizing car, transit, paratransit, walking, and other modes—each one in its most effective role.

2. Because the car-based city is not considered to be a desirable form of human settlement by most peer countries, the policies of those countries have been concentrated on achieving intermodal balance. The main problem in achieving such a balance is underpriced car use and its cost structure—that is, very low out-of-pocket costs.

3. Alleviation of the problems of car dominance and the city–car collision requires the following three policy goals.

   a. *Make car use less attractive* by eliminating direct and indirect subsidies and introducing user charges that better reflect the full cost of driving, as well as various driving disincentive measures.

   b. *Provide viable alternatives to car travel* wherever that is physically and economically feasible.

   c. *Apply integrated and coordinated planning* of urban form and transportation with land-use controls to ensure its implementation.

The first two policies, referred to earlier as, respectively, *car-use disincentives* and *transit-use incentives,* applied in most peer countries, have produced good results: cities with multimodal systems are distinctly more human-oriented and livable than car-based cities. The third policy, coordinated planning of urban form with transportation, has resulted in the reconstruction of many city centers (Hannover, Portland [Oregon], Rotterdam), which has redefined the relationships among pedestrians, cars, and transit. It also created suburban developments and towns that are efficient, livable, and environmentally sustainable, as exemplified by the new towns in the metropolitan areas of Cologne, Stockholm, and Toronto.

4. Since the use of the private car—the dominant mode of transport—is grossly underpriced, particularly on an out-of-pocket basis, introduction of charges directly related to car use and the costs it imposes on others would be the most effective measure to correct the present imbalance among modes. Consequently, road pricing, tolls, parking, and other charges would represent the most appropriate and effective measure to increase efficiency of urban transportation.

5. Despite its basic logic, equity, and effectiveness, however, road pricing has thus far been limited because of two major obstacles to its introduction: the technical problems of collecting charges, and political opposition to such measures. The former problem (method of collection) has now been practically solved by the simple prepayment method used in Singapore, as well as by the invention of smart cards and other electronic devices. The latter issue (political acceptability) remains, limiting its implementation to only a few cities at this time, such as Singapore, Oslo, and a half-dozen others. Great Britain has been advanced in studying and preparing a specific plan for road pricing as a solution for London, but it failed to implement it because of political opposition and pressures by lobbies.

   A lively discussion of road pricing has been intensifying, however, in both academic and political circles. Many reputable publications, including *The Economist* (1997), have noted the distortions created by current underpriced car use and have argued forcefully for more realistic charges for car use in cities, as well as for the application of generated revenues to improvements of transit and other alternative systems.

6. The consensus is increasing that providing good transit and other alternatives is a sine qua non for any major effort to control car use, achieve a balanced transportation system, and prevent continuing deterioration of accessibility in metropolitan areas. For example, Neil Kinnock, European Union Secretary of Transport, noted that "there have to be 'push' factors such as road pricing and parking controls, but to introduce restraints would be politically untenable until we have affordable, acceptable alternative transport in place" (Hope 1996).

   At local levels—such as in CBDs, neighborhoods, and campuses—walking, bicycling, and paratransit can effectively reduce the use of cars. In many cases, this is achieved by partial redesign of the street network. For longer trips, high-quality, attractive transit supplemented by paratransit represents the only viable alternative.

7. In small and medium-sized metropolitan areas, transit can be made attractive by various priority measures for transit vehicles on streets and highways. In large metropolitan areas, transit can be truly competitive with the car only if it is independent of general traffic—that is, if it operates on ROW category B or A.

8. The choice of transit modes (bus, LRT, metro, and others) follows the selection of ROW category (rather than vice versa). Usually, for operation on streets in mixed traffic, paratransit and buses are most efficient; on separate rights-of-way, rail systems generally offer the highest capacity, speed, quality of service, and operating efficiency. For this reason there has been extensive construction of rail transit systems in recent decades in large and medium-sized cities around the world.

   Since 1980, LRT has become the fastest-growing rail transit mode. Requiring lower investments than metro while offering a broad range of options, LRT is being planned and built in dozens of cities. Moreover, regional rail has seen a resurgence in North America, as well as in many other countries. Construction of busways has also been increasing around the world in spite of the setbacks in several countries, such as their massive conversions into HOV facilities in the United States and their degradation due to bus deregulation in Lima, Peru, and some British cities.

   The development of high-performance transit systems is a result not only of efforts to develop attractive alternatives to the private car, but also of the numerous technological innovations of rail and bus transit systems.

9. The car continues to be used extensively in all cities of developed countries, but its operation is more efficient and its negative impacts are lower in metropolitan areas that utilize intermodal transportation systems—that is, alternative means of travel—than in car-based areas.

   The most serious transportation problems and deterioration of quality of life are found in the rapidly growing cities of developing countries that have failed to build or organize any high-capacity transit systems. Bangkok, Bogota, New Delhi, Lagos, and many of their peers suffer from chronic congestion, waste of personal time and energy in travel, extremely polluted air, accidents, and deteriorated quality of life in general. The conditions in their streets symbolize to the extreme the failure of modern civilization to understand transportation as a complex system that interacts with the city and that must be planned comprehensively.

10. Lack of understanding of urban transportation characteristics and their long-term impacts is likely to lead to these serious problems in all cities and countries that simplistically follow the policy of "satisfying people's desire to drive cars." The problems will be compounded in countries such as China and some countries of the former Soviet Union where the automobile manufacturing industry is now seen as a major element of industrial and economic progress. Allowing unlimited satisfaction of the micro phenomenon—the individual's desire for driving—without solving the resulting macro problem of congestion by controlling car use and offering attractive alternatives, inevitably leads to deterioration of transportation systems and of the livability of cities.

THE NEED FOR DISCUSSION AND VISION ABOUT THE FUTURE OF METROPOLITAN AREAS

The diversity among cities and countries in terms of their historic, geographic, social, and other conditions points to the need for a variety of approaches and solutions to urban transportation problems. Policies and solutions cannot be directly transferred from one city to another; however, many fundamental problems are similar, and the exchange of experiences can be useful in resolving the complex problems faced by cities and metropolitan areas.

Extensive coverage and references to urban transportation in peer countries have been presented here because some of the developed countries have made significant progress toward resolution of the collision between cities and cars. Many of these achievements are either unknown or misrepresented in the United States. Just as Europe and Japan learned a lot from

PHOTO 8.1
Intermodal system: pedestrians, bicycles, cars, and buses in Boulder, Colorado. *(Mario Semmler)*

U.S. experiences in developing highways and traffic engineering several decades ago, the United States can now learn from the more diversified experiences and sophisticated solutions in balancing different urban transportation modes that have been achieved in peer countries.

As interesting as the specific technical and organizational solutions may be, an even more important lesson to be learned from some peer countries is the need for a comprehensive and coherent approach to total transportation systems and to cities in general.

The transportation problems and urban decay that U.S. metropolitan areas are experiencing stem largely from the lack of consensus on what the urban America of tomorrow should be. Strong pressures by interest groups that benefit from the present excessive dependence on cars lead to laissez-faire governmental policies, thus aggravating the problems. Studies that point out that long-term social interests should be considered and policies introduced to change some of the present undesirable trends are ignored or bypassed. Most importantly, there is no clear picture of what type of metropolitan areas—not only with respect to transportation, but also in terms of quality of life and social relations—the country should work toward.

PHOTO 8.2
Coordinated land-use and transportation planning: high densities around metro stations in Toronto. *(Toronto Transit Commission)*

Because there is limited understanding of the basic characteristics of transportation modes and their impacts on metropolitan areas, many of the present policies are mutually conflicting, and some tend to exacerbate the problems rather than resolve them.

The basic conclusion of this book is that the urban transportation problem is so serious and has such far-reaching consequences that a comprehensive study should be undertaken to consider the future of cities and metropolitan areas. As discussed in chapter 2, rational planning should start at Planning Level I—reaching consensus on general guidelines about the type of city and society. That should be used as the basis for determining transportation mode composition (Planning Level II), and only then should specific plans for different modes be developed. The study must therefore involve persons with a deep understanding and broad vision of the complex city–transportation system relationships. It should not be another attempt to justify the present trends as inevitable and immutable.

In considering the transportation policies that affect the future of cities (Levels I and II), the differences between car-based cities and cities with balanced intermodal transportation should be fully understood. They are briefly summarized here.

Car-based cities are characterized by convenient travel by auto to any location in large, predominantly low-density areas. Traffic congestion on highways is a frequent phenomenon, and all travelers are subjected to it. Personal living comfort and privacy are very high for all car owners and users. Social life in public spaces is limited. Groups of people who do not own cars or do not drive (teenagers, students, low-income people, the elderly, and so on) have distinctly inferior living standards and opportunities for jobs and all other activities. Expansion of cities and spacious housing involve low costs but consume considerable land areas.

Cities with balanced intermodal systems provide mobility for all population groups. The use of cars is discouraged through various measures. Availability of high-quality transit and other alternatives allows a far greater diversity in land-use densities and concentrations of activities that offer economies of agglomeration. Residential conditions are less spacious, and privacy is lower, than in car-based cities. Pedestrian and human-oriented areas that generate social and public activities, preservation of historic areas, and so forth, are provided. Overall, the advantages of cities with intermodal systems result in more economically efficient, socially integrated, and environmentally livable cities than car-based, unimodal cities.

National hearings on transportation policy organized to prepare the ISTEA in 1990 showed that emphasis must be shifted away from separate funds for different modes and palliative solutions strongly influenced by interest groups, toward a clearer definition of overall long-term goals. To achieve these goals, innovative solutions, some of which require significant changes in travel habits and behavior, must be promoted. Many such innovative solutions have been described in this study. It would be delusional to ignore such solutions under the pretense that they are "not transferable" from cities that are more advanced in the development of policies and their implementation. Setting clear goals, application of a systems approach to urban transportation, and pursuit of coordinated rather than mutually conflicting policies are valid steps in all countries, regardless of how different their local conditions are.

The intellectual challenge and social responsibility with respect to cities and their transportation is to examine present conditions and trends critically; to develop a consensus about the future character, form, and quality of life in metropolitan areas; and then to devise the policies needed to achieve such goals. These efforts must be followed by the process of implementation, which is complex and difficult but more rational and less costly in the long run than complacent continuation of present trends, many of which obviously lead to a much less desirable (if at all physically and economically feasible) future state of metropolitan areas—the centers of contemporary society and civilization.

References

Buchanan, Colin, et al. 1964. *Traffic in towns.* London, UK: HMSO.

(The) Economist. 1997. Jam today, road pricing tomorrow (pp. 15–16); No room, no room (pp. 21–23). December 6.

European Commission. 1996. *Transport research – APAS – Public transport prioritization.* Luxembourg: Office for Official Publications of the European Communities.

Hope, Richard (interviewer). 1996. Kinnock charts path to rail's comeback. *Railway Gazette International* (February): 74-76. Interviewer.

Leibbrand, Kurt. 1970. *Transportation and town planning.* Cambridge, MA: MIT Press.

Replogle, Michael A. 1997. Comments on Draft Interim Atlanta Regional TIP, FY1998-2000. Washington, DC: Environmental Defense Fund.

Schaeffer, K.H., and E. Sclar. 1975. *Access for all: transportation and urban growth.* Hammondsworth, UK: Penguin.

Smeed, Reuben J. 1961. The traffic problem in towns. *Manchester Statistical Society.* February.

Tehan, Brian J. 1999. An evaluation of U.S. Employer Trip Reduction programs: urban transportation planning and policy implications. Ph.D. dissertation, University of Pennsylvania.

Transportation Research Board (TRB). 1995. *Expanding metropolitan highways.* Special Report 245. Washington, DC: Transportation Research Board.

_____. 1997. *Toward a sustainable future.* Special Report 251. Washington, DC: Transportation Research Board.

Union Internationale des Transports Publics (UITP). 1995. *Public transport: the challenge.* 51st International Congress of Union Internationale des Transports Publics (UITP), Paris, France. Brussels, Belgium: UITP.

Vuchic, Vukan R., et al. 1994. *The bus transit system: its underutilized potential.* Final Report No. DOT-T-94-20. Washington, DC: Federal Transit Administration.

Wachs, Martin. 1993. Learning from Los Angeles: transport, urban form, and air quality. *Transportation* 20: 329–54.

World Bank. 1996. *Sustainable transport.* Washington, DC: World Bank.

Bibliography

Appleyard, Donald, with M. Sue Gerson and Mark Lintell. 1981. *Livable streets.* Berkeley, CA: University of California Press.

Aschauer, David Alan. 1991. *Transportation spending and economic growth – the effects of transit and highway expenditures.* Washington, DC: American Public Transit Association.

Associação Nacional de Transportes Públicos (ANTP). 1997. *Transporte humano – cidades com qualidade de vida.* Sao Paolo, Brazil: ANTP.

Bank of America et al. 1995. *Beyond sprawl: new patterns of growth to fit the new California.* San Francisco, CA: Bank of America.

Black, Alan. 1995. *Urban mass transportation planning.* New York: McGraw-Hill.

Bovy, Philippe. 1999. Urban structure and modal distribution. *Public Transport International* 48,1: 8–15.

Burden, Dan. 1997. *Walkable communities.* Lansing, MI: Tri-County Regional Planning Commission. March.

Cervero, Robert. 1988. *Suburban gridlock.* New Brunswick, NJ: Center for Urban Policy Research, Rutgers University.

Delucchi, Mark. 1998a. The annualized social cost of motor vehicle use in the U.S., 1990–1991: summary of theory, data, methods, and results. UCD-ITS-RR-96-3(1). Davis, CA: University of California, Institute of Transportation Studies. September.

_____. 1998b. Summary of the nonmonetary externalities of motor vehicle use. UCD-ITS-RR-96-3(9). Davis, CA: University of California, Institute of Transportation Studies. September.

Edwards, John D., ed. 1992. *Transportation planning handbook.* Institute of Transportation Engineers (ITE). Englewood Cliffs, NJ: Prentice-Hall.

Felz, Herbert. 1989. *Revitalizing city centers by public transport.* Report 1, 48th Congress of UITP, Budapest, Hungary. Brussels, Belgium: Union Internationale des Transports Publics (UITP).

Fruin, John J. 1971. *Pedestrian planning and design.* New York: Metropolitan Association of Urban Designers and Environmental Planners.

Girnau, Günter; Adolf Müller-Hellman; and Friedhelm Blennemann, eds. 1997. *Zukunftsfähige Mobilität – sustainable mobility.* Düsseldorf, Germany: Alba.

Gomez-Ibanez, Jose A., and Kenneth Small. 1994. Road pricing for congestion management: a survey of international practice. *NCHRP Synthesis of Highway Practice 210.* Washington, DC: Transportation Research Board, National Cooperative Highway Research Program (NCHRP).

Goodwin, Philip B. 1996. *Extra traffic induced by road construction: empirical evidence, economic effects, and policy implications.* Roundtable 104, European Conference of Ministers of Transport, Paris, France. November.

Gray, George, and Lester Hoel, eds. 1991. *Public transportation: planning, operations and management.* Englewood Cliffs, NJ: Prentice-Hall.

Homburger, Wolfgang S., et al. 1989. *Residential street design and traffic control.* Institute of Transportation Engineers (ITE). Englewood Cliffs, NJ: Prentice-Hall.

Jacobs, Jane. 1961. *The death and life of great American cities.* New York: Vintage Books.

Lee, Douglass B. 1995. Full cost pricing of highways. Paper presented at the 74th annual meeting of the Transportation Research Board (TRB), Washington, DC.

Lehner, Friedrich. 1969. Regional organisation of transport and urban development. Report Ia. 38th International Congress of UITP, London, UK. Brussels, Belgium: Union Internationale des Transports Publics (UITP).

Leibbrand, Kurt. 1970. *Transportation and town planning.* Cambridge, MA: MIT Press.

Litman, Todd. 1995. *Automobile dependency as a cost.* Victoria, B.C., Canada: Victoria Transport Policy Institute.

Newman, Peter, and Jeffrey Kenworthy. 1989. *Cities and automobile dependence: an international sourcebook.* Aldershot, UK. Gower.

_____. 1998. *Sustainability and cities.* Washington, DC: Island Press.

1000 Friends of Oregon. 1997. *Making the connections: a summary of the LUTRAQ project.* Portland, OR: 1000 Friends of Oregon. February.

Project for Public Spaces, Inc. 1997. *The role of transit in creating livable metropolitan communities.* TCRP Report 22. Washington, DC: Transportation Research Board.

Pucher, John. 1995. Urban passenger transport in the United States and Europe: a comparative analysis of public policies. *Transport Reviews* 15, 2 (April–June): 89–107; and 15, 3 (July–September): 261–283.

Replogle, Michael A. 1983. *Bicycles and public transportation: new links to suburban transit market.* Washington, DC: The Bicycle Federation.

Shoup, Donald C. 1997. The high cost of free parking. *Access* 10 (Spring): 2–9. Berkeley, CA: University of California Transportation Center.

Smerk, George M. 1991. *The federal role in urban mass transportation.* Bloomington, IN: Indiana University Press.

Topp, Hartmut H. 1993. Parking policies to reduce car traffic in German cities. *Transport Reviews* 13, 1: 83–95.

Union Internationale des Transports Publics (UITP). 1995. *Public transport: the challenge.* 51st International Congress of Union Internationale des Transports Publics (UITP), Paris, France. Brussels, Belgium: UITP.

Vuchic, Vukan R. 1973. Quo vadis, ASCE? *Civil Engineering* (June): 59–61.

_____. 1977. Integrated urban transportation—a major challenge for transportation engineers. *Proceedings* of the 47th Annual Meeting of ITE, Mexico City (October). Washington, DC: Institute of Transportation Engineers (ITE).

_____. 1981. *Urban public transportation systems and technology.* Englewood Cliffs, NJ: Prentice Hall.

_____. 1984. The auto versus transit controversy: toward a rational synthesis of urban transportation policy. *Transportation Research* 18A, 2 (Spring): 125–133. Special Issue on Public Policy.

_____. 1987. Urban transit: a public asset of national significance. *Urban Resources* 4, 1: 3–6, 63.

_____. 1988. Design, evaluation, and selection of transit systems: theory and practice. *Proceedings* of the Conference on Les Transports Collectifs Urbains, École Nationale des Ponts et Chaussées, Paris, France. pp. 287–299.

———. 1991. Recognizing the value of rail transit. *TR News* 156 (Sept.–Oct.): 13–19. Washington, DC: Transportation Research Board.

Vuchic, Vukan R., S. Kikuchi, N. Krstanoski, and Y. E. Shin. 1995. Negative impacts of busway and bus lane conversions into high-occupancy vehicle facilities. *TR Record* 1496: 75–86. Washington, DC: Transportation Research Board.

Vuchic, Vukan R., and Antonio Musso. 1998. Increasing potential of road pricing for improved efficiency of urban transportation. *Proceedings* of the 8th World Conference on Transport Research, Antwerp, Belgium.

Weyrich, Paul M., and William S. Lind. 1996. *Conservatives and mass transit: Is it time for a new look?* Washington, DC: Free Congress Foundation and American Public Transit Association.

Index

A

accessibility, 198-201
Adelaide, Australia, 41
Advanced Traffic Management Systems (ATMS), 122
Advanced Vehicle Control Systems (AVCS), 122
air pollution, 18, 52, 74, 119, 123, 252, 301, 322
 attention to, 203
 driving restrictions and, 287
 in Sweden, 152
 quality standards, 104, 108
air transport mode, 96
Alaskan Way Viaduct (Seattle, Washington), 99
Alexandria, Virginia, 198
Altshuler, Alan, 18
American Association of State Highway Officials (AASHO), 100
American Association of State Highway and Transportation Officials (AASHTO), 100
American Automobile Association (AAA), 74, 79, 80, 196
American Society of Civil Engineers (ASCE), 304
Americans with Disabilities Act (ADA), 120, 123
Amsterdam, the Netherlands, 15, 16
Amtrak, 106, 183, 271, 322
Anderson, J. Edward, 221
Area Licensing Scheme (ALS), 155-156, 272, 281-282
Aschauer, D. A., 195
Asia, 128, 155-157, 170
AT&T, 30
Atlanta, Georgia
 balanced transportation, 243
 freeway design, 118
 MARTA, 302
 rail system, 124, 189, 217
 transit studies, 210
Atlanta Interim 1998-2000 Transportation Improvement Program, 321
Austin, Texas, *20*
Austria
 auto use, 164
 Klagenfurt, 50
 regional rail, 304
 Salzburg, 292
 transit federation, 134
 Vienna, xxii, *95*, 175
Australia, 1
 Adelaide, 41
 auto travel policies, 14
 auto use, 159, 163
 "Better Cities Program," 15
 bus mode, 158
 Melbourne, xxii, 129, 158-159, 200
 pedestrian mode, 158-159
 policy studies, 167
 Sydney, 16, 51, 158, 159-160
 traditional neighborhood development, 293
 traffic-calming, 52
 transit mode, 158-160, 170
 urban planning, 157-160
 urban transportation problems, 128, 157
Autobahn, 271-272
auto-free zones, 1
automated guided transit (AGT), 220-221, 304
automobile use, xx-xxi, xxiii, 54
 and suburbs, 4
 auto-restricted zones (ARZ), 291-292
 car ownership, 1, 7, 9, 36, 98, 141, 149, 163-167
 congestion and, 6, 7, 52-60

Note: Page numbers in italics refer to figures, photographs, and tables.

costs of, xxi, xxiv, 60-65, 67-79, *236*, 241
disincentives (CD), xx, xxii, xxiii, 63, 121, 150, 174, 175, 202, 240-244, 247, 252, 270-271, 285-286, 327
driving restrictions, 286-287
fosters spatial separation, 19
impact on cities, 7-10, 74
impact on pedestrian traffic, 74
in
Austria, 164
Australia, 159, 163
Canada, 4, 162, 163
developed countries, xxii
England, 141, 174, 175
Europe, 12, 14, 163, 175
Finland, 154-155
France, 74, 137, 141, 175, 177, 252, 287
Germany, 130, 132, 175
Hong Kong, 156
Japan, 12, 14, 156, 157, 176
Netherlands, the, 141-142, 174
Norway, 149
Singapore, 12, 175
Sweden, 152, 163
Switzerland, 143, 174
incentives (CI), xxiii, 240, 242, 244
inspection requirements, 229
misconceptions of, 198-201
occupancy, 55, 59
optimal role for, 268-293
policy dilemmas, 10-14
pricing, 271-286
reduction of, 270-271
registration fees, 285
reliance on, 2-3, 10, 17, 25, 35-37, 99, 100, 169, 192, 202, 230, 239, 299, 306
restrictions, 286-287
shift to, 9
street layout and design, 291
subsidies, 19, 67-69
travel restrictions, 11-12
vehicle types, 178-179
See also highway mode
auto-restricted zones (ARZ), 291-292

B

Baltimore, Maryland, 202, 211-212, 243, 263
Bangkok, Thailand, 245, 330
Bay Area Rapid Transit (BART). *See* San Francisco, California
beltways, 262-263
Bergen, Norway, 175
Berkeley, California, 197
Berlin, Germany, 182, 184
Besançon, France, 136, 141
Bicycle Laws of 1977 and 1980 (Japan), 157
bicycle mode, 32-37, 255-256, 257, 267, 309-310
costs of, 66
in
California, 309
Europe, 310
Finland, 154-155
Germany, 33, *34*, 51, 130, 133, 206, 255, *256*
Japan, 157, 255, 309, 310
large cities, 51
Netherlands, the, 33, 51, 141, 255, 309
New Jersey, 118
Norway, 149
peer countries, xxii
Pennsylvania, 118, 206
Scandinavia, 255
small cities, 50
lanes, 310-311
laws and regulations, 310
maps, 311
misconceptions of, 205-207
neglect of, 103, 112
parking and storage, 310
promotion of, 118
Birmingham, England, 149
Bogota, Colombia, 215, 242, 245, 330
Bonn, Germany, 51, 135
Boston, Massachusetts, 202
Amtrak service, 183
automobile disincentives, 175
Central Artery construction, 125
congestion, *6*
elimination of freeways, 173
freeway development, 262
Green Line, 40
land availability, 60
LRT service, 41
parking, 149, 228, 287
pedestrian mode, 257
rail system, 124
reexamination of transportation plans, 103
transit mode, 209
transit study, 125
Boulder, Colorado, 34, 207, 288, 331
Bovy, Philippe, 31
Brazil
Curitiba, 41, 208-209, 212, 300
Sao Paolo, *35*, 245
Bremen, Germany, 135-136, 141, 152, 292
Brookings Institution, The, 97
Brussels, Belgium, 1
Bruun, Eric C., 54
Buchanan, Colin, 144
Buenos Aires, Argentina, 51
Buffalo, New York, 28, 211, 301
Burden, Dan, 291
Burrington, Stephen H., 74, 270
bus transit, 46, 54, 95, 200, 300
Bus Transit Systems (BTS), 41, 42, 43
cessation of service, 36
deregulation of, 86, 329
improvements, 200
in
Australia, 158
Canada, 36
developed countries, xxii
England, 145, 147, 148
Germany, 130
New Jersey, 210-211
New York, 200, 211
Washington (state of), 200
Washington, D.C., 200, 210

- increase in use, 113
- lanes, *47*
- misconceptions about, 207-211
- -rail intermodal network, *107*
- Semi-rapid Bus Systems, 41
- separated rights of way, 41
- *See also* high-occupancy vehicles (HOVs)

C

Calgary, Canada
- automobile use, *4*
- favoring transit vehicles, 291
- livability, 223
- low-density suburbs, *4*, 193
- LRT, 41, 200, 211-212, 301

California
- Berkeley, 197
- Davis, 207, 309
- Department of Transportation (Caltrans), 113
- Highway-91, 114, 280, 281, 284
- Los Angeles, 1, 2, 12, 15, 60, 73, *94*, 97, 99, 103, *107*, 113, *117*, 118, 132, 162, 200-201, 212, 213, 227, 234, 263, 277
- Modern Transit Society, 173
- Oakland, 197
- parking "cashout" schemes, 277
- pedestrian mode, 257
- Sacramento, 40, 119, 173, 211-212, 301
- San Diego, 10, 28, 41, 119, 171, 200, 202, 211-212, 213, 217
- San Francisco, 5, 10, 12, *25*, *26*, 28, 59, 60, 99, 103, 118, 119, 124, 129, 164, 171, 173, 193, 197, 198, 200, 201, 202, 211, 216, 252, 262, 266, 280, 302, 309, 322
- San Jose, 1, 173, 243
- Santa Monica, 65, 202

Campbell, E. C., 195

Canada
- auto mode, 162, 163
- auto travel policies, 14
- Calgary, *4*, 41, 193, 200, 211-212, 223, 291, 301
- cessation of bus service, 36
- Edmonton, 51, 162, 173, 223
- Montreal, 51, 162, 198, 211, 252
- Ottawa, 41, 51, 208, 212, 227, 228, 300
- pedestrian mode, 162, 163
- policy studies, 167
- rail mode, 162
- Toronto, xxii, 1, 40, 51, 59, 161, 162, 198, 209, 228, 243, 267, 327, *332*
- traditional neighborhood development, 293
- traffic calming, 289
- transit mode, 170
- urban transportation problems, 128
- Vancouver, 51, 162, 210, 221, 223, 289
- Waterloo, 50

Caracas, Venezuela, 245, 313

carpooling, 255, 307-308

Cato Institute, 219

central business districts (CBDs), 28, 99, 262, 302
- *See also* city

Cervero, Robert, 274

Channel Tunnel, 183

Chicago, Illinois, 305
- automobile dependence, *265*
- CATS, 97
- inner-city area, 2
- "inner loop," 99
- LRT and metro combination, 40
- Metra, 47
- pedestrian malls, 177
- PRT system, 29
- site selection, 5
- transit mode, 51

China. *See* People's Republic of China

Cisneros, Henry, 5, 112

city
- competitiveness, 183-184
- crisis in, 1-22
- future of, 320-333
- human character, 97, 100, 141, 169, 189, 233
- low-density, 193
- metropolization, 167
- need for, 192
- planning and development, 189-193
- size, 50-52, 202, 236
- spatial spreading, 166
- -transportation relationship, 23-25
  - causes and consequences of congestion, 52-60
  - family of urban transit modes, 40-49
  - four levels of planning, 82-87
  - optimum in travel choice, 60-65
  - private, public, and for-hire, 30-39
  - transportation represents a system, 26-30
  - transport's composition to urban size, 50-52
  - travel costs, charges, and subsidies, 65-81
- *See also* livable cities

Clean Air Act, 74, 104, 203, 229, 277

Clean Air Act Amendments, xxii, 74, 104, 108, 322

Cleveland, Ohio, 16, 42, 218

Clinton, Bill, 111, 121

Cologne, Germany, 41, 135, 184, 327

Colorado
- Boulder, *34*, 207, *288*, *331*
- Denver, 28, 29, 73, 200, 209

Columbus, Ohio, 1, 99, 262

commuter systems, 46-49, 98

congestion, xxiii, 1, *6*, 26, *26*, 167-168
- and reconstruct-the-city policy, 13
- automobile use and, 6, 7, 52-60
- causes and consequences of, 52-60, *116*
- in small cities, 50
- misconceptions of, 192-193, 197
- pricing, 284

Congestion Mitigation and Air Quality (CMAQ), 108

Congressional Budget Office, 280

contracting, 147

Copenhagen, Denmark, 212, 253

crime, 3, 112

Croydon, England, 149

Curitiba, Brazil, 1, 41, 208-209, 212, 300

Czech Republic, Prague, 252

D

Dallas, Texas, 1, 12, 262
Damascus, Syria, 215
Davis, California, 207, 309
Dayton, Ohio, 173, 205, 287
Deen, Thomas, 217
De Gaulle Airport, Charles, 183
demand-responsive services, 39, 255
Denmark, 33, 51, 207, 309
  Copenhagen, 212, 253
Dennis Agreement (Sweden), 151
Denver, Colorado, 28, 29, 73, 200, 209
deregulation
  and disintegration of services, 146, 168, 296, 329
  in England, 86, 144-148, 244
  versus contracting, *147*
Detroit, Michigan, 1
  auto-dependent city, 37, 199, 234
  automated rail system, 221
  difficulty of travel in, 13
  disutilities of travel, 241
  freeway development, 263
  inner-city areas, 299
  transportation system, 51
dial-a-ride services, 39, 135, 308-309
"Diamond" lanes. *See* high-occupancy vehicle lanes
disabled population, 104, 120, 308
Does America Need Cities? (Persky, Sclar, Wiewel), 192
Dole, Robert, 110
Dortmund, Germany, 135
Downs, Anthony, 124, 216, 223
Duisburg, Germany, 135
Dunlay, William J., 259, 295
Düsseldorf, Germany, 135

E

economies of aggregation, xix, 2
Economist, The, 18, 203, 328
ecotaxes, 285
"edge cities," 4, 17
Edmonton, Canada, 51, 162, 173, 223
education, 3, 223
Eindhoven, the Netherlands, *21*
elderly population, 104, 308
electric tramway. *See* streetcar
electronic road pricing, 156
  See also road pricing
Embarcadero Freeway (San Francisco, California), 99, 103
Employer Trip Reduction (ETR) program, 121, 252, 269, 322
England (Great Britain)
  automobile use, 141, 174, 175
  Birmingham, 149
  British Department of Transport, 145
  bus deregulation, 86, 144, 148, 244
  Croydon, 149
  gasoline taxes, 81
  highway mode, 203
  invention of railway, 5
  Leeds, 51, 149
  Liverpool, 144
  London, 12, 144, 145, 147, 149, 175, 182, 183, 184, 213, 221, 222, 228, 287, 328
  Manchester, 148, 303
  Newcastle, 144, 301
  Nottingham, 149
  parking, 149
  Railway Conversion League, 215
  reliance on car travel, 18
  road pricing, xxi, 280, 281, 328
  Royal Commission on the Environment, 148
  Sheffield, 149
  transit deregulation, 86, 144-145, 244
  transit federations, 168
  transit mode, 144-149
  urban planning, 144-149
environmental concerns, 285
  changing attitudes toward, 103, 104, 119, 123
  costs (EC), 73, 70, 237
  in
    Sweden, 152
    Switzerland, 143
  major construction and, 167
  neglect of, 97, 98
Environmental Defense Fund, 321
environmental impact statement (EIS), 104, 106
Environmental Protection Agency (EPA), 104
Erie Canal, 96
Essen, Germany, 135
Europe, xxiv, 1
  auto mode, 163
  auto travel policies, 14
  auto travel restrictions, 12, 175
  bicycle storage, 310
  older cities, 260
  pedestrian zones, 168
  public transportation, 184-185
  "push measures," 241
  traffic calming, 51-52, 290
  transit costs, 66, 170
  transit priority, 295
  urban transportation problems, 128, 326, 330-331
European Commission, 324
European Union, 285, 328
externalities, xviii, 149, 252

F

Farsta, Sweden, 151
Fay, William, 11
Federal Aid Highway Act
  of 1956, 93-97
  of 1962, 100-101, 103, 107, 109, 112, 321
Federal Railways (Germany), 134
Federal Transit Administration (FTA), 101, 123
Felz, Herbert, 267
Finland
  automobile use, 154-155
  bicycle mode, 154-155
  Helsinki, 155

    metropolitan organizations, 167
    pedestrian mode, 154-155
    planning studies, 167
    urban planning, 154-155
Fitch, Lyle, and Associates, 100
Florence, Italy, 292
Fort Worth, Texas, 141
France
    automobile use, 137, 141, 175
    Besançon, 136, 141
    gasoline taxes, 177
    Grenoble, 139, 140, 301
    Lille, 139, 221
    Lyon, 139
    Marseilles, 139
    Nantes, 40, 139, 140
    Paris, 40, 51, 74, 137, 139, 175, 182, 183, 200, 209, 213, 243, 252, 287
    pedestrian mode, 141
    regional rail, 304
    road pricing, 281
    Rouen, 139
    St. Etienne, 139
    Strasbourg, 139
    toll roads, 175
    Toulouse, 139, 221
    transit mode, 51, 137, 139-141, 200, 209, 213
    urban planning, 137, 139
Frankfurt, Germany
    central city areas, 135
    pedestrian malls, *131*
    rail transit, 16, 40, 41
    traffic calming, *131*
    urban planning, 267
    versus New York City, 182, 184
"freeway revolt," xxi, 103, 119
Fruin, John J., 31
"Future Highways and Urban Growth," 98

G

gasoline taxes, 177, 277-279, 298, 323
    for highway investment, 10-11, 67-68
    in
        France, 177
        England, 81
        Germany, 130, 278
        Italy, 177
        Netherlands, the, 177
        Norway, 81
    misconceptions about, 195-196
    raising, xxiii, 81, 106, 110-111, 123, 238
Gatwick Airport, 184
General Motors, xi
gentrification, 3
Germany
    Autobahn, 271-272
    automobile use, 130, 132, 175
    Berlin, 182, 184
    bicycle mode, 33, 51, 130, 133, 206, 255, *256*
    Bonn, 51, 135
    Bremen, 135-136, 141, 152, 292
    bus mode, 130
    car travel costs, 81
    Cologne, 41, 135, 184, 327
    congestion, 168
    Dortmund, 135
    Duisburg, 135
    Düsseldorf, 135
    Essen, 135
    Frankfurt, 16, 40, 41, *131*, 135, 182, 184, 267
    gasoline taxes, 130, 278
    Hamburg, 133-135, 149, 168, 228, 252, 287
    Hannover, 15, 40, 136, *136*, *137*, 180-182, 253, 327
    Karlsruhe, 136-137, *138*, *139*, 303
    lack of tolls, 175
    metropolitan organizations, 167
    multimodal operations, 169
    Munich, 1, *34*, 129, 133, *134*, 168, 202, 222, *222*, 243
    planning studies, 167
    Ruhr Region, 135
    Saarbrücken, 137, 304
    S-Bahn, 133-134, 184
    Stade, *13*
    Stuttgart, 135, 222, *222*
    traffic calming, 130, *131*, 289
    traffic engineering, 96-97
    transit mode, 130, 133-137
    U-Bahn, 133-134, 184
    urban planning, 129-137
    user costs, 273
    Wiesbaden, 212
Giuliani, Rudy, 206
Glasgow, Scotland, 5, 144
Gomez-Ibanez, Jose, 125, 184
Gordon, Deborah, 259
Gothenburg, Sweden, 29, 41, 136, 152-154, 292
Great Britain. *See* England
Great Lakes (United States), 5
Grenoble, France, 139, 140, 301
Group Rapid Transit (GRT), 29
growth management laws, 118
Gruen, Victor, 141

H

Hamburg, Germany
    intermodal planning, 252
    parking supply, 149, 228, 287
    transit federations, 168
    urban planning, 133-135
Haneda Airport, 183
Hannover, Germany
    city center, 327
    contrasted to Seattle, Washington, 180-182
    efficient transportation system, 253
    historic buildings, 15
    LRT, 40
    modal split, *137*
    pedestrian malls, 180, *181*
    pedestrian mode, *136*
    urban planning, 136
Hartford, Connecticut
    freeway design, 1, 96, 99, 262
    I-84, 115, *115*, 117
Heathrow Airport, 184

Helsinki, Finland, 155
high-occupancy vehicles (HOVs)
  favoring of, 277
  lanes, 112-118, 295
    conversion of busways, 47, *47*, 65, 176, 208, 215, 301, 321, 329
    misconceptions of, 204-205, 208-209, 216
    preference for, 124
highway mode
  building, xviii, 10, 13, 14, 93-108, 195, 228, 262-264
  categories of, 33
  costs of, 10, 67, *174*
  federal policies, 93-108
  high-capacity radial freeway, *25*
  in England, 203
  misconceptions about, 201-205
  network, 253, 270
  redesign of, 118
  related taxes, 11
  street layout and design, 291
  subsidies, xxi, xxii
  See also automobile use
Highway Revenue Act of 1956, 93-97
Highway Trust Fund (HTF), 93, 194, 277
  concept of, 67-68, 96
  for transit projects, 104
  Mass Transportation Account, 106
Highway Users Federation, 11
Hirschman, I., 259
historic conservation, 119
Hollatz and Tamms report, 129
Homburger, Wolfgang, 290
home ownership, 2, 162
Hong Kong
  automobile use, 156
  metro stations, 198
  rapid transit system, 218
  urban planning, 155-156
  versus New York City, 182, 184
Honolulu, Hawaii, 99, 189, 200, 262
Hook, Walter, 157, 245
Horn, Burkhard, 295
housing
  diversified, 19, 305
  federal support for, 17, 95
  high-density, 5, *265*
  single-family, 167
Houston, Texas, 261
  auto-dependent city, 37, 227, 234
  commuter transit services, 47, *47*
  difficulty of travel in, 13
  freeway development, 262
  parking supply, 287
  reconstruct the city policy, 12, 96
Hylton, Thomas, 190

I

IBM, 30
India, 32, 309
  New Delhi, 330
Indianapolis, Indiana, 13
individual equilibrium (IE), 60-62, 228, *246*
Institute of Transportation Engineers (ITE), 52, 259, 267, 268, 291
insurance coverage, 285
"Integrated Transport Strategy for Greater Sydney" (ITS), 159
Intelligent Transportation Systems (ITS), 29-30, 122, 211, 269-270, 324-325
  and international cooperation, 168
  and jitneys, 308
  improvements for vehicular travel, 125
  misconceptions of, 204
  objectives, 266
  policy considerations, 229
  transit mode, 298
Intelligent Transportation Systems (ITS) Act, 108
Intelligent Vehicle Highway System (IVHS) Act, 107
intercity express (ICE) lines, 184
intermodalism. *See* transportation, multimodal; Intermodal Surface Transportation Efficiency Act (ISTEA), integrated multimodal requirements
Intermodal Surface Transportation Efficiency Act (ISTEA), xxiii, 213, 221, 321-322, 333
  bypassing, 112-118
  highway congestion, 175, 203
  integrated multimodal requirement, xxii, 11, 84, 86, 107-108, 118, 169, 173, 307
  parking exemption, 275
  progress by—and its obstacles, 109-112
  revitalization of TSM, 103
  stimulated construction of bikeways, *34*
  toll road financing, 280
International Study of the Population Crisis Committee, 158
Interstate Highway Act, 119
Interstate Highway System
  completion of, 106
  construction of, 244
  design of, 94
  financing of, 68, 213, 280
Italy
  automobile use, 164, 175
  car travel costs, 81
  Florence, 292
  gasoline taxes, 177
  Naples, 5
  Rome, 241, 292
  Salerno, 51

J

Jacobs, Jane, 112
Japan, xxiv
  auto travel policies, 14
  auto travel restrictions, 12, 175
  auto use, 156, 157
  bicycle mode, 157, 255, 309, 310
  Kobe, 221
  monorails, 220
  Osaka, 200, 221
  Tokyo, 16, 144, 157, 182, 183, 213, 218, 252, 266, 309
  toll roads, 177

transit mode, 156-157
urban planning, 156-157, 330-331
jitneys, 39, 308
Johnson, Elmer, xix, 125, 203, 270

K

Kain, J., 217-218
Urban Transportation Problem, The, 27-28, 29, 98, 216, 217
Kanafani, Adib, 211
Karlsruhe, Germany, 136-137, *138*, *139*, 303
Kennedy Airport, John F., 144, 183
Kennedy, John F., 100
Kenworthy, J., 267, 290
Kinnock, Neil, 328
Klagenfurt, Austria, 50
Kloten Airport, 144, 184
Kobe, Japan, 221
Komanoff, Charles, 284, 285
Korea, Seoul, *9*, 74, 213, 287
Kuala Lumpur, Malaysia, 245
Kuhn, Tillo, 99
Kuranami, Chiaki, 311
Kyoto Conference on World Climate, 121

L

Lagos, Nigeria, 245, 330
LaGuardia Airport, 183
Lancaster, Pennsylvania, 50
land-use, *230*, 250, 257, 304-306
and rail transit, 197-198
controls, xxii, xxiv, 97, 118, 161, 253
in
Hannover, Germany, 182
Seattle, Washington, 182
Lantau Island, Hong Kong, 156
Lee, Douglass, B., 194
Leeds, England, 51, 149
Lehner, Friedrich, 132
Lewis, Nigel C., 280, 284
light rail transit (LRT), 40, 41, 46, 59, 173, 211-212, 215-218, 266, 300, 301, 329
competing investments, 243-244
diversity, *302*
efficiency of, 251-252
funding, 119
in
California, 211-212, 217, 266
Canada, 41, 162, 200, 211-212, 301
England, 148-149
Finland, 154
Germany, 40, 135-137
Illinois, 40
Missouri, 41, 301
Oregon, 65, 119, 173, 211, 301, 302
Sweden, 153
Washington, 182
Light Rail Rapid Transit (LRRT), 41
Los Angeles Blue Line, *107*
ROW categories, 43
See also rail mode; transit mode
Lille, France, 139, 221
Lima, Peru, 245, 329
Lind, William S., 86, 219-220
Litman, Todd, 74, 311
livable cities, xix, 125, 150, 158, 179, 205-207, 327
and contemporary societies, 6
creation of, xix, xxiii
definition of, 7, 158, 233
determining, xvii
intermodality and, 9-10
See also quality of life
Liverpool, England, 144
London, England
automobile disincentives, 175
Channel Tunnel, 183
-Docklands, 221
ease of travel in, 12
operation of buses, 144, 145, 147
parking provision, 149, 228, 287
road pricing, 328
transit mode, 213
urban planning, 149
versus New York City, 182, 184
zonal fares, 222
Los Angeles, California, 60, *117*
Blue Line, *107*
car-based city, 15, 132, 162, 227, 234
Central Freeway, 213, 277
congestion in, 73
freeways in, 1, 118, 263
inner-city areas, 2, 99
LARTS, 97
low-density metropolis, 212
Metrolink, 200-201
parking provision, *94*
reconstruct the city policy, 12
reexamination of transportation plans, 103
Santa Monica Freeway, 113
Lyon, France, 139

M

Macao, 155
Madison, Wisconsin, 309
Maine, 60
Manchester, England, 148, 303
Manhattan. *See* New York City, New York
Manila, Philippines, 41, 215, 245, 266
marginal pricing, 79-81
marine mode, 5
Marseilles, France, 139
Matoff, Thomas, 211
Melbourne, Australia, xxii, 129, 158-159, 200
Mercer Island, Washington, 120
metro. *See* rapid transit
metropolitan areas. *See* city
metropolitan planning organizations (MPOs), 84, 108, 110
creation of, 101, 167
impotence of, 107, 167
innovative action, 118,121
stronger role of, 109
Metropolitan Transit Development Board (MTDB), 259, 267, 295
Mexico, *53*

Mexico City, Mexico, 73, 74, 245, 287, 313
Meyer, J., *Urban Transportation Problem, The*, 27-28, 29, 98, 216, 217
Miami, Florida, 221, 241
minibus, 46, 145-146
Ministry of the Environment of Finland, 267, 295
Minneapolis, Minnesota, 29, 97, 227
mobility, 198-201
Moktarian, Patricia L., 193
Monheim, Rolf, 130, 290
monorails, 220
Montana, 60
Montreal, Canada, 51, 162, 198, 211, 252
Moore, T., 216, 218
Moscow, Russia, 266
motorcycles, 29
Munich, Germany
  balancing modes, 222, *222*, 243
  bicycle mode, *34*
  livability, 1, 129
  modal choice, 202
  transit federations, 168
  urban planning, 133, *134*

N

Nantes, France, 40, 139, 140
Naples, Italy, 5
Narita Airport, 144, 183
National Economic Crossroads Transportation Efficiency Act (NEXTEA), 121
National Environmental Policy Act (NEPA) of 1969, 104
National Highway System, 68
National System of Interstate and Defense Highways, xxi, 93
neighborhoods, 205-207, 293
  See also traditional neighborhood development (TND)
Netherlands, the, 190
  Amsterdam, 15, 16
  automobile use, 141-142, 174
  bicycle mode, 33, 51, 141, 255, 309
  congestion, 168
  Eindhoven, *21*
  gasoline taxes, 177
  metropolitan organizations, 167
  multimodal operations, 169
  road pricing, 281
  Rotterdam, 40, 327
  traffic calming, 289
  transit mode, 141-143
  urban planning, 141-143
  user costs, 273
  woonerf concept, 141, 292-293
New Delhi, India, 330
New Haven, Connecticut, 183
New Jersey
  bicycle mode, 118
  bus versus rail transit, 210-211
  Garden State Parkway, 280
  intermodal system, *106*
  suburbs, 16
  Turnpike, 280
New Jersey Transit, 47
New Orleans, Louisiana, 164, 166, 202, 252
New South Wales (NSW), 159
New York, 313
  Buffalo, 28, 211, 301
  New York City, 3, 5, 12, 16, 40, 59, 144, 164, 172, 173, 180-185, 200, 202, 204, 206, 211, 213, 215, 252, 257, 261, 262, 266, 280, 282
  Syracuse, 205, 287
New York City, New York, 16, 144, 173, 361
  bus mode, 200, 211
  car-free travel, 252
  Committee for Better Transit, 172, 204
  ease of travel in, 12
  freeway development, 262
  gentrification, 3
  higher performance metro, 40
  metro lines, 266
  pedestrian mode, 164, 202, 206, 257
  site selection, 5
  subway, 215
  toll roads, 280, 282
  train capacity, 59
  transit mode, 213
  "Transportation Alternatives," 172
  versus its peers, 182-185
Newark Airport, 183
Newcastle, England, 144, 301
Newman, Peter, 267, 290
1988 Metropolitan Area Transportation Study (Finland), 154-155
noise pollution, 152
  and traffic calming, 289
  changing public attitudes, 119
  installation of noise barriers, 120
  negative environmental impact, 52, 252
non-motorized vehicles (NMVs), 309, 311
Norway, xxii
  auto use, 149
  Bergen, 175
  bike mode, 149
  gasoline taxes, 81
  Oslo, 1, 150, 175, 200, 222, 252, 282, 328
  pedestrian mode, 149, 150
  road pricing, 149, 175, 281, 282, 328
  transit mode, 149, 200
  Trondheim, 150-151
  urban planning, 149-151
  user costs, 273
"Not In My Backyard" (NIMBY) attitude, 15, 119, 120
Nottingham, England, 149

O

Oakland, California, 197
Ogden, Kenneth, 211
Ohio
  Cleveland, 16, 42, 218
  Columbus, 1, 99, 262
  Dayton, 173, 205, 287
Olympic Games, 133, 287
1,000 Friends of Oregon, 172, 259, 267, 290, 291

Oregon
growth management laws, 118
Portland, 10, 51, 65, 119, 124, 149, 173, 175, 200, 202, 210, 211, 222-223, 228, 243, 267, 288, 301, *302*, 322, 327
Organization for Economic Cooperation and Development (OECD), 7, 324
Orly Airport, 183
Osaka, Japan, 200, 221
Oslo, Norway
intermodal planning, 222, 252
livability, 1
road pricing, 175, 282, 328
transit mode, 200
urban planning, 150
Ottawa, Canada
busways, 41, 51, 208, 212, 227, 300
parking limitations, 228

P

paratransit mode, xxii, 39, 46, 101, 255, 308-314
subsidies, xxii
park-and-ride facilities, 201
parking, 294
"cashout," 276-277, 298
charges for, 271, 274
costs, 69, 77, 238, 323
free, 77, 111, 123, 169-170, 194, 249, 277
in
England, 149, 228, 287
France, 243
Germany, 149, 228, 287
Oregon, 149, 288
Singapore, 155
Texas, 287
provision for, *95*, 97, 98, 205, 228, 252
rates, 275-276
reducing, xxiii, 274-275
supply standards, 287-288
use of smart cards, 298
validation schemes, 276
Paris, France
automobile disincentives, 74, 175, 252
driving restrictions, 287
Metro, 137, 139
parking provisions, 243
rail system, 40
transit mode, 51, 200, 209, 213
versus New York City, 182, 183
Parsons Brinckerhoff Quade and Douglas, Inc., 314
"pay as you drive" (PAYD), 285
Pedestrian Environment Factor (PEF), 314
pedestrian malls
and LRT services, 301
in
Germany, 130, *131*, 180, *181*
Illinois, 177
Seattle, Washington, 177, 180
reopening—for vehicular traffic, 177
traffic-calming measure, 168
pedestrian mode, xx, xxii, xxiii, 31-32, 52, 55, 168, 202, 256-257, 267, 312-314
costs, 66
designs, 1, 13
impact of car travel on, 74
in
Australia, 158-159
California, 164, 257
Canada, 162, 163
Europe, 168
Finland, 154-155
France, 141
Germany, *136*
large cities, 51
medium cities, 51
New York, 164, 202, 206, 257
Norway, 149, 150
Pennsylvania, 206
small cities, 50
Sweden, *31*, 151, 152
misconceptions about, 205-207
neglect of, xxiii, 9, 12, 14, 103, 112, 312
reliance on, 2
safety, 95
Pennsylvania, 190
bicycle mode, 118, 206
bus mode, 210
Lancaster, 50
pedestrian mode, 206
Philadelphia, 3, 16, 41, 47, 51, 98, *102*, 103, *105*, *106*, 183, 206, 210, 211-212, 213, 243, 261, 262, 305, *313*
Pittsburgh, 5, 97, 208
Turnpike, 280
Pennsylvania Environmental Council (PEC), 259, 274, 280, 284, 285
people movers. *See* automated guided transit
People's Republic of China, 32, 155, 282, 309, 330
Persky, J., 192
Personal Rapid Transit (PRT), 29, 125, 220-221, 324
Philadelphia, Pennsylvania, 16, 261
Amtrak service, 183
bicycle mode, 206
bus mode, 210
"freeway-dominated" plan, 98, *102*, 103, 262
gentrification, 3
highway design, *105*, 213
Logan Circle, *313*
Main Line, 305
multistory parking garages, 243
Norristown Line, 41
PATCO line, *106*, 211-212
regional rail, 47
transit's mode, 51
Phoenix, Arizona, 13, 51, 199, 313
Pittsburgh, Pennsylvania, 5, 97, 208
Place Ville Marie (Montreal, Canada), 162
planning. *See* transportation, planning
Portland, Oregon
automobile disincentives, 175, *202*
bus mode, 200, 210
city center, 327
intermodal coordination, 228, 243
livability, 322
LRT system, 65, 119, 173, 211, 301, 302
modal split, 222-223

parking, 149, 288
rail system, 51, 124
time-transfer system, 210
transit mode, 10
urban planning, 267
poverty, 2
Prague, Czech Republic, 252
privacy, 198-199
private transportation, 30-37
privatization, 146, 147, 296
Project for Public Spaces, 233, 259, 267
public transportation. *See* transit
Pucher, John, 259
Puget Sound Regional Council, 117
"push-pull measures," 247, 261
See also Travel Demand Management (TDM)

Q

quality of life, 321
and contemporary societies, 6
detrimental impacts on, 169
England and—, 144
neglect of, 9
spatial spreading and, 191
trend toward, xxi, 104
See also livable cities

R

rail transit, xx, 99, 124, 171
-bus intermodal network, *107*
anti—campaigns, 214-220
diversification of, 40
federal assistance, 96
growth of cities around, 5, 16
high-speed, 211
in
Austria, 304
Canada, 40, 51, 59, 161, 162, 221
California, 124, 128
developed countries, xxii
France, 40
Georgia, 124, 189, 217
Germany, 16, 40, 41, 133
Japan, 183
Michigan, 221
Missouri, 213
Oregon, 51, 124
Sweden, 198
Switzerland, 40, 304
Washington, D.C., 124, 189, 213, 217
investments in, 195
misconceptions of, 211-214
rail diesel cars (RDCs), 303
rail rapid transit (RRT), 45, 59, 99, 133, 182, 302
regional, 46, 133, 303-304
See also light rail transit (LRT); transit mode
rapid transit, *106*, 218
characteristics of, 41
time-area consumption, 54-55, 59, 99
See also transit mode
Reagan, Ronald, xxi, 104, 106
Reason Foundation, 219
regional rail, 46, 133, 303–304
Regional Transportation Plan for the Philadelphia Tri-State Area, 103
Rendell, Edward, 3
Replogle, Michael A., 311
Réseau Express Régional (RER), 139
Reston, Virginia, 16
reverse commuters, 47
right-of-way (ROW), 40-42, 218, 265, 300-301
category A, *43*, 43, 45, 88, 130, 135, 171, 210, 255
category B, 43, 45, 88, 130, 171, 210, 255
category C, 42, 43, 45, 88
road pricing, xxiii, 281-285
costs, 323
in
England, xxi, 280, 281, 328
Netherlands, the, 281
Norway, 149, 175, 281, 282, 328
peer countries, 175
Singapore, 175, 328
Sweden, 281
obstacles, 328
underpriced, xxiv
See also tolls
Robinson, L., 267, 290
Rockwell, 30
Rome, Italy, 241, 292
Roosevelt, Theodore, 15
Rotterdam, the Netherlands, 40, 327
Rouen, France, 139
Rubin, J. E., 216, 218
Ruhr Region (Germany), 135

S

Saarbrücken, Germany, 137, 304
Sacramento, California, 40, 119, 173, 211-212, 301
Salerno, Italy, 51
Salomon, Ilan, 193
Salt Lake City, Utah, 65, 243
Salzburg, Austria, 292
San Antonio, Texas, 262
San Diego, California, 10, 41, 119, 200, 202
LRT system, 211-212, 213, 217, 301
Trolley, 28, 171
San Francisco, California, 60, 118, 129
Bay Area Rapid Transit (BART), 28, 124, 171, 197, 200, 201, 211, 216, 302
bicycle mode, 309
ease of travel in, 12
Embarcadero Freeway, 99, 103
freeway revolt, 103, 119, 173
high-capacity radial freeway, *25*, 262
high-quality transit, 10
highway congestion, *26*
light rail transit, 266
livability, 322
low-density city, 193
modal choice, 202, 252
pedestrian mode, 164
rail system, 124, 198

site selection, 5
toll roads, 280
train capacity, 59
San Jose, California, 1, 173, 243
Santa Monica, California, 65, 202
Santa Monica Freeway, 113
Sao Paolo, Brazil, *35*, 245
Sarajevo, Bosnia-Herzegovina, 73
Scandinavia
bicycle mode, 255
traffic engineering, 97
transit federations, 134
urban planning, 175, 190, 293
Schaeffer, K. H., 325
Schneider, Jerry, 221
Sclar, E., 192, 325
Sea-Bus (Vancouver, Canada), 162
Seattle, Washington, 120
Alaskan Way Viaduct, 99
bus mode, 200
commuter transit, 47
contrasted to Hannover, Germany, 180-182
freeway building, 96, *266*
HOV lanes, 205
pedestrian malls, 177, 180
transit mode, 51, 179-182, 211
trolley bus tunnel, 41, 301
Second Comprehensive Transport Study, The (Hong Kong), 156
Seoul, Korea, *9*, 74, 213, 287
Sheffield, England, 149
shopping malls, *32*, *33*
Shoup, Donald, 277
Singapore
Area Licensing Scheme (ALS), 155-156, 281-283
auto travel restrictions, 12, 175
parking, 155
road pricing, 175, 328
tolls, 155
transit mode, 155, 202
single-occupancy vehicles (SOVs)
add-a-lane popularity, 114, 204-205
alternatives to—travel, 108, 307-308
discouraging, 109, 111, 175, 208, 277, 322
increasing, 112, 115, 117, 121
inefficiency of, 251, 252
pressure from—drivers, 65
Skytrain (Vancouver, Canada), 162
Small, Kenneth, 284
smart cards, 156, 283, 294, 298
social behavior, xvii, xxiv
social costs (SC), 73, 79, 89, 237
Socialdata, 170
social optimum (SO), 60-65, 228, *246*
soundwalls, *254*
Soviet Union, states of the former, 330
Soyk, Thomas J., 259, 295
spatial spreading. *See* sprawl
Sperling, Daniel, 18, 203
sprawl, 118, 151, 193
departure from, 52
inefficiency of, 17
misconceptions of, 189-193
result of affluence, 166
trend, 4, 167
Stade, Germany, *13*
Stanstead Airport, 184
State Implementation Plan (SIP), 104
St. Etienne, France, 139
St. Louis, Missouri, 189
LRT system, 41, 301
Metrolink, 171
rail systems, 213
site selection, 5
Stockholm, Sweden
automobile disincentives, 175
environmental concerns, 152
multimodal approach, 16, 228
new towns, 327
pedestrian mode, *31*
rail transit, 198
urban planning, 151, 267
St. Paul, Minnesota, 97
Strasbourg, France, 139
streetcar/tramway, 5-6, 40, 158
Stuttgart, Germany, 135, 222, *222*
subsidies (SS), 76-77, 111, 194, 237, 239, 249
automobile, 19, 67-69
companies/agencies, 71, 72
government, 71, 72
suburban growth, 3, 192
along streetcar and railway lines, 6
planning of, 4-5
sprawl, 4, 52, 267
Surface Transportation Assistance Act (STAA) of 1982, 106-107
Surface Transportation Policy Project, 172
Sweden
air pollution, 152
auto use, 152, 163
car travel costs, 81
environmental concerns, 152
Farsta, 151
Gothenburg, 29, 41, 136, 152-154, 292
metropolitan organizations, 167
pedestrian mode, *31*, 151-152
road pricing, 281
single-family housing, 167
Stockholm, 16, *31*, 151, 152, 175, 198, 228, 267, 327
traffic calming, 153
transit mode, 151-154
urban planning, 151-154, 267, 293
Vällingby, 151
Switzerland, 190
automobile use, 143, 175
Bahn 2000 plan, 143
congestion, 168
environmental concerns, 143
metropolitan organizations, 167
multimodal operations, 169
regional rail, 40, 304
single-family housing, 167
traffic engineering, 96-97
transit federation, 134
transit mode, 143, 209
urban planning, 143-144
Zürich, 15, 40, 144, 168, 182, 184, 209, 222, 253

Sydney, Australia, 16, 51, 158, 159-160
Syracuse, New York, 205, 287
Syria, Damascus, 215

T

Taipei, Taiwan, 221
Taiwan, Taipei, 221
taxes, 275, 285. *See also* gasoline taxes
taxis, 39, 308
telecommunications, 192-193
tendering. *See* contracting
Texas Transportation Institute, 73
TGV lines, 183
3C planning process, 100-101, 109, 321
time-area consumption, 54-55, *56*, *57*, *58*
timed-transfer system, 162
Tokyo, Japan
  bicycle mode, 309
  car-free travel, 252
  metro lines, 266
  multimodal services, 16
  transit mode, 213, 218
  urban planning, 157
  versus New York City, 182, 183
tolls, xxiv, 155, 280
  collection, 151
  costs, 323
  disincentives for auto use, 175
  HOVs and, 114
  in
    California, 280
    France, 175
    Japan, 175
    New York, 280, 282
    Singapore, 155
  medium-term transit measure, 294
  use of smart cards, 298
  See also road pricing
Topp, Hartmut H., 290
Toronto, Canada
  Eaton Center, 198
  Greater Toronto Area (GTA), 161
  intermodal coordination, 228, 243
  livability, xxii, 1
  metropolitan organizations, 167
  new towns, 327
  rail systems, 40, 51, 59, 161
  transit mode, 162, 209
  urban planning, 267, *332*
Toulouse, France, 139, 221
traditional neighborhood development (TND), 293, 305
traffic calming, xxiii, 168, 173, 288-290
  in
    Australia, 52
    Canada, 289
    Europe, 51-52, 290
    Germany, 130, *131*, 289
    Netherlands, the, 289
    Sweden, 153
traffic cells, 135-136, 152-153, 292
traffic controls, 270, 310
traffic engineering, 268
Traffic in Towns (Buchanan), 144
traffic taming. *See* traffic calming
tramway. *See* streetcar
"transit cities," 6
Transit Federation (Germany), 134
Transit First, 295
transit mode, xix-xx, xxiii, 19, 37-39, 253-255
  and ITS, 298
  and low-density cities, 193
  assistance, 121
  "captives," 37, 262
  "choice riders," 39
  commuter, 46-49, 303
  contracting services, *147*
  costs, xxiii, 60-65, 66-74, *174*, 236, 237-238
  deregulation of, 86, 146, *147*, 147-148
  deteriorating, xxiii
  disincentives (TD), 241, 243-244
  family of urban—, 40-49
  fare collection, 135, 294, 303
  fare policy, 297-298
  federal involvement in, xxi, 322
  financing, 100, 106, 175, 244, 249-250, 299
  high-performance, 299-300
  improvements, xxiii, 170-171
  in
    Australia, 158-160
    Canada, 162, 170, 209
    developed countries, xxii, 1
    England, 144-149, 213
    France, 51, 137, 139-141, 200, 209, 213
    Germany, 130, 133-137
    Illinois, 51
    Japan, 156-157, 213, 218
    Netherlands, the, 141-143
    New Jersey, 47, 210-211
    New York, 213
    Norway, 149, 200
    Oregon, 10
    Pennsylvania, 51
    Singapore, 155, 202
    Sweden, 151-154
    Switzerland, 143, 209
    Texas, 37, 227, 234
    Washington, 51, 179-182, 211
    Washington, D.C., 10
  increasing the role of, 293-306
  incentives (TI), xxii, xxiii, 63, 150, 202, 241, 243, 247, 252, 294-306, 327
  independent, 255
  integration of, 168-173
  large cities and, 51-52, 88
  medium cities and, 51, 88
  performance investment cost characteristics, *44*, 45
  priority, 295, 329
  privatization, 146, 147
  promotion of, 304
  provision of, xxiv, 9-10, 264-267
  regular, 46, *48*, 49
  reliance on, 3
  shift to private automobile, 9, 12, 94-95
  small cities and, 50-51, 88

street, 255
subsidies, xxii, 77
technologies, 40-41, 101, 298
See also automated guided transit (AGT); bus transit; light rail transit (LRT); rail transit; rapid transit; regional rail
transit-oriented developments (TODs), 52, 193, 293, 305, 314
Transport Act of 1988 (Sweden), 153
transportation, xviii
and livable cities, 5-9
and the functioning of cities, 229-232
balanced – system, xix, xxii, xxiii, 12, 13-14, 52, 124, 129, 149, *160*, 189, *222*, 235-258, 259-319, 327
costs, xviii, xxiii
definition of efficient system, 234-235
economic aspects, 193-198
funding, 238
future of, 320-333
intermodal system, 235–258, 259
modes, xix, 8, 24, 27-30, 66-67, 307-314
multimodal, xx, xxiii, 9-10, 12, 27, 136, *138*, *139*, 168-169, 202, 235, 238, 295-296. *See also* Intermodal Surface Transportation Efficiency Act (ISTEA), integrated multimodal requirements
planning, xxi-xxii, 49, 93-108
and development, 189-193
changes in, xxiv
levels, 82-87, 90
policies, xi
aggravating problems, 120-126
changes in, xxiv
changing public attitudes, 119-120
dilemmas, 10-14
diverging, 14-17
federal policies, 1956–1991, 93-108
for livable cities, 227-229
freeway widening, 112-118
international, xxii
progress by ISTEA and its obstacles, 109-112
United States and peer countries, 128-186
relationship with city, 23-25
causes and consequences of congestion, 52-60
family of modes, 40-49
four levels of planning, 82-87, 90
optimum in travel choice, 60-65
private, public, and for-hire – , 30-39
– represents a system, 26-30
transport's composition to urban size, 50-52
travel costs, charges, and subsidies, 65-81
role in economy, 5
role in growth of cities, 5
studies, 97
systems approach, 27, 109
technologies, 28-30
See also urban transportation
Transportation Equity Act for the 21st Century (TEA-21), *34*, 120, 322
Transportation Improvement Plan (TIP), 108
Transportation Research Board (TRB), 18, 203, 270, 301, 324
Transportation System Management (TSM), 103-104, 268, 321
Transport Structure Plan Project Team, 284
travel choice, 60-65
Travel Demand Management (TDM), 241, 268-269
See also "push-pull measures"
Trondheim, Norway, 150-151
Tunis, Tunisia, 245

U

Ulberg, Cy, 275
Union Internationale des Transports Publics (UITP), 170, 324
Transit First measures, 295
transportation in urban planning, 259, 267, 290
United Nations, 7
United States
crisis of cities and metropolitan areas, 1-5
diverging transportation policies, 14-17
the automobile, 7-10
transportation and livable cities, 5-7
urban transportation policy dilemmas, 10-14
vitality of cities, 17-21
versus peer countries, xxii, xxiii, xxiv, 14-17, 128-129, 221-223, 330-331
comparison of conditions, trends, and attitudes, 163-173
developments in peer countries, 129-163
diverging directions, 173-179
policy implementation and results, 179-185
Urban Mass Transportation Act of 1964, 101
Urban Mass Transportation Administration (UMTA), 101, 292
Urban Mass Transportation Assistance Act of 1970, 104
Urban Transport Financing Act (West Germany), 129-130
urban transportation
aggravating problems 120-126
costs, 67-79, *78*, *236*
future of, 320-333
goals, requirements, and composition, 232-235
in
Australia, 128, 157-160
Canada, 128, 162, 267, *332*
England, 144-149
Europe, 128, 326, 330-331
Finland, 154-155
France, 137, 139
Germany, 129-135, 136, 154-155, 267
Hong Kong, 155-156
Japan, 156-157, 330-331
Netherlands, the, 141, 143
Norway, 149-151
Oregon, 267
Scandinavia, 175, 190, 293

Sweden, 151-154, 267, 293
Switzerland, 143-144
misconceptions about, 188-189
bus transit, 207-211
highway transportation, 201-205
mobility and accessibility, 198-201
non-conventional transit modes, 220-221
pedestrians, bicycles, and neighborhood livability, 205-207
peer countries and the United States, 221-223
planning and development, 189-193
rail transit, 211-220
transport and economic aspects, 193-198
planning, 261-268
policy dilemmas, 10-14
United States and peer countries, 128-186
shift of travel modes, *8*
3C planning process, 100-103
"vicious cycle of—," *8*, 9, 244
See also city; transportation
Urban Transportation Problem, The (Meyer, Kain, and Wohl), 27-28, 29, 98, 216, 217
U.S. Department of Housing and Urban Development, 4
U.S. Department of Transportation, 26, 30, 121, 123, 221
user costs, 65, 111, 271-286
by different modes, 66-67
direct (UD), 71, *75*, *76*, 237, 271, 322-323
estimates of, 67-69
fixed (UF), 237
indirect, 71-72
marginal pricing, 79-81
structure of, 69-79
U.S. Office of Technology Assessment, xxi, 69

V

Vällingby, Sweden, 151
Vancouver, Canada
bus mode, 210
livability, 223
rail systems, 51, 221
traffic calming, 289
urban planning, 162
vanpooling, 199, 255, 307-308
vehicle-kilometers traveled (VKT)
growth of, xx, 117, 121, 142-143, 167, 267
reduction of, xxii, xxiii, 108, 114, 122, 175, 196, 241, 252, 270, 271, 279, 282, 286-293, 322
vehicle-miles traveled (VMT)
growth of, xx
reduction of, 108
Vickrey, William, 283
Vienna, Austria, xxii, *95*, 175
Vuchic, Vukan R., 40, 42, 54, 299

W

Wachs, Martin, 223, 323
walking. *See* pedestrian mode
"walking cities," 5
Walters, Alan, 215
Wardrop, John, 60
Wardrop's Principle of Traffic Flow Distribution, 60-61
Washington
Department of Transportation, 117
growth management laws, 118
Mercer Island, 120
Seattle, 41, 47, 51, 96, 99, 120, 177, 180-182, 200, 205, 211, 266, 301
Washington, D.C., 16
Amtrak service, 183
Ballston, 198
benefit-sharing programs, 299
bus mode, 210
Crystal City, 198
freeway development, 263
low-density city, 193
MARC, 47
Metro, 28, 124, 171, 197, 200, 201, 211, 227, 243, 302
Metropolitan Area Transit Authority, 214
modal choice, 202
Pentagon City, 198
rail system, 124, 189, 213, 217
reexamination of transportation plans, 103
taxi service, 308
train capacity, 59
transit mode, 10
Waterloo, Canada, 50
water pollution, 123
Webber, Melvin, 124, 197, 211, 216
Weyrich, Paul M., 86, 219-220
Wiesbaden, Germany, 212
Wiewel, W., 192
Wilcox Commission, 9
Willson, Richard, 274-275
Winston, Bruce P., 311
Wohl, M.
Urban Transportation Problem, The, 27-28, 29, 98, 216, 217
woonerf concept, 141, 291-292
World Bank, 215, 245, 270
Worldwatch Institute, 178
World War II, 10
post—highway policies and trends, xxi, 7, 280
in Germany, 132
in Japan, 156
Wright, Alan Armstrong, 215

Z

Zein, Sandy R., 289
Zürich, Switzerland
airport facility, 144, 184
balancing modes, 222
historic preservation, 15
rail transit, 40
transit federations, 168
transit network, 209
transportation efficiency, 253
versus New York City, 182, 184